The Japanese Today

The
JAPANESE
TODAY

Change and Continuity

ENLARGED EDITION

Edwin O. Reischauer

and Marius B. Jansen

The Belknap Press of
Harvard University Press
Cambridge, Massachusetts
London, England

Copyright © 1977, 1988, 1995 by the President and Fellows of Harvard College
All rights reserved
Printed in the United States of America
Second printing, 1996
Library of Congress Cataloging-in-Publication Data

Reischauer, Edwin O. (Edwin Oldfather), 1910–1990
    The Japanese today : change and continuity / Edwin O. Reischauer
and Marius B. Jansen. — Enl. ed.
        p.   cm.
    Originally published, 1977.
    Includes bibliographical references and index.
    ISBN 0-674-47184-9 (pbk.)
    1. Japan.   I. Jansen, Marius B.   II. Title.
DS806.R35   1995
952—dc20   94-31346
                                                                             CIP

Preface to the Enlarged Edition

Since this book was last revised Japan, like the rest of the world, has undergone enormous changes. The impact of the end of the Cold War has combined with a world-wide recession to create a fluid situation in which long-held assumptions about politics and policies no longer hold. For this reason the editors have asked me to add a concluding chapter describing the changes that have rocked Japan since 1990. Where events have made it necessary I have also made minor changes in other chapters to avoid confusion, and I have added two paragraphs to the Suggested Reading to show how the literature about Japan is changing in response to new concerns.

Marius B. Jansen
April 1994

Preface

A decade has passed since Harvard University Press first published *The Japanese,* making the editors feel that an updated revision would be appropriate. But it soon became evident that a few alterations and the addition of materials on the past ten years would not be adequate. It is true that the Japanese themselves have not changed greatly in so short a period, but knowledge about Japan among foreigners and attitudes toward the Japanese have changed enormously. Japan is now looked upon as one of the three or four most important countries in the world. In writing about Japan, one must realize that readers probably know a great deal more than they did a decade ago and their concepts of Japan are likely to be far different.

That is why *The Japanese Today: Change and Continuity* is essentially a new book. While some sections are virtually identical with the earlier volume, others are almost completely rewritten. At one extreme, the historical background has not been greatly modified; at the other extreme, a chapter on business has been expanded to a whole new fifth part, and the final, sixth part on Japan and the world is also largely rewritten. The subtitle of the new book, "Change and Continuity," in a sense expresses the relationship between the two volumes, while further emphasizing a major theme that runs through both.

A book of this size clearly cannot discuss all aspects of so large and diverse a subject as the Japanese. Fortunately, there are many specialized books covering areas that I do not attempt to treat, such as the fascinating minutiae of day-to-day life in Japan; the literature, art, drama, and other cultural achievements of the Japanese; and the details of Japan's economic development. I have concentrated instead on the Japanese people themselves—their present society, political system, business organization, and increasingly crucial relations with the rest of the world.

In writing a book of this sort one depends not just on one's own observations and research but also on the studies of a vast number of Japanese and foreign scholars and writers. They are so numerous that it would be quite impossible to list even the most important ones. In *The Japanese,* I expressed my indebtedness to certain friends for suggesting corrections and also for typing the manuscript. In this volume I wish to add my thanks to Ella L. Rutledge and Ruiko Connor for a great deal of typing, and to the two of them and also to Nancy Deptula for help in checking some names and details. My gratitude is also due Ann Hawthorne for her skillful editorial work, Dr. Steven Ericson for compiling the "Suggested Reading" section, and Pembroke Herbert/Picture Research Consultants for providing the illustrations, which together with the maps are almost entirely new.

Edwin O. Reischauer
May 1987

Author's Note

For the December 1989 reprint of the paperback edition, I have made certain changes reflecting contemporary politics, the position of women, and the accession of the Heisei emperor, Akihito.

Contents

The Japanese Today

Part One ———————————————

The Setting

Japan's modern signature: Mount Fuji, the Shinkansen (the "New Main Line" or "Bullet Train"), and rice stubble in a traditional paddy field. (Courtesy Japan National Tourist Organization)

1 The Land

The Japanese, like all other peoples, have been shaped in large part by the land in which they live. Its location, climate, and natural endowments are unchangeable facts that have set limits to their development and helped give it specific direction.

Most people think of Japan as a small country. Even the Japanese have this idea firmly in mind. And small it is if seen on a world map—a mere fringe of scraggly islands off the east coast of the great continental land mass of Eurasia, looking outward to the vast sweep of the Pacific Ocean. It is certainly dwarfed by its near neighbors, China and the Soviet Union, and by the two North American colossi, the United States and Canada, which face it across the Pacific. But size is a relative matter. Japan would look far different if compared with the lands of Western Europe. It is less revealing to say that Japan is smaller than California or could be lost in a Siberian province than to point out that it is considerably larger than Italy and half again the size of the United Kingdom. For Americans the best comparison, in terms of both terrain and population, might be to New York, New Jersey, Pennsylvania, and all of New England, minus Maine.

National size can be measured in various ways, and square mileage is certainly not the most important of these. In fact, it can be very misleading. A thousand square miles in Antarctica, Greenland, or even New Guinea are not to be equated with ten square miles on the lower Rhine or in the rich agricultural lands of Illinois. The vast stretches of terrain that separate the mineral resources of Siberia, Alaska, or the Canadian northwest from more habitable regions are economic liabilities rather than assets.

A more meaningful measure of a nation's size is population. In this category, there are four giants: China's population is around a billion and India's close to 800 million; the Soviet Union and the United States have grown far above the 200 million mark. Indonesia and Brazil have the geographic size to become of giant rank, with populations beginning to approach 200 million. But Japan, though less than a fifth the geographic size of Indonesia, the smallest of these six nations, comes seventh in population, far ahead even of those countries in Western Europe that until recently have been considered the great powers of the world. As far back as the early seventeenth century, Japan had around 25 million inhabitants, considerably more than France, which was then the largest country of Europe, and several times as many as England. Today its population exceeds 122 million, meaning that it is more than twice the size of any of the Western European big four—West Germany, Italy, the United Kingdom, and France.

Another important measure of a country's size is its productive power, or gross national product (GNP), which is the multiple of its exploited resources, its population, and, most important, their skills. In this category Japan is one of the giants, ranking behind only the two superpowers, the United States and the Soviet Union. It is well ahead of the great nations of Western Europe and is closing in fast on the Soviet Union, despite the latter's more than two-to-one edge in population and sixty-to-one advantage in area. (The omission of specific figures for GNP and the like here and elsewhere in this book is deliberate. Nothing is less memorable than an outdated statistic. Most numbers move quickly toward oblivion in the present age of rapid population and economic growth, magnified in the latter case by galloping inflation. I have preferred for the most part to stick to broad numerical generalizations and comparative ratios, which are less likely to become quickly out of date.)

We are so conditioned to judge national size by our conventional maps that it may be useful to insert at this point two other types of map. In the one on page 6, the size of countries is drawn proportionately to their populations, in the one on page 7 to their GNP. I first devised maps of this sort in 1964 in order to point out to the Japanese, who were still suffering from a gross underestimation of their country following their defeat in World War II, that Japan was a relatively large country. The maps on pages 6 and 7 are revisions of the earlier ones. They show how gigantic Japan has become in economic terms in recent years, now possessing close to a tenth of the world's total GNP though less than a fortieth of its population.

The statistics underlying these maps, particularly the one of GNP, are often quite shaky, but even if we allow for a wide margin of error, the two maps taken together reveal a great deal about our present world. Much of its population is in China, India, Indonesia, Brazil, and a host of other so-called developing countries in Asia, Africa, and Central and South America, but its productive power is overwhelmingly concentrated in the industrialized nations of Europe, North America, and Japan. The details of these maps will change over time, but the basic imbalance between the populous but nonindustrialized poor lands and the industrialized rich ones will certainly remain for many years and may even grow greater. On the whole, it is the poor countries that are increasing fastest in population and the rich in GNP. Herein lies perhaps the most intractable of all international problems.

Despite its largeness by some measurements, Japan is actually a smaller country in geographic size than the figures on square miles would suggest. The whole country is so mountainous that less than a fifth of it is level enough to permit agriculture or other economic exploitation other than forestry, mining, or hydroelectric power. Belgium and the Netherlands have a higher ratio of people to total land area than does Japan, but figured on the basis of habitable land Japan is much more crowded than either of them. In fact, with the exception of city states like Hong Kong and Singapore, Japan has by far the highest density of both population and production per square mile of habitable land of any country in the world.

The mountains of Japan are almost uniformly precipitous, being relatively young, but in most parts of the country they are to be measured only in hundreds or a few thousands of feet. Most of Japan is made up of long stretches of forest-covered hills interlaced with narrow valleys that form slim strips of agriculture and habitation. Here and there, active or extinct volcanic cones rise much higher, and in the central part of Honshu, the largest island, there are several ranges, collectively known as the Japanese Alps, that attain heights of around 10,000 feet. In this region also stands Fuji-san (Mount Fuji), a perfect volcanic cone, last active in 1707, which soars 12,385 feet, on one side directly out of the sea. Because of its majesty, it has always been much in the Japanese artistic and literary consciousness.

There is only one relatively extensive plain in Japan—the Kanto Plain around Tokyo—which stretches a mere 120 miles at its longest point. Otherwise the habitable portions of Japan consist of small seacoast

POPULATION

□ Represents one million people

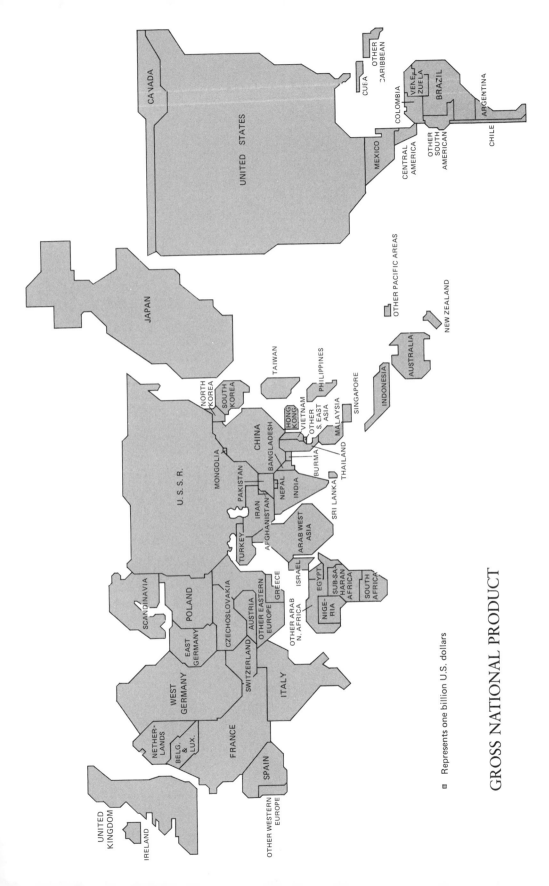

GROSS NATIONAL PRODUCT

▪ Represents one billion U.S. dollars

floodplains, relatively narrow river valleys, and a few basins in the mountains, each separated from the others by rugged hills or impassable mountains.

The division of the country into many small units of terrain has been conducive to local separatism and may have contributed to the development of a decentralized, feudal pattern of government in medieval times. These topographical divisions certainly underlay the division of the land in antiquity into a number of autonomous petty "countries," which became institutionalized by the eighth century as the traditional sixty-eight provinces of Japan. It is significant that more than nine-tenths of the borders of the forty-seven prefectures into which the country is now divided still follow precisely the mountain ridge delimitations of these early provinces.

Despite the natural division of the country, however, unity and homogeneity characterize the Japanese. As early as the seventh century, probably influenced by the example of a unified Chinese empire, already close to a thousand years old, the Japanese saw themselves as a single people, living in a unified nation. This has always remained their ideal, despite long centuries of feudal divisions. Today few if any large masses of people are as homogeneous as the Japanese. There is little of the ethnic divisiveness that persists in the British Isles, even though geographic barriers there are much less formidable than in Japan.

Until the building of railroads and paved highways in modern times, communication by land within the country was difficult. Only short stretches of any of the rivers are navigable. But sea transport has always been relatively easy around all the coasts and particularly on the beautiful, island-studded Inland Sea, which has always been the great central artery of the western half of Japan. Leading from the chief point of contact with the continent in north Kyushu to the ancient capital district at the eastern end of the Inland Sea, it was the main axis for much of Japan's early history.

Agricultural people everywhere have developed a close attachment to the soil that has nourished them, but among the Japanese there is in addition to this universal feeling a particularly strong awareness of the beauties of nature. No part of Japan is more than seventy miles from the sea, and mountains are within view almost everywhere. With ample rainfall, the whole country is luxuriantly green and wooded, and the play of the seasons brings wondrous variety. The earliest Japanese literature shows a keen appreciation of the beauties of seascapes, mountains, and wooded dells, and today Japanese are avid visitors to renowned beauty spots, sometimes all but destroying them in their enthusiasm. In addition to peerless Fuji, there are the famous "three landscapes of Japan" *(Nihon sankei)*—Miyajima, a temple island in the Inland Sea near Hiroshima; Ama-no-hashidate, or "Bridge of Heaven," a pine-covered sandspit on the Japan Sea coast north of Kyoto; and Matsushima, a cluster of picturesque pine-clad islands in a bay near the city of Sendai, in northern Japan. Most localities in Japan are likely to have their own three or eight landscapes, and there are thousands of other beauty spots and hot spring resorts, as well as innumerable less-known places of beauty.

Unlike the vastness of the untamed American West, the scale of Japan's natural beauty is for the most part small and intimate. The smallness of scale has perhaps lent itself to the Japanese effort to capture and preserve nature in small bits, as in their miniaturized gardens, in which within the narrow confines of their crowded cities a small area of carefully selected rocks and stones, some skillfully pruned trees and bushes, and a few pools of water suggest the grandeurs of nature. The chief exceptions to the smallness of scale in Japan's landscape are the high mountains of central Japan and the long vistas of the northern island of Hokkaido. Not fully absorbed into Japan until the latter part of the nineteenth century, Hokkaido has stretches of landscape and a thinness of population that are more reminiscent of North America than of the rest of Japan.

Ironically, the Japanese, for all their love of nature, have done as much as any people to defile it. This may have been inevitable in a country with the highest levels of population and production per habitable square mile. Beautiful green hills have been hacked down for factory or living sites and to provide fill for land recovered from the sea. More distant mountains for a while disappeared behind industrial smog. Urban blight sprawls across much of the agricultural countryside. Mountains have been defaced by so-called "skyline drives" to accommodate the city tourist. Renowned beauty spots are half buried in hotels, restaurants, and trinket shops. But the greater part of Japan today is thinly populated, and anywhere off the beaten track it remains a land of great natural charm and beauty.

Japan's dense population and phenomenal agricultural production can in part be explained by the climate, which contrasts quite sharply with that of Europe. Whereas European agriculture is limited by summers

The main *torii*, the gateway to all Shinto shrines, at the Itsukushima Shrine on Miyajima ("Shrine Island"), in the Inland Sea a few miles west of Hiroshima. Twice daily the tides sweep beneath it. Miyajima is considered one of the "three landscapes of Japan" *(Nihon sankei)*. *(© Burt Glinn / Magnum Photos)*

that are overly dry in the south and too cool in the north, Japan has both hot summer weather and ample rainfall, which comes for the most part during the growing season from early spring to early autumn. This has permitted a much more intensive form of agriculture than in Europe, with consequently heavier agricultural populations.

The climate of Japan resembles that of the east coast of North America more than that of Europe, largely as a result of the similar relationship among land masses, oceans, and prevailing winds. One way to gain a general idea of Japanese temperatures and climate would be to superimpose the Japanese islands on a map of the east coast of North America at the same latitudes. The four main islands of Japan—Hokkaido, Honshu, Shikoku, and Kyushu—would stretch from northern Maine, or Montreal in Canada, almost to the Gulf of Mexico. Okinawa (the Ryu-

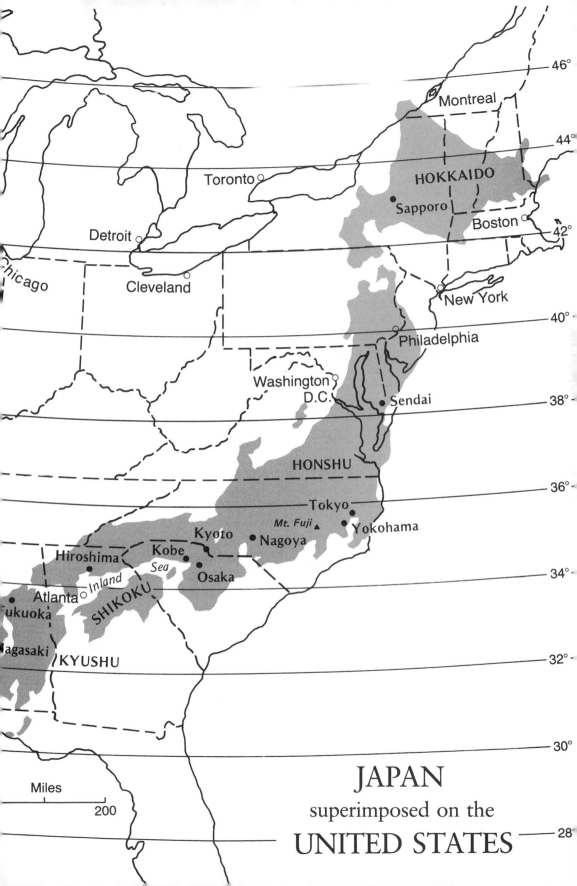

46°

Montreal

44°

Toronto ○

HOKKAIDO

● Sapporo

Boston ○
42°

Detroit ○

Chicago

Cleveland ○

New York ○

40°

Philadelphia ○

Washington
D.C. ○

● Sendai
38°

HONSHU

36°

Tokyo

Mt. Fuji ▲

● Yokohama

Kyoto

● Nagoya

Kobe ●

34°

Hiroshima ●

Sea

Inland

Osaka ●

Atlanta ○

SHIKOKU

●
ukuoka

agasaki KYUSHU

32°

30°

Miles

200

JAPAN

superimposed on the

UNITED STATES
28°

kyu Islands) is in the latitude of Florida, and the Kuril Islands, which Japan lost to the Soviet Union after World War II, parallel Newfoundland. Tokyo and the bulk of metropolitan Japan, however, lie at the latitude of North Carolina.

Since Japan is not part of the continental land mass but lies several hundred miles offshore, it has a somewhat more oceanic climate, with less severe heat in summer and cold in winter than do parallel latitudes along our east coast. There is also more precipitation, ranging from around 40 to 120 inches per year. Late autumn and winter are relatively dry, with long stretches of delightful sunny weather in most parts of Japan. This is because during the colder months high pressures build up over frigid Siberia and Mongolia, causing cold, dry winds to flow outward from the continent.

There is one major exception to this rule, however. The winter winds from Siberia pick up considerable moisture from the Japan Sea and dump it as snow as they cross the central mountainous backbone of Honshu. It is the same phenomenon as the "snow shadow" on the eastern shores of the Great Lakes in North America, only on a much larger scale. As a result, the northwestern coastal regions of Honshu, which are known as the "snow country," have prodigious winter snows, giving a steady ground cover of five or six feet in many areas—the heaviest snowfall in the world for any region with a dense population.

The contrast can be striking between deep snow and gloom on one side of the mountainous backbone of northern Japan and sunshine and bare ground on the other, sometimes only a few miles apart by railway tunnel. These conditions, together with the concentration of all the great cities on the Pacific side of the islands, have given a certain sense of inferiority and resentment to the residents of what they themselves call the "backside of Japan" (Ura Nihon). In contrast, the peninsulas that jut into the Pacific on Japan's south coast have a particularly benign, almost subtropical, climate, thanks to the Japan Current (or Black Current, Kuroshio, as the Japanese call it), which bathes that coast in much the same way that the Gulf Stream does the southeast coast of the United States.

Except for Hokkaido, the growing season in most of Japan averages between 200 and 260 days, but the period of oppressive summer heat is relatively short, usually lasting only from early July to early September. However, during this period it is indeed oppressive, not so much because of high temperatures as because of excessive humidity.

Winters are not very severe, but they can be quite uncomfortable if one does not have adequate heating, which was the prevailing situation in Japan until well after World War II. Except in the north and the higher mountains, temperatures rarely fall more than a few degrees below freezing, but in most parts of Japan they do dip during the night below freezing for a month or two in the winter, and snow does fall at least occasionally in all parts of Japan except Okinawa. Since winter temperatures are not severe enough to kill sheltered humans, the premodern Japanese, like other peoples living in comparable climatic zones, developed heating systems that lessened the rigors of winter only a little. Traditionally the construction of their houses was light and drafty, more fitted to admit cooling breezes in summer than to keep out the frost of winter. The chief heating device was a charcoal brazier, or *hibachi,* where one could warm one's wrists for supposed circulation of the heated blood throughout the body, though in some farmhouses one could warm one's feet in a sunken heating pit, or *kotatsu.* A nightly scalding bath would bring real warmth from then until bedtime, and in the middle of the day glorious winter sunshine might heat the house to tolerable levels for a short while. A good southern exposure was therefore important. Today, central heating is still not the general rule in private homes, but electric, gas, or oil heaters have replaced the old charcoal brazier and together with more solid house construction make winter living more tolerable. For most Japanese, however, winter still means heavy long underwear.

Thus, summer and winter can be unpleasant in Japan, but they are not extreme and are relatively brief. The remaining eight months of the year are very pleasant. The four seasons are clearly differentiated, and the progression of temperature changes is slow and quite regular, unlike that in most of the United States.

Japan's climate is typically temperate, contrasting with the tropics, where the growing season is year round and temperatures make a relatively slow pace of life advisable. To survive the colder months, food surpluses have always had to be built up by hard, concentrated work during the more productive parts of the year, and daytime rest periods or a leisurely work pace have not seemed necessary to escape the midday heat. The same is true for Japan's East Asian neighbors, Korea and China. Such climatic conditions may help explain why the people of all three of these countries are noted for their hard work and unflagging energy. Simple necessity at first, reinforced over the centuries by well-established custom and insistent moral precept, seems to have produced among the Japanese and their neighbors in East Asia what may be the most deeply ingrained work ethic in the whole world.

One outstanding feature of Japanese weather is the series of great cyclonic storms, called typhoons, that devastate parts of the country in late summer and early autumn. These are identical in nature with the hurricanes that occasionally ravage the east coast of the United States, both being products of the same general relationship between land and water at comparable latitudes. Typhoons, however, strike Japan with somewhat greater frequency and usually with more destructiveness to life and property, since the greater part of the Japanese population is concentrated on the southeastern seacoast, where the typhoons first come ashore.

Typhoons have accustomed the Japanese to expect natural catastrophes and to accept them with stoic resilience. This sort of fatalism might even be called the "typhoon mentality," but it has been fostered by other natural disasters as well. Volcanic eruptions sometimes occur, since Japan has many active volcanoes that are part of the great volcanic chain that encircles the Pacific Ocean. The largest active volcano, Asamayama, devastated hundreds of square miles of central Honshu in 1783. There are also numerous fault lines throughout the islands, and destructive earthquakes are frequent. Tokyo and its port of Yokohama were in large part leveled by fires resulting from a great earthquake that struck at noon on September 1, 1923, taking 130,000 lives. Since Edo, as Tokyo was earlier called, has been periodically hit by severe earthquakes about every sixty years, there is a popular belief that another is about to strike now that more than sixty years have passed since 1923, and people wonder how well the city will survive with its modern subways, towering buildings, and traffic-jammed streets. In any case, the Japanese have a fatalistic acceptance of nature's awesome might and a great capacity to dig themselves out after such catastrophes to start afresh.

2 Agriculture and Natural Resources

Between the ever present mountains and the sprawling cities, less than 12 percent of Japan's land area is under cultivation. The soils of Japan, moreover, are on the whole not very fertile. Nonetheless, a relatively long growing season, plentiful rainfall, unlimited hard work, and high agricultural skills have made it a very productive country despite its narrow geographic base.

Agriculture reached Japan quite late—only two or three centuries before the time of Christ. Whereas millet grown in unirrigated fields characterized farming in North China, the homeland of most East Asian civilization, the type of agriculture that came to Japan was wet-field rice cultivation, which seems to have originated somewhere to the south of ancient China. By the second century A.D. it was practiced in Japan in its essentially modern form in small dike-surrounded, water-filled plots of land, fed by an intricate man-made system of small waterways. Seedlings normally are grown in dense profusion in special seedbeds and later transplanted to the main fields; in earlier times transplanting was performed by hand, but today it is normally done by machine. Transplanting assures more uniform growth and also frees the main fields longer for the maturation of winter crops in the warmer parts of Japan, where double cropping is possible.

In the small floodplains and narrow valleys of Japan, this sort of agriculture did not require the massive water control efforts needed to harness the destructive forces and agricultural potential of great river systems. Large-scale water-control projects in Egypt, Mesopotamia, and North China are thought by some to have contributed to the development of mass authoritarian societies in these regions. In Japan, however, what was needed was close cooperation in the sharing of water among smaller groups. Probably such cooperative efforts over the centuries contributed to the notable Japanese penchant for group identification and group action.

Irrigated rice cultivation as practiced in Japan in the past demanded enormous amounts of labor, but it produced much higher yields per acre than the dry-field wheat farming of the West. As much of the land as possible was converted into irrigated paddies. Marshes, swamps, and coastal flats were carefully drained, diked, and turned into productive areas. Elsewhere rice fields followed each stream or rivulet almost to its source and, where water was available, ascended the hillsides in man-made terraces. Unirrigated dry fields for other crops stretched still higher up the slopes or wherever water could not be made to flow. Today rice is grown as far north as the western half of Hokkaido, and roughly 40 percent of farmland is devoted to paddy.

The productivity of the land has been further increased by double cropping wherever possible, usually between summer rice and various winter grains or vegetables. This sort of double cropping can be practiced in the half of Japan southwest of a line running from a little north of Tokyo to the west coast of Honshu north of Kyoto.

As a result of intensive wet-field rice cultivation and double cropping, Japan, like the rest of East Asia, has supported since antiquity much heavier concentrations of population than the drier or colder lands of West Asia and Europe. At least since Roman times China alone has equaled or outdistanced the population of all of Europe, and the Japanese population as long as three centuries ago had grown well beyond that of European states of comparable size. Thus the Japanese have been living together for many centuries in much larger and more concentrated masses than have Westerners. These conditions may have helped develop their propensities for group action and their skills in group organization.

Japanese agricultural methods, involving as they once did an immense amount of labor, were relatively primitive when compared with the large-scale, highly mechanized agriculture of the United States. Even with the aid of modern machines, it is still not very productive per man-hour, but it is extremely productive per acre—perhaps the most productive in the world. For example, until recently Japanese rice yields per acre were two to four times those of Southeast and South Asia. This emphasis on productivity per acre rather than per man is understand-

Facing page: Mountains, sea, and intensive agriculture characterize most of Japan's countryside. Here farmers cultivate by hoe wheat and vegetable patches on terraced fields by an inlet from the sea on the island of Shikoku. (© *Bob Davis / Woodfin Camp & Associates*)

able because Japan has long been richer in people than in land. As a result, well over a hundred times as many people work a square mile of farmland as in the United States and almost ten times as many as in West Germany.

Japanese agriculture, however, is very efficient and even scientific in its own way. Almost every square foot of tillable land is exploited as fully as possible. The rice seedlings or other crops are planted in careful straight rows that fill every square inch of space. The soil is carefully tilled to a depth of one or two feet, in earlier times by the long-bladed hoe of East Asia. The fields are meticulously weeded, and fertilizers are used in abundance. Originally these were organic materials, including until shortly after World War II night soil from the urban areas, which was as malodorous as it was economically beneficial. More recently night soil has virtually dropped out of use, and the Japanese farmer has come to depend largely on chemical fertilizers, which he applies lavishly. He also makes extensive use of vinyl coverings to form a type of simple greenhouse for vegetables.

Even before modern times Japanese agriculture had become self-consciously "scientific," and many treatises on improved seeds and superior agricultural methods were written by eighteenth-century farmers. Virtually all the suitable agricultural land had been put under cultivation (except in Hokkaido, which then was still a largely undeveloped border land), and both the government and farmers sought by every means to increase production. Thus, the population of around 30 million with which Japan entered the nineteenth century was perhaps almost the maximum that could be supported by the country in its preindustrial isolation.

The opening of Japan to world trade in the middle of the nineteenth century and the centralization and modernization of its government dramatically changed the situation, permitting a surge forward in agricultural production. Advanced agricultural techniques now could spread more rapidly from more progressive areas to backward regions; cheap transportation by steamships and then railroads made possible a greater regional specialization of crops; Hokkaido came under the plow; eventually government agricultural institutes made available more modern scientific agricultural knowledge; and in the twentieth century Manchurian soybean cakes and other sources of foreign fertilizers became available. Most of Japan's political modernization and industrial growth in the late nineteenth century was financed by surpluses achieved in agriculture. Population growth, however, in time outdistanced agricultural production, and by the beginning of the twentieth century Japan had developed a deficit of almost 20 percent in its food supply.

In the early years after World War II food was in extremely short supply, and hungry people tried to grow crops among the ruins of the cities and on any other scraps of unutilized land, but as the country slowly restored itself such desperate efforts were abandoned and some particularly uneconomic pieces of agricultural land were allowed to fall out of use. Meanwhile a rush of new technology brought another leap in agricultural productivity. Chemical fertilizers, which were already widely used, became available in even greater quantity, and mechanization at last came to agriculture, permitting a sharp decline in the farming population. In the depressed conditions of the early postwar years, close to half the Japanese remained engaged in agriculture, but thereafter the percentage declined drastically. At present only about 8 percent of Japanese live in farming households, and a mere quarter of these devote themselves exclusively to agriculture. The great majority combine seasonal work on the ancestral farm with other employment or, more frequently, perform their farming chores on weekends and in the early mornings and late evenings while holding down nonagricultural jobs

Harvesting rice by machine. The "farmer" appears to be dressed for his main job in town. (© *Michal Heron / Woodfin Camp & Associates*)

within commuting distance in factories, offices, or stores. For a while the farm work was done primarily by wives and retired parents, but the parents have mostly died, and the wives have joined their husbands in taking other positions, leaving very few full-time farmers.

The pattern of mechanization in Japanese agriculture is far different from that of the United States. In Hokkaido the size of farms is relatively large, though still very small by American standards, but elsewhere in Japan farms average only about two and a half acres, or about one hectare, the unit the Japanese themselves now use. A further drop in farm population may eventually produce a consolidation of farm holdings, but this has not yet started on a significant scale. In any case, regardless of the amount of land the individual farmer cultivates, the terrain dictates that most of the rice paddies and dry fields must be extremely small, better measured in square yards than in acres or hectares. Their size does not permit the use of great combines or large tractors. Instead the Japanese have developed an extremely different set of tractors, threshers, rice transplanters, and other machines, better suited to their type of agriculture and the smallness of their fields, and incidentally more suitable for the small fields and agricultural methods of most other parts of East, Southeast, and South Asia. The desire of each farm family to own its own machinery despite lack of adequate land to make much use of it has made Japanese agriculture perhaps the most overmechanized in the world.

Despite the drastic decline of agricultural labor, Japan witnessed a postwar surge in agriculture resulting in annual new records of rice production. Since per capita consumption of rice declined at the same time, because higher living standards permitted a more varied diet, the Japanese, to their amazement, suddenly found themselves with a surplus of rice. But with a population four times the Malthusian limit that was reached in the eighteenth century, the Japanese now face an even greater overall deficit in food of about 30 percent, or more than half if one counts imported feed grains used in domestic meat production.

Such shortages in food make the Japanese nervous. This anxiety, together with political sensitivity to the farm vote and a desire to avoid upsetting social changes in rural areas, has induced the government to continue to put emphasis on agriculture, even though it is much less productive per capita than most other forms of economic activity, contributing only about 3 percent to GNP. Generous farm subsidies keep food prices much higher in Japan than on the world market. For example, American rice identical to that produced in Japan could be unloaded in Japanese ports at only a fifth of the cost of domestic rice. To keep Japanese agriculture from being swamped by cheaper foreign produce, agricultural imports are strictly controlled, and the government has raised the price of rice to artificially high levels in order to maintain production and help farm families keep up with the rapid general rise in living standards. On the other hand, most farmers cling to their land, not just out of traditional devotion to it but also because, in the land-short, industrialized country that Japan has become, land prices have shot up astronomically, far beyond their agricultural value.

The Japanese farm population, as we have seen, has dropped precipitately, and the sprawling cities continue to gobble up surrounding tracts of the most productive agricultural acreage. But the Japanese will probably attempt to maintain their present degree of self-sufficiency in food. The resulting economic drag of inefficiently small-scale agriculture will probably be offset in their minds by the insurance value and psychological satisfaction of not being almost totally dependent on foreign sources for food, especially rice.

The diet and cuisine of the Japanese have been strongly influenced by the nature of their agriculture. Rice has always been the staple food and until recent times was eaten in large quantities at all three meals each day. In fact, the word for cooked rice *(gohan)* is also the word for meal. *Sake,* the chief traditional alcoholic beverage, is made from rice by a brewing process that gives it an alcoholic content of 15 to 20 percent—a trifle stronger than most wine. All land that can be brought under irrigation, almost regardless of the effort required to do so, has been devoted to rice cultivation. Nonirrigable fields are used for dry-field crops of other grains, vegetables, and justly renowned fruit, including most of the temperate zone varieties as well as a great abundance of Mandarin oranges.

Of the total land area of Japan, less than 2 percent, largely in the colder north, is pastureland used for the less efficient production of food through animal husbandry. In the past, cattle were used to haul carts or plow fields but not for food. Their relative scarcity, together with the Buddhist prejudice against the taking of animal life, made the Japanese for most of their history nonmeat eaters. They obtained their protein instead from the fish that abound in the waters which bathe the country and now largely from worldwide fisheries and imports. Much of the fish is eaten raw either in small slices called *sashimi* or as *sushi,* which combines it with seaweed and vinegared rice in a tidbit that has won wide popularity in the United States in recent years. Another important source of protein has always been the versatile soybean, which is now largely imported from abroad and is used to make *tofu* (bean curd), *miso* (fermented bean paste), and *shoyu* (soy sauce).

The traditional Japanese cuisine is simple and fairly bland, especially when compared with the world-famous cooking of the Chinese. Polished white rice, uncontaminated by sauces or condiments, is not just the belly filler in a traditional Japanese meal but also the most highly prized component. Large mouthfuls of rice are alternated with small bites of fish, vegetables, or pickles. Whereas a Chinese banquet consists of a series of rich dishes with a variety of sauces, a Japanese banquet is made up of a great number of small servings of individual things—a piece of cooked fish, a few slices of sashimi, some vegetables, pickles, and the like—all artistically served, often with more obvious attraction to the eye than to the palate. Chinese cooking is an overwhelming gustatory experience; traditional Japanese cooking appeals more to delicate tastes and to esthetic charm.

Of course, like everything else in Japan, eating habits have been changing rapidly in recent decades. Per capita consumption of rice has declined as the Japanese have developed more catholic tastes. Cheap imported wheat is baked into excellent European-style bread, which is commonly substituted for rice at breakfast. Meat, either imported or produced from imported feed grains, has become a significant part of the modern diet, though per capita consumption remains less than a fifth that of Americans. The Japanese have even taken to dairy products, which until recently were anathema to all East Asians. Even sake is gradually yielding place to excellent German-type beer, Scotch-type whiskey, and other Western beverages.

The Japanese enjoy a great variety of noodle dishes; Chinese cooking is widely prevalent; and Western dishes from French *haute cuisine* to American fast foods, such as McDonald's and Kentucky Fried Chicken, are very popular. The Japanese have also developed a number of specialty dishes that are quite unlike their traditional cuisine and perhaps for that very reason have achieved a degree of international fame. Among these are *sukiyaki,* a beef dish said to have been invented by iconoclastic medical students in the mid-nineteenth century, and *tempura,* or deep-fried prawns, thought by some to have been borrowed in the sixteenth century from the Portuguese. Japanese beef is known for its excellence, attributed by popular myth to beer mash and massage, though a more plausible explanation may be the fact that the animals are often stall raised and lack a range or even pasturelands in which to toughen their muscles.

The traditional Japanese diet of rice, vegetables, and fish, which contrasts with the heavy consumption of meat and fat in the West, would be almost a perfect health diet if it were less salty and the Japanese did not insist on polishing the nutritious bran off their rice. This diet may account in part for the low Japanese incidence of heart disease as compared with Americans. On the other hand, something about it, possibly the polished rice, may produce the high rate of stomach cancer in Japan.

In earlier days the diet was perhaps too austere for optimum childhood growth. Since World War II, Japanese children have increased several inches in height and many pounds in weight. Part of the increased height may be attributed to the straightening out of legs as Japanese sit less on the floor and more on chairs, but, like the weight, it may be chiefly due to a richer diet, which now includes dairy products and more meat and bread. Young Japanese today are quite visibly a bigger breed than their ancestors, and fat children, which formerly were never encountered, have become a commonplace sight.

Japan's meager supply of arable land is not offset by any other great natural riches. Water is the only resource with which it is well endowed. Plentiful rainfall makes possible its intensive agriculture and produces a dense forest cover on two thirds of the area. Much of this forest land is now scientifically planted for maximum growth. As a result, Japan, despite its small size, ranks relatively high among the wood-producing nations of the world, though the yield meets less than half its own voracious appetite for pulp for industry and lumber for its private housing. Traditionally almost all Japanese buildings were constructed of wood, since stone or brick structures were extremely vulnerable to earthquakes, and even now most private homes and small shops are made of wood. The small but precipitous rivers of Japan are also a significant source of hydroelectric power. Despite almost full exploitation, however, water power supplies less than 5 percent of Japan's present gargantuan consumption of electricity.

The surrounding seas are a major economic asset. They are the source of Japan's chief protein supply—fish—and also vitamin-rich seaweeds, which the Japanese use extensively in their cooking. Coastal waters have always provided vital food resources, and today there is considerable cultivation of fish, shellfish, and seaweed. Japanese fishing fleets also harvest the seven seas. In fact, Japan is the leading fishing nation in the world, which is appropriate for a large country with the highest per capita consumption of fish.

The oceans also provide the Japanese with easy communication within their country and constitute their highways to the resources and markets of the world. With the exception of the old capital of Kyoto, all of Japan's six biggest cities and a majority of its middle-sized cities are located directly on the sea. In most cases, they have themselves been extended seaward by the construction of new docking facilities and factory sites through the filling in of large stretches of shallow water. The bulk of Japanese heavy industry thus can be located efficiently for transportation purposes, not on inland waterways and railroads, but directly on the sea.

In mineral resources Japan is poorly endowed to meet its modern needs. The volcanic origin of the islands has provided an abundance of sulphur, and there are plenty of limestone, clays, sands, and the like, but otherwise Japan is short of almost every important mineral resource. A wide variety of minerals is to be found in the islands and these were adequate for Japanese needs in preindustrial times, but today they provide for the most part only marginal support to Japanese industry. There is, for example, sufficient coal to have been of critical importance in Japan's early industrialization, but the seams, being thin and broken, are not easily exploited, and today Japan imports more than five times as much coal as it produces. Once Japan was a copper exporter, but even in this commodity it is now almost entirely dependent upon the outside world, and more than two thirds of its zinc and six sevenths of its lead, two other minerals with which the islands are reasonably well supplied, must come from abroad. In most other important minerals, including iron ore, Japan is entirely or almost entirely dependent on imports. Worst of all, it is virtually lacking in the key energy resource of petroleum, which accounts for roughly three fifths of total Japanese energy consumption. Moreover, it has only very meager prospects for offshore oil and no appreciable fuels for nuclear power.

Despite its paucity of natural resources and extremely limited agricultural base, Japan's population has more than doubled since the beginning of the twentieth century and its standard of living has increased many times over. Obviously, this sort of growth has been possible only because of rapid industrialization. But because of Japan's narrow and poorly endowed geographic base, this industrialization has brought with it a heavy dependence on foreign sources of energy and raw materials and therefore an equal dependence on foreign markets for industrial exports to pay for necessary imports. Japan is the world's largest importer of oil, coal, iron ore, a large number of other ores and metals, cotton, wool, lumber, and a great variety of other commodities. Although Japan once grew its own cotton, it has long since converted the land used for cotton to food crops and buys its cotton abroad. It has even become a net importer of silk, a labor-intensive semiagricultural product (because of the mulberry leaves on which silk worms are fed), which was its greatest export item from the 1860s until the 1920s. Japan's dependence on global trade for its very survival is the single most important fact about its economic geography and the chief determinant of its relationship with the rest of the world.

Industrialization naturally means cities, and Japan is indeed a heavily urbanized land today. But in fact, even the preindustrial, isolated Japan of the eighteenth century was economically and politically centralized

A small corner tower on one of the moats surrounding the old Edo castle, now in large part the imperial palace grounds, which provide a spacious island of greenery in the center of Tokyo. *(Courtesy Morris G. Simoncelli / Japan Air Lines)*

enough to have had surprisingly large cities. Edo, as Tokyo was then called, had a population of about a million and may have been the largest city in the world around 1700. Osaka, the great trade center, and Kyoto, the ancient capital, both had several hundred thousands. The rest of Japan was dotted with castle towns which ranged up to 100,000 in population and were the seats of the roughly two hundred and sixty-five semiautonomous feudal lords.

In the middle of the nineteenth century there was already a sizable urban population, and the growth since then has been prodigious. Tokyo alone now has more than 8 million people in its main urban areas (the portion divided into wards) and over 11 million counting the suburban cities of Tokyo Prefecture. Packed alongside it are Yokohama, with about 3 million; Kawasaki, with over a million, squeezed between Yokohama and Tokyo; and heavy industrial and suburban populations in the adjacent portions of surrounding prefectures. The whole population node rivals metropolitan New York and is one of the four or five largest in the world.

The Kansai region, around Osaka, is another great metropolitan area of more than 12 million people. Meaning "west of the pass," the Kansai is the one great regional rival to the Kanto area ("east of the pass"), around Tokyo. In addition to Osaka, which has more than 2.5 million people, the Kansai includes the great port city of Kobe and the old capital of Kyoto a little way inland, each with close to 1.5 million, and a host of smaller cities.

Nagoya, midway between the Kanto and the Kansai, is the center of another major node of well over 2 million people. Sapporo, the capital of Hokkaido, has 1.5 million; Fukuoka, the old capital of northern Kyushu, and Kitakyushu, a large industrial center made up of a number of once separate municipalities and located as its name, "North Kyushu," indicates, both exceed a million; and Hiroshima, on the Inland Sea, has close to a million. Besides the cities named above, there are 194 other municipalities ranging from 100,000 to over 800,000, and an industrial sprawl permeates most of the countryside wherever there are a relatively heavy rural population and adequate transportation facilities.

Japanese industry is located in the nonmountainous fifth of the country, but it is particularly thick along the old main line of Japanese history, which extends westward from the Tokyo area along the Pacific coast through Nagoya to the Kansai region and then along the northern side of the Inland Sea to northern Kyushu. Here lies an almost continuous band of factories and houses, interspersed at places with agriculture and broken only occasionally by mountain ridges. This coastal band is comparable to the strip city of the American east coast and contains close to half Japan's total population.

As a result of political centralization and then industrialization during the past 120 years, Japan now has excellent internal communications. The metropolitan areas are serviced by superb networks of commuting railway lines and the cities of Tokyo and Osaka by fine subway systems as well. Where commuting lines converge, large secondary "downtown" areas have developed, as at Shinjuku, five miles west of downtown Tokyo. Despite these scattered downtowns and the fine commuting systems, the size of the Tokyo and Osaka metropolitan areas forces millions of people to commute to work or school between one and two hours each way.

The whole of Japan is now tied together by a complex and efficient railway network, and modern high-speed highways are beginning to spread to most areas. The water breaks between the main islands are being overcome by giant bridges and tunnels. These already connect Kyushu with Honshu; a tunnel to Hokkaido, longer than the English Channel tunnel, is in use, and bridges connect Shikoku with the main island. Airlines cover the islands, but a series of "New Main Lines" (*Shinkansen*) railways running from Tokyo through the Kansai to Fukuoka and also to the west coast and northern Japan carry the bulk of the traffic at speeds averaging well over a hundred miles an hour. They run with incredible punctuality and frequency, about every 15 minutes between Tokyo and Osaka, covering the 343 miles on this run in a mere three hours. Planes are much less reliable and, counting the time needed to travel between city centers and airports, not much faster.

Japan's cities and general industrial sprawl are scarcely its most attractive features. Industrialization came rapidly to Japan, and under adverse conditions. During World War II most of the cities were in large part destroyed, and they had to be rebuilt in a period of great economic stress. Many of their structures, as a consequence, were flimsy and tawdry. Little effort was put into city planning; economic necessity seemed to override all other considerations.

Today the rate of growth is more leisurely, and attention can be given to matters other than economic production, but Japan still faces great problems. As the world's most crowded land in terms of habitable area, it suffers acutely from a general lack of space, and this situation is, of course, worst in the cities. Land prices are extremely high, and crowding

A typical city street, jammed with cars and pedestrians. Overpasses are common for people who prefer stairs to the hazards of crossing large streets on foot. As in England, traffic keeps to the left. (© *Sonia Katchian / Photo Shuttle: Japan*)

is inevitably severe in personal living accommodations and public facilities. Almost all Japanese would prefer small individual houses, but many city dwellers have been forced to find accommodations in the groups of four- to ten-story concrete apartment buildings (called *danchi*) that ring most of the large cities. In these an apartment is usually no larger than a good-sized room in an American home, though it may be divided into two small sleeping and living rooms and an even tinier

Facing page:

Above: Tokyo viewed eastward from downtown. The city and its satellites stretch from its center some fifteen to thirty miles in all directions, making greater Tokyo one of the largest nodes of population in the world. (© *Michal Heron / Woodfin Camp & Associates*)

Below: Rush hour on one of the platforms of a Tokyo railway station. The signs with large arrows say "Up" and "Down." The "No Smoking" sign is self-explanatory. (© *Michal Heron / Woodfin Camp & Associates*)

kitchen and bathroom. A third of housing facilities in Tokyo average only eleven by eleven feet in size, and most Japanese still lack flush toilets. The Japanese were deeply wounded when an outspoken British journalist a few years ago compared their apartments to "rabbit hutches," and irritation still rankles over the comment.

The roads of Tokyo and Osaka occupy only 12 and 9 percent of the land space, compared with 35 percent in New York. Residents are allowed to have a car in Tokyo only if they can prove they have offstreet parking, with the result that the entrances to many homes look like small garages. Tokyo residents have less than a tenth as much park space per person as residents of New York and hardly more than a twentieth that of Londoners. In comparison with Japanese urban conditions, even the most crowded cities of the United States seem almost like the proverbial wide open spaces.

The net result is that Japanese cities and their surrounding areas of urban sprawl are not only terribly crowded but also form a vast esthetic wasteland. Although private homes often wall off quiet islands of beauty, and many small side streets are quite charming, the outer face of most cities is almost unrelievedly ugly, contrasting sharply with the beauties of sea, mountain, and the rural countryside, where these remain undisturbed by industrialization. The great moats and castle walls of the imperial palace grounds have always given charm and dignity to the center of Tokyo, but otherwise Japanese cities are only just beginning to take on some shape and grandeur, as broad thoroughfares are cut through the jumble of houses and handsome new buildings rise, sometimes to a height of forty or fifty stories.

The scarcity of space in Japan, combined with a much smaller investment in the past in permanent, paved roadways and in longer-lasting structures of brick and stone, means that actual "living standards" in Japan may be quite a bit lower than per capita GNP figures would suggest. Space up to a certain point is a vital element in well-being. Though it cannot be factored into our statistics, its scarcity justifies the Japanese in their argument that they are quite a bit poorer in "gross national living standards" than the GNP figures would indicate. In any case, in Japan's cities, with their vast industrial production, vibrant life, but deplorable overcrowding, one encounters as clearly as anywhere in the world the mixture of triumphs and mounting problems that characterize industrialized society today.

3 Isolation

One final, vital fact about the geographic setting of the Japanese is their relative isolation. Japan lies off the eastern end of the Old World in much the same way the British Isles lie off its western end, though at considerably greater distance. The more than 100 miles that separate the main Japanese islands from Korea is roughly five times the width of the Straits of Dover. In the time of primitive navigation it constituted a considerable barrier, and the roughly 450 miles of open sea between Japan and China were even more formidable.

Throughout most of its history Japan has been perhaps the most isolated of all the major countries of the world. Until the dawn of oceanic commerce in the sixteenth century it was fitfully in contact with its two closest neighbors, Korea and China, and influences from further afield came to Japan only as filtered through these two lands. In more modern times, Japan's rulers took advantage of their natural geographic isolation to fix on the country a firm policy of seclusion from the outside world. For more than two centuries, from 1638 to 1853, the Japanese were almost completely sequestered from foreign contacts. It was a unique experience at a time of quickening international and inter-regional relations elsewhere in the world.

Thus natural geographic isolation, magnified later by human design, forced the Japanese to live more separately from the rest of the world than any other comparably large and advanced group of people. Or perhaps one should say that this combination of natural and artificial isolation enabled them more than most other peoples to develop on their own and in their own way. Certainly the Japanese throughout history have been culturally a very distinctive people, diverging sharply even from the patterns of nearby China and Korea, from which much of their higher civilization originally came. Even today, Japan occupies a unique place in the world as the one major industrialized and fully modernized nation that has a non-Western cultural background.

Isolation has had a number of important by-products. It has made other people, even the nearby Koreans and Chinese, look on the Japanese as being somehow different and has produced in the Japanese a strong sense of self-identity and also an almost painful self-consciousness in the presence of others. Such things are hard to measure, but the Japanese do seem to view the rest of the world, including even their close cultural and racial relatives in Korea and China, with an especially strong "we" and "they" dichotomy. Throughout history they have displayed almost a mania for distinguishing between "foreign" borrowings and elements regarded as "native" Japanese.

Isolation thus has ironically caused the Japanese to be acutely aware of anything that comes from outside and to draw special attention to its foreign provenance. The civilization of any country is much more the product of external influences than of native invention. If one subtracted everything from English culture that had foreign roots or antecedents, there would be little left. But borrowing from abroad has usually been a slow and unconscious process or at least has gone unrecorded. The Japanese, on the other hand, have always been sharply conscious of the distinction between "foreign" and "native" and made the fact of cultural borrowing a major theme of their history. Thus they have given themselves and others the impression that they are somehow uniquely cultural borrowers. A myth has grown up that, unlike other peoples, the Japanese are mere mimics, incapable of invention themselves and unable to understand the inner essence of what they have borrowed. In actuality, their isolation has probably forced them to invent a greater part of their culture and develop a more distinctive set of characteristics than almost any comparable unit of people in the world. What distinguishes them is not their imitativeness but rather their distinctiveness and their skill at learning and adapting while not losing their own cultural identity. Others have tried to do the same but with less success.

Another by-product of isolation may be Japan's unusual degree of cultural homogeneity, which has already been remarked upon. Of course, isolation and homogeneity do not necessarily go together, as can be seen in the case of the British Isles. But prolonged separation from the outside world perhaps aided in the spread of uniform cultural patterns throughout the Japanese islands, despite their internal barriers of terrain.

The theme of homogeneity will reappear frequently in our story, but one striking illustration of it is the racial composition of the Japanese people, which might be regarded as part of the natural setting for Japanese civilization. The Japanese, like all other peoples, are the product of long and largely unrecorded mixtures. In fact, the diversity of facial types in Japan suggests considerable mixing in the past. But the important point is that, whatever their origins, the Japanese today are the most thoroughly unified and culturally homogeneous large bloc of people in the world, with the possible exception of the North Chinese. There are few important physical variations throughout the islands, and, while there are differences in folkways and accents, not unlike those among the English, French, Germans, and Italians, there are none of the sharp divisions as between Gaelic and English speakers and Protestants and Catholics in the British Isles, between speakers of French, Breton, German, and Basque in France, or the profound differences of all sorts between north and south Italians.

Actually the Japanese islands form a sort of cul-de-sac into which various peoples drifted over time and, finding no exit, were forced to mix with later comers. Among these peoples were the Ainu, who may represent an early type of man dating from a period before the modern races became clearly differentiated. In any case, they combine some characteristics of the white race, notably hairiness of face and body, with characteristics associated with other races. Thus the Ainu may account for the somewhat greater hairiness of some Japanese as compared to most other members of the Mongoloid race. At one time the Ainu, or people who at least were in part their ancestors, occupied either all or most of the Japanese islands, and until the eighth century they still controlled the northern third of the island of Honshu. But bit by bit they were conquered and absorbed by the main body of Japanese, until today fewer than 20,000 Ainu survive as a culturally identifiable group in the northern island of Hokkaido, and even these are on the brink of complete absorption.

Basically the Japanese are a Mongoloid people, much like their neighbors on the nearby Asian continent. Both archaeology and historical records attest to a broad flow of peoples from northeastern Asia through the Korean Peninsula into Japan, especially during the first seven centuries of the Christian era. There may also have been an earlier flow of people or at least cultural traits from more southerly regions, which gave rise to certain "southern" characteristics that Japanese culture shares with the peoples of Southeast Asia and the South Pacific. An early diffusion of peoples and cultures may have occurred from South China southward but also eastward to Japan by way of Korea. These "southern" strains may account for some of the mythology of Japan, the flimsy, tropical nature of its early architecture, and the fact that Japanese in physical build are more like the South Chinese than their somewhat taller and sturdier neighbors in Korea and North China.

Hints in the historical records suggest that there was some ethnic diversity in Western Japan up until the eighth century, and there is solid evidence of a heavy flow of people from Korea up until that time, but there has been no major infusion of new blood since that time. In fact, for over a thousand years immigration of any sort into Japan has been only infinitesimal. There has thus been a long time for racial mingling and the development of a high degree of cultural homogeneity. This process was no doubt aided by the artificial seclusion of Japan from the seventeenth to the nineteenth centuries and has been further fostered by strong centralized rule since then. But long before this the Japanese had developed a picture of themselves as a racially distinct and "pure" group, often portrayed in terms of a single great family. It is a concept more frequently encountered among primitive tribal peoples than among the citizens of a large modern nation.

Japan's imperial conquests in modern times and its present global trade have attracted some foreigners into the islands in recent decades. The only sizable group, however, is a Korean community of about 700,000 left over for the most part from the much larger numbers imported during World War II to replace Japanese workers gone off to war. There are also a few tens of thousands of Chinese, mostly merchants, from Japan's former colony in Taiwan or from the mainland, and a few thousand other outlanders from more distant parts of Asia and the West.

Altogether, these outsiders number much less than 1 percent of the population, and only the Koreans constitute any sort of a real ethnic problem. Since they are physically all but identical with the Japanese and are closely allied to them in language, they could be readily absorbed both culturally and physically, and Koreans born in Japan usually do lose the language of their parents in much the same way that people of non-English-speaking origin become linguistically absorbed in the United States. The Japanese, in their extreme ethnocentrism, however, tend to reject Koreans as full members of their society, while the

Koreans, resentful of this attitude and of Japan's colonial domination of their homeland in the past, often cling to their ethnic identity. In fact, the Korean community injects a disruptive element into Japanese society and politics by its passionate adherence to one or the other of the two rival Korean regimes and the respective supporters of these regimes in Japanese politics. The Korean problem, however, is a tiny one compared to that of ethnic diversity in North America or even the problems caused by floods of postwar immigrants and temporary workers into the countries of northern Europe.

One extraordinary exception to Japanese homogeneity, however, deserves mention. This is the survival from feudal times of a sort of outcast group, known in the past by various names, including the term *eta,* but now usually called *burakumin,* or "hamlet people," a contraction from "people of special hamlets." This group, which accounts for less than 2 percent of the population, probably originated from various sources, such as the vanquished in wars or those whose work was considered particularly demeaning. Clearly they included people engaged in leather work or butchery, since the Buddhist prejudice against the taking of all animal life made others look down on such persons, though, it should be noted, not on the butchers of human life in a feudal society dominated by a military elite.

The *burakumin* have enjoyed full legal equality since 1871, but social prejudice against them is still extreme. While they are in no way distinguishable physically from the rest of the Japanese and are not culturally distinct except for their generally underprivileged status, most Japanese are reluctant to have contact with them and are careful to check family records to ensure that they avoid intermarriage. In the highly urbanized Japan of today, the *burakumin* are becoming progressively less recognizable, but their survival as an identifiable group is a surprising contrast to the otherwise almost complete homogeneity of the Japanese people.

Japan's isolation is now only a psychological remnant. Japan, in fact, is in a sense the least remote of all nations. None is more clearly dependent on a massive worldwide flow of trade simply to exist. As a result, it has developed strong trade relations with almost all parts of the world. The seas that once cut it off now bind it effectively to all regions. The great distances that once lay between it and all other countries have now shrunk to insignificance. Military destruction can be projected across the oceans in a matter of minutes. Floods of words and visual images are transmitted instantaneously throughout the world. A person can be in both Tokyo and New York on the same calendar day. With the coming of giant tankers and container vessels, the costs of oceanic transportation have plummeted compared with those of land transport. Mountain ranges, deserts, tropical jungles, and arctic tundra can still be serious barriers to commerce, and man-made barriers can be even greater, but oceans are now the cement that binds the world together economically. It is for these reasons that, in drawing my population and GNP maps, I largely eliminated the oceans and seas, leaving only enough of them to help demarcate the various countries and continental land masses, and I placed Japan, not on the periphery as it seemed to be in the past, but in the center, a spot to which it is as much entitled as any nation because of its massive involvement in worldwide trade.

The shift from almost complete isolation little more than a century ago to complete involvement today has, in historical terms, been sudden. The impact of outside economic and military power as well as of culture and ideas was once cushioned by what were then great intervening distances and also by firm man-made barriers. The psychological effects of isolation still linger on among the Japanese and in the attitudes of other peoples toward them. Linguistically the Japanese remain quite separate, having a most unusual and difficult writing system and a very distinctive language. But the original geographic isolation and the self-imposed isolation of more recent times exist no more.

This has been a huge and upsetting change for the Japanese. Attitudes and skills once suitable to their position in the world do not serve them as well today. The adjustment to the new conditions is not an easy one to make. The Japanese feel grave uncertainty about their position in the world and even about their identity. What does it mean to be Japanese today, and what should Japan's role be in the contemporary world? These are questions the Japanese frequently ask themselves, and I shall return to them in the final section of this book.

Part Two

Historical
Background

The Daibutsu ("Great Buddha") of Kamakura dates from the thirteenth century, when Kamakura, near Tokyo, was the military capital of Japan. It and a similar figure in Nara in West Japan are the two largest bronze statues in the world. The temple that once housed it was swept away by a tidal wave in 1495. (Courtesy Morris G. Simoncelli / Japan Air Lines)

4 *Early Japan*

Japan's location and natural endowments helped determine the path the Japanese took, but these physical features alone can
scarcely account for what they are today. Without some knowledge of
their past experience, the contemporary Japanese and their potentialities
cannot really be understood. And there is another reason for looking
back at Japanese history. Unlike Americans but like the other peoples of
East Asia, the Japanese have a strong consciousness of history. They see
themselves in historical perspective. They will delve a thousand years
and more into their past in analyzing their contemporary traits. To
understand Japan and its problems as these appear to the Japanese
themselves, we must know something about their background. Thus,
before concentrating on the present scene, we would do well to take a
quick look at the past.*

The islands of Japan were reached relatively late by the higher civilization of the Old World. Some of the oldest pottery in the world has
been found in Japan, but the islands were thousands of years behind
Europe, the Middle East, the Indian subcontinent, and China in the introduction of agriculture and centuries behind in the use of bronze and
iron. These metals seem to have begun to enter the islands at the same
time as agriculture in the third and second centuries B.C.

Our first clear view of the Japanese is afforded by Chinese records of
the third century A.D. They are described as having sharp class divisions
and living by agriculture and fishing. They were divided into a hundred
or more tribal units under female or male chieftains of semireligious
status. What the records call the "queen's country" had a certain hegemony over the others. The presence of women rulers suggests an origi-

* For those who desire a more detailed consideration of Japanese history, I suggest my
book *Japan: The Story of a Nation* (New York: Knopf, 1981).

nally matriarchal system, which fits well with the mythological tradition of the descent of the historical imperial line from the sun goddess.

Starting around 200 A.D., Japan seems to have been overrun by waves of mounted invaders from the Korean Peninsula, or at least by cultural influences from Korea. During the next three centuries many large burial mounds were built throughout the western two thirds of the islands, suggesting considerable concentrations of wealth and power in the hands of a military aristocracy. By the sixth century a group centered in the small Yamato or Nara Plain, which lies across a range of hills a little to the east of Osaka, had established clear leadership over most if not all of western Japan. The political and economic organization of the country had become complex but was still relatively primitive. Most of the land remained under the control of semiautonomous tribal units called *uji*, which were bound to the ruling family of the Yamato group by mythological ties and real or fictitious bonds of kinship. These *uji* had their own chiefs and their own *uji* shrines. Each also controlled a number of subordinate *uji* and pseudo-family groupings of farmers, fishermen, weavers, and other types of workers.

The religious practices of these early Japanese were later given the name Shinto, "the way of the gods," to distinguish them from the imported religion of Buddhism. Shinto centered on the worship of the gods, or *kami*, which were natural phenomena or mythological ancestors, the latter often nature gods as in the case of the sun goddess. The line between man and nature was not drawn sharply, and unusual or awesome men were easily made into deities. The leaders were both high priests and temporal rulers—in fact the same words were used for "religious worship" and "government" and for "shrine" and "palace." There were no ethical concepts associated with these religious ideas, except for a sense of awe and reverence before nature and a concept of ritual purity, which some believe may have contributed to the Japanese insistence on cleanliness and love of bathing.

Already by the sixth century there had been a heavy flow of cultural influences into Japan from the nearby continent. Agriculture as well as bronze and iron were examples of this. But in the middle of the sixth century the flow quickened, and the Japanese became conscious of it in a way they had not been before. It started with a fight at the Yamato court over the acceptance of Buddhist images and beliefs as a magical system of equal or possibly greater power than Shinto. The supporters

The five-storied pagoda of the Horyuji Temple near Nara. The Horyuji was founded by Prince Shotoku early in the seventh century, but the pagoda and some other buildings probably date from late in that century. They are the oldest wooden buildings in the world and illustrate the classic simplicity of the T'ang Dynasty architecture of China. (*Courtesy Japan Information Center*)

of Buddhism won out, and a generation later Prince Shotoku, from 593 to 622 the regent for his reigning aunt, proved a great champion of the new religion and the continental civilization that accompanied it.

Shotoku himself wrote commentaries on Buddhist scriptures and erected Buddhist monasteries. One of them, the serenely beautiful Horyuji near Nara, is noted for having the oldest wooden buildings in the world and a wealth of beautiful Buddhist images dating from this period. Shotoku also dispatched embassies to the Chinese capital to learn directly from this source of high culture, and he began to copy Chinese political institutions and drafted a so-called constitution, embodying Buddhist and Chinese precepts.

In the next generation a group of innovators, seizing power at the court during the so-called Taika Reform of 645, promoted the borrowing of Chinese technology and institutions with increased vigor. The effort continued at full flood for almost two centuries more, tapering off only in the ninth century. It transformed Japan from a backward, tribal area into a full participant in the higher civilization of the Old World, modeled, even if imperfectly, on China, which at that time was embarking on what was to be almost a millennium of leadership as the economically and politically most advanced nation in the world.

Western history shows no parallel to the conscious Japanese effort at massive cultural borrowing, with the possible exception of the much later and far less difficult and ambitious attempt of Peter the Great of Russia at the beginning of the eighteenth century. There were somewhat similar efforts, however, among other peoples in the penumbra of Chinese civilization, such as the Koreans and the tribal peoples of Manchuria. This difference from the West may have been more the result of the glory and appeal of Chinese civilization than of some special characteristic of the Japanese or the other peripheral peoples. Rome at this time was by comparison a tragically decayed model. In any case, from the sixth to the ninth centuries the Japanese, who had in earlier times been decidedly behind the peoples of northern Europe, surged ahead of them in art, literature, technology, and political and social skills. They also developed a clear awareness of the distinction between borrowed and "native" elements in their culture, thus achieving an early realization of the value of learning from other countries but also laying the foundation for the myth that they were an uncreative race of borrowers.

The Chinese since antiquity had seen their civilization as centering around the political unit, and the Japanese and other peoples of East Asia accepted this concept of the primacy of a unified political system. This concept contrasted with the emphasis on religion as the unifying element in South and West Asia and the acceptance in the West, after the fading of Rome, of religious unity but political diversity. The East Asian emphasis on the political unit may help account for the fact that among the nations of the contemporary world those that first took shape as recognizably the same political units they are today are China in the third century B.C. and Korea and Japan in the seventh century A.D.

The Japanese also accepted the Chinese concept of an all-powerful monarchy, attempting to transform their native, semisacred leader into a secular ruler of the Chinese type. Ever since, the Japanese emperor has in theory had the dual character and functions of a religious leader of the native Shinto cults and the secular monarch of a Chinese-type state. In actuality, however, he rarely operated in the second capacity. The Japanese emperors had not in remembered times come to power as conquerors, and already by the seventh century they were largely symbols of authority rather than wielders of personal power. As time went on, an occasional strong man on the throne might attempt to rule as well as reign, but for the most part emperors were manipulated by other members of the extensive imperial clan, by the broader court aristocracy, and in time by the feudal nobility of the provinces. Under these circumstances, the onerous ceremonial functions of the emperors overshadowed their exercise of power, and it is therefore not surprising that early abdication had become almost the rule by the ninth century. The present status of the emperor as merely the "symbol of the State and the unity of the people" is no modern anomaly but has more than a millennium of history behind it.

Below the emperor, the Japanese borrowed the Chinese organs of a centralized state. The country was divided into provinces administered by officials dispatched from the capital. The Chinese law codes were taken over almost verbatim. At the capital, an elaborate bureaucratic form of government was created, though with innovations on the Chinese model to fit it better to Japanese conditions. For example, the traditional six ministries of Chinese government were increased to eight in order to accommodate an Imperial Household Ministry and a central secretariat, and a Council of Deities, representing the native religious side of the emperor's functions, was set up to balance the political Council of State.

An elaborate system of court ranks of the Chinese type was instituted to supersede the traditional ranking system of the court families and local *uji*, and innumerable bureaucratic posts were created. In the Chinese system, particularly as it developed after the late seventh century, the higher posts in government were filled in large part by bureaucrats who had displayed their qualifications through elaborate and highly scholastic state-administered examinations. But this system had not developed fully at the time the Japanese started to borrow the Chinese model, and in any case it was probably too foreign to their highly aristocratic society to be acceptable. Both rank and position in the Japanese bureaucracy quickly became determined by inherited family status rather than by individual merit.

One of the most amazing aspects of the Japanese borrowing from China was the adoption of the extremely complex landholding and tax system. According to this, all land in theory belonged to the central government and most of it was to be periodically assigned in equal proportions to all peasant families, so that each could bear a uniform tax burden, assigned largely by head and divided into the three categories of agricultural products, textile products, and labor. This cumbersome system worked only imperfectly in China and broke down periodically. In a still relatively backward Japan, it is surprising that it worked at all, but it clearly was applied to a large part of the land and operated after a fashion for several centuries, though reassignments of land probably never took place. One other feature of the system never was put into effect. This was the creation of a large draft army as part of the labor service due the government as taxes. In their island fastness, the Japanese had no need for large foot-soldier armies, and military service remained for the most part an aristocratic profession.

A centralized political system required a central capital city. Until this time the Japanese had not even had towns, but now they attempted to build capitals in the Chinese style, centered around extensive palace and government buildings. The first city to have much permanence was Heijo, or Nara, as it was later known. It was laid out in the Yamato Plain in the checkerboard pattern of the Chinese capital. Since it served as the seat of government from 710 to 784, the eighth century is commonly known as the Nara Period. A second permanent capital, Heian, was founded in 794 in a small plain north of Yamato, and the next few centuries are known as the Heian Period. Heian too had a Chinese checkerboard plan, which is still to be seen in the main streets of Kyoto, as this city later came to be called.

While political innovation lay at the heart of the borrowings from China, all of Japan's higher culture was affected. The scholarship, philosophy, and literature of China were much studied and deeply influenced styles of thought and even habits of life. There was a great surge forward in technology in such diverse fields as weaving, lacquer ware, and metallurgy. An orchestral court music and dance were learned from China and Korea and are still preserved in Japan as probably the world's oldest authentic music and dance traditions. The arts of Japan were completely transformed, and in architecture, sculpture, and painting Japanese created works of art in the Chinese style that were comparable to the best in China.

Most of the art centered on the new religion, Buddhism, which unlike Shinto was a highly sophisticated religion of universal appeal. It had started in India a millennium earlier and stressed the concepts that life, made perpetual by an endless cycle of reincarnations, was basically painful but could be escaped through careful self-cultivation and the achievement of enlightenment, leading to Nirvana, or the blissful merging of the individual identity with the cosmos. In its course through the centuries and spread throughout the eastern two thirds of Asia, Buddhism had acquired a huge literature, a rich art, a tremendous pantheon, and a wide variety of doctrines and beliefs. It was the magical aspects of some of these beliefs and the glory of Buddhist art, rather than the austere early doctrines, that initially appealed to the Japanese court. The new religion was at first limited largely to court circles, and it was not until the eighth and ninth centuries that it began to spread widely throughout the country.

The Japanese were lucky to be able to learn from China, then the most advanced nation in the world, but it was most unfortunate for them that the Chinese had a writing system that was ill adapted to Japanese needs. Any of the phonetic scripts, which by that time had spread over all regions west of China, could have been easily applied to the writing of Japanese. The Chinese writing system, however, consisted of unique symbols, or characters, for each of the thousands of Chinese words, and these could not easily be adapted to other languages, especially a highly inflected one like Japanese. As a consequence, the Japanese were forced to keep their records and conduct the written aspects of government in a foreign language. The great cultural advance in Japan during these centuries is all the more remarkable for having been achieved through the medium of an entirely different type of language and an extraordinarily difficult system of writing.

Despite these handicaps, the Japanese of this period produced voluminous writings. The Chinese considered the compilation of an accurate historical record to be an important function of government, since past experience was seen as a valuable guide to the present. The Japanese dutifully recorded their own meager history, attempting to make it stretch back to a respectable age—in fact, all the way back to 660 B.C. From this effort emerged two early histories, the *Kojiki* of 712 and the *Nihon shoki* (or *Nihongi*) of 720, which recorded Japanese mythology in its relatively pristine, primitive form, as well as more sober recent history.

Despite the massive wave of influences that swept over the Japanese between the seventh and ninth centuries, they seem to have managed to retain a clear sense of their own identity. One is reminded of the survival of Japanese self-identity despite the waves of Western influence during the past century. In both cases, geographic location and language probably helped account for the outcome. Because of their island position, the Japanese were never subject to invasion from China, as the Koreans repeatedly were, and therefore they could maintain a sharper sense of separateness. Their language also helped insulate them from absorption into the Chinese cultural unit. It is as radically different from Chinese as it is from English, and, even though the Japanese of the time were forced to write in Chinese, they spoke only Japanese. They also expressed their poetic emotions best through their own language. Although they did compose some poetry in Chinese, their greatest early poetic achievement was the *Manyoshu*, an anthology of some 4,516 native Japanese poems, collected shortly after 759 and laboriously written down syllable by syllable in Chinese characters used phonetically.

The Japanese not only survived the cultural flood from China but by the ninth century were beginning to blend it with their own culture to form a new synthesis. After several generations of acclimatization in the Japanese environment, borrowed Chinese institutions and culture had taken on a life of their own and, when further modified by native traits, produced an essentially new culture. Although it showed clearly the Chinese origin of many of its components, it was basically different both from what existed in China and from the earlier culture of Japan.

One of the clearest signs of the emergence of this new culture was the development in the ninth century of efficient ways to write Japanese. These were the *kana* syllabaries, in which Chinese characters were simplified and used phonetically to represent Japanese syllables. *Kana* permitted the Japanese to record with ease prodigious amounts of native poetry, almost exclusively in the form of brief 31-syllable *tanka*, or short poems. The best of these they collected in imperially commissioned anthologies. They also began to write extensively in prose. The ladies of the court often kept long diaries—the Japanese have ever since been the world's most enthusiastic diarists—and from these developed the world's first novels. The monumental *Tale of Genji* by Lady Murasaki, written around the year 1000, remains not only the world's first great novel but also one of the literary masterpieces of all time. It portrays in brilliant detail and psychological subtlety a court life that could hardly have been more different from that of China—or for that matter from the roughness of life in Europe at that time. All that seemed to matter for these lady diarists and novelists was the sensitivity of esthetic feelings and the style in which the participants in this life conducted themselves, dressed, and wrote down their poems. The world of economic and political strife and its commonplace people did not seem to exist at all—and perhaps it really did not for these sheltered members of the high aristocracy.

Back of the refined and gentle court life portrayed in the literature of the tenth and eleventh centuries was a series of profound changes that had greatly altered the borrowed Chinese economic and political system. Much of the land had gradually gravitated from state control into the hands of private owners, who often were completely free of tax burdens. This trend had started already in the eighth century, when private ownership of new agricultural lands was permitted, first for a specified period and then in perpetuity, as an incentive for the large investments required to make wild lands suitable for paddy irrigation. The trend was accelerated in the ninth century by the hold of the court aristocrats on the high posts in government and their willingness to bend the laws in favor of their own economic interests. More and more of the land became the permanent and increasingly tax-free holdings of the great court families or of influential Buddhist monasteries or Shinto shrines associated with the court. Sometimes smallholders in the provinces would commend their lands to these families or institutions in order to assure their freedom from the tax collector. By the twelfth century a great part of the agricultural land of the country had been divided into tax-free private estates, usually made up of scattered agricultural fields, and even the remaining taxed lands were becoming a form of private property, since the right to appoint provincial governors and control the tax yield was becoming a hereditary privilege of certain families.

The resulting pattern of land ownership was a complex one. At the bottom was the actual cultivator, above him a local strong man who managed the estate for its absentee owner, above him a powerful court family or institution that had titular ownership, and above it possibly a still more powerful patron who could guarantee the estate's tax-free status. Each had a specific share in the income. As this system developed, the flow of goods in the country became less a product of the tax system and more a matter of the payment of agricultural dues from provincial estates to owners or patrons in the capital area.

These developments starved the central government of both revenues and functions. As a result, the elaborate Chinese structure of centralized government began to atrophy, and simpler organs of government developed to take its place. But that did not mean that the old system disappeared. All the ranks and bureaucratic positions continued in existence but tended to become symbols of prestige and factors in court ritual rather than the instruments of real power. It was this situation that permitted the great emphasis on outward show and style that *The Tale of Genji* portrays. Meanwhile the private administrations maintained by the great court families and religious institutions became more and more the real government of the land.

Another change from the Chinese system was that during the ninth century one of the aristocratic court families established its dominance over the imperial family. This was the Fujiwara, descended from one of the leaders in the Taika Reform of 645. The basic reasons for Fujiwara dominance were their ownership of the greatest number of private estates and their growing monopoly of high government posts. Their technique of control was to have successive Fujiwara family heads named as regents for the emperors and to marry their daughters to the monarchs and put the resulting issue on the throne. Only retired emperors, freed of the ritual burdens of reigning, could challenge Fujiwara supremacy, as some who happened not to be the sons of Fujiwara mothers did with considerable success in the late eleventh and twelfth centuries.

The whole system that was evolving in Japan had indeed strayed far from the Chinese model. It was perhaps a system possible only in an isolated country like Japan. In China, a comparable decentralization of power would have invited conquest by nomadic neighbors or a usurpation of the throne by some vigorous new dynastic founder, better able than the old emperors to defend the country from invasion. In a Japan relatively free from outside pressures, there could be both a diffusion of control and a transfer of actual power at court without a change in the imperial line. Isolation permitted the Japanese to hold onto outmoded forms and institutions even when reality had passed them by. The result was a curious form of cultural conservation in Japan.

The change in Japanese society during the ninth to twelfth centuries was not limited to economics, politics, and court life but affected all aspects of the culture. Japanese literature was creatively forging new paths quite distinct from Chinese prototypes. In the arts, the Japanese also displayed their own particular genius. For example, in painting, while still using the techniques learned from the Chinese, they developed what they themselves called *Yamato-e,* or Japanese painting, in which they experimented in a bold use of color and a sense of design that still help differentiate Japanese artistic tastes from those of the Chinese. The Japanese thus demonstrated not only that they had maintained their cultural identity but also that they were indeed an extraordinarily creative people.

5 Feudalism

By the twelfth century Japan was on the threshold of an even greater departure from East Asian norms. This was the development of a feudal system, which over the next seven centuries was to go through phases that had many striking parallels to the feudal experience of Western Europe between the ninth and fifteenth centuries. These similarities to Europe cannot be laid to mutual influences, since there was no contact between the two. The parallels are more likely to have been the result of similarities in the social and cultural ingredients that became mixed together in these two areas—namely, tribal societies and relatively advanced political and economic systems. In the West, tribal German groups fell heir to the wreckage of the administration and land system of the Roman Empire. In Japan, the tribal islanders adopted the political institutions and land system of the Chinese Empire. In both cases, these two elements worked on each other over a long period in relative isolation, and out of the amalgam emerged a complex political system based on bonds of personal loyalty in a military aristocracy and the fusion of public authority and personal property rights to land.

As the authority and power of the central government declined in Japan, various groups of local leaders in the provinces banded together for mutual protection. These groups were made up of the officers of the old provincial administrations and the local managers or owners of estates. At first such groups consisted of relatives or neighbors, centered frequently around some charismatic figure who inspired loyalty. Because of the strong Japanese sense of hereditary authority, nothing was more prestigious than imperial descent. Thus, many of the groups came to be led by cadet branches of the imperial family that had received the family names Taira or Minamoto and had moved out to the provinces to make their fortunes as the representatives of central authority.

Organized to protect their own interests, the local groups were in essence vigilante bands of warriors. Their members formed a petty local aristocracy, somewhat like the knights of early feudal Europe, for they too were mounted, armored warriors. Their chief weapons were the bow and arrow, skillfully used from horseback, and the curved steel sword, which came to be the finest blade in the world. Their armor was quite different from that of the West, being much lighter and more flexible and therefore probably more efficient. It consisted largely of small strips of steel, bound together by brightly colored thongs and fitted loosely over the body.

These warrior bands slowly grew in the provinces and in the twelfth century became involved in the affairs of the central government at Kyoto. Succession rivalries within the main Fujiwara family and the imperial line induced the two sides to call on the armed support of warrior bands associated with their provincial estates. These fought two brief wars between 1156 and 1160, from which a Taira leader emerged as clearly the dominant military power over the court. He settled down at the capital, took for himself high positions in the central government, and, in the Fujiwara manner, married his daughter to the emperor and put the resulting grandson on the throne.

Meanwhile Yoritomo, the heir of the defeated Minamoto leader, raised the standard of revolt in the Kanto region in eastern Japan. By 1185 his forces had swept the Taira into oblivion, and he had become the undisputed military master of the land. Instead of establishing himself in Kyoto or taking high civil office there, he made his base at Kamakura, today a seaside suburb of Tokyo in East Japan, and took only the title of *shogun,* or generalissimo of the emperor's army. He rewarded his followers with the estates once managed or owned by the members of the defeated faction, creating for them the new managerial position of steward *(jito)* and grouping the stewards together for defense purposes by provinces under the leadership of a "protector" *(shugo).*

In theory Yoritomo left the old central government intact, with the court aristocrats still occupying the high civil posts and drawing income from the estates they owned; but within this somewhat hollow shell of the old imperial system, he had established effective control over the whole land by spreading throughout its estates a thin layer of warrior families from the Kanto who were personally loyal to him. Simple organs of family government in Kamakura gave direction to the whole group and administered justice on the basis of local customary law rather than the old Chinese-type law codes of the imperial court. Be-

A section of a thirteenth-century scroll painting, illustrating the burning of the Sanjo Palace in the Heiji War of 1159–60, which brought the provincial warrior Taira family to power in Kyoto. The mounted knights and foot soldiers wear efficient, flexible Japanese armor and are armed with swords and longbows; the foot soldiers also carry pikes. They are making off with the retired emperor Go-Shirakawa in an ox cart. The explanatory accompanying text is written in Japanese in a mixture of Chinese characters and *kana*, the native Japanese phonetic syllabary. The *kana* can be identified by their much greater simplicity and smaller size. (*Courtesy Museum of Fine Arts, Boston: Fenollosa-Weld Collection*)

cause so much of the old prefeudal government and economy remained unchanged, the Kamakura system was only proto-feudal, but it was efficient and lasted almost a century and a half, surviving during this period two very serious challenges.

One challenge was the early disappearance of the main Minamoto family, the focus of personal loyalty on which the whole system theoretically depended. First Yoritomo's suspicions of his close relatives and then the machinations of his widow and her Hojo family, ironically of Taira descent itself, led to the extinction of the line by 1219. Thereafter Hojo shogunal "regents," utilizing figurehead shoguns of Fujiwara or imperial origin, demonstrated once again the Japanese tendency to al-

low supreme authority to become purely symbolic. They also demonstrated the persistent Japanese preference for group over individual leadership. Power was usually shared by paired officers or collegial groups.

The other great challenge to the Kamakura system was the one serious invasion Japan faced between unrecorded antiquity and World War II. The Mongols had overrun Korea, Central Asia, much of the Middle East, and eastern Europe and then, more slowly and with much greater difficulty, the powerful Chinese Empire. They next attempted to invade Japan, sending against it in 1274 and again in 1281 the greatest overseas expeditions the world had as yet seen. These were turned back more by the weather than by the relatively small groups of Japanese knights who tried to beat them off. The fortuitous intervention in 1281 of a great typhoon—called the *kamikaze,* or "divine wind"—strengthened the Japanese in their belief in the divine uniqueness of their land.

The Kamakura system, depending as it did on the personal loyalty of a single warrior band spread thinly throughout the nation, eventually succumbed to the ravages of time. Repeated divisions of patrimonies impoverished many of the descendants of the original stewards, and they became increasingly dependent on local strong men, often the descendants of the original provincial "protectors." Moreover, loyalty to the central symbol of authority in Kamakura wore thin over the generations and came to be replaced by loyalty to better-known local leaders.

These trends resulted in a sudden breakdown of the whole system in the fourteenth century. The emperor Go-Daigo, who was an anomaly for his age, attempted in 1333 to take back political control, and the Kamakura general sent down to Kyoto to chastize him defected to his cause. The once unitary warrior clique immediately fell apart into a number of more localized bands of lords and vassals.

The turncoat Kamakura general, Ashikaga Takauji—Japanese family names precede personal names—soon broke with Go-Daigo, set up another member of the imperial family as emperor in Kyoto, and himself assumed the title of shogun. But there was no possibility of reestablishing the unity of the warrior class under a single lord. Instead Takauji and his descendants, who settled down in Kyoto and held on to the title of shogun until 1573, attempted to create a three-tiered feudal system. They asserted their supremacy over the various local warrior leaders and left it up to these supposedly vassal feudal lords to attempt to maintain control over the warriors of their respective regions as their own subvassals.

In practice, no such neat system emerged. Until 1392 Go-Daigo and his descendants maintained a rival imperial court in the mountains south of Kyoto, and the various local lord and vassal groups battled one another, ostensibly in behalf of the rival claimants to the throne but in reality over their own conflicting interests. After the reunification of the imperial court, the Ashikaga for several decades did exercise considerable authority in the central part of Japan around Kyoto, but leaders in more distant areas paid little or no attention to their claims of overlordship.

In 1467 a prolonged war broke out between the great lords active at the shogun's court in Kyoto, and the rest of Japan also disintegrated into chaotic fighting. In fact, warfare became endemic throughout Japan for the next century, and during this time an almost complete turnover in power took place. The authority of the Ashikaga shoguns faded entirely, and most of the great lords were destroyed by new military families. The lords of the early Ashikaga period, who were largely the descendants of provincial "protectors" of the Kamakura system, usually claimed authority over a wider area than they really controlled. During the prolonged fighting that started in 1467, these families were for the most part replaced by new leaders who had established complete control over the warriors of smaller but more tightly knit domains. It was men of this type who became the *daimyo,* or feudal lords, of later Japanese feudalism. In absolute control of their own vassals and lands, they appeared to the Europeans who arrived in Japan in the sixteenth century to be petty kings.

During all the fighting that swept Japan from the fourteenth century on, the warrior holders of power in the provinces had ample opportunity to whittle away at the residue of tax payments and dues from estates that had formerly gone to the Kyoto government and its aristocratic families, and by the late fifteenth century these payments had ceased entirely. As a result, the imperial court and its aristocracy, though maintaining as best they could the old court ranks, positions, and ceremonials, sank almost out of sight into relative poverty. The descendants of the once all-powerful Fujiwara subsisted mostly on dues paid them by Kyoto merchant guilds, and emperors were even known to discreetly sell samples of their calligraphy. With the virtual disappearance, except in vague theory, of the old imperial system, Japan had become a fully feudal land.

Feudal Japan was in many basic ways more like Europe than like China. The warriors, who were known by the generic term *samurai,* or "servitors," placed great emphasis on the military virtues of bravery, honor, self-discipline, and the stoical acceptance of death. Lacking any religious injunctions against suicide, in defeat they commonly took their own lives rather than accept humiliation and possible torture in captivity. Suicide by the gruesome and extremely painful means of cutting open one's own abdomen became a sort of ritual used to demonstrate willpower and maintain honor. Vulgarly called *harakiri,* or "belly slitting," but more properly known as *seppuku,* this form of honorable suicide has survived on occasion into modern times, and suicide by other, less difficult means is still considered an acceptable and basically honorable way to escape an intolerable situation.

The Japanese feudal system, like that of Europe, depended on bonds of personal loyalty. Of course, loyalty was in actuality the weakest link in both systems, and the medieval histories of both Japan and Europe are full of cases of turncoats and traitorous betrayals. In Europe, with its background of Roman law, the lord-vassal relationship was seen as mutual and contractual—in other words, as legalistic. In Japan, the Chinese system had placed less emphasis on law and more on morality— that is, on the subordination of law to the moral leadership of the ruler, since his right to rule was theoretically based on his superior wisdom and morality. Hence, the lord-vassal relationship was seen as one of un-limited and absolute loyalty on the part of the vassal, not merely one of legal contract between the two. There was thus no room for the devel-opment of the concept of political rights, as happened in the West.

Loyalty to the ruler was important in the Chinese Confucian system, but it was usually overshadowed by loyalty to the family. In fact, three of the five basic Confucian ethical relationships had to do with filial piety and other family loyalties. In Japan, loyalty to the lord was more central to the whole system and, despite the importance of the family, took precedence over loyalty to it. Thus in Japan the suprafamily group early became established as more fundamental than the family itself, and this made easier the transition in modern times to loyalty to the nation and to other nonkinship groupings.

Still, family lineage and honor were of great importance in medieval Japanese society, because inheritance determined power and prestige as well as the ownership of property. Family continuity was naturally a matter of vital concern. The Japanese avoided many of the problems of Western hereditary systems by permitting a man to select among his sons the one most suitable to inherit his position and also by using adoption when there was no male heir by birth. The husband of a daughter, a young relative, or even some entirely unrelated person could be adopted as a completely acceptable heir. While inheritance is no longer a key-stone of Japanese society, these types of adoption are still common.

Japanese feudal society differed from that of Europe in two other re-vealing ways. In Japan there was no cult of chivalry that put women on a romantic pedestal, though as fragile, inferior beings. The Japanese warriors expected their women to be as tough as they were and to accept self-destruction out of loyalty to lord or family. Also, Japanese warriors, though men of the sword like their Western counterparts, had none of the contempt that the Western feudal aristocracy often showed for learn-

A section of a fifteenth-century scroll showing a warrior with his bow and sword placed behind him, engaged with a scholar in the refined literary art of composing alternating lines of a poem. Medieval Japanese warriors, unlike their feudal counterparts in Europe, prided themselves on their mastery of literary skills. (*Shashinka Photo Library*)

ing and the gentler arts. They prided themselves on their fine calligraphy or poetic skills. Perhaps the long coexistence of the culture of the imperial court with the rising warrior society of the provinces had permitted a fuller transfer of the arts and attitudes of the one to the other.

The political and social organization of medieval Japan is extremely remote from that of contemporary Japanese society, but many of the attitudes developed then, and preserved and reshaped in the later phases of Japanese feudalism, have survived into modern times. Thus the warrior spirit and its sense of values were easily revived by the modern Japanese army, and a strong spirit of loyalty, duty, self-discipline, and self-denial still lingers on from feudal days, shaping the contemporary Japanese personality.

The long, slow decline of the Kyoto court has given rise to a picture of feudal times as the dark ages, but this is even less true of Japan than of

Europe. Literature, art, and learning showed remarkable continuity, and the high culture that once had been largely limited to the capital region spread throughout the nation. Naturally new themes and new styles also appeared in both literature and art. Stirring war tales recounted the military exploits of the twelfth century. These as well as the histories of Buddhist monasteries and the lives of Buddhist saints were graphically portrayed in marvelous scroll paintings. The thirteenth century witnessed a brilliant renaissance of sculpture. The Great Buddha at Kamakura, one of the largest bronze figures in the world, remains as a symbol of this age. In the late fourteenth and fifteenth centuries a sophisticated dramatic form was developed at the court of the Ashikaga shoguns in Kyoto. This was Nō, in which a handful of masked and costumed actors presented, through sonorous chanting, measured movements, and stately dance, historical stories and early myths, usually based on Buddhist concepts of the vanity of life or Shinto ideas of the permeation of nature and man by the spirit world of the gods. The use in Nō of a chorus accompanied by musical instruments to fill out the story is reminiscent of ancient Greek drama.

Under the rule of the provincial warriors, the peasants sank from taxpayers to the status of serfs but probably gained in security in the process. In any case, the common man at this time began to make his appearance in both art and literature, and he seems to have found new self-expression through the spread and spiritual resurgence of Buddhism. The court aristocrats had been most interested in a form of Buddhism that emphasized magic formulas and rituals, but during the eleventh and twelfth centuries a new emphasis developed, especially among more plebeian Japanese. This was belief in salvation and entrance into paradise through simple faith—that is, through reliance on the grace of one of the many Buddhist deities. Such concepts were an almost complete reversal of the original Buddhist doctrine of the merging of the personal ego into the cosmos through austere self-cultivation leading to enlightenment. Popular preachers spread the idea that, in this supposedly corrupt "latter age" of Buddhism, people no longer had the strength to achieve enlightenment through their own abilities but must rely through faith on "the strength of another."

These concepts gave rise in the twelfth and thirteenth centuries to new sectarian movements that were to become the largest Buddhist sects of Japan. One of these, which emphasized the Pure Land, or Western Paradise, of the Buddha Amida, championed the congregational, instead of monastic, organization of the church and the marriage of the clergy, a custom that in time spread to most sects. Another sect, which emphasized the Lotus Sutra as the central object of faith, is popularly known by the name of its founder, Nichiren. His thinking also took a peculiarly nationalistic bent, emphasizing that Buddhism had declined in India and China in turn and that Japan was now the central land of the religion. These sects in the fifteenth and sixteenth centuries developed religious congregations that in some places contended with the feudal warriors for local political power.

Many of the warriors preferred a different sort of Buddhism. This was Zen, which was introduced from China in sectarian form in the early Kamakura period. Zen emphasized concepts of meditation, simplicity, and closeness to nature. The austere life of its monasteries appealed to the Spartan warriors, and they saw in the rigorous self-discipline of the

The garden of the Tofukuji in Kyoto, a temple founded in 1236. (*Courtesy Japan Information Center*)

A sixteenth-century ceramic bowl for use in the tea ceremony. In its simplicity, roughness, and purposeful imperfections, it demonstrates medieval Japanese tastes, which seem sophisticated and modern to contemporary Westerners. The tea ceremony itself illustrates a love of grace and serenity, which modern men find harder to emulate. (*Shashinka Photo Library*)

practice of Zen meditation a way to develop the self-control and firmness of character their way of life demanded. Under the patronage of the feudal leaders, Zen monasteries around Kamakura and Kyoto became the great intellectual centers of medieval Japan. Zen monks were used by the Ashikaga shoguns as advisers, particularly in their contacts with China. Through these men there was a great resurgence of interest in Chinese scholarship and literature and a revival of skill in the writing of the Chinese language. Zen monks also imported the then relatively new Sung style of monochrome landscape painting, which Japanese artists mastered as they had the earlier Chinese styles. Other Zen imports were landscape gardening and tea drinking, introduced to keep the Zen meditator awake.

Around Zen there grew up a whole esthetic system that became a lasting element in Japanese culture. The small, the simple, the natural, even the misshapen were valued over the large, the grandiose, the artificial, or the uniform. In architecture, natural wood textures and twisted trunks were esteemed more than precisely shaped and painted pieces of wood, and simple, irregular structures, fitted to the lay of the land, were preferred to the stately, balanced majesty of Chinese buildings. Small gardens were designed to represent in microcosm the wild grandeur of nature, contrasting sharply with the Western love of great geometric patterns. The epitome of Japanese taste can be seen in the famous rock garden of the Ryoanji in Kyoto, dating from the fifteenth century, which in a tiny space evokes through sand and a few scattered rocks a majestic seascape. In painting, a few bold, expert strokes in black India ink caught more of the essence of nature than could be portrayed in realistic paintings replete with color and detail. The tea ceremony was developed as an esthetic cult, gracefully performed in simple surroundings and with simple utensils. This medieval Zen esthetic was well suited to the austere life of feudal Japan, but, curiously enough, it also has great appeal in the modern West, surfeited as it is with abundance, machined regularity, and unlimited technical skills.

The close contacts of the Zen monks with China were made possible by a great increase in trade with the continent, which in turn was the product of considerable development of Japanese technology and growth in its economy. The increasing export of manufactured goods, such as folding fans, screens, and the highly prized swords of Japan, shows that the islands were beginning to draw abreast of China in technology. The development of guilds of merchants and artisans within the country was a sign of commercial growth. As in feudal Europe, such guilds were needed to give artisans and merchants some protection against the tax barriers and many other restrictions on trade in a divided, feudal land.

Since the ninth century, there had been relatively little contact with the continent, but overseas trade began to pick up in the thirteenth century. For a while in the fifteenth century, the Ashikaga shoguns attempted to monopolize it by allowing it to be fitted into the Chinese pattern of tributary relations, including even the "investiture" of the shoguns as the "kings" of Japan by the Chinese emperor—to the lasting shame of Japanese nationalists. A more significant feature of overseas commerce was the fact that Japanese traders commonly turned to piracy when frustrated in their commercial objectives, taking by the sword what they were unable to gain by trade. Japanese pirates started along the nearby shores of Korea, then became a scourge along the coast of China, and by the sixteenth century were roaming the seas of all Southeast Asia.

6 Centralized Feudalism

In the sixteenth century, the more efficient of the new type of tightly organized feudal domains grew through the subjugation and incorporation of less successful ones, until by the end of the century Japan had again become politically unified. It had in fact achieved a type of centralized feudal system that seems almost the antithesis of the decentralized feudalism that had existed in Europe. The basic pattern was the one attempted but never attained by the Ashikaga. A supreme overlord kept close rule over a large number of vassal lords, who in turn controlled their respective vassals and samurai retainers.

The appearance of the Europeans at this time may have contributed to the process of reunification, because they brought with them new military technology. After rounding Africa and reaching India in 1498, the Portuguese pushed on rapidly eastward, and in 1542 or 1543 some reached an island off the southern tip of Kyushu. The Portuguese were seeking trade, but they were accompanied by Jesuit priests, who embarked on missionary activities, winning close to a half million converts by the early seventeenth century. This was a much larger percentage of the Japanese population of the time than are Christian today.

The Japanese, however, showed an even greater interest in the guns the Portuguese brought with them. Firearms spread rapidly throughout Japan, contributing to the success of the more efficient feudal realms. Castle building also increased, possibly under European influence. The white-walled wooden structures of the castles of this period were largely decorative, but they were surrounded by broad moats and huge earth-backed stone walls that were quite impervious to the cannon fire of the time. These Japanese castles were more like sixteenth-century European fortifications than like castles. Many built around the turn of the sixteenth century still stand, including beautiful Himeji, a short distance west of Osaka. The imperial palace grounds of downtown Tokyo constitute a good example of the central core of one of these great fortresses.

The political reunification of Japan was largely the work of three successive military leaders. The first, Oda Nobunaga, seized Kyoto in 1568, ostensibly in support of the last Ashikaga shogun, and then subjugated the lesser lords of central Japan and destroyed the power of the great Buddhist monasteries. After Nobunaga was assassinated in 1582, his mantle fell to the ablest of his generals. This was Hideyoshi, who once had been a common foot soldier and was of such humble origin that he originally lacked a family name. By 1590 Hideyoshi had established his authority over the whole country, destroying all his rival lords or forcing them to become his vassals.

Hideyoshi never took the title of shogun, but he did assume high posts in the old imperial government and by his patronage brought it back into modest affluence. He monopolized foreign trade, which by this time had become very lucrative. He had the whole land surveyed and assigned fiefs on the basis of a clear knowledge of the areas and agricultural yields involved. He confiscated the arms of the peasantry, drawing a sharp line between them and the samurai, who were increasingly becoming a salaried, professional military, living not on the land but at the castle towns of their respective lords.

Hideyoshi also embarked in 1592 on the conquest of Korea, ostensibly as the first step in an effort to conquer the world, which to him really meant China. The Japanese were stopped by Chinese armies in northern Korea and, after a long stalemate, withdrew upon Hideyoshi's death in 1598. This Japanese invasion has been emphasized in the historic memories of the Koreans and still contributes to the bitterness between them and the Japanese.

Since Hideyoshi did not leave an adult heir, a scramble for power followed his death. The victor at a great battle in 1600 was his foremost vassal, Tokugawa Ieyasu, who had been enfieffed by Hideyoshi at Edo, the present Tokyo. Ieyasu, instead of moving to Kyoto, retained his base of power in eastern Japan and devoted his energies to consolidating the supremacy of his family on the basis of the pattern already established by Hideyoshi. He was successful in this, and his heirs remained the rulers of Japan until the middle of the nineteenth century.

Ieyasu assumed the old title of shogun and divided up the country between his own domain and those of his vassals. He saved for himself a fourth of the agricultural land and all the great cities, ports, and mines.

The 245 to 295 vassal lords, or daimyo—the number varied over time—had domains ranging in size from tiny areas that produced only 10,000 *koku* of rice (a *koku* being about five bushels and the equivalent of what a person would eat in a year) to the largest, which in theory produced 1,022,700 *koku*. The domains were divided into three categories. Some went to Ieyasu's sons or relatives—the collateral daimyo. A large number of relatively small domains were assigned to men who had been Ieyasu's vassals already before 1600, and these were known as *fudai* or hereditary daimyo. His major allies and some of his enemies in the battle of 1600, who were called *tozama,* or "outer" daimyo, were allowed to retain relatively large domains on the western and northern periphery of the nation. The shogun in addition maintained a large body of direct samurai retainers, as did each of the daimyo.

The central Tokugawa administration at Edo developed into a large bureaucracy, staffed by the hereditary daimyo and the shoguns' direct retainers. It showed the old tendency toward shared authority and group decisions. At the top were two councils, the "elders" and "junior elders," under which paired officers or groups of four officials administered the various branches of the shogun's government and supervised the whole country. The shoguns themselves in time became largely figureheads, thus serving basically as symbolic authority figures, like the emperors, in whose behalf the military government of Edo theoretically ruled.

The domains followed the same general pattern and trends of development, with daimyo often becoming no more than figureheads and samurai bureaucrats governing through councils and group decisions. The domains were in theory entirely autonomous and paid no taxes to the central government, but they were in actuality held on a tight string. They were assigned costly duties of castle or palace construction or coastal defense, and a system soon developed whereby all the daimyo spent alternate years in attendance on the shogun at Edo and left their families there as permanent hostages. The daimyo were also held strictly

Facing page: Himeji Castle (Shirasagi-jo, "the White Heron Castle"), forty-five miles west of Osaka, is one of the best preserved of the castles of the late sixteenth and early seventeenth centuries. These castles were the headquarters of the major *daimyo,* or feudal lords. They were more like early modern European forts than medieval castles, since their broad moats and earth-backed stone walls provided ample defense against the gunnery of the day. Their crowning white-walled towers were more for show than for defense. Around them developed castle towns that have grown into many of the cities of contemporary Japan. (*Courtesy Japan Information Center*)

accountable for the peace and efficient administration of their domains and, particularly in the early years, might be expropriated for misdeeds or demoted to lesser domains.

In order to assure the stability of their regime, Ieyasu and his successors were eager to eliminate all sources of possible challenge. They viewed the activities of European Catholic missionaries and their converts as particularly dangerous, since they involved a foreign source of authority and object of loyalty. First Hideyoshi and then the Tokugawa persecuted the religion, until it was virtually stamped out by 1638. Foreign trade also fell victim to the anti-Christian mania. Overseas Japanese were prohibited in 1636 from returning to Japan for fear that they might reintroduce the virus of Christianity, and Japanese ships were limited to coastal vessels unsuitable for ocean voyages. Relations with the outside world were limited to a few contacts with Korea and, through Okinawa, with China and to a small Dutch trading post and a group of Chinese merchants, both confined to a strictly supervised trade in the Kyushu port of Nagasaki. Thus Japan embarked on its more than two centuries of self-imposed seclusion.

Since the two centuries that followed witnessed the rise of modern science in Europe, the commercial revolution in world trade, and the start of the industrial revolution in the West, a Japan that had been abreast of most developments in the world in the early seventeenth century had fallen technologically far behind by the nineteenth. But isolation did contribute to internal stability. For more than two centuries the country enjoyed absolute peace. The political history of the time is marked only by periodic reform efforts and occasional riots by oppressed peasants. The most exciting political event was the incident in 1703 of "the forty-seven *ronin*," or masterless samurai, in which the former retainers of an expropriated petty daimyo revenged themselves on the Edo official who they felt had caused their lord's downfall and then paid the price for this act by committing suicide through *seppuku*. Despite its old-fashioned feudal pattern, Japan in the seventeenth and eighteenth centuries was certainly more orderly and in many ways more uniformly and efficiently ruled than any country in Europe at that time.

Peace and stability also permitted the Japanese to work over and perfect their own rich cultural heritage. During this period they became culturally more homogeneous and developed an extremely strong sense of national identity. At the same time, the continuation of a basically feudal system into the nineteenth century permitted the somewhat anachronistic survival into modern times of medieval feudal attitudes,

A sixteenth-century Japanese folding screen depicting Portuguese debarking in a Japanese port. They have with them a Jesuit priest, black servants from Africa, and curiosities, including a tiger, to present to the local feudal lords. The Portuguese first reached Japan in 1542 or 1543, and the Japanese were fascinated by their strange costumes and physiognomies as well as by their firearms, which they were soon manufacturing for themselves in great number. In 1549 St. Francis Xavier inaugurated a missionary movement, which at first was highly successful, converting a higher percentage of the population than is Christian today. Subsequently the Japanese, fearing that Christians would prove subversive, virtually stamped the religion out of existence by 1638. (*Shashinka Photo Library*)

such as respect for military leadership, unquestioning loyalty, and emphasis on group organization. Group identification in particular was strengthened by the tight organization and long continuity of the various feudal domains.

The political pattern established in the early decades of the seventeenth century remained basically unaltered until the middle decades of the nineteenth. Although it was well suited to conditions as they had existed at the end of the sixteenth century, it became increasingly ill adapted to conditions as they developed in Japan after that. However, within this rigid political structure, great economic, social, and cultural changes did take place.

The most fundamental change was a huge growth of the economy. Peace and stability permitted a great initial leap in production during the seventeenth century. Another spur to economic development was the system of alternate residence of the lords in Edo, which forced each domain to maintain at least one large establishment at the Tokugawa capital and to spend a great part of its revenues to pay for this establishment and the travel of the lord and his retinue to and from it. This situation required the domains to produce excess rice or specialized local crops for sale to the cities and the nation at large in order to acquire the liquid assets they needed for travel and in Edo. The result was considerable regional specialization in production and the development of a national, monetized economy of a more advanced type than existed in any other Asian land.

These conditions also led to the appearance of large cities. Edo, where half the feudal lords and a large percentage of the whole warrior class were congregated at any one time, grew to be a city of around a million, while Osaka, as the great commercial center for West Japan, and Kyoto, the imperial capital with its fine industries, each came to have populations numbering in the hundreds of thousands.

Economic growth in preindustrial societies has usually been accompanied by a corresponding growth in population. This did occur during the economic surge of the seventeenth century, when the Japanese population rose to 25 or 30 million, but subsequently population remained relatively steady, despite a slow continuing rise in technology and production. The result was that living standards for most Japanese rose above mere subsistence levels. The Japanese, like the early modern Europeans, in a sense had got a step ahead of Malthus. The reasons for this are not clear, but one factor may have been the combination of feudal patterns of inheritance, in which a man had only one heir, and Japanese practices of adoption, which made it unnecessary for this heir to be his natural child. As a result, a man did not need a large number of children for financial security and family continuity and, in fact, usually found a big family more of a liability than an asset. In any case, Tokugawa peasants are known to have practiced infanticide to keep down the number of mouths to be fed, and the population did remain quite static for a century and a half despite the growth of the economy. This rise beyond subsistence levels may help account for the relatively high levels of literacy and of economic, social, and political integration of the Japanese in the nineteenth century and the vigor and dynamism they displayed at that time.

The natural agrarian bias of a feudal society produced a curious irony during the Tokugawa period. The political leadership esteemed agriculture and therefore taxed it heavily, while it despised trade and therefore taxed it only indirectly and lightly. This situation, together with the nationwide integration of the economy, permitted the growth of a prosperous urban merchant class, particularly in the large cities under the direct rule and protection of the shogun's government. During the seventeenth century, great merchant houses developed out of such economic activities as sake brewing, the retailing of dry goods, and money lending. An example is the house of Mitsui, which was to become in modern times one of the greatest private business enterprises in the world.

The various domains as well as their samurai retainers, tied as they were to fixed incomes in rice from agricultural taxes, fell increasingly in debt to urban merchants. This situation was corrosive to the whole Tokugawa system, because in theory society was divided into four classes—the warrior rulers; the peasants, who were the primary producers of wealth; the artisans, who were the secondary producers; and at the bottom the merchants, who were deemed to perform a role in society that was more parasitic than productive. This concept of a four-way division of society was a borrowing from early Chinese thought, but it was quite natural to a feudal system. The shogun's government and the individual domains periodically attempted to reverse the growing indebtedness of the ruling class by cutting down on expenses, including salaries to their retainers, and placing sumptuary laws and other restrictions on the merchants. In desperation, they also created commercial monopolies but all to no avail. The indebtedness of the ruling class to the theoretically lowest class continued to grow.

The sharp line that had been drawn in Hideyoshi's time between peasants and warriors led to a freeing of rural Japan from close supervision by the feudal rulers. In effect, Hideyoshi had forced the warriors of rural Japan to decide whether they would follow their lords to their castle towns as salaried samurai or stay with their lands and become classified as peasants. Many who had the most land to lose took the second option, becoming village headmen and the leaders of rural society. The villages thus had a strong local leadership with many of the attitudes and ethical values of the samurai class, and they were allowed a considerable degree of autonomy in running their own affairs and assigning and collecting taxes.

As the national economy developed during the Tokugawa period, villagers in the more advanced central parts of Japan increasingly shifted from subsistence farming to the growing of commercial crops, and richer peasants often found it more advantageous to let out much of their land to tenant farmers and concentrate their own energies on the processing of foodstuffs, silk, and other agricultural products. In the late eighteenth century there was a veritable outburst of entrepreneurial activity of this sort in rural Japan, and poorer peasants increasingly became accustomed to supplementing their incomes by working for wages in the enterprises of their richer neighbors or in nearby towns. Thus rural as well as urban Japan was developing far beyond the normal limits of a feudal society.

During the long Tokugawa peace the warrior class too underwent great changes. It constituted about 6 percent of the total population, including as it did the common soldiery and the clerks and underlings of the feudal establishments. Although it was basically a fighting force at the outset of the Tokugawa period, it became in time more a hereditary civil bureaucracy than a standing army. The samurai wore their traditional two swords as their badges of rank, and they still attempted to maintain their martial prowess, but in actuality they had become men of the writing brush rather than the sword.

Virtually the whole of the samurai class became literate, and so did most merchants and the richer peasants. Chinese scholarship once again had a great appeal to a Japan at peace, and during the seventeenth century the Japanese for the first time delved deeply into Confucian doctrines as these had become standardized in twelfth-century China. Confucian scholars flourished in Edo and in the domains of the great daimyo, and there was a great surge forward again in skills in the Chinese language. For the first time also there was a wide use of printing, which actually had been known to the Japanese ever since the eighth century.

The rapid growth of intellectual and scholarly activities in the seventeenth century was greatly furthered by the nationwide intellectual cross-fertilization made possible by the system of alternate residence of the lords and their retainers in Edo. Leaders from all over Japan came into constant contact with one another, and a large flow of students and teachers developed between Edo and the various domains. Just as Japan had become a single economic unit, it also became a single intellectual unit in a way no other Asian nation was.

Chinese Confucian philosophy and the historical scholarship it inspired, however, injected some intellectual elements that were subversive to the feudal system. The Chinese ideal was rule by men of superior education and morality, rather than by men merely of superior birth. In the Tokugawa system status was fundamentally determined by birth, and individual merit played only a subsidiary role. The two systems were obviously in sharp conflict with each other, and by the nineteenth century there were increasing demands by ambitious but low-ranking samurai that greater responsibilities should be given to men of talent.

Confucian philosophy and historical studies also called attention to the fact that China was ruled by emperors, not by feudal lords, and that Japan too had once had this system. As a result, increasing attention was focused on the emperor, and doubts were raised regarding the shogun's relationship to him. Among the common people, too, a movement arose, called "national learning," which started in the eighteenth century with the study of early Japanese poetry, *The Tale of Genji,* and the *Kojiki,* the eighth-century work of history, and increasingly came to emphasize the concept that the true glory of Japan was its unbroken imperial line of divine descent. Such ideas were of course potentially inimical to Tokugawa rule.

Isolation is usually associated with cultural stagnation, but the long peace, stability, and economic growth of the Tokugawa period led instead to a veritable cultural explosion. There was a great diversity of Confucian and other philosophical schools of all sorts, and men in touch with the Dutch traders at Nagasaki in the eighteenth century developed an interest in Western science, particularly medicine, metallurgy, and gunnery. Since this knowledge was laboriously mined from books and encyclopedias in the Dutch language, it was called "Dutch learning." Thus the isolated Japanese remained intellectually very much alive.

The early Tokugawa period witnessed an architectural outburst of lavishly decorated buildings, best seen today in the mausoleums of the early

Tokugawa shoguns at Nikko. Many schools of painting, derived from Chinese styles or from native concepts of design, flourished at the courts of the shogun and daimyo, and a school of painting that experimented with the use of Western oil paints and perspective emerged from "Dutch learning" in the late eighteenth century. Porcelain making also became for the first time a great art in Japan, and artistic skills were lavished on lacquer ware, weaving, and brocades.

Perhaps the most interesting cultural development in the Tokugawa period, however, was the rise of an urban merchant culture quite distinct from that of the ruling samurai class. It centered on the amusement quarters of the cities, where the merchants, who were essentially hard-working, sober moneymakers and family men, went to relax in the company of professional female entertainers, called *geisha* in modern times. Here they were free from family and business responsibilities and the oppressive regulations of the feudal rulers. In this demi-monde milieu grew up a rich art, theater, and literature quite distinct from the arts cultivated by the samurai. This new merchant culture matured in Osaka and Kyoto in the late seventeenth century and subsequently became centered chiefly in Edo.

The art of this merchant culture was known as *ukiyo-e,* or "pictures of the fleeting world." The fleeting world was a Buddhist concept in origin, but it had come to connote "up-to-date." The *ukiyo-e* style was reminiscent of the emphasis on color and design in the *Yamato-e* painting of some seven centuries earlier, but the subject matter was quite different—largely stylish courtesans, popular actors, and familiar scenes of urban life. From it developed multicolored woodblock prints, also called *ukiyo-e,* which met the greatly increased demand of a prosperous urban society for works of art. These, too, featured beautiful courtesans and actors but in time also added famous scenes of nature, such as Mount Fuji, and spots of interest in the cities and along the highways of Japan. In a sense, these woodblock prints were the world's first true mass art and the forerunners of the picture postcard.

The theater of this merchant culture was at first limited largely to

Facing page: Gateway of the mausoleum and shrine erected at Nikko, seventy-five miles north of Edo (Tokyo), for the first Tokugawa shogun, Ieyasu, who died in 1616. Baroque in style, the structures are ornate and elaborately decorated with carvings, including the famous three monkeys who "see, hear, and speak no evil." The setting of towering cryptomeria trees (related to the redwoods) is majestic. Nikko is a favorite with both Japanese and foreign sightseers. (*Courtesy Morris G. Simoncelli / Japan Air Lines*)

A scene from Kabuki, the popular theater developed during the seventeenth century in urban merchant society. Kabuki utilizes elaborate scenery, a revolving stage with rising and sinking parts, and a runway through the middle of the audience for dramatic entrances and departures. The men seated on a low platform constitute an orchestra and chorus to heighten the drama and help recount the story. All parts, including the dancing damsel above, are played by men (*onna-kata*). (*Courtesy Japan Information Center*)

puppets, but in time *kabuki* dramas with human actors won out in popularity. Kabuki, while very stylized in its own way, was much more lively and realistic than the medieval Nō and developed elaborate and extremely realistic stage settings and even the revolving stage for quick shifts of scene.

The literary activities of the samurai were largely scholarly and philosophical, but poetry was popular with them as well as with other groups, especially the witty, epigrammatic seventeen-syllable *haiku*. Most other new literary trends came entirely out of merchant society. Guidebooks to the amusement quarters developed into amusing descriptions of urban social types and these into spicy or picaresque novels.

Thus Japan, though isolated from most foreign stimuli, was large and diverse enough to have a very lively society with a richly creative culture. Packed together in great numbers in big cities and a crowded countryside and bound down by a complex, oppressive feudal system of government, the Japanese developed great skills in social and political organization and group cooperation. While the general political pattern remained rigidly unchanging, beneath the surface there were great dynamic tensions between Confucian and feudal values and between economic growth and a frozen class society. Japan, far from becoming a stagnant society in its isolation, remained capable of great change, as it was to demonstrate brilliantly in the second half of the nineteenth century.

7 The Meiji Restoration

Despite the many problems and tensions within the Tokugawa system, it still showed no signs of collapse in the first half of the nineteenth century, and it might have continued for much longer if Japan could have maintained its isolation. But rapid technological advances in the West made this no longer possible. Industrialization and steampowered ships were beginning to bring Western economic and military power around the shores of Japan with a pressure incomparably greater than that exercised by the early seventeenth-century Europeans, whom the Tokugawa had driven away.

By the middle of the nineteenth century the European maritime powers had completed the subjugation of the Indian subcontinent, had taken over much of Southeast Asia, and were beating down the doors of China and foisting on it a semicolonial system of unequal treaties. The Russians had extended their hold over all of Siberia and were pushing southward into the islands north of Japan. American ships sailed past the shores of Japan on their way to the China trade or frequented Japanese coastal waters in search of whales.

Various Western nations had repeatedly tried to persuade the Japanese to open their doors, before the United States in 1853 dispatched about a quarter of its navy, under the command of Commodore Matthew C. Perry, to force the Japanese to give American ships access to their ports. The Japanese had to bow to *force majeure*. Perry's ships with their more modern cannon could have destroyed Edo and could even more easily have cut off its essential food supplies by blockading the entrance to Edo Bay. The treaty signed in 1854 achieved only a limited success, but Townsend Harris, the American consul permitted by this agreement to reside in Japan, finally managed to negotiate a full trade treaty in 1858, using the threat of British naval power then engaged in war in China to persuade the shogun's government to comply. In both cases, the principal European powers followed suit with similar treaties.

Through these treaties and subsequent agreements, the full unequal treaty system developed in China was applied to Japan. Foreign traders became ensconced at the new port of Yokohama, near Edo, and at other treaty ports, protected by European military forces and the extraterritorial privilege of trial by their own judges under their own laws, while treaty limitations on Japanese tariffs left the whole economy open to the machine production of the West. Japan, with its purely preindustrial economy and its archaic feudal system of autonomous domains, seemed as defenseless before Western imperial expansion as the other countries of Asia that had already succumbed.

Trade developed more slowly than the Westerners had hoped. The Tokugawa authorities threw up every possible obstacle, and the people were not very receptive to strange foreign goods. A silk blight in Europe also produced a strong demand for Japanese silk, which helped the Japanese with their trade balance. Nonetheless, the sudden opening of the country was disruptive to domestic markets and the monetary system, and the political repercussions were even worse. The shogun's military dictatorship was in theory justified by his role as military protector of the emperor and nation, but he had been proved incapable of fulfilling this role. The shogunate thus was laid open to attack by all those discontented with current conditions or resentful of Tokugawa overlordship, as some of the "outer" domains had been ever since 1600.

The Edo government, in the face of Perry's demands, had sought broad national support for its policies by taking the unprecedented step of consulting the daimyo. The response, though mixed, was generally negative, and this breach of precedent together with the national crisis opened the gates to a flood of criticism. When subsequently Edo felt constrained to sign the commercial treaty of 1858, it again consulted the lords, and it also asked for the emperor's approval, but without success.

Popular sentiment ran high against the opening of the country, and there was a growing feeling that, in order to meet the foreign menace, the nation would have to rally itself more effectively around the emperor, as the legitimate symbol of unity. Moderates called for "a union of court and military," that is, of Edo and Kyoto, but some radicals advocated a refurbished imperial regime to replace the Tokugawa. The slogan of this policy, "honor the emperor," was joined with the cry "expel the barbarians" to form a pithy four-character motto, *sonno joi,* "honor the emperor and expel the barbarians." Young samurai hotheads, inspired by these only vaguely defined concepts, sometimes cut loose from their domains as *ronin,* or "masterless samurai," and assassinated shogunal officials or even an occasional Western diplomat or trader.

Some Japanese had realized from the start that the only defense against the West was to adopt its superior military and economic technology and thus to "expel the barbarians" in the modified sense of achieving security from the West and political equality with it. The leaders of two particularly large "outer" domains, Satsuma, at the southern end of Kyushu, and Choshu, at the western tip of Honshu, were won over to this view by demonstrations of Western naval might. When Satsuma samurai killed an Englishman near Yokohama, a British fleet in 1863 destroyed Kagoshima, its capital city. Similarly, when Choshu fired on Western ships passing through the Straits of Shimonoseki, an allied fleet in 1864 leveled the Choshu forts.

The Tokugawa system had been shaken to its foundations by the events since 1853, and the whole antiquated structure began to disintegrate. All policies had become subject to debate by samurai from all over Japan. Some of the great domains vied with one another and with Edo for influence over the Kyoto court, and Choshu openly defied Edo's authority. A military expedition sent in 1864 to chastise it produced only a compromise settlement, and a second expedition in 1866 ended in complete failure. Finally a coalition of Satsuma, Choshu, and some other "outer" and collateral domains seized control of the imperial court and in the name of the emperor announced the resumption of direct imperial rule on January 3, 1868. The shogun's forces and a few loyal domains put up a half-hearted resistance, but a so-called imperial army seized Edo, putting an end to more than two and a half centuries of Tokugawa rule.

The leadership of the "imperial" forces was ostensibly provided by imperial princes, court nobles, and a few feudal lords, but actually the initiative for policies and their execution was seized by a group of able young reformers of largely middle or lower samurai rank and mostly from Satsuma and Choshu. These men realized that, although the cry of "expel the barbarians" had been useful in their attainment of power, it would be disastrous for Japan to attempt to carry out such an unrealistic policy. Instead they made clear at once their acceptance of the Western treaties negotiated by the Tokugawa. They also took the contemporary

West as their model under a new motto, "rich country, strong military" (*fukoku kyohei*). Men knowledgeable about Western technology through their study of "Dutch learning" were helpful in this attempt, and, as the country opened up to Westerners, the "barbarians" themselves were used in growing numbers.

The new leaders, however, faced a herculean task in attempting to replace the old feudal system with a more effective centralized rule and starting Japan on technological modernization that would give it security from the powerful and predatory nations of the West. They had fallen heir to no more than the broken-down, bankrupt shogunal domain, in a country long divided into autonomous feudal units and still limited to a purely preindustrial economy.

Although the theory of imperial unity had had little practical content for almost a thousand years, a major asset of the new government was its control over the fifteen-year-old emperor, which it utilized to the full. He was moved in 1869 to the great shogunal castle in Edo, which was accordingly renamed Tokyo, or "Eastern Capital," and everything was done in his name. The whole great transformation came to be known as the Meiji Restoration, named after the Meiji "year period" inaugurated in 1868, which became also the posthumous name of the emperor when he finally died in 1912. (Year periods, corresponding in length to reigns since 1868, are still used in Japan. For example, the year World War II ended is known in Japan both as 1945 and as the twentieth year of Showa, the year period of the man known in the West as Hirohito.)

Replacing the old feudal domains by more centralized rule proved relatively easy because of the largely symbolic role of the daimyo. Already in 1869 the new regime persuaded them to return their land registers to the emperor and receive appointment as governors of their domains, and two years later it simply replaced the old domains by new prefectures of roughly uniform size, administered by officials appointed by the central government. The feudal lords were recompensed generously with government bonds, which ensured their continuing prosperity but also their financial dependence on the success of the new order.

It was a more difficult task to wipe out the class divisions of the old system and the special privileges of the samurai. With the disappearance of the domains, the samurai lost their position as a hereditary bureaucratic class, and in 1873 universal military conscription was substituted for the old class basis for military service. In 1876 the samurai were even prohibited from wearing their swords, their badge of distinction. Samurai stipends were also drastically reduced and by 1876 were entirely

A portrait of the Meiji emperor. The seizure of power from the Tokugawa and the subsequent modernization of the country were done in his name and so became known as the Meiji Restoration. Meiji was the name of the period of his reign (1868–1912) and later was given him as his posthumous title. The military uniform, medals, Western style sword, haircut, mustache, beard, and stuffed chair were all innovations borrowed from nineteenth-century European royalty. (*Shashinka Photo Library*)

commuted into relatively small lump-sum payments of cash or government bonds. Thus the samurai in a brief nine-year period were deprived of all their special privileges, and Japan was started on a great change that was to transform its society in a mere generation or two from one in which status was determined primarily by heredity to one in which it depended largely upon the education and achievements of the individual.

Meanwhile the government was being modernized, largely on the model of the nineteenth-century West. Ministries like those of Western governments were formed. These included a Finance Ministry, which was the most powerful because of its control over the pursestrings; Army and Navy Ministries, which in 1878 were paralleled by general staffs on the German model; and an Education Ministry, which embarked on an ambitious program of universal education that took some three decades to be put fully into effect. A modern court and legal system, based first on French and then on German models, was laboriously built up but, being closely tied to social realities, was not perfected until 1899. To stabilize revenues and clarify land ownership, fixed monetary taxes were substituted in 1873 for the traditional percentages of agriculture yield, and the payers of the tax, who were the peasants themselves, were confirmed as the outright owners of the land. Modern Japan, unlike postfeudal Europe, has had no continuing problem of land ownership by the old feudal classes.

At the same time, efforts were being made to modernize the economy. A modern banking system was created, and the monetary system was reformed with the yen as its unit, worth roughly half an American dollar. Lighthouses were built, and port facilities improved. The country was tied together by a telegraph network. Railroads were constructed, and a line between Tokyo and its port at Yokohama was completed in 1872. Silk production was improved by the mechanical reeling of silk, a simple innovation achieved largely through private capital. Other industries were more costly and took long years to become profitable. The government itself built up strategic industries in the production of weapons and ammunition, developed mining, and pioneered with pilot plants in a variety of other fields. In order to secure the northern island of Hokkaido from Russian penetration, the government also embarked on a costly program of building up the population and agriculture of the island, largely on an American model, complete with silos and herds of cattle.

To carry out all these innovations, the government needed a great deal of Western technical knowledge. It dispatched students abroad to acquire new skills and hired Western experts at great expense to come to Japan. In these efforts, the Japanese were carefully selective, utilizing the specific national model they felt was best in each field. Since they paid for foreign assistance themselves, they appreciated it more and used it better than have many countries that in more recent times have received aid gratis. But some assistance was free even then. Much of the teaching of English, the necessary language of contact with the West, was provided by Protestant missionaries, largely from the United States.

The restructuring of the government and economy was not accomplished without confusion, much trial and error, serious setbacks, and a great deal of opposition. The most dangerous opposition came from elements of the large samurai class, which had the most to lose. There were several samurai uprisings, culminating in a great revolt in 1877 in Satsuma itself. This was put down only with great difficulty by the new conscript army, but Tokyo's victory in 1877 made it clear that the new government was now safe from military challenge at home.

Meanwhile, however, the new regime was drifting toward financial collapse. Its many costly undertakings, the commuting of samurai pensions, and finally the suppression of samurai resistance had produced a serious inflation by the late 1870s. The government was forced in 1881 to start a program of stringent fiscal retrenchment, including the sale of the pilot industrial plants, mines, and the enterprises in Hokkaido, which were transferred at whatever prices they would bring to whoever gave promise of being capable of operating them successfully.

These drastic measures brought Japan financially back to an even keel, and at much the same time the new industries began to pay for themselves. The first success in the early 1880s was in cotton spinning, which within another decade had become competitive with the West and began to enter the export market. Success in other fields followed. Thus, within two decades of its shaky start, the new government had achieved military and financial stability at home, and the country was well launched on its effort to win military and economic security from the West.

Told in this brief way, the so-called Meiji Restoration may seem to have been an almost inevitable development. In fact, many scholars make of it simply the expression of supposed laws of history, according to which "absolutist" trends or "bourgeois revolution" automatically followed in the same sequence as in modern Europe. But when the history of Japan from the 1850s to the 1880s is compared with that of other non-Western countries, it stands out as a truly extraordinary experience. No other country responded quickly and successfully to the challenge of superior Western economic and military technology. China, for example, starting a dynastic collapse in the 1840s, did not achieve a unified and stable new political system until a full century later, and it is still to a large extent a preindustrial country. Most of the other lands of Asia succumbed to colonial rule. They were not stirred by a national awakening until inspired by the Japanese defeat of the Russians in 1904–05, did not regain their independence until the middle of the twentieth century, again in large part thanks to the Japanese destruction of Western imperialism during World War II, and for the most part are still only partially industrialized in their economies or modernized in their institutions.

The relatively quick success of the Japanese is not to be attributed mainly to external factors, such as the nature of the impact of the West or the relative size of Japan, for other countries of comparable experience or size reacted quite differently. The reasons should rather be sought in internal characteristics, such as the great homogeneity of the Japanese people and their strong self-identity. Their clear awareness of the possibilities of learning from abroad was also a distinct advantage. Even the social tensions of late Tokugawa times were an asset to a country facing great changes. And it should be remembered that, though preindustrial in economy and feudal in political pattern, Japan's economic and political institutions were highly complex and sophisticated. The country had standards of bureaucratic rule that did not suffer by comparison with the West in either honesty or efficiency. With perhaps 45 percent of its men and 15 percent of its women literate, Japan also had literacy levels not far behind the leading countries of the West. Another important factor was that the whole great change could be justified in Japanese minds, not through newly learned foreign concepts, such as democracy or, later, communism, but by Japan's own ancient system of imperial rule. The utilization of a native ideology undoubtedly smoothed an otherwise wrenching change and made it somewhat less traumatic.

No one can be sure just what combination of traits best explains the extraordinary contrast between Japan and all other non-Western lands in the nineteenth century, but there can be no question of the advantages Japan gained by its early start in modernization. For one thing, the technological gap with the West was not as great in the nineteenth century as it was to become in the twentieth. More important, the lack of precedent and the general skepticism at the time about the possibility that any non-Western country could achieve standards comparable to those of the West permitted the Japanese some freedom from unrealistic expectations of instant industrialization or overnight democracy, and more chance for pragmatic experimentation. The lead in modernization over other non-Western lands already achieved by the end of the nineteenth century allowed a further widening of the gap in succeeding decades, until Japan seemed to stand more with the world powers of the West than with the colonial or semicolonial lands of Asia.

8 The Constitutional System

By the 1880s Japan had survived the birth pangs of its new order, and its leaders, now settling into middle age, were eager to consolidate the gains of two decades of rapid improvisation into a permanent system that would continue after they were gone. Born in the stable certainties of Tokugawa days, they longed to have once again an unchanging order that would be clearly known to all and accepted by everyone. Influenced by the experience of the leading countries of the West, they decided that such a system should be embodied in a constitution.

A more surprising decision was to include in the new constitutional system a popular assembly on the Western model. Popular political movements had always been regarded as subversive in Japan, but Western experience suggested that an elected assembly strengthened a government by giving it wide popular support or at least served as an ingenious safety valve for popular discontent. A parliament would also be useful in gaining the respect of the Western powers, which was needed if Japan was ever to get out from under the unequal treaties that had been imposed on it. Another factor was the need to broaden the base of government. Under the old system a large proportion of the samurai class had been involved in the administration of the shogunate or the domains, but in the new system many former leaders had been frozen out of the government and were demanding a chance to participate.

One of the original leaders of the Meiji Restoration, a man named Itagaki Taisuke from the Tosa domain in Shikoku, fell out with his colleagues in 1873 and, returning to Tosa, formed his samurai supporters into a political party, which was soon joined by urban merchants and peasant taxpayers. Drawing its ideas from liberal French thought, this group came to be known as the "freedom and people's rights movement" (jiyu minken undo). A second popular party, which gained considerable support from the rising business community, was founded by Okuma Shigenobu, another government leader, who was ousted by his colleagues in 1881 because he had advocated immediate adoption of the British parliamentary system. These two movements were the start of lasting streams in Japanese politics that are still discernible today.

When Okuma was dropped in 1881, the government issued a promise in the emperor's name that a constitution would be in force by 1890. Ito Hirobumi, a former samurai from Choshu, took the lead in a detailed study of European systems, particularly the conservative German one. He also experimented carefully with elements in the proposed new system. After much meticulous preparation, the new constitution was finally issued in 1889.

The constitution naturally centered on the emperor and his authority, since a restoration of his supposedly direct rule had been the justification for the overthrow of the Tokugawa. In actuality, however, the emperor was not expected to rule but merely to validate the decisions made by his ministers. There was, of course, an ambiguity as to who appointed the ministers, but this was not perceived at first, because the surviving members of the group who had been in control since 1868 went on performing this task in the emperor's name, even though the constitution made no mention of them. Their numbers reduced through deaths and their prestige greatly enhanced by their long leadership, this select group was in effect a Satsuma and Choshu oligarchy, as its critics claimed, and it came in time to be known as the genro, or "elder statesmen."

Below the emperor and the oligarchy, the ministries of the government were grouped together in a Western-style cabinet under a prime minister. The early cabinets constituted little more than rotating rosters of the genro themselves. Under the cabinet a thoroughly modernized civil service was created on the then most progressive German model. At first graduates of Tokyo University, the government institution founded in 1877, automatically qualified for the higher civil service posts, but a system soon developed of qualification for these positions by examination, and under it Japan built up an elite, highly independent, and extremely efficient civil service bureaucracy.

The constitution had a number of articles granting broad rights to the people, but each clause was qualified with phrases such as "within the limits of the law," which greatly reduced the protection afforded. The judicial system, though highly centralized, was given an admirable degree of independence, and it administered justice with scrupulous adherence to the laws.

The most revolutionary innovation of the constitution was the creation of a bicameral national assembly, which was in part elective. The upper house, or House of Peers, modeled on the British House of Lords, was filled almost entirely by heredity or appointment. It required a peerage, which was created in 1884 out of former court nobles, feudal lords, and the members of the new leadership group. The House of Representatives was elected by male taxpayers who paid more than 15 yen in taxes—a very select group constituting not much more than 1 percent of the population. A majority vote of both houses was required for the budget and for any law to remain permanently on the books.

This was a very limited sort of popular government and has been frequently described as a great setback or "betrayal" of democracy, but the Japanese had no intention of creating a full democratic system, and informed Westerners at the time felt that they were if anything rushing too fast on a path suitable only for Occidentals—trying to run, as one commentator put it, before they could walk. In view of the lack of popular experience with elections or understanding of parliamentary institutions, it is extremely doubtful that a more democratic system would have worked at all in 1890. In any case, limited though it was, the Japanese Diet, as it is called, turned out to be the first successful parliamentary experiment outside the West, and, despite a shaky start, the system survived and proved itself flexible enough for remarkable evolutionary growth.

In 1894, not long after the introduction of the new constitutional system, the British, impressed by Japan's modernization, agreed to relinquish their extraterritorial privileges by 1899, and the other nations followed suit. Within a few years, the Japanese had also regained full control over their tariffs. They also fought in quick succession two successful wars which demonstrated that, on the basis of their new economic strength and institutional reforms, they were winning their effort to achieve military security from the West.

The first of these wars was in 1894–95 against China over the control of Korea. To the surprise of the world, Japan easily defeated its giant neighbor. Chinese influence was eliminated from Korea, and Japan annexed the Chinese island of Taiwan, thus starting to build its own empire in imitation of the Western powers. It also acquired the southern tip of Manchuria, but Russia, covetous of this strategic piece of terrain, persuaded Germany and France to join it in forcing Japan to disgorge the peninsula. This lesson in power politics was made all the more bitter for the Japanese when the Russians appropriated the area for themselves three years later.

In 1902 Japan negotiated a pact with Great Britain that strengthened the British in their rivalry with Russia and assured the Japanese that the other European powers would not gang up on it again. This was the first truly equal alliance between a Western and non-Western nation. It set the stage for a showdown between Japan and Russia over control of Korea, which soon came, in the Russo-Japanese War of 1904–05. To the world's amazement, Japan once again emerged victorious, acquiring the southern tip of Manchuria, the southern half of the Russian railways in Manchuria, the southern half of the island of Sakhalin in the north, and such complete control over Korea that it quietly annexed the country in 1910.

Japan was becoming a major colonial power, and it continued the process during World War I. The involvement of the European nations on the other side of the globe left Japan the paramount power in East Asia, and it took advantage of this position in 1915 to force new concessions from China through the so-called Twenty-one Demands. It also seized the German holdings in Shantung Province in China and acquired control over the German islands of the North Pacific in the form of a mandated territory. At the Versailles Peace Conference, Japan sat as one of the five major victors—the first non-Western nation to have made it into the club of the Western great powers.

Meanwhile great changes had been taking place within Japan. Although the constitution of 1889 had been meant to embody a permanent, unalterable system, it proved but one step in the unending series of changes that seems to characterize modern life in Japan as elsewhere in the world. In 1889 industrialization had only just begun, and with each succeeding decade it moved at a faster pace. The shift from a leadership determined by class to one determined by education and examinations was only just taking hold. Universal education for six years became a full reality only in 1907. University education was expanding rapidly. A white-collar middle class of relatively well-educated people was beginning to form. Newspapers were growing to great size and influence. Life in the cities was beginning to approximate that of the urban West.

The framers of the constitution had not counted on such basic changes, and they had even misread existing conditions. The small body of voters proved to be far more politically conscious and cantankerous than expected. In preparation for a national assembly, the government had experimented with various elected local assemblies, and through these antigovernment politicians had gained experience in elections. As a consequence, they dominated the first national election in 1890 and every succeeding one—even the second election in 1892, when the government did all it could to win a majority through brutal police suppression and bribery. Far from proving a meek debating society and government claque, the Diet became something of a Frankenstein monster, attacking its makers on the grounds that they were nothing more than a "domain clique" made up of men from Satsuma and Choshu. And it proved to have more power than had been intended. On the advice of German scholars, Ito had put into the constitution a provision that, if the Diet failed to vote the budget, last year's budget continued in effect; but this supposed trump card proved almost useless. In a rapidly growing economy, last year's budget was never enough. Utilizing their control over the size of the budget, the politicians in the Diet did their best to wrest a share of real political power from the oligarchs, not accepting the original concept of the constitution makers that the cabinet should be "transcendental" and above politics.

The first four years of the Diet's existence was a period of open battle between it and the government, eased at the end only by a patriotic outburst over the war against China. Then for a few years a sort of compromise was worked out, with either Itagaki or Okuma, the two former oligarchs now in leadership of the parties, admitted into the cabinet in return for the support of their following in the Diet. This compromise was further developed in 1900, when Ito and his bureaucratic supporters joined with the politicians of the Itagaki line to found a new party, called the Seiyukai. For the next twelve years the Seiyukai served as a sort of government party, securing a number of cabinet seats and other plums for the politicians and getting its views taken into account in the formulation of policies in return for the assurance that the cabinet would have majority support in the Diet.

By this time the original leadership was growing old and tired of the unexpected turmoil of parliamentary politics. Ito resigned the prime ministership for the fourth time in 1901, and thereafter none of the original oligarchs, except for the ousted Okuma, ever took the top position again. In their place, their bureaucratic followers took over as prime ministers and cabinet members. Between 1901 and 1913 two men alternated as prime minister. One was Saionji Kimmochi, a member of the old court aristocracy who had developed a strong liberal tendency as a student in France, had become Ito's protégé in the bureaucracy, and succeeded him as leader of the Seiyukai party. The other was General Katsura Taro, a man of Choshu samurai background. Katsura was the protégé of Yamagata Aritomo, a former Choshu samurai who was the chief shaper of the army and the main rival of Ito among the oligarchs.

The period between 1900 and 1912 was one of relative political tranquility, but this was destroyed by a political blowup in the winter of 1912–13. It started with the army's removal of the army minister from a Saionji cabinet in pique over the cabinet's refusal to go along with the army's desires for expansion. This situation revealed another ambiguity in the system. Yamagata had seen to it that the army and navy in theory would be directly under the emperor and free of civilian control, in order to be sure that venal and disloyal politicians, as he saw them, would not emasculate the armed forces. But as the oligarchs aged and shrank in number, their control in the name of the emperor over the military and civilian branches of government began to wane, permitting this military challenge to cabinet leadership.

General Katsura was brought back in as prime minister to work out a compromise, but the Seiyukai men in the Diet refused to accept him, even defying an "imperial" request to do so. Katsura desperately attempted to organize a new party to gain the needed Diet support but failed. The press and the public clamored for "normal constitutional government," by which they meant not the original "transcendental" concept, but cabinets responsive to Diet majorities. The upshot was the appointment of a neutral navy admiral as prime minister, with a substantial increase of Seiyukai representation and power in the cabinet.

This political incident, named the "Taisho political change" for the new reign and year period that had just started, was a clear sign of the changes that were sweeping Japan. The cabinets that followed were usually more dominated by the parties than those before the incident had been. The party formed originally by Katsura gradually grew into a second contender for power in the Diet and served as the "government party" under the Okuma cabinet of 1914–1916. In 1918 Yamagata, who, after Ito's assassination by a Korean in 1909, had become the chief wielder of the emperor's prerogatives, accepted as prime minister the head of the Seiyukai party, who was a party politician by profession. This man was Hara Kei, who, though of very high samurai origin, came from North Japan and thus was an outsider in the Satsuma- and Choshu-dominated central government and had had to fight his way to power through parliamentary politics.

Hara was assassinated by a deranged youth in 1921, and from 1922 to 1924 the cabinets were briefly headed by nonparty men. In 1924, however, Kato Komei, a retired Foreign Ministry bureaucrat who was the head of the other major party, was appointed prime minister, and for the next eight years the respective presidents of the Seiyukai and of this newer party, renamed in 1927 the Minseito, alternated as prime minister. The Diet thus had increased steadily in power since 1890, until it had come to assume leadership in the civil government and had replaced "transcendental" cabinets with openly party ones.

Meanwhile the electorate for the Diet had expanded along with its powers. The tax qualification for the franchise was reduced substantially in 1900 and again in 1919, and finally in 1925 the vote was given to all adult males. Japan seemed well on its way to becoming a full democracy. In fact, the period between 1913 and 1932 is generally known as the time of "Taisho democracy."

Behind these political changes lay great economic growth and social and intellectual development. The European powers, by becoming involved in World War I, had left their Asian markets to Japan, which prospered greatly. The victory of the democracies in the war also brought a new wave of liberalizing ideas and ways from the West. This contributed to the victory of universal male suffrage in 1925 and produced in the cities a Japanese variant of the flapper and jazz age. As a result of the Russian Revolution, radical ideas won a small following among intellectuals, and a growing labor movement appeared and even stirrings among tenant farmers. Business interests became more influential through their financial support of the parties, and the expanding middle class increasingly set the tone for the new Japan.

In response to the leading role of the Diet and its business backers, Japanese foreign policy shifted from its earlier military orientation to policies more in line with business interests. The imperialistic expansion of the Meiji period had been undertaken basically for strategic reasons. The new foreign policy was more concerned with the need of Japan's growing industries for foreign raw materials and markets to pay for them. Hara's government in 1921 was responsive to an American invitation to a conference in Washington to limit naval expansion and stabilize the Far East. Japan accepted a ratio in capital ships of three to five with the United States and Great Britain, in return for American and

British promises not to build bases beyond Hawaii and Singapore, and it agreed to return to China the German rights it had seized in Shantung. It also backed out of an expedition into Siberia, launched together with smaller American and British contingents on the grounds of maintaining an eastern front against the Germans after the Russian Revolution. A cut in the standing army in 1924 and drastic reductions in the military share of the budget further showed the tendency of the party governments to rely for Japan's security on trade with the outside world rather than on military expansion.

9 The Militarist Reaction

During the 1920s, Japan seemed to be approaching the norms of the democracies of the West, but beneath the surface lurked grave problems. For one thing, the Japanese version of the British parliamentary system had certain notable imperfections. Prime ministers were not produced by parliamentary majorities but were chosen by the few men who exercised the imperial prerogative, and only after appointment did they hold elections in which they usually won their parliamentary majorities. The "king makers" were the remnants of the old oligarchy—principally Yamagata until his death in 1922 and thereafter the court noble Saionji, who came to be classed with them as the "last genro." In other words, Diet control over the prime ministership and cabinet was by no means part of the established constitutional system but merely a political convenience.

An even more serious imperfection was the division between the military and civil branches of government, which the "Taisho political change" had revealed. Army and navy ministers remained military men, outside party discipline. To be sure, the Diet was gradually establishing control over the military, since it had to vote the military as well as the civilian budgets. Ambitious military men, like civil bureaucrats, sometimes joined the parties after retirement in order to achieve ultimate political power, as happened in the case of General Tanaka Giichi, who as president of the Seiyukai party became prime minister in 1927. Still, the armed forces were in theory and in their actual internal operations completely free of civilian control.

Japan's economic underpinnings were also far from firm. World War I had permitted phenomenal industrial growth, but the adjustment after the war to resumed competition by European industry proved extremely painful. Japan grew economically more slowly during the 1920s than at any other time in its modern history, except for the period of World War II and its immediate aftermath. The whole world was in economic doldrums, and international trade stagnated. Rural Japan was particularly hard hit by a drastic fall in price of its two most important crops: rice, because of competition from its own empire in Taiwan and Korea; and silk, because of the virtual disappearance of the American silk trade following the stock market crash of 1929 and the subsequent development of nylon and other substitute fibers for silk stockings. The plight of tenant farmers, who tilled some 45 percent of the soil, was especially serious. In many parts of Japan the poorer peasants fell into dire want and in some cases were forced to sell their daughters into prostitution to avoid starvation.

Even in urban Japan there were serious economic difficulties. A great gap in productivity had appeared between the new industries, with their modern technology, and the more traditional industries, including agriculture, which were still largely unmechanized. This "dual structure," as the Japanese call it, in the economy is a common feature of countries during the early stages of industrialization but was particularly marked in Japan because of the speed with which industrialization had come. The leadership was not attuned to such problems of the industrial age and was slow to pass remedial social legislation.

Another weakness of Japan in the 1920s was the unevenness of the social and political terrain on which its parliamentary institutions stood. The dual structure of the economy was paralleled by a dual structure throughout society. Modernization had progressed much more rapidly in urban Japan than in rural areas, which lagged behind as great reservoirs of past attitudes and ways. The products of higher education had achieved ever broader intellectual horizons and were abreast of the ideas of the whole world, but the much larger number of people who had gone no further than the six years of compulsory schooling had not been educated so much as indoctrinated in ideas of strict loyalty and conformity. Some Japanese looked eagerly forward to all that was new; others looked nostalgically back to the past.

People who were dissatisfied with the economic record or other policies of the party governments and their businessmen supporters yearned for the more patrician and supposedly less self-serving leadership of the past. A great deal of corruption and self-seeking pork-barrel politics did characterize the Japanese parliamentary system, and the whole contentious nature of electoral democratic politics was distasteful to many Japanese, who had in mind the old ideal of harmonious decisions achieved through consensus and executed by dedicated, loyal servants of the state. The influence of capitalistic businessmen in government seemed particularly corrupting, and there was increasing criticism of the great business magnates, who by this time were pejoratively known as the *zaibatsu*, or "financial clique." The peaceful, trade-oriented foreign policy of the party governments was seen by some as a betrayal of Japan's real strategic interests for the selfish benefit of the captains of industry.

Tradition-minded Japanese tended to regard parliamentary institutions, big business, individualism, and the liberal style of life emerging in the cities as related signs of the corrupting influence of the West. The new radical left shared these prejudices, but this did not prevent conservatives from showing particular fear and hatred for it. In 1925, ironically the year that universal male suffrage was instituted, the Diet passed a repressive Peace Preservation Law, making it a crime to advocate a basic change in the political system or the abolition of private property. Thus, despite the seeming triumph of democracy in Japan, it did not have as firm an institutional framework as in the West and lacked wide emotional and intellectual support.

It is impossible to say whether these conditions would have led to a breakdown of the system if Japan had not encountered what was perceived as a foreign policy crisis. As international trade shrank following the outbreak of the world depression in 1929 and countries resorted to nationalistic economic policies of attempted self-sufficiency, the Japanese realized that their new industrial economy was dangerously extended beyond what their own small empire could support. Great Britain, France, and the Netherlands had huge overseas possessions and the Russians and Americans vast continent-wide territories, but Japan had only a relatively small geographic base. To many Japanese, it appeared that they had started their empire building too late and stopped too soon, unwisely influenced by the attitudes of the already satiated Western nations.

The situation was commonly described as a population problem. The white race had appropriated for itself the lightly inhabited, desirable lands in the Western Hemisphere and Australia and was excluding the Japanese from them. By the early twentieth century Japanese had been effectively banned on openly racial grounds from the United States and the British Dominions, and the United States made this policy brutally clear in 1924 in a new exclusion act based on race. As the Japanese saw the situation, they were not only being discriminated against in a humiliating way but were also being economically bottled up. The only answer, some felt, was military expansion on the nearby Asian continent.

China was the obvious target, but nationalism was at last on the rise there, and the days of easy colonial pickings were clearly over. In fact, the newly founded Nationalist government of Chiang Kai-shek was attempting to gain back some control over Manchuria, which the Japanese by now had firmly in their economic grip. Rising Chinese nationalism made it clear that time was fast running out for any further cutting up of the Chinese melon. It was, in a sense, now or never.

The relative independence of the Japanese armed forces made it possible for them to transform this sense of national crisis into an actual change in foreign policy and a shift in political structure. Already in 1928 certain elements of the Japanese army in Manchuria had engineered the assassination of the Chinese warlord of the area and, protected by the army as a whole, had escaped censure by the civil government. In 1930 the cabinet forced the navy to accept the London Naval Treaty, which extended to heavy cruisers the three-to-five ratio with the United States and Great Britain that was first established at the Washington Conference, but this was achieved only at the cost of almost open insubordination by the navy. Then on September 18, 1931, a group of army officers in Manchuria, with the tacit approval of their superiors in Manchuria and Tokyo, staged an incident on the railway near Mukden, the Manchurian capital, which gave an excuse to the Japanese army to overrun the whole of Manchuria during the next few months and set up the puppet state of Manchukuo the next February. The civil government, unable to control the situation for fear of provoking an army coup d'état, was forced to accept the abrupt return to empire building and attempted to justify it before the rest of the world. It also found itself swept along by a huge outpouring of popular patriotic fervor. When the League of Nations condemned Japan's actions in Manchuria, the Japanese simply walked out, thus sealing the fate of the League.

The shift in foreign policy and the change of mood within Japan soon brought an end to party cabinets. Small bodies of ultrarightists among military officers and civilians had for some time been agitating for a military coup. The prime minister who forced through the London Naval Treaty in 1930 was shot by a fanatic and subsequently died. Other leaders were assassinated early in 1932, and the prime minister was killed by a group of young naval officers in May of that year. Saionji selected in his place a moderate naval admiral, who was followed by a similar figure in 1934. Party men continued in the cabinets, and the parties continued to win overwhelming victories in the elections in 1932, 1936, and 1937. In the 1936 election, the Minseito actually won a strong plurality under the slogan "Will it be parliamentary government or fascism?" Even the new leftist vote was rising rapidly. But parliamentary control was waning. The military virtually dictated foreign policy, and the cabinets, now called "national unity" cabinets, had drifted back toward the "transcendental" concept of the early constitutional system.

National euphoria over the seizure of Manchuria strengthened the hand of the military leaders immensely, and pressures by rightest zealots, particularly among the younger officers, gave them arguments for tilting national policies in the directions these men advocated. The ultrarightists tended to champion the impoverished peasantry, who provided the bulk of the soldiers, and to excoriate the privileged classes of rich businessmen and powerful politicians. They saw their own function to be the assassination of "evil leaders" around the throne, thus clearing the way for a military seizure of power and an undefined "Showa restoration," named for the year period of the new emperor, which had started in 1926. Young army officers almost brought off a coup d'état on February 26, 1936, when they killed a number of government leaders and seized part of downtown Tokyo, but, after some indecision, the army and navy commands suppressed the movement and executed its leaders. The more moderate element in the army then reimposed sterner control over its officers and put an end to the factionalism among the higher officers, which had become severe in recent years. At the same time, the 1936 incident resulted in another decline in the powers of the Diet, and in 1937 all party participation in the cabinet was eliminated under a prime minister who was an army general.

The army meanwhile had been extending its control over parts of Inner Mongolia and North China. On the night of July 7, 1937, unplanned fighting broke out between Japanese and Chinese forces near Peking. Chiang Kai-shek's government demanded an overall settlement of Japan's creeping aggression, and the Japanese military dug in its heels in response. World War II had started. The Japanese military machine won an almost uninterrupted series of victories, pushing deep into North and Central China and seizing the southern coast in an effort to knock out or strangle the Chinese government, but the Chinese kept fighting on as they withdrew inland, and guerrilla warfare and lengthening lines of communication began to take their toll on the Japanese. The Japanese army was sinking into what subsequently came to be known as the quagmire of Asian nationalism.

Full-scale war in China heightened patriotic fervor in Japan, and many trends that had been observable since 1931 became accentuated. The military increasingly came to dominate the government and pushed its men into various newly created civilian agencies. The government extended its control over industry in an effort to strengthen the economic base for war. Parliamentary power continued to decline, and in 1940 the government forced all the parties to disband and enter the political wing of the Imperial Rule Assistance Association, a large, amorphous organization that was meant to be a nationwide popular movement, like the Nazi or Fascist parties. Indoctrination of the people through education and the mass media became increasingly narrow and virulent, and deviant ideas were suppressed with growing vigor, often more by neighborhood enthusiasts than by the government or police. A turning point in free thought had been the suppression in 1935 of the works of Professor Minobe Tatsukichi of Tokyo University and his expulsion from the House of Peers on the grounds that his once accepted theory that the emperor was an "organ" of the constitution was now lese majesty.

The Japanese experience is often compared to the fascism of interwar Europe, and certainly the resemblances are in some ways striking. But, unlike the Italian and German cases, there was no dictator and the system was not the product of a well-defined, popular movement, but more a vague change of mood, a shift in the balance of power between the elite groups in Japanese society, and a consequent major shift in national policies, all occurring within the framework of the constitutional system established in 1889. There was no revolution, no successful coup d'état, no formal change of the political system. The military-dominated government of the late 1930s was fully as constitutional as the parliamentary-dominated government of the 1920s, though neither was at all what the designers of the constitution had intended. Not many people had stood out boldly in opposition to the trends of the time and gone to prison for their beliefs. Quite a few of those who did—and these were largely Communists—were persuaded to recant. For the most part, opponents were cowed into silence and unhappy conformity to the new consensus.

The war in China stretched on, and the Japanese eventually found no escape from it, except by expanding it into a broader and ultimately disastrous conflict. The outbreak of war in Europe in 1939 and the eventual involvement of the Soviet Union in that conflict freed Japan from pressures from the European powers but increased American opposition to Japan's conduct in China. All along the United States had adopted the moralistic attitude of not recognizing the fruits of Japanese aggression but had been unwilling to take any but verbal measures. The growing threat that Hitler would establish his hegemony over Europe, however, put in a new light the threat of Japanese hegemony in East Asia, which the Japanese came to describe as the Greater East Asia Co-Prosperity Sphere. Pacts signed with Germany and Italy heightened the association in American minds of these twin menaces to American hopes for a more open world order and raised the specter of a world dominated largely by Nazis and Japanese.

Following the fall of France, Japan seized North Vietnam in the summer of 1940 in order to strengthen its stranglehold on South China, and the United States reacted with economic sanctions. When Japan occupied South Vietnam the next summer in order to gain bases for a possible push southward, the United States took the further step of banning oil shipments. Faced with the prospect of a dwindling oil supply with which to prosecute its war in China and meet possible attack by the United States, the Japanese were forced to make a quick choice among three courses: backing down in China, negotiating a compromise settlement with the United States, or waging a war to seize the oil of Indonesia, then called the Dutch East Indies. The government was unwilling to do the first and unable to achieve the second and therefore settled on the third choice, striking brilliantly at Pearl Harbor on December 7, 1941, in order to neutralize the American navy while Japan pushed south. Before starting the war, the military consolidated its political position at home. The army minister, General Tojo Hideki, became also the prime minister, thus putting the civilian government fully under the military.

The Japanese knew that the United States had far greater economic and military capacities than Japan, but they thought that if they struck rapidly and seized the whole of the Western Pacific, Americans would find the road back to victory too long and arduous to be worth pursuing, especially if the Nazis had in the meantime won in Europe. Within a few months the Japanese overran all Southeast Asia and a vast region stretching from the borders of India to New Guinea and Guadalcanal. But the "sneak" attack on Pearl Harbor, timed to be simultaneous with the delivery of a declaration of war in Washington, helped drive the Americans to a determined and sustained response. Building vastly greater naval and military power than the Japanese were capable of, they fought their way slowly and painfully across the Pacific. Meanwhile their submarines and aerial mines sank the greater part of the Japanese merchant marine, immobilizing the Japanese army in its far-flung military conquests and cutting off the necessary flow of raw materials to the factories of Japan. By November 1944 American air power was close enough in the islands south of Japan to start a systematic destruction by firebomb raids of its highly inflammable cities, driving the work force away from the already faltering factories. It was a double kill of Japanese industry, and Japan's military strength began to falter.

The situation was hopeless, but the Japanese social order remained surprisingly strong, and the military continued in its proud tradition of no surrender. Only after the Americans dropped two atomic bombs, which all but wiped out the cities of Hiroshima and Nagasaki on August 6 and 9, 1945, and the Soviet Union came crashing into Manchuria on August 8 in an eager effort to get in on the kill and the disposition of the Japanese carcass, did an anguished Japanese government bow to the inevitable. On August 14 it accepted the "unconditional" surrender demanded, though on the basis of clear but stern conditions set forth by the United States on July 26 in the so-called Potsdam Proclamation. Japan had risked all and lost all. Eighty years of prodigious effort and extraordinary achievement lay in ruin. For the first time in history Japan felt the tread of a foreign conqueror.

10 The Occupation Reforms

Defeat in World War II brought great and sudden shifts to Japan, comparable only to the changes of the Meiji Restoration. The war itself had been a traumatic experience. At its end Japanese industry was at a virtual standstill, and even agricultural production had fallen off about one third because of long years without new tools, adequate fertilizer, or sufficient labor. All of Japan's great cities, with the exception of Kyoto, and most of its lesser cities had been in large part destroyed and their populations scattered throughout the country. Around 668,000 civilians had been killed in aerial bombardments. The economy, critically maimed, cut off from its normal flows of trade, and disrupted by the uncertainties of foreign rule, recovered only very slowly—much more slowly than in war-devastated Europe. It took a full decade for per capita production to creep back to the levels of the mid-1930s.

The psychic damage to the Japanese was even more severe. They had been under mounting psychological pressure for fifteen years and had lived under full wartime conditions for eight. Life had become constantly more difficult. First ersatz materials replaced normal fabrics; then all consumer goods slowly disappeared, food ran short, and finally urban housing vanished in flames. Forced to scrounge on the black market just to stay alive, city dwellers suffered a collapse of morale. A people punctilious in their observance of the law became accustomed to petty legal infractions. The leaders had expected to win through the superiority of Japanese will power, and the people had responded with every ounce of will they possessed, until they were spiritually drained. Not just the cities but the hearts of the people had been burned out.

There was a great popular revulsion against the war, against the leadership that had steered the nation into this disaster, and against the past in general. Instead of feeling guilt, the people felt that they had been betrayed. To their surprise, they discovered that their armies, far from being welcomed in Asia as liberators, were universally hated. The great respect for the military as selfless patriots and servants of the emperor turned to anger and contempt. In the early postwar months, most Japanese were absorbed in the struggle to keep body and soul together, but underneath these immediate concerns there was a great longing for peace and a determination to avoid any repetition of this great catastrophe. People wanted something new and better than the old Japan that had come to grief. They were confused but open to change in a way they had never been before.

It was these Japanese attitudes that made the American military occupation of Japan, which lasted until the spring of 1952, an effective shaper of change. The United States in its determination to stop the Japanese militarists had not overlooked planning for postwar Japan, and the American forces thus entered the country on September 2, 1945, with broad policy directives for sweeping reforms. They were under the command of General Douglas MacArthur, who acted not just for the United States but for the coalition of victorious nations, under the title of Supreme Commander for the Allied Powers, or SCAP, as both he and his headquarters came to be called.

The Allied aspect of the occupation, however, was more theoretical than real. The defeat of Japan had been almost completely the work of the United States, and although the British sent an Australian contingent to serve under MacArthur in Japan, the Chinese were too involved in their own civil war to do so, and the Soviet Union demanded a separate zone of occupation and, when this was refused, declined to put its troops under an American commander. A Far Eastern Commission of all the victorious nations was created in Washington early in 1946 to set the general policy of the occupation, and an Allied Council for Japan made up of the four chief powers was established in Tokyo to advise on its execution, but neither body was permitted by the United States to have any real influence. Thus, the occupation was almost entirely an American show and was regarded as such by the Japanese.

MacArthur was an extremely self-willed, dynamic, and charismatic leader, who brooked only general guidance from Washington and none at all from the Allied nations. His messianic cast of mind and phrase appealed to the Japanese, who in their desperation looked for inspiring guidance. The Japanese, to their surprise, also found the American troops to be not vindictive but essentially well intentioned and benevolent. Since the United States had apparently proved its superiority by defeating Japan, the disillusioned, demoralized Japanese, instead of reacting to the army of occupation and its leader with the normal sullen resentment of a defeated people, regarded the Americans as guides to a new and better day.

The Americans, for their part, found the Japanese people not the die-hard fanatics they had expected from their experience with the Japanese army in the battlefields of the Pacific, but a well-educated, disciplined, docile people, eager to cooperate in reforming and rebuilding their nation. Even the more sophisticated leaders, realizing the completeness of Japan's defeat and the necessity of bending to the American will if Japan were to recover its independence, proved surprisingly cooperative. American tendencies of didactic self-confidence and benevolent patronage and the old Japanese habits of effective cooperation and loyalty to leaders blended well. The military occupation of one advanced, modernized nation by another, instead of proving the unmitigated disaster that most people might have expected, turned out on the whole to be a resounding success.

The first and most basic objective of the American occupation was the demilitarization of Japan, since Japanese military expansionism was viewed at the time as the one overriding problem in East Asia. The country was flooded with Allied troops and was shorn of all its conquests. In fact, it was even deprived of territories to which no other country had a valid claim. The Kuril Islands, north of Hokkaido, were given to the Soviet Union, and the United States took Okinawa for itself. Japanese troops and civilians were rounded up from all over East Asia and the Pacific, and more than 6.5 million were dumped back into Japan. Next the army and navy were completely demobilized and their ships and weapons destroyed. Members of the military who were convicted of committing atrocities were punished, and seven men, including General Tojo and one civilian former prime minister, were executed on the dubious grounds that they had brought about the war through their personal plotting.

In the flush of the postwar mood of pacifism and MacArthur's enthusiasm for Japan as the Switzerland of Asia, as he described it, both the Japanese leaders and the American authorities happily agreed to an article in a new constitution that in very specific terms renounced war and the maintenance of any war potential forever. By the time a peace treaty was finally negotiated in 1951, however, it was deemed more realistic to make no mention in it of any military restrictions on Japan. On the economic side, all excess industrial capacity beyond the needs of a completely demilitarized country was declared available for reparations to the countries that Japan had despoiled. Little, however, came of this program, for three reasons: no one could agree on how these industrial facilities should be divided; there was almost nothing in a war-destroyed Japan worth transporting and setting up elsewhere; and Japan had no remaining excess industrial power but instead a huge industrial deficit for its own civilian needs. In fact, during these years Japan was kept alive only by injections of American aid.

If the occupation had stopped with this program of demilitarization, it would not have differed much from previous historical cases of punitive settlements of wars. But it went far beyond this. The American thinking was that demilitarization was only a temporary cure for Japan's militaristic ills but that a democratization of the government might produce a Japan that would be less likely to go to war in the future. To this end, ultranationalistic groups were banned, all repressive laws were rescinded, political prisoners—who were mostly Communists—were released, and all former army and navy officers and whole categories of the top leadership in government and even in business and education were banned from occupying any positions of significant responsibility. The most important aspect of the democratization policy, however, was the adoption of a new constitution and its supporting legislation.

When the Japanese government proved too confused or too reluctant to come up with a constitutional reform that satisfied MacArthur, he had his own staff draft a new constitution in February 1946. This, with only minor changes, was adopted by the Japanese government in the form of an amendment to the 1889 constitution and went into effect on May 3, 1947. The American origin of the new constitution naturally raises skepticism as to its suitability and durability. But the American drafters wisely made their work not a new creation based on the American political system but a perfection of the British parliamentary form of government that the Japanese had been moving toward in the 1920s. As such, it was compatible with Japanese political experience and was enthusiastically embraced by the bulk of the Japanese people.

The new constitution focused on the ambiguities and weaknesses of the old one. The emperor was unequivocally defined as the powerless symbol of the unity of the nation—which is what he had long been in fact. Supreme political power was assigned to the Diet, and all competing sources of power were eliminated or clearly subordinated to it. Cabinets were made responsible to the Diet by having the prime minister elected by the lower house. The House of Peers was replaced by an elected House of Councillors. However, the operations of the Diet and the electoral system, except for the enfranchisement of women, remained largely unchanged from what they had been in the late 1920s.

The constitution also included a greatly expanded list of popular rights—all that exist in the American constitution and a good many more recently formulated ones, such as the equality of the sexes, the right of labor to bargain and act collectively, and the right of everyone to receive an equal education. The judicial system was made as independent of executive interference as possible, and a newly created supreme court was given the power to review the constitutionality of laws. Local governments were given greatly increased powers, and the governors of prefectures were made elective officials, as mayors of municipalities had long been.

The occupation did not stop at political reform. It also boldly attempted to reform Japanese society and the economy in order to create conditions that were thought to be more conducive to the successful functioning of democratic institutions than the old social and economic order had been. Curiously, the American authorities held to the Marxist interpretation that the real villain behind Japan's imperialism had been the excessive concentration of industrial wealth and power in the hands of the zaibatsu, which was thought to have necessitated an aggressive foreign policy. Although Japan's prewar history scarcely bears out this theory, it led to a remarkable display of socialist zeal by MacArthur and his staff. Revolutionary reforms are easier and more fun to make in someone else's country.

The wartime destruction had been a great economic leveler, since it had impoverished almost everyone, and the occupation confiscated most of the remaining personal wealth through a capital levy. It also disbanded the great zaibatsu firms, dispossessed the owning families, and started to break up the industrial and commercial units of which these great combines were made. By that time, however, it had become clear that further surgery to improve the Japanese economy for social and political reasons might kill it instead. The program was therefore terminated, and the emphasis shifted to attempts to revive Japanese industry.

Japan was plagued by high rates of tenancy, which had stood at around 45 percent of the land since the end of the nineteenth century.

Much thought in Japan had gone into plans to reduce tenancy, and the injection of the American external *force majeure* now made possible an extraordinarily radical and effective land reform. Absentee ownership of agricultural land was banned completely, and a village landowner was permitted to hold only a small area beyond what he himself farmed. The transfer of land to former tenants was effected on extremely easy terms—actually, at prewar prices, which meant virtual confiscation— and tenancy was reduced to only about 10 percent of the land.

The occupation also put into effect enlightened laws in behalf of urban labor and encouraged union organization as a balance to the power of management. The labor leaders surviving from the 1920s quickly built up a tremendous new labor movement, which ultimately grew to more than 12 million members. To the surprise of the American authorities, however, this movement took a decidedly more radical turn than in the United States. In the desperate economic conditions of early postwar Japan, there was little room for successful bargaining over wages, and many labor unions instead made a bid to take over industry and operate it in their own behalf. Moreover, because large numbers of workers in Japan were government employees, such as railroad workers and teachers, whose wages were set not by management but by the government, direct political action seemed more meaningful to these people than wage bargaining.

The occupation reforms spread to many other fields. Women were enfranchised and given full legal equality. The authority of a main family over branch families and of the family head over adult children was ended. Compulsory education was extended to nine years, there were efforts to make education a training more in thinking than in rote memory, and the school system above the six elementary grades was revised to conform to the American pattern. This last mechanical change produced great confusion and dissatisfaction but became so entrenched that it could not be revised even after the Americans departed.

Some of the occupation reforms thus were not very successful or much appreciated, but on the whole they were welcomed, and they inevitably brought huge changes. The transformation of postwar Japan, however, should not be viewed as largely the work of foreign intervention. The whole war experience—the failure of the bid for empire and the national collapse that had resulted—would in any case have forced Japan to move in the directions it took under the occupation. It had no way to survive economically except through reliance on peaceful international trade. Parliamentary democracy, whatever its faults, seemed the obvious alternative to the disasters of authoritarian rule. And the social changes that the militarists and ultranationalists had dammed up or diverted for a decade and a half would inevitably have swept across Japan once these barriers had collapsed. The occupation reforms succeeded in large part because they were headed in the same direction in which forces within Japan were pushing. The dynamic leadership of external military authority perhaps channeled these forces more narrowly and thus made them flow more swiftly than might otherwise have been the case, but basically the occupation facilitated rather than determined the postwar development of Japan.

The Japanese people went through the traumatic experiences of war and occupation with the same great social discipline that they had evinced a century earlier during the even more basic shift from feudalism and isolation to centralized rule and international contacts. The Americans, lacking adequate language skills and trained personnel to run Japan directly, exercised their authority through the Japanese government. They had at first left the way open for a revolution in Japan and had half expected one, but nothing of the sort occurred. There was confusion but no breakdown of law and order. Most Japanese shied away from violence whenever it was attempted by the more radically inclined. Government servants continued to perform their specific duties as best they could, teachers kept teaching, students kept studying, and everyone tried to adjust to the new conditions. Despite the whirlwind of change, Japanese society continued in its orderly ways, as it had for the past several centuries.

The major streams of change, as these had shown themselves in the early decades of the twentieth century, reemerged after the war almost as if the experiences of military dictatorship, war, defeat, and occupation had never occurred. In no field was this clearer than in politics. All the old parties were quickly reconstituted in the autumn of 1945, and the voting trends of the 1920s and 1930s picked up almost where straight-line projections would have placed them. The two traditional prewar parties were revived and, faced by a rising leftist vote, merged in 1955 to form the Liberal Democratic Party, a name that reveals its dual origin. The members of this party had been the liberals of prewar days, but in the postwar situation they were considered the conservatives. The parties of the left, which were from left to right the Communists, the Socialists, and the Democratic Socialists, all had prewar antecedents.

The only major postwar party with no prewar roots did not develop until the 1960s. This was the Komeito, sometimes translated as the Clean Government Party, which started as the political wing of a new religious movement, the Soka Gakkai. It and the three parties of the left, by splitting the opposition vote, have contributed to keeping the Liberal Democratic Party in power ever since its founding.

The early postwar years were a time of great political as well as social and economic uncertainty and turmoil. Organized labor made a bid for the control of industry and direct political power. Socialists and Communists, under the tolerance of MacArthur, agitated for the early establishment of a fully socialist or communist society. Leftists, intellectuals, and the urban white-collar classes, who had suffered most from repression by the militarists, were extremely suspicious of the intentions of the conservatives in power. Political rhetoric tended to imply all-out confrontation, not reasoned debate, and this spirit of confrontation was not confined to elections and Diet politics but overran into the streets. People rallying in huge numbers and marching under inflammatory banners, usually proclaiming "absolute opposition" to something or other, became a highly visible part of the whole process. While everyone acclaimed democracy, *demo,* the most ubiquitous postwar political term, was an abbreviation not of democracy but of demonstration.

The early honeymoon between the occupation forces and the Japanese people gradually turned sour. Conservatives became progressively more irked with American meddling, which in its details often seemed uninformed and needlessly damaging to the economy, while leftists became entirely disenchanted when the emphasis in occupation policies shifted between 1947 and 1949 from further reform to economic recovery. This shift was natural, for the original American reform program was nearing completion and the continued economic weakness of Japan was coming to be seen as the chief threat to its success. But a shift in American perceptions of the world outside Japan was also involved. The Cold War was developing, China was being "lost" to communism, and Japan no longer appeared the unique threat to peace in East Asia but rather a base for democracy and American military power in that part of the world.

There were several turning points in the attitude of the left toward the occupation. One was when the labor unions, in a bid for political power, planned a nationwide general strike for February 1, 1947, and MacArthur, fearing the resulting damage to the economy and his own reform program, banned the strike. Another was when the occupation early in

1949 insisted on a stringent financial retrenchment in government and business, which gave an excuse to the conservatives for a wholesale firing of troublesome leftists—the so-called Red Purge. And finally there was the sudden invasion of South Korea by Communist North Korea on June 25, 1950, and the American military response from bases in Japan. Japanese leftists came to the conclusion that the occupation had made, as they put it, a 180-degree shift in policy and had changed from patron to enemy.

Ever since, the political fight between left and right in Japan has focused to a large extent on the relationship with the United States. This situation, in a sense, has merely been a reflection of the fact that the fate of a Japan vitally dependent on foreign resources and markets was likely to be determined more by its foreign relations than by what happened within the country. The predominant role of the United States in these relations was magnified in Japanese eyes by the whole occupation experience as well as by continuing dependence on the United States for Japan's military security and roughly 30 percent of its foreign trade. The leftists argued that heavy dependence on the United States tied Japan to capitalism and therefore prevented the achievement of socialism. They saw American bases in Japan as dangerously involving Japan in the Cold War and running the risk of reviving militarism. The presence of American bases and troops also led to endless friction that could be exploited by the opposition parties to their political advantage.

The termination of the occupation through a peace treaty was delayed longer than the United States had planned because of the obvious unwillingness of the Soviet Union to accept the sort of treaty the Americans believed to be necessary. Eventually, however, the United States went ahead with a "separate peace treaty," without Soviet endorsement or Chinese participation. It also concluded at the same time a bilateral Security Treaty providing for American bases in Japan and a commitment to defend the islands. The two treaties were signed in September 1951 and went into effect the next March.

11 Post-Occupation Japan

Japan's history since the occupation can be presented more briefly, for the rest of this book deals mainly with this period. During the early post-occupation period, a major source of political controversy was the desire of the conservatives to revise the constitution in order to make clear the sovereignty of the emperor—a largely theoretical point—and to get rid of the limitations on military defense, which was a much more practical issue. Lacking a two thirds majority in both houses of the Diet, they failed in the face of determined opposition by the left, but a tacit reinterpretation of the no-war clause did occur. A modest military establishment was built up and was named in 1954 the Self-Defense Forces. Some modifications of the occupation reforms were also made during the early post-occupation years. The purge of the war-time leaders was ended, and the police and educational systems were reconsolidated under central government leadership. The opposition parties put up a tremendous fight against this return toward centralized controls, fearing that these moves would start a general erosion of the liberties guaranteed in the new constitution. A running battle between left and right has continued ever since over controls the ruling party felt were necessary for administrative efficiency and the left feared might open the way to a return to the prewar system.

During these years, the Japanese government also reestablished its relations with the outside world and won a place for itself again in the community of nations. Starting in 1954 it began to make reparation settlements with most of the countries it had despoiled. In 1956 a termination of hostilities, though not a full peace treaty, was negotiated with the Soviet Union, which then dropped its veto of Japan in the United Nations, permitting it to gain membership. Contact with Japan's closest neighbors, Korea and China, remained less satisfactory. It was not until 1965 that relations with South Korea were normalized on the basis of large financial payments by Japan, and not until 1972, following the Sino-American rapprochement, that Japan established full diplomatic relations with Peking.

The biggest political crisis in the postwar period came in 1960 over a revision of the Security Treaty with the United States, necessitated by Japan's growing self-confidence and status in the world. This produced a violent political explosion and massive demonstrations in the streets, but once the new treaty had been ratified, excitement subsided, and the next few years proved to be the calmest politically between the end of the war and the late 1970s. Ikeda Hayato, the new prime minister, adopted a "low posture" of not forcing political decisions against determined opposition and instead drew popular attention to Japan's eco-

Demonstrators from a nearby prefecture protest the new Security Treaty with the United States on May 26, 1960, in front of the Diet building. Hundreds of thousands of citizens protested day after day during this greatest political crisis in postwar Japanese history. The Security Treaty did go into effect on June 19, but a planned visit to Japan by President Eisenhower had to be canceled and Prime Minister Kishi Nobusuke was forced to resign. *(AP / Wide World Photos)*

nomic success, promising a doubling of incomes within ten years. President John Kennedy also had a charismatic appeal for many Japanese, particularly the young, thus reducing some of the political heat over relations with the United States.

Tensions over these relations, however, mounted again as the Americans became deeply involved after 1965 in the war in Vietnam. Most Japanese were opposed to the American position in Vietnam and saw it as threatening to involve Japan in American military adventures. Such attitudes merged in the late 1960s with growing excitement once again over the Security Treaty, since the initial ten-year term of the revised treaty was coming to an end in June 1970 and either side would then be able to demand its revision or termination. Student unrest, which was at its height around 1968 in Japan as elsewhere in the world, contributed to the political turmoil, and by then demands for the return of Okinawa to Japan had become strong, injecting a very pronounced nationalistic overtone to the attack on the relationship with the United States.

The mounting foreign policy crisis, however, just as in 1960, dissolved once more, and Japan continued on its remarkably steady course. The United States pulled slowly out of Vietnam; the Security Treaty problem never came to a head, since neither government proposed termination or revision and the treaty simply continued in effect; and in November 1969 the reversion of Okinawa to Japan was announced and went into effect in May 1972. Japan steamed into the 1970s on a more even keel than ever before.

Behind Japan's relatively stable political course in the years following the occupation lay the so-called economic miracle that had made Japan by the end of the 1960s the third largest economic unit in the world and had brought the Japanese people a personal affluence that they had never dreamed of before. Economic recovery began to be evident in the early 1950s. The severe retrenchment policies of the occupation in 1949 had created a sound financial foundation, and American offshore procurement for the war in Korea provided a strong stimulus. Once revived, Japan's economy began to move at an accelerating pace, and by the mid-1950s the Japanese had regained their per capita production levels of the prewar years and were humorously talking about the "Jimmu boom," meaning the greatest economic boom in their history since the mythical founding of the nation by the Emperor Jimmu in 660 B.C.

By the late 1950s the Japanese economy was racing ahead and for more than a decade thereafter averaged annual growth rates around 10 percent in real terms—a record no other major nation had ever attained. Ikeda's talk in 1960 of the doubling of incomes in ten years proved a gross underestimate; the Japanese economy actually was doubling every seven years. By the 1960s the Japanese were feeling downright prosperous, and the country was swept by a mood of consumerism. Fine cameras, stereos, refrigerators, washing machines, air conditioners, even cars became possessions almost anyone could aspire to, in rural areas as well as the cities. Japanese basked in a sense of pride in their country, which they had not felt for some years, and enjoyed the wonderment of the rest of the world. They showed off their country to foreigners with self-satisfaction at the Olympic Games in Tokyo in 1964 and the Osaka International Exposition of 1970. They talked of a leisure boom, going in enthusiastically for golf, skiing, and bowling, and, when exchange controls were eased, they stampeded abroad as tourists. Per capita GNP passed that of southern Europe and rose to more than two thirds that of the United States.

Growth in per capita GNP was aided by a decided slowdown in population growth, after an initial postwar baby boom. During the 1950s and 1960s the rate of births slowed rapidly to only a little over 1 percent population growth per annum and gave promise of producing a stable population of around 135 million in the year 2000. Public and private advocacy of birth control—there were no religious scruples about it—and lax abortion laws, which were not enforced in any case, contributed to this decline, but the basic reason, as elsewhere in the world, was probably the rapid urbanization of Japanese society. The typical city family became limited to two children, which is usually all there is room for in a small urban apartment and all the family can afford to see through the long years of university education. The rural birth rate, however, slowed even more, because most people of childbearing age had deserted the countryside for the city. But, whatever the reasons, the Japanese who saw themselves as facing a population crisis in the 1930s now saw no population problem at all, for the small annual increase in population took only an insignificant bite out of the much more rapid growth of the economy.

Meanwhile Japan's industrial success was flooding the world with Japanese cameras, radios, television sets, ships, steel, automobiles, and all sorts of other electronic and industrial goods. Already by the late 1960s Japan had become the largest or at least the second-largest trading partner of almost every country, capitalist or Communist, in East

Asia and the Western Pacific. It began to build up huge trade surpluses. With the United States alone the trade balance rose from being slightly unfavorable in the mid-1970s to a staggering $50 billion surplus only a decade later. Naturally Japan began to invest heavily abroad, particularly in the United States, Western Europe, and East Asia. During the 1980s it became the world's largest creditor nation.

Helping to account for this spectacular economic surge was a general perception of Japan's manufactured goods as being among the best though cheapest in the world. Until well after the end of World War II Japan retained its prewar reputation of being a producer of shoddy, second-rate goods, but in the 1970s and 1980s the assumption took hold that Japanese manufactures, particularly in the fields of high technology, were in general superior, more reliable, and cheaper than comparable American products. This extraordinary turnabout in the meaning of "made in Japan" caused a tremendous rise in interest about Japan, particularly in the United States. The world also began to expect more from Japan. Its aid to the less developed lands came to be looked on as crucial and its participation in international bodies as a matter of importance to all.

As Japan's economy rushed rapidly ahead, the new prosperity eased internal frictions, and some of the fire went out of political controversy, even though the old rhetoric and style of confrontation lingered on. With the exception of the Communists, the opposition parties began to accept the defense relationship with the United States, hitherto the most bitterly contested point, and even joint Japanese-American military exercises were undertaken without serious protest. Rural Japanese were clearly well satisfied with conditions, and blue-collar workers in private industry shifted gradually to the pattern of collective bargaining for economic interests, leaving direct political action to white-collar and government workers. The great annual May Day demonstration by the left became a sort of good-natured folk festival. While some of the discrepancies in the "dual structure" of the economy remained, general prosperity and an increasingly tight labor market made them less marked. Moreover, rural affluence together with an explosion of communications, particularly through television, wiped out much of the social and intellectual differences that had existed before the war between modernized urban areas and a stagnant, old-fashioned countryside. Without this brilliant economic advance, postwar Japan would probably not have proved politically so stable nor its democratic institutions so successful.

Economic vigor was paralleled by comparable but less measurable social and cultural achievements. Regardless of the bitterness of political debate, a general feeling developed that Japan had a happy society— "bright" (*akarui*) was the word Japanese liked to use. The rights guaranteed by the constitution were well observed. Despite vast increases in urban population, crime rates remained low—actually less than half those of any major industrialized country in the West—and Japan was free of any serious drug problem. By the 1980s it had achieved the highest rates of longevity in the world. Meanwhile educational levels had soared, giving perhaps the best statistical evidence of social health. School dropouts were practically unknown, and the percentage of the age group that completed the twelve rigorous years of education leading to graduation from senior high school grew to 94 percent, while about 30 percent of these continued on to some form of higher education. These were percentages well above those of most Western countries.

Culturally Japan was also experiencing a boom. It was vibrantly alive. There were great creativity and tremendous vitality in literature, art, and music. Traditional cultural currents ran strong in all these fields, but at the same time Japan participated fully in worldwide cultural trends. For example, while traditional Japanese music showed more vigor than for many decades, Japanese musicians and conductors of Western-type music won worldwide acclaim, and Tokyo supported six full professional symphony orchestras. Japanese films achieved international renown, and Kawabata Yasunari, one of the more traditional writers, won the Nobel Prize for Literature in 1968.

There was some slowing of the rate of growth and change in the 1970s and 1980s, but this increased the sense of stability and general feeling of well-being. The country had clearly succeeded in its long, desperate scramble to catch up with the West and had become the world leader or at least one of the leaders in many fields. The Japanese not unnaturally felt an unaccustomed sense of self-confidence—even euphoria sometimes bordering on arrogance. Under these circumstances, it is not surprising that old political tensions within Japan relaxed, and the country became even more orderly and smooth-running.

Japan's very success, however, contributed to the rise of a whole new set of problems. In their headlong industrialization after the war, the Japanese had despoiled their natural environment and created conditions of terrible crowding and pollution in the urbanized areas. In all industrialized countries people were becoming conscious of these problems, but the Japanese suddenly realized that they faced perhaps the most serious conditions of pollution and overcrowding in the whole world. It was no easy matter to change gears from the long accepted policy of industrial growth at any price, but they managed to effect a sharp decrease in pollution. Through strict laws, underlined by a series of landmark legal decisions beginning in 1978, they improved conditions greatly by the 1980s. Crowding, however, remained a problem less amenable to correction.

The astounding success of the Japanese in international trade had also made their dependence on the outside world all the more obvious. Despite their new pride and self-confidence, they felt even more helpless in the face of developments in the rest of the world. They did not even dare to establish formal relations with Peking until President Richard Nixon suddenly reached a rapprochement with China in July 1971. Nixon did this without consulting the Japanese or even informing them in advance, despite numerous promises to keep them fully informed. The resulting "shock"—the Japanese use the English word—was reinforced in the summer of 1973, when Washington, fearing a soybean shortage, suddenly imposed an embargo on soybean exports despite the key role they played in the Japanese diet. In the autumn of 1973 a worse blow fell when the Organization of Petroleum Exporting Countries (OPEC), made up largely of Iran and the Arab states of the Middle East, quadrupled the price of oil. No major nation was harder hit than Japan, which relies on imported oil for more than 60 percent of its total energy resources. It was thrown into panic, and soaring oil prices contributed for a while to two-digit inflation. In the long run Japan weathered the crisis as well as any other country, but the lesson of Japan's extreme economic vulnerability to external forces remained clearly etched on Japanese minds. Even more disturbing was the fact that Japan, for all its wealth and its central position in the world economy, still had no influence on the most menacing international situation—the confrontation between the Soviet Union and the United States.

Greater expectations of Japan by other countries were another unwelcome result of Japan's achievement of economic superpower status. The less developed lands, particularly Japan's neighbors in East Asia, demanded that it open its markets more fully to them and provide them with more generous aid. The intensity of this feeling first came home to the Japanese when Prime Minister Tanaka Kakuei, on a goodwill tour of Southeast Asia in January 1974, was greeted by widespread rioting in Indonesia.

The industrialized countries of the West, particularly the United States, also began to insist on economic reciprocity from Japan in place of the strongly restrictionist policies under which the Japanese economy had grown so fast and had come to build up large trade surpluses. Such restrictive policies, though understandable when the country was still weak and attempting to restore its economy, were no longer justifiable for a rich and economically powerful nation. Some European countries had all along been openly hostile to Japan, and the United States became increasingly insistent on the lowering of Japanese trade barriers. Many unemployed American workers bitterly accused the Japanese of having stolen their jobs, and trade frictions became a major element in Japanese-American relations.

The Japanese saw the situation differently. They visualized themselves as living precariously on a narrow geographic base, more threatened by external forces than were other industrialized nations and therefore requiring stricter economic controls and a larger economic cushion. They correctly pointed out that they had lowered tariff barriers to levels equal to or below those of most other industrialized countries and that they ran the risk of being squeezed to death between threatened restrictions on high-technology exports to the advanced nations and demands for increased imports of low-technology goods from their newly industrializing neighbors. They attempted to refute American charges that they were continuing their earlier restrictionist policies through less visible nontariff barriers of petty administrative regulations and long-established business practices that tended to exclude foreigners. They claimed that the problem lay more in the inefficiencies of American industry, the failure of Americans to learn either the Japanese language or Japanese business practices, and the general Japanese feeling, shared by many Americans, that most American manufactured goods were inferior to Japanese products. Japan had no alternative but to forge ahead in technology and depend increasingly on "postindustrial," knowledge-oriented products that would not require great quantities of raw materials or energy. But it was clear even to the Japanese that mounting economic competition between Japan and the United States injected an abrasive new element into the relations between these two leaders in world trade. Clearly the time had come for them to rethink their whole position in the world.

In the early postwar decades, a self-confident United States had taken a weak, dependent Japan for granted as a safe even if somewhat reluctant ally, while Japan had meekly accepted the protection and benevolent support of the United States. Now Americans thought the Japanese were being "unfair" in their economic relations with them and were taking a "free ride" in defense at American expense, while the Japanese for their part looked on the United States, after its debacle in Vietnam and the faltering of its economy, as losing its leadership of what they had once thought of as a "Pax Americana." The United States, they felt, could no longer be trusted as a strong protector; the Western Europeans seemed downright hostile because of Japan's economic success; and the less-developed countries made unreasonable demands for aid. Japan obviously would have to play a much more active role in world affairs in order to ensure its own security and maintain its prominent role in the world economy.

The Japanese moved cautiously and somewhat reluctantly to measure up to their new position. Already in 1966 they played a major part in establishing the Asian Development Bank. They accepted voluntary restraints on certain exports and in 1971 started to ease pressures on their trading partners by revaluing the yen upward from 360 to the dollar to over 60 percent of that value by the late 1980s. Aid to the developing countries was increased markedly. Starting in 1975 the Japanese prime minister joined the American president and the prime ministers or presidents of the other major industrialized nations — West Germany, the United Kingdom, France, Italy, and later Canada — in annual summit conferences. Japan became recognized as the second largest industrial power in the world and financially the strongest. But by this point in our historical account, we have come too close to the present for clear perspective. It is time to shift to a broader, more analytic consideration of what the Japanese are like today and where they may be heading.

Part Three _____

Society

Flower viewing (hanami) *picnickers. Enjoying the cherry blossoms, sadly depleted by urban fumes and sprawl, is still a rite of spring. (Courtesy Morris G. Simoncelli / Japan Air Lines)*

12 *Diversity and Change*

The preceding brief account of Japan's historical heritage reveals a story of considerable diversity and constant change. It should suffice to correct some of the facile stereotypes with which the rest of the world tends to explain the Japanese and write them off. Perhaps their isolation and extreme sense of distinctiveness have left the Japanese particularly open to such stereotyping.

Some have seen the Japanese as complete esthetes—the descendants of the delicate and sensitive courtiers and ladies of *The Tale of Genji*, or of medieval Zen artists, or of the gentle folk who so attracted Lafcadio Hearn in the late nineteenth century. Others have seen them as merely the modern version of the arrogant, punctilious, rule-bound samurai of Tokugawa times. A common view among Japan's East Asian neighbors is that they are basically militarists, as shown by the long dominance of feudal military leadership and the brutal conquests by the Japanese army in modern times. A more recent stereotype, contrasting with militarism in content but paralleling it in the emphasis on single-minded fanaticism, is of the Japanese as "economic animals," incomparably efficient in their organization and absolutely ruthless in their willingness to sacrifice all else to their own economic gain.

Our brief run-through of Japanese history should show that the Japanese have changed over time as much as any other people, and considerably more than most. They have been extremely responsive to changing external conditions. Of course, there are cultural continuities and the persistence of some traits, but no more so than elsewhere in the world. Contemporary Japanese are no more bound by the patterns of feudal warriors, Tokugawa samurai bureaucrats, or prewar militarists than Swedes are bound by Viking traditions or early modern military conquests, Germans by their premodern political disunion or their more recent Nazi experience, or Americans by their Puritan heritage or traditions of isolationism. Japan since the war differs in many fundamental ways from what the country was in the 1930s, just as it differed greatly in that period from what it had been a half century earlier, and in the late nineteenth century from the early, and so on back through history.

Our historical account, highly simplified though it is, should also have revealed that Japan does not have a simple, uniform society, but an extremely complex one. Though a homogeneous people culturally, the roughly 122 million Japanese display great variations in attitudes and ways of life according to age group and their diverse roles in society. A teenager and an octogenarian, a day laborer and a corporation executive, a bank clerk and an artist show about as much diversity in attitudes as would their counterparts in any Western country. Almost anything that might be said about the Japanese in general would not be true of many and might be flatly contradicted by some.

But despite this complexity and the rapid changes that have swept Japan, foreign observers have commonly sought to find some one trait or tightly knit group of traits that would explain everything in Japan as it is today and was in the past. Japanese, too, in their self-consciousness have endlessly sought to do the same. Perhaps it is the feeling both share—that Japan is somehow unique—that encourages this search for some one simple explanation for this uniqueness.

In the past, Japanese frequently cited the unbroken line of emperors since antiquity as explaining everything about Japan, though our historical sketch has shown how little that had to do with most developments. Some scholars have singled out the samurai ethics of the Tokugawa period, seen through the militarism of the 1930s, as the key to modern Japan, and others have emphasized the hierarchical groupings in a so-called vertical society or the sense of dependence in human relations as the central elements in Japanese society. Such one-dimensional interpretations do offer some keen insights, but they are basically distorting for such a complex and fast-changing society as that of contemporary Japan.

The speed of change makes sharp analysis particularly difficult. The firm generalization of one decade may start to break down in the next and be almost gone by the one after. The salient features of Japanese life in the 1930s seemed quite different from those in the 1920s and even more different from those of the 1950s and 1980s. Japanese who have received their total education since the end of World War II appear to be almost a new breed when compared with their prewar parents, who continually complain that the younger generation has lost the old virtues. The speed of change shows some signs of slowing at last, but what the Japanese will be like in the future no one can tell. If one thinks about how much has changed in American life and attitudes decade by decade since Civil War days, one can realize how much Japanese too have changed during the same period, for they have been living through greater and more sudden shifts in their foreign relations and far more traumatic transitions at home.

A final problem in analyzing Japanese society is the uncertain ground from which we view it. Any study like this one is inescapably comparative, for one can make no statement about things in Japan being either great or small without having in mind some standard by which they are being judged. But what is that measuring stick? No two Americans have exactly the same attitudes or standards, and if we include other Westerners the diversity becomes still greater. And norms keep changing in America as elsewhere in the world. Whereas Westerners were scandalized by Japanese openness about exposing the human body in the nineteenth century, today they might consider the Japanese in some ways slightly prudish in such matters. Over time the picture of war-mongering Japanese and peace-loving Americans of the 1930s has been transferred into almost a mirror image.

Modern technology also tends to produce considerable convergence between Japan and the West. Without doubt, basic trends in Japan are flowing for the most part in the same direction as in the United States and Western Europe. Individual variations also are almost as great in Japan as within the lands of the West—for example, from very bold to very timid or from wildly ambitious to extremely passive.

Still, when all is said and done, the Japanese do remain a very distinctive people with norms in some fields quite different from those that prevail in the West. Significantly, some of these norms have behind them long historical antecedents and therefore may be all the more likely to persist into the future. Tocqueville a century and a half ago, in attempting to explain to Europeans the Americans of that time, made certain generalizations that have some applicability even today. We cannot hope to do the same for this faster-moving country in this more volatile age, but, in attempting to describe Japanese society as it now exists, we may lay bare some characteristics of continuing relevance.

One thing, however, is certain. Japanese society is too complex and too rapidly changing to fit into any tight, neat model. Certain traits obviously mesh more closely than others, though they all hang together in a relatively smoothly operated whole. I begin my analysis with some of the elements that are most compatible with one another.

13   *The Group*

A good place to start our analysis is the balance between the individual and the group. The human race is made up of individuals, but each is born and for the most part lives his life in a group context. Various societies differ greatly in the relative emphasis placed on the individual and the group. Certainly no difference is more significant between Japanese and Americans, or Westerners in general, than the greater Japanese tendency to emphasize the group at the expense of the individual.

The Japanese are much more likely than Westerners to operate in groups or at least to see themselves as operating in this way. Whereas Westerners may at least put on a show of independence and individuality, most Japanese will be quite content to conform in dress, conduct, style of life, and even thought to the norms of their group. Maintaining "face," originally a Chinese term but one of universal applicability, is much on Japanese minds, but it is face before the other members of the group that most concerns them.

Part of this difference between Japan and the West is myth rather than reality. We have so idealized the concept of the independent individual, alone before God, the law, and society, that we see ourselves as free and isolated individuals far more than the facts warrant. Prevailing Japanese attitudes have tended to make the Japanese do the reverse. Group affiliations in Japan are very important, but the Japanese tend to emphasize these even beyond reality, attempting to interpret everything in terms of such things as personal factional alignments (*habatsu*) in politics, family interrelationships, university provenance (the "academic clique," or *gakubatsu*), and personal patronage and recommendations. They like to insist that what counts is not one's abilities but one's *kone*, an abbreviation of the English word "connections." The actual situations in Japan and the West, however, are much less different than the American Lone

Ranger myth, for example, or the traditional Japanese ideal of selfless merging with the group would lead one to believe.

The balance between group and individual is in flux in Japan as else-where, and there are signs of convergence in this regard between Japan and the West. Modern technology in the Occident clearly produced conditions in which more individuals could win economic and other forms of independence from their families or other groupings than in earlier ages. In fact, the trend in this direction has become so extreme that the isolation and anomie of contemporary urban life are giving Westerners pause and are causing a sort of groping once again for closer group relationships. In Japan the effects of modern technology have by no means gone so far, but they have had the same general effect as in the West, deemphasizing the group somewhat in favor of the individual.

When the Japanese first confronted the superior technology of the Occident, they comforted themselves with the idea that they would adopt "Western science" but stick to "Eastern ethics." The Chinese and other Asian peoples had much the same concept. But the Japanese soon learned that there was no clear dividing line between techniques, institutions, and values. They tended to be all of a piece. Fukuzawa Yukichi, who took a leading role in the 1860s and 1870s in popularizing knowledge about the West, stressed the importance of individual self-reliance as the secret of Western success, and two very influential translations of the time were Samuel Smiles' *Self-Help* and John Stuart Mill's *On Liberty.*

The Meiji leaders recognized the necessity of putting more emphasis on the individual and rapidly got rid of strict class barriers and the whole feudal system, making of the citizenry individual taxpayers and candidates for universal education and military service. Individual rights were written into the 1889 constitution, even though they were strictly limited by the provisions of law; industrialization bit by bit produced greater individual economic freedom as in the West; and the 1947 constitution brought a great number of clearly defined and unrestricted individual rights, which the courts have rigorously enforced since then. Thus the balance between the group and the individual has shifted greatly in Japan during the past century, but, nonetheless, great differences from the West still persist both in attitudes and in realities.

Once these differences were clearly embodied in the family, though this is no longer the case. The premodern Japanese family, known as the *ie,* might include subordinate branch families under the authority of the main family and other members who were distant kin or not related at all. It also gave absolute authority over the individual members to the father or else the family council. This sort of family was to be found particularly among the more prominent members of the feudal warrior class, rich merchants, and certain peasant groups.

The traces of this system lingered on in modern times but have largely disappeared since the war and the adoption of the new constitution. In any case, the bulk of the population even in premodern times held to a simpler family pattern. This was the nuclear family of parents and children, or more properly the stem family variant in which one child, usually the eldest son, and his spouse remained with the parents to inherit the farm or business and then gradually took over from the old folks, who went into retirement while still living in the old home.

The modern Japanese family is in structure not very different from the American nuclear family, though with a strong survival of the stem fam-

A three-generation family playing *uta karuta,* in which verses of famous poems are matched. This is a favorite diversion at New Year's. The word *karuta* is from the Portuguese *carta,* but *torampu* ("trump") is now used for Western playing cards. The spacious, purely Japanese style room, with its rush mat *tatami* floor, indicates that the family is well-to-do. In the rear of the room is the *tokonoma,* an alcove for the display of one or a few works of art. (© *Michal Heron / Woodfin Camp & Associates*)

ily system. The Japanese have never emphasized ancestor worship   the term applies better to Chinese society than to Japanese—but the tablets of a few recent ancestors may be kept on a shelf in a Buddhist shrine and be passed on to one of the children, usually the eldest son, thus symbolizing continuity of the family through him, while the other children are considered to have entered or established separate families. The retired parents are likely to live with the child who receives the ancestral tablets whether or not there has been a farm or business to pass on. Those families who can afford it may have a separate but adjoining house or wing of the family residence for them. This situation is not only a reflection of old customs but is also necessitated in part by inadequate retirement pay and social security benefits, which make retired persons more dependent on their children for support than in the West. Tiny urban apartments, however, may preclude live-in grandparents, often to the open relief of the daughter-in-law, and there is growing resistance to accommodating the old people in this way. Nevertheless, some three quarters of retired persons still live with their children, though with urban crowding growing worse and old people becoming a larger proportion of the population—about a tenth of the people are now over the age of sixty-five—isolated living for the aged and old people's homes are beginning to become prominent features of Japanese society.

The nuclear family in contemporary Japan is somewhat less eroded than its American counterpart. Parental authority is stronger, and family ties on the whole are closer. But these are not structural differences. Beyond the nuclear family, ties of kinship, as with uncles, aunts, and cousins, are as varied and vague as in the United States. Basically the Japanese nuclear family is reminiscent of the American nuclear family as it existed a half century or so ago. The differences are more of degree than of kind, and the trends in both countries are in the same direction, toward smaller units and less binding ties.

The differences from the West come out more clearly in extrafamily groupings. Even in premodern times these often took precedence over the family, though familial terms were sometimes used to describe these relations. For example, the ruler or lord was the "father" of his people. Even today in gang parlance a boss is known as the *oyabun,* or "parent status," and his followers as *kobun,* or "child status." In everyday speech the term *uchi,* meaning "within" and by extension one's home or family, is also commonly used for the business firm to which one belongs. But the important point is that the key groupings even in premod-

A typical middle-class family at dinner in a typically small, overcrowded apartment.
(© *Tadanori Saito / Photo Shuttle: Japan*)

ern times were not essentially kinship units. They were instead such groups as the agricultural village, which shared water resources for the rice fields and cooperated in handling its taxes and other administrative problems, or at a higher level the tight lord-and-vassal units of feudal society. The groups that play such a large role in Japanese society today are more the echo of units of this sort than of the family.

The original village group, organized on a basis of households rather than individuals, is still strong, though it is a much smaller part of society as a whole than it once was and even in rural Japan has been overshadowed by other, larger units, such as the powerful agricultural cooperative or, in politics, the administrative village, which is a grouping together for efficiency of a number of natural villages. The term "village" (*mura*) is now used for these artificial larger units, while the original village has slipped to the informal status of *buraku,* or "hamlet."

For the great majority of Japanese who are not village dwellers, the neighborhood associations of towns and cities have little significance and loomed large only when fostered by the government in the 1930s and the war years as a means of political and economic control from above. There is, however, a great variety of other groupings that are important in their lives. Of these, the firm where one works is probably the most important.

A job in Japan is not merely a contractual arrangement for pay but means identification with a larger entity—in other words, a satisfying sense of being part of something big and significant. Employment for both management and labor is likely to last until the normal age of retirement. For both, this brings a sense of security and also pride in and loyalty to the firm. There is little of the feeling, so common in the West, of being an insignificant and replaceable cog in a great machine. Both managers and workers suffer no loss of identity but rather gain pride through their company, particularly if it is large and famous. Company songs are sung with enthusiasm, and company pins are proudly displayed in buttonholes.

Whereas the American tends to see himself as an individual possessing a specific skill—a salesman, accountant, truck driver, or steamfitter—and is ready to sell this skill to the highest bidder, the Japanese is much more likely to see himself as a permanent member of a business establishment—a Mitsui Trading or Mitsubishi Heavy Industry man—whatever his specific function may be. The same spirit applies to other work groups, as in the various ministries of the government. As we shall see later, this identification of the worker with his work group has had a profound influence on how Japanese business and the economy operates.

Japanese business is also pervaded by other sorts of groupings. Associations of business enterprises, from groups of petty retailers by street or ward to nationwide associations of the great banks or steel producers, are more widespread and more important a feature in Japan than in America. Such associations are pyramided together into comprehensive and effective national organizations, culminating in the Japan Chamber of Commerce for smaller businesses and the Federation of Economic Organizations, the famous Keidanren, for big business. Doctors, dentists, and other professional groups are closely organized in a similar way, and agricultural cooperatives and the federations of labor unions fit into this pattern. The Japanese, in short, are almost the perfect "organization men."

Schools, particularly at the college level, are another important area in which individuals find group identification. Americans, too, talk nostalgically about their alma mater, but links established in school days are likely to be far more important in Japanese life, and university provenance often determines hiring patterns in business. Major universities have the ideal of staffing themselves exclusively from their own graduates and achieve this goal to a surprising degree. Very few students attend more than a single university, and throughout life individuals identify themselves and are identified by others on the basis of the university they attended in a way that finds only a pale reflection even among Ivy League schools in the United States.

Groups of every other sort abound throughout Japanese society and usually play a larger role and offer more of a sense of individual self-identification than do corresponding groups in the United States. There are great congeries of women's associations, pyramided into prefectural and national associations. Youth groupings are important. The Parent Teachers Association, known in Japan as in the United States as the PTA, is a far more influential and well-organized body, particularly in rural Japan, than is its American prototype. There are numberless hobby groups for everything from *judo* and the other martial sports to the gentler arts of flower arrangement and tea ceremony, all tightly organized and occupying a larger role in the lives of their members than would usually be the case in the United States. Rotary is organized on a huge scale, larger than anywhere else in the world except for the United States and the United Kingdom, and instead of being mostly a small-town movement goes right up to the captains of industry in the metropolitan centers.

Naturally, large groups are often subdivided into smaller ones. The work team or office group is an important social as well as operational subunit within a factory or business. There is a particular solidarity among persons of the same age in villages, business firms, and the bureaucracy. Political parties and ministerial bureaucracies often are divided into sharply contending factions. Student life in universities centers on "circles" or interest groups, whether these be for various organized sports, hobbies such as photography, more academic concerns such as the English Speaking Society, or political action groups. Students for the most part develop the bulk of their social contacts within the one such group they choose to join. In society as a whole, artistic and intellectual life tends to break up into small, exclusive, clublike groupings, which support their own publications and do not mingle much with one another.

Some people on the periphery of society do not fit into any of the various types of groups described above, but for them the so-called new religions often fill the void. As we shall see in more detail later, religion as a whole plays less of a role in group life in Japan than an American might expect, but during the past century and a half a number of tightly organized new religions have arisen, perhaps in response to the uncertainties of an age of rapid change and unquestionably serving to give a sense of group identity to those who otherwise lack it. The most outstanding example of such new religions in postwar Japan is Soka Gakkai, which may have around 6 million members, many of whom are casual workers in small enterprises or other persons without any strong identification with work groups or other well-organized bodies. Characteristically Soka Gakkai is made up, not of large congregations, but of small groups that meet together.

The emphasis on the group has had a pervasive influence on Japanese life styles. The Japanese love group activities of all sorts, such as the school or company field day or the association outing. College boys and girls tend to go hiking, skiing, or on other expeditions as groups, and there is correspondingly less getting together on a one-to-one basis. Male groups from work habitually stop at a bar on the way home for a bit of relaxation, and parties are characterized by group drinking and group games rather than by tête-à-tête conversations with shifting partners, as at Western dinners and cocktail parties. Nowhere is group activity clearer than in sightseeing, to which the Japanese have always been addicted. Groups predominate over individuals or families—groups made up of school classes, associates at work, village organizations, women's societies, and the like—each herded along by a tour guide or bus girl carrying a little flag. With the growth of world tourism, the Japanese tourist group has become a common sight abroad. In fact, in Southeast Asia, where many groups from agricultural cooperatives have gone in recent years for sightseeing, local merchants have been known to call out to any passing Japanese tourist *Nokyo-san*, or "Mr. Agricultural Cooperative."

Some people feel that the Japanese are especially prone to the herd instinct. This is a common enough phenomenon everywhere, particularly noticeable when a society is viewed from the outside, but it does seem stronger in Japan than in many other places. The Japanese have always been very susceptible to fads and styles. The postwar Japanese are continuously describing themselves in terms of prevailing "booms" or "moods," using the English terms. An unkind commentator has likened the Japanese to a school of small fish, progressing in orderly fashion in one direction until a pebble dropped into the water breaks this up and sets them off suddenly in the opposite direction, but again in orderly rows.

The group emphasis has affected the whole style of interpersonal relations in Japan. A group player is obviously appreciated more than a solo star, and team spirit more than individual ambition. Whereas the American may seek to emphasize his independence and originality, the Japanese will do the reverse. As the old Japanese saying goes, the nail that sticks out gets banged down. A personality type that in the United States might seem merely bluff or forceful but still normal is defined in Japan as a neurotic state. Cooperativeness, reasonableness, and understanding of others are the virtues most admired, not personal drive, forcefulness, and individual self-assertion.

The key Japanese value is harmony, which they seek to achieve by a subtle process of mutual understanding, almost by intuition, rather than by a sharp analysis of conflicting views or by clear-cut decisions, whether made by one-man dictates or majority votes. Decisions, they feel, should not be left up to any one person but should be arrived at by consultations and committee work. Consensus is the goal—a general agreement as to the sense of the meeting, to which no one continues to hold strong objections. One-man decrees, regardless of that man's authority, are resented, and even close majority decisions by vote leave the Japanese unsatisfied.

To operate their group system successfully, the Japanese have found it advisable to avoid open confrontations. Varying positions are not sharply outlined and their differences analyzed and clarified. Instead each participant in a discussion feels his way cautiously, unfolding his own views only as he sees how others react to them. Much is suggested by indirection or vague implication. Thus any sharp conflict of views is avoided before it comes into the open. The Japanese even have a word, *haragei*, "the art of the belly," for this meeting of minds, or at least the viscera, without clear verbal interaction. They have a positive mistrust of verbal skills, thinking that these tend to show superficiality in contrast to inner, less articulate feelings that are communicated by inference or nonverbal means.

In a highly homogeneous society like Japan's, such nonverbal forms of communication may have been easier to develop than in the countries of South and West Asia and the Occident, where greater cultural diver-

Recording a class outing at a favorite spot in front of the two successive bridges that connect the public part of the imperial palace grounds to the restricted area where the palace itself is located. A guard tower of the old castle can be seen in the background. Junior and senior high school students usually wear uniforms to discourage distinctions of class or wealth. (© *Inge Morath / Magnum Photos*)

sity made verbal skills more necessary and therefore more highly prized. To Americans the Japanese style of negotiation can be confusing and even maddening, just as our style can seem blunt and threatening to them. An American businessman may state his case clearly from the start and in maximal terms for bargaining purposes. The Japanese may be appalled at this as an opening gambit, wondering what more the American may really have in mind. And the American in turn may feel that the cautious indirection of the Japanese is not only unrevealing but also smacks of deceit.

To avoid confrontations and maintain group solidarity, the Japanese make extensive use of go-betweens. In delicate transactions a neutral person scouts out the views of the two sides and finds ways around obstacles or else terminates the negotiations without the danger of an open confrontation or loss of face on either side. The go-between is particularly employed in arranging marriages, thus obviating the hurt to pride and feelings that so commonly occurs in mating procedures elsewhere.

The group skills and virtues that the Japanese have developed contribute to a personality type that is at least superficially smooth, affable, mild, and formally correct. Their deep reluctance ever to utter a flat no causes foreigners to feel that they are dishonest. Westerners seem to them by contrast a little rough, unpredictable, and immature in their frankness and ready display of emotions. In the West unpredictability in a person may be seen as amusing or spirited, but to the Japanese it is a particularly reprehensible trait. Their society does indeed run in more clearly fixed channels and is relatively placid and tranquil, at least on the surface. Aside from labor and political demonstrations, voices are rarely raised, except in convivial group activities. There is little of the scolding mother, loud-mouthed youth, or cursing fishwife that one finds elsewhere in the world.

The Japanese have a strong aversion to most open displays of feelings, whether of anger or love, though like most rules this has its exceptions in their toleration of maudlin drunkenness and their unabashed sentimentality. The Japanese actually are a deeply emotional people, but they strictly hide their emotions as much as possible. The effort to do this may account for their ubiquitous smiles in sorrow and embarrassment as well as in pleasure. In public, physical demonstrations of affection, except toward small children, are avoided, and kissing, which traditionally is associated with the sex act, is little seen or even practiced except in this restricted context. In a country in which a mother would not even kiss her grown daughter, the ritualized and sometimes indiscriminate embracing and kissing of the West and the Middle East seem strange indeed.

Whether all these characteristics are really the result of their group orientation is hard to say. Perhaps they, as well as the emphasis on the group itself, may more basically be the product of a dense population living in little space over a long period. In particular, it may be the result of cramped and relatively flimsy living quarters that require great personal restraint and consideration for others if living conditions are to remain tolerable. Under these conditions, the development of skills in cooperation and in avoiding confrontations was virtually necessary, as was also the toning down of individual whims and idiosyncrasies. But whatever the origins, there can be no doubt that the Japanese are more group oriented than most Westerners and have developed great skills in cooperative group living.

There can also be little doubt that the Japanese have benefited greatly from their identification of themselves with small groups. To Westerners they may appear to have lost much of their individuality in doing this and become all the more faceless, as they seem to people unaccustomed to their quiet style of personal relations and the uniformity of their straight black hair and brown eyes. But as we shall see, they have other ways of maintaining a sense of individuality, and by soft-pedaling individual idiosyncrasies and pooling their efforts they make themselves more effective in most endeavors.

Through consensus decisions achieved by negotiation and compromise, they tend to avoid the losses of open conflict and much of the wasteful friction produced by litigation, to which Americans are so prone. They also build up a solidarity that is invaluable both to small groups and to the nation as a whole. Japanese business prowess depends heavily upon this solidarity, and group identification lies at the heart of their national strength. When confronted by overwhelming Western economic and military power in the middle of the nineteenth century, no Japanese sought to make common cause with outsiders against their fellow Japanese for their own personal gain. Many of the leaders of other developing countries facing crises and disasters such as the Japanese experienced have built up huge personal fortunes abroad at the expense of their countrymen, but there is no case of a Japanese acting in this way. Profits, whether ill gotten or legitimate, are not squirreled away in some safe haven or lavished on conspicuous consumption abroad but are reinvested in Japan or in some nationally beneficial enterprise elsewhere. The firm group identification of the Japanese has on the one side proved comforting to the individual and on the other has strengthened all groups, including the nation as a whole.

14 *Relativism*

In a society that sees itself as made up of independent and equal individuals, any organizing principles must almost perforce be universalistic, applying to all individuals equally. Right and wrong, whether in ethics or in law, must be clear and invariable, regardless of one's personal status. This is indeed the way the West sees itself, harking back for justification to the Christian emphasis on the individual soul, though for long periods, as under feudalism, universalism was honored more in the breach than in the observance. In a society in which people see themselves primarily as members of groups, specific intragroup and intergroup relationships may reasonably take precedence over universal principles. In other words, ethics may be more relativistic or situational than universal.

Group orientation also tends to suppress individual self-expression. Universalistic principles, group orientation, and individual self-expression are all three present to some degree in all societies, but the Japanese may differ from other modernized peoples in recognizing more openly their conflicting pulls and bending more clearly than most in the direction of group solidarity. They accept the need to conform to general principles, calling it *tatemae,* but at the same time they recognize *honne,* or a person's own internal motivations. They do not have as clear a set of words for the dichotomy between universal principles and actions accommodated to particular group relations, but they comprehend this too. Since they admit to themselves these internal inconsistencies and conflicts, they may adjust to them more easily, doing less harm to their psyches than Westerners do by trying to make universal principles, the need for group accommodation, and personal selfish motives all a single rational whole.

These contrasts between Japanese and Westerners should not be drawn too sharply. They are differences in degree, not in kind. In Japan, Buddhism, the most important religion historically, emphasized the salvation of the individual soul on the basis of universal principles, much in the manner of Christianity in the West. In modern times, moreover, there has been growing emphasis on the individual and his rights and an increasing tendency to see things in universalistic terms, as in the West. Still, there undoubtedly remains a deep underlying difference from the West in the greater emphasis on particularistic relations and relativistic judgments. Not only did the whole social organization of feudal times lean heavily in that direction right up into the nineteenth century, but so also did the influence of Chinese thought.

The Chinese clearly recognized universal principles but tempered them by strong particularistic considerations. The five basic Chinese relationships were all specific ones and not applicable universally. They were those between ruler and subject, father and son, husband and wife, elder brother and younger brother, and friend and friend. Among the virtues most emphasized were filial piety, loyalty, and love, or humanheartedness. To the Chinese, however, this love was not to be applied uniformly but was carefully graded according to the nature of the specific relationship. There was no thought of loving one's neighbor as oneself. It would be grossly immoral to treat a stranger as one would a relative. Ethics was a harmonious part of the cosmos, but the centerpiece of that cosmos was human society itself, with all its many specific relationships. There was no sharply drawn line between individual men and a wholly different, all-powerful God, applying clear and inflexible laws to all men alike.

It is interesting that both the East Asians and Westerners saw the world in terms of a basic duality, but there was a significant difference. In the West the division was between good and evil, always in mortal combat with each other. In East Asia the division of *yang* and *yin* was between day and night, male and female, lightness and darkness—that is, between complementary forces that alternate with and balance each other. There was no strict good-bad dichotomy but rather a sense of harmony and a balance of forces.

Much of the flavor of these Chinese attitudes as well as of the particularism of Japanese feudalism lingers on in contemporary Japan, though it is important to remember that it is just a vestige rather than a wellorganized system of ideas contrasting with Western norms of rigid law codes and universalistic ethical principles. Most Japanese have pretty clear concepts of right and wrong basically defined in universal terms.

Their law codes are as universalistic as our own. In 1973 the courts overturned the concept of heavier punishments for patricide than for other forms of murder—an old concept in keeping with ideas of the importance of filial piety—as being discriminatory between individuals. The Japanese revere the individual rights defined in their present constitution as if they were the Ten Commandments. But still, the whole tone and feel of the way society operates in Japan is often quite different from ours.

Some observers have characterized Japan as having a shame culture rather than a guilt culture like that of the West; that is, shame before the judgment of society is a stronger conditioning force than guilt over sin in the eyes of God. There is considerable validity to this concept, though it should not be pushed too far. Shame and guilt easily blend in the feelings of the average person. For example, all too many Westerners are worried more about being found out by neighbors or the law rather than by a sinful act itself. Or again, a Japanese fearing shame in the judgment of his family or society may develop a guilt complex over his failure to live up to expectations. The end effects of shame and guilt may not be very different. Still, there can be no doubt that the Japanese on the whole think less in terms of abstract ethical principles than do Westerners and more in terms of concrete situations and complex human relations. To the Westerner the Japanese may seem weak or even lacking in principles; to the Japanese the Westerner may seem harsh and self-righteous in his judgments and lacking in human feeling.

This difference between Japanese and Westerners is probably not the result of formal education, which in Japan is about as didactic about good and bad or right and wrong as in the West. It probably stems more from child-rearing techniques. We have seen that structurally the Japanese family is much like the American, but the inner relationships are often quite different. During World War II there was a rash of speculation by Western psychologists that harsh toilet training practices produced the Japanese personality as it was perceived at that time. Unfortunately for these theories, they contradicted the facts of toilet training and had an extremely biased view of Japanese personality. But other aspects of child rearing do seem to be significant.

Japanese infants and small children are treated quite permissively, are in almost constant contact with their mothers, and are practically never left alone. This contrasts sharply with the American tendency to put

A mother out shopping with her child strapped to her back. Her destination is a McDonald's and her shopping bag is labeled *Dai gifuto senta* ("Big Gift Center"). (© *Richard Kalvar / Magnum Photos*)

children on strict sleeping and eating regimes, to have them sleep alone from the start, to separate them in their own rooms, to hand them over on occasion to the care of unknown babysitters, and to have more verbal interplay with them than body contact. Japanese children are nursed for a relatively long period, are fed more at will, are constantly fondled by their mothers, are still often carried around on the back when mothers go out—once an almost universal practice—and often sleep with their parents until quite large. Even after that, Japanese tend to sleep in groups rather than singly in individual rooms. Instruction is not by generalized verbal rules reinforced by punishment so much as by intimate contact and patient example. In short, Japanese children are babied rather than treated as small, incipient adults. The result, not surprisingly, is a degree of dependence, especially on the mother, that would be unusual in the West.

Out of this situation emerges a child and then an adult who is accustomed to bask in the affections of others. This attitude is defined in Japanese as *amae,* the noun form of the verb *amaeru,* which is cognate with the word for "sweet" and means "to look to others for affection." It begins with physical and psychic dependence for gratification on the mother and grows into psychic dependence for gratification from the warmth and approval of the group. The child develops an expectation of understanding indulgence from the mother but also an acceptance of her authority, and in time this attitude becomes expanded into an acceptance of the authority of the surrounding social milieu and a need for and dependence upon this broader social approval. In this way, the Japanese child moves with surprising ease from the permissiveness of his earlier years to the acceptance of strict parental and school authority in later years and then to acquiescence in the judgments of the groups to which he belongs or of society as a whole. Parental disapproval, backed up by admonitions that "people will laugh at you," becomes a devastating threat for the child, and later the sanction of the group has the same effect. In the traditional village, ostracism (*mura hachibu*) was the extreme punishment, and in ancient times exile from the court to a distant island or province was the most feared penalty.

Amae blends easily with a concept derived from Chinese philosophy and Japanese feudalism known as *on.* Actually *on* means the benevolence or favor of the ruler, feudal lord, or parent but has been turned around in most usage to signify the unlimited debt of gratitude or obligation of the recipient to the bestower of this grace. As such it has been much emphasized in formal expositions of traditional Japanese ethics.

Both *on* in premodern times and *amae* today underlie the Japanese emphasis on the group over the individual as well as the acceptance of constituted authority and the stress on particularistic rather than universal relationships.

The general relativism of Japanese attitudes shows up in a number of ways in modern Japanese society. Despite the didacticism of their education, the Japanese certainly have less of a sense of sin than do Westerners or of a clear and inflexible demarcation between right and wrong. There are no obviously sinful areas of life. Most things seem permissible in themselves, so long as they do not do some damage in other ways. Moderation is the key concept, not prohibition. There is no list of "Thou shalt nots." Homosexuality has always been accepted and was quite openly acknowledged among feudal warriors and Buddhist monks in medieval times. The Japanese, despite their tendency to be hypochondriac and much interested in psychological and psychiatric problems, have not found Freudian psychoanalysis, with its strong orientation to sex and sin, of much relevance.

Except for a small number of Christians, whose attitudes derive from late nineteenth-century Protestant missionaries, there is no objection to drinking or even drunkenness, so long as they do not get out of hand. With such relaxed attitudes, Japanese easily and happily get drunk on very small quantities of liquor. Liquor shows almost at once in their flushed faces for physical reasons—reportedly the lack of an enzyme and possibly also the low fat content of their diet—but more important is the fact that they good-naturedly tolerate inebriation. Drunks are treated like children and forgiven almost anything but drunken driving. Significantly, alcoholism has never been a serious problem in Japan.

Contemporary politics in Japan may be couched in harsh, absolute terms, but people on the whole remain both relativistic and lenient in their judgments. In cases in which Westerners might feel unmitigated indignation, contempt, or condemnation, Japanese are more likely to emphasize extenuating circumstances and the pitifulness of the miscreant. Young officers who murdered political leaders in the early 1930s and student radicals who wrecked their universities in the 1960s were forgiven by much of the public because of their youth and the "purity" of their motives. Laws in Japan have always been relatively lenient for the time and the social system. For a long period before the development of feudalism, there was no capital punishment—a truly remarkable situation for that day and age. Today great efforts are made to solve disagreements by compromise or conciliation in terms that give something to both sides, rather than by a black-and-white legal decision in favor of one party. In legal sentencings, the culprit's degree of penitence is considered as important as his original motives and, if felt to be sincere, will lead to surprisingly lenient sentences.

The emphasis on particularistic relations rather than universal principles naturally leads to a great number of specific rules of conduct rather than a few clear ethical signposts. Ethics blends into politeness and good manners. There is little esteem for "diamonds in the rough." Instead the good man shows his worth by the shine of each facet of his many relationships, each specific to the situation. There are thousands of rules, all to be meticulously observed. Japanese are the most punctilious people in the world, even if not necessarily the most polite.

The multiplicity and complexity of the rules of conduct were much greater in premodern times. Relations between the various classes and their subgroups were carefully prescribed and scrupulously observed. In today's mass society, the rules have been considerably simplified and generalized. Still, to the Westerner, the Japanese seem extraordinarily formal in all but their most intimate relations. A decorum that would seem stiff to Americans is observed even between members of the same family. The lengthy bowing, all carefully graded as to depth of bows and duration of the exchange according to the relative status and the relationship of the participants, is the most obvious and, to Westerners, the most amusing outward expression of this Japanese politesse. Gift giving on a great variety of occasions, such as formal calls, major events in one's life, New Year's, and midsummer, has been elaborated into a very complex and extremely onerous art of reciprocity. The Japanese language has endless gradations of politeness, and these are carefully used to fit each occasion. Humble forms are reserved for oneself and what belongs to one, and increasingly polite forms are used for persons of higher status and of greater remoteness from oneself. The various levels of politeness in Japanese words usually obviate the need to employ pronouns, to the great confusion and annoyance of foreigners attempting to speak Japanese. But older Japanese constantly complain that young persons are losing these verbal skills.

One result of the emphasis on detailed codes of conduct is a tendency toward self-consciousness on the part of the Japanese—a worry that they may not be doing the right thing and thus are opening themselves to criticism or ridicule by others. This is particularly marked in their relations with foreigners, whose mores are not fully known, but it also exists in dealings between Japanese. Each Japanese seems to be constantly worrying about what the other person thinks of him. He tends to be painfully shy in many of his personal relations and bound down by *enryo,* "reserve" or "constraint." One of the commonest polite phrases is "please do not have *enryo,*" but it seems to have little effect. This self-consciousness, of course, makes Japanese often ill at ease with others and may help account for the tendency of young girls to giggle and simper and men to suck in air while speaking, producing a sound foreigners sometimes describe as hissing. Many Japanese—at least those of the older generation—seem to be at ease only in their most habitual contacts. This makes the familiar group all the more dear to them.

For these various reasons, Japanese do not develop new associations lightly. It may be easier for two people to continue to pass as strangers than to take on the burdens of a recognized relationship. Japanese on the whole are less inclined than Westerners to enter into casual contacts and are likely to seem forbiddingly formal in any new encounter. Pauses in conversation can be agonizingly long, at least to the Western participant. The Japanese, with their low estimate of the value of verbal communication, seem almost oblivious to them. Friends are less easily made, but once made may be held onto with a strength that the more socially casual Westerner finds puzzling. Japanese are inclined to stick to already established group contacts and to put all other persons into a well-defined category of "others." This clearly reduces both public-spiritedness and casual involvement in the problems of other people. These are tendencies that are growing in the urban West as well, but they seem much stronger in Japan.

One result of an ethical system oriented more to specific relationships than to abstract principles is that in an unfamiliar situation it gives less clear guidance. When confronted by something new, a Japanese is more likely to feel unsure of himself than a person who is smugly confident of the universality of his own principles. This is particularly true of a Japanese abroad, but even in Japan itself there are fields where the traditional relativistic ethics do not seem to have been successfully applied to modern conditions. For example, the commuting stampede on and off trains turns the mild, polite Japanese into wild scramblers and shovers.

In wartime the soldiers of any nation may find difficulty in applying their peacetime ethics to the new situation and are likely to act abroad in ways that would not be condoned at home, but the problem seems to be especially difficult for the Japanese with their particularistic emphasis. Certainly there seems to have been an especially wide gap between the brutalities of the Japanese army in World War II and the gentleness and orderliness of life in Japan. Of course, in the treatment of prisoners another factor entered in. The Japanese soldiers had been deeply indoctrinated to believe that surrender was the ultimate disgrace, which they must never suffer, and their contempt for prisoners and harsh treatment of them was no worse than what they would have expected themselves. A better example of loss of ethical bearings under strange circumstances may be the massacring of many Koreans by rampaging crowds at the time of the great Kanto earthquake of 1923, merely on the basis of unfounded rumors. A loss of ethical bearings of this sort may be a more likely possibility among Japanese than among some Western peoples. On the other hand, carefully reasoned atrocities, like the extermination of millions of Jews by the more principle-oriented Germans, would seem less of a possibility than in the West. But this dichotomy should not be too sharply drawn. Seventeenth-century Japanese coldly exterminated the Christians of Japan, and Americans in the past exterminated whole tribes of Indians and, more recently, entire villages in Vietnam.

15 *Hierarchy*

One obvious contrast between Japanese and American society, though by no means all of Western society, is the much greater Japanese emphasis on hierarchy. Despite clear allocations of authority to individuals in the United States, often to a degree that seems almost dictatorial to Japanese, Americans have a strong sense of equality or at least a compulsion to feign equality—"Just call me Joe." Japanese, with their recent feudal background and a society that emphasizes particularistic relationships, consider differing ranks and status natural and inevitable. In fact, their interpersonal relations and the groups into which they divide are usually structured on the assumption that there will be hierarchical differences.

Some groups do consist of equals, as, for instance, men of the same age who form groups within a business or government bureau, or former school classmates among women. Most groups, however, are clearly made up of leaders and followers in the pattern of the traditional family, or *ie*. Even where there is no obvious ranking order, such as between teacher and students or company president and common workers, a hierarchical structure is often achieved through the election of officers and the recognition of status by age and length of membership.

This emphasis on hierarchy undoubtedly derives in part from the long history of hereditary power and aristocratic rule in Japan. Class divisions, hereditary authority, and aristocratic privileges characterized all of Japan's premodern history. The imperial line is a good case in point. Clearly traceable back to the fifth century, it has always been the symbol of the unity of the nation and until quite recently the unique source, at least in theory, of all legitimate authority. When in the seventh and eighth centuries the Japanese borrowed the Chinese system of bureaucratic administration, they could not accept the Chinese method of choosing bureaucrats on the basis of their merit as determined by education but slipped back to the native concept that all ranks and positions should be determined by birth. Subsequently, the whole feudal system depended from start to finish on inherited authority. By Tokugawa times, a very sharp line had developed between the samurai class and all others, and the samurai were divided into dozens of hereditary ranks, which largely determined the level of the jobs for which each person qualified. A small degree of flexibility remained among the samurai, because an excess of candidates for all the higher posts allowed some choice according to merit among those who were eligible for a post by heredity, and in time a system developed permitting supplementary salaries and even permanent promotions for particularly talented individuals who were needed for more important jobs than they qualified for by birth. But by and large the two and a half centuries of Tokugawa rule witnessed one of the most hierarchical and carefully enforced hereditary systems that the world has ever seen.

Even the arts during feudal times fell into the hereditary pattern. All artistic skills came to be regarded as secret family possessions to be passed down from father to son. Schools of painting and of theatrical performance were organized on this hereditary principle, though the almost filial teacher-disciple relationship and the lenient system of adoption actually meant that artistic skills were more often passed on through talented adopted disciples. Curiously, it is in the traditional arts that hereditary authority persists perhaps most strongly in contemporary Japan. Schools of tea ceremony or flower arrangement, for instance, may be tightly organized on a family pattern, and the supreme authority in them may still be transmitted by inheritance.

With this strong and recent background of class distinctions and hereditary authority, one might suppose that Japan still has sharp class divisions. The continuing emphasis on hierarchy, in fact, is often interpreted by foreigners as part of a class system. But this notion is quite wrong. Hierarchy is taken for granted. Status is vastly important. But a sense of class and actual class differences are both extremely weak. In most essential ways, Japan today has a very egalitarian society—more so in fact than those of the United States and many European countries.

By the late Tokugawa period considerable restiveness against the rigidities of the hereditary system had developed, but the real break with this pattern did not come until the Meiji period, when it was achieved with amazing rapidity. Legal distinctions within the samurai class and between it and the other classes were wiped out within a few years, and the category of samurai in census records became a grouping of only historical significance. The samurai who lived through the great change of the nineteenth century often remained distinct from other Japanese in their attitudes and pride, and the elite in Japanese society continued to be drawn heavily from the 6 percent of the population that had constituted the samurai class. It has been estimated that half the elite were of samurai origin as late as the 1930s and around a fifth even at the end of the 1960s. But the great majority of the samurai in the Meiji period were unable to make a successful economic transition and sank into the commonality. Perhaps they disappeared more rapidly than the feudal classes in the West because the samurai had already lost their direct hold on agricultural land in the late sixteenth and early seventeenth centuries. Unlike the West, there was no survival of feudal estates into modern times, and the peasantry from the early 1870s on became the complete and undisputed owners of the soil.

With each succeeding generation the distinction between samurai and commoners became less meaningful. Eventually the samurai category was dropped entirely, and the difference between samurai and non-samurai origins became largely irrelevant to the average Japanese. Some families may on occasion make reference to their distinguished antecedents but much less than do the supposed descendants of Mayflower passengers or plantation owners in the antebellum South. Young Japanese seem no more interested in such matters than young Englishmen in the proportions of Celtic, Saxon, Danish, or Norman blood in their veins.

The one class distinction that was maintained in the modern period was that between the nobility and commoners. The old Kyoto court aristocracy, the feudal lords of Tokugawa times, and some of the new leaders were constituted into a modernized nobility in 1884 in order to staff the House of Peers of the new Diet. For sixty years a great deal was made of this nobility, but the pressures of World War II forced it to adopt more egalitarian ways, and at the end of the war, when the American authorities decreed its abolition, it disappeared almost without a ripple. Even the various branches of the imperial family became commoners. Older people, especially those with a historical cast of mind, may still pay attention to aristocratic pedigrees, and there have been cases in which a descendant of feudal lords found his name an important electoral asset in the home prefecture where his ancestors once ruled. But today all the old nobility, unlike that of France and other European countries, are known simply as Mr. and Mrs.—except among some foreigners. Most of the Japanese could not be less interested in the former nobility and simply ignore it in a completely unselfconscious way.

Class distinctions can exist even in the absence of a nobility and legal class lines. But consciousness of any sort of class distinction is relatively weak in Japan. Actually the type of group identification the Japanese emphasize works against class feeling. The Japanese group, unlike the Indian caste, is normally not made up of people of the same status and function. The two major exceptions to this rule, as noted earlier, are the *burakumin* and possibly the recent Korean immigrants, but these account for only a tiny part of the population. Otherwise, group associations, by emphasizing discrete hierarchical relationships and reducing lateral contacts with groups of similar function and status, play down class feelings as these are known in the West.

The Japanese do not tend to identify themselves in class terms, and when asked to do so, about 90 percent opt vaguely for the middle class, for the most part the "upper" middle class. The lack of class feeling in a sense mirrors reality. The spread of incomes in Japan is roughly similar to that of the United States in the middle brackets but differs markedly from it at the two ends, since there is much less great wealth at the upper end of the scale and a much smaller "underprivileged" group at the other. A recent study ranks Japan with Sweden and Australia as the three industrialized democracies with the least spread in income between the rich and the poor.

The war and the American reforms wiped out most wealth, and the top management of Japanese big business is on the whole more moderately paid and participates less in the ownership of the company's stock than is the case with comparable groups in the United States. Windfall profits, particularly those resulting from a fabulous rise in real estate values, have created some new fortunes, but sharply progressive income taxes and extremely stiff inheritance taxes make the accumulation and transmission of wealth far more limited than in America. At the other end of the scale, great cultural homogeneity and a relatively small and uniform geographic environment have meant that there are no large ethnic or regional groups of "underprivileged" persons, as in the United States. The *burakumin* and the Koreans offer some problems, and there are a few other people who become derelicts or drift into crime. But few people are classified as needy, and a large proportion of them are widows and their children who have lost their chief economic support but are by no means destined to remain underprivileged.

Another sign of the relative classlessness of the Japanese is the lack of class differences in speech. Regional differences can be detected, particularly among the less educated, and there are obvious differences in the quality of a person's vocabulary depending on his degree of education, but there are no class accents, such as are so pronounced in the United Kingdom and are discernible even in parts of the United States.

Starting in 1868 far behind the British in terms of strong class lines and hereditary authority, the Japanese have swept well past them in only a little more than a century. It is indeed an amazing achievement. While part of it may be attributed to the special characteristics of group affiliation in Japanese society, the greater part can be explained only as a conscious product of education. The Japanese adopted the Western concept of universal education open at least in theory to everyone on an equal basis and used this system to sort people out for their respective roles in society. The result has been steadily growing social mobility ever since the Meiji Restoration, until Japan today has at least as high a degree of social mobility as the United States or any country of Western Europe. We shall look at the role of education in more detail in a later chapter, but here we need note only that the shift from a hereditary to an educational system for determining hierarchical status is now virtually complete. The Japanese achieve their various functions in society and find their respective status levels, not chiefly through inheritance or class and family considerations, but through formal educational achievements, followed by rigorously equal qualifying examinations for most of the positions of greatest prestige.

There are some survivals of the older system in Japan, as there are almost anywhere in the world, even in most socialist countries. Children of well-educated parents, because of environment and family tradition, usually have advantages in the whole educational and examination process. Small family businesses as well as the family farm are commonly passed on by inheritance. Even a big business, if it was recently founded by some successful entrepreneur, may be handed on to a son. The great Matsushita firm, which produces under Panasonic and other trade names for the foreign market (its domestic trade name, National, would not be very appropriate), is a good case in point. The presidency of the firm was passed on to an adopted son-in-law, but judging from the experience of similar companies in the past, transmission by inheritance is not likely to go on for more than a single generation or two. Doctors' sons commonly take over their father's practice. Certain artistic activities still recognize hereditary principles, as does an occasional private school or "new religion." But that is about it. There being much less inherited wealth than in the United States, inheritance probably figures quite a bit less in Japanese society than in American and distinctly less than in some countries of Western Europe.

Hierarchy, however, remains fundamental and pervasive throughout Japanese society, giving it its shape and character. Japan is divided up into numberless groups, each organized into multiple layers of status. This vertical, hierarchical arrangement is quite natural to many institutions, such as government bureaucracies and business firms, but it shows up in other groupings too. Even the village (now "hamlet") organization, though a somewhat egalitarian grouping by households, had in earlier days a clear pecking order, from households that traditionally provided the head men down to tenant farmers. Many modern groupings, such as agricultural cooperatives or women's associations, which have, beneath the hierarchy of officers, an egalitarian mass membership, achieve a sort of hierarchical pattern through a strong sense of age distinctions.

In government bureaucracies as well as in big business firms, age groups reinforce the hierarchy of rank, since those who have entered in any given year form a "class" that will stay in step in both salary and rank through most of their careers. One may enter a business firm or government service at different levels leading to different careers, but each career consists of a sort of age escalator of pay and status on which everyone advances together. The factory worker, for example, is on a lower escalator of pay and status, while the executive has qualified by higher education and a competitive entrance examination for a higher escalator that may lead all the way to the boss's job; but within each category, status as well as pay is determined primarily by age and length of service.

It is as natural for a Japanese to shape his interpersonal relations in accordance with the various levels of hierarchy as for an American to attempt to equalize his interpersonal relations despite differences of age and status—in fact the Japanese approach may be considerably more natural. Older people or persons otherwise recognized as having higher status walk first. People are seated in clear order of precedence on any formal occasion. In a Japanese-type room the seat of honor is at the opposite end from the entrance and in front of the *tokonoma,* or alcove for art objects. As a result, entrance ways not infrequently get seriously jammed with people who, in either doubt or humility, insist on sitting in the place of least honor. One addresses a person who is recognized as being of higher status with regard to wisdom by the title *sensei,* a general term for "teacher." Among men, intimates of the same age or younger will be addressed as *kun,* instead of *san* or very formally *sama,* which are used for everyone else, male or female, single or married, and are thus equivalent to Mr., Mrs., and Miss. (Persons are almost never addressed by their first names, except for children, younger members of the family, and persons who have known each other intimately since childhood.)

Actually one of the commonest forms of interpersonal address is by specific status appellations. Within the family, these go beyond such terms as "daddy" and "grandma," familiar to Americans, to include such categories as "elder sister" or "older brother." In addition, any intimate older person may be addressed as "uncle" or "auntie," or, if the age is appropriate, "grandpa" or "grandma." But what is much more significant is the prevailing use in direct address of such terms as *okusan* or *okusama* (lady of the household), *kocho-sensei* (teacher-principal), *Kyokucho-san* (Mr. Bureau Chief), and *Shacho-san* (Mr. Company President). The only equivalent American usages, aside from military ranks, are a few rarified terms such as "Mr. President" or "Mr. Ambassador," which most people never have occasion to use.

Unlike the American propensity for the elderly person to try to act young or the company president to be one of the boys, the Japanese try to live up to their status. In earlier times, the concept of taking one's proper station in life had to do with unchanging hereditary status, but now it means to act in accordance with one's age and position as one moves up in life. A good part of personal self-identification derives from one's status role. Others will treat a person according to his status, and there is nothing less becoming than for the person himself not to act accordingly. To ignore or break the order of status on either side is felt to be extremely awkward. A foreigner's attempt to show equality across status lines, though forgiven as an outsider's ignorance, is embarrassing to Japanese.

The importance of hierarchy and status is one of the reasons for the constant exchanging of *meishi,* which we call by the antiquated term of "calling cards." It is true that some Japanese names are extremely difficult to read in the Chinese characters with which they are always written, and a card with the name clearly printed, and possibly with a phonetic gloss to help the reading, can be of help. Addresses and phone numbers, which are usually included on the card, may also be useful for later reference. But the main significance of the exchange of *meishi* is that they make clear a man's specific position and group affiliation—Managing Director of the Fuji Bank, Director of the Treaty Bureau of

Men being introduced to each other or simply exchanging greetings. Bowing is customary between Japanese; handshaking is largely reserved for foreigners. The depth and number of bows generally reflect differences in status, relationships, and age. (© *Richard Kalvar / Magnum Photos*)

the Foreign Ministry, Professor of Economics at Tokyo University—and this then helps establish the nature of the relationship with the other person and the degree of politeness and deference to be shown.

The hierarchical arrangement of society retains some of the flavor of earlier days. Those in the top ranks of any hierarchy are expected to show a sort of benign paternalism to those further down on the scale, including a personal concern for their private lives that might in the West be considered an infringement of privacy. For example, bosses in government or business are commonly asked to serve as go-betweens in marriage arrangements. In return for this benevolence, those in inferior positions are expected to demonstrate respect and loyalty. There is an overtone here of the old concepts of *on,* or benevolence by the superior, and *giri,* the reciprocal sense of loyalty and duty from the inferior person.

The pattern of hierarchy within groups is paralleled by a hierarchy between groups. Japanese are prone to think in terms of rank order. Almost anyone has a pretty clear idea of the informal order of universities, with Tokyo University unquestionably at the top, Kyoto University next, and so on down to a broad base of undistinguished private universities and below them the junior colleges. Business firms fall into the same patterns in people's minds, with great, prestigious firms at the top and small, weak ones at the bottom. To speak of a country as number one or as a third- or fifth-rate power is not just vaguely figurative, as in the American mind, but is a much more precise and meaningful statement to the Japanese.

Strong hierarchy to a Westerner suggests firm, almost autocratic, authority, but this is not the situation in Japan. In fact, some of the emphasis on hierarchy is purely symbolic, as is most strikingly shown by the role of the emperor in the greatest Japanese hierarchy, the state. Another example is that, in organizing almost any activity, the Japanese set great store by honorary committees of big names that are used for prestige purposes. Below these top committees will be the real operating committees of junior and more active persons. This is a common enough pattern in the United States too, but it is even more pervasive in Japan. Another sign of the symbolism of hierarchies is that the person at the top of any organization, regardless of his actual function and authority, may feel such a sense of responsibility for all that transpires under his supposed jurisdiction that, in the event of any major untoward occurrence, he is likely to "accept responsibility" formally and resign from his post, even though in Western eyes there may have been not the slightest suggestion of his legal or moral culpability. In an earlier age, suicide might have been the expected response.

Even in the case of actual, not symbolic, leadership roles, the Japanese approach is quite different from the American. Leaders are expected to be not forceful and domineering, but sensitive to the feelings of others. Their qualities of leadership should be shown by the warmth of their personalities and the admiration and confidence they inspire rather than by the sharpness of their views or the vigor of their decisions. What the American might consider as desirably strong leadership causes suspicion and resentment in Japan. Consensus through prolonged consultation is the norm. The purported boss more often seems to be just the chairman of the committee. Subordinates, who are lifetime members of the group and who in time will be carried to higher posts and status by the escalator of age, expect to be in on decisions and not just receive them as dictates from above. They expect to be treated as junior associates or even disciples rather than as mere underlings. I shall explore such matters further in my discussions of Japanese business and the government bureaucracy; here I need only emphasize what seems to Westerners to be the surprising contrast between the great emphasis on hierarchy in Japan and the relatively wide sharing of authority and decision-making powers.

One final point about Japanese hierarchy is that it breeds fewer of the tensions and resentments that are caused in the West by differences in status. This is not surprising for a number of reasons. Those higher on the career escalator are seen merely as older persons who got on the escalator earlier, not as persons who have scrambled unfairly to the top. One's own time will come in due course. Or if they are on a higher career escalator than one's own, this is because of their superior achievements in education and examinations. In a homogeneous society, differences in educational performance are more likely to be seen as the result of differences in personal ability, not of an unfair society. The lack of dictatorial authority on the part of the leaders and the wide consultations and sharing of decision-making powers tend to make a subordinate's position in Japan less irksome than in the West. The close solidarity of the group, the lingering sense of paternalistic concern on the part of those on top, and the personal loyalty on the part of those below give a feeling of warmth and intimacy across status lines. And finally the sense of belonging—of achieving a self-identity through membership in the group—makes the individual more willing to accept his status, whatever it may be. Not that restiveness against superiors and infighting among cliques do not exist. The young officer problem of the 1930s almost led to open revolt, and today there is much grumbling about old men blocking the way to promotions for their juniors. Still, the traditional sense of hierarchy of the Japanese has been fitted very smoothly into what is now a basically egalitarian society, and thus it remains a major and efficiently functioning feature of contemporary Japanese society.

16 *The Individual*

We should not stress the group orientation, relativistic ethics, and hierarchical structure of Japanese society too much. To do so would be to suggest that Japan is made up of a uniform race of pliant, obedient robots, meekly conforming to rigid social rules and endlessly repeating the established patterns of their society. This is a concept widely held in the West, but all Japanese history contradicts it. The Japanese have shown themselves to be extremely dynamic and capable of rapid and purposeful change. Their art reveals them to be both very sensitive and creative. Their literature shows them as painfully self-conscious individuals. There clearly is another side to the picture. Although the Japanese subordinates his individualism to the group more than the Westerner does, or at least thinks he does, he retains a very strong self-identity in other ways. He is devoted to emotional self-expression, even if he channels it more than does the Westerner. Most important, he appears to develop at least as much individual drive and ambition.

The clash between personal self-expression and social conformity naturally exists in Japan as elsewhere in the world. In fact, the greater uniformity and strictness of Japanese social patterns leads to a widespread sense of malaise, especially among the young, and sometimes to open revolt. It takes more daring and determination to be a social rebel in Japan than in a society of looser weave, and the result is thus likely to be more violent, as in the political assassinations by young military officers in the 1930s, the explosiveness of the student movement in the late 1960s, and the atrocities of the Red Army (Sekigun) and other small terrorist bands of young people in the 1970s—though it should be noted that even the rebel against society is usually a member of his own closely knit little group and not a lone operator or individual eccentric.

Below the level of open revolt, there is a general restiveness. Young men express their nonconformity by forming motorcycle gangs, and groups of young people, predominantly girls, organize dancing groups that meet in public in outlandish costumes and perform their own special dances with blaring electronic music but utter solemnity. The park outside the entrance to the Meiji Shrine in Tokyo is a favorite place on Sunday afternoons for these rites of rebellious youth. The 1980s have witnessed a sharp increase in schoolboy delinquency, leading to physical harassment of unpopular children and occasional acts of violence against teachers. Such conduct deeply disturbs adults even though it is milder and less frequent than school delinquency in the United States. Young Japanese in general seem to be seeking for ways to break out of the strict molds of Japanese society. They often feel that they must get out of Japan at least once in their lives to savor the supposedly fresher atmosphere of the outside world. They freely express resentment at the limitations imposed on their lives by a tightly organized educational and employment system. In fact, public opinion surveys often show Japanese young people as ranking highest among the industrialized nations in their avowed dissatisfaction with the way their society works, though it seems probable that this is in part just a conventional group reaction that is contradicted by the obvious satisfaction they show for most aspects of their society.

Still, a pervasive restiveness and constant straining for change do characterize Japanese youth, making the older generation fear that the young are losing their Japaneseness. Such conditions go back at least to the 1920s, though they have become much more marked since the end of World War II. As elsewhere in the world, there is a gap between generations that makes true communication between them difficult, though this situation is often concealed in Japan by outward social conformity and a discreet silence on matters of consequence. The university student may eat breakfast quietly with his parents before setting out with his comrades to destroy his university.

Despite the search for individual self-expression and freedom from social restraints, the word "individualism" (*kojin-shugi*) itself has always been in ill repute in Japan. It suggests to the Japanese selfishness rather than personal responsibility. As a consequence, they have tended to avoid it by using other terms. For a while students used the word "subjectivity" (*shutaisei*) in the sense of one's being the active subject rather than passive object in one's life. Another popular phrase was "my-home-ism" (*mai-homu-shugi*), expressing the passionate desire of young Japanese to own their own homes—by no means an easy thing to do where land values are so high—and to lead their own private lives, free of family or group pressures.

Despite these various efforts to avoid conformity, even the relatively free and spontaneous younger Japanese of today seem extraordinarily conformist to Westerners. The American cliché of the college radical becoming in time the corporate executive in a three-piece suit is even truer of Japan, where the businessman's white shirt and blue suit become almost a uniform for adult men. The great majority of Japanese pass smoothly from permissive childhood through rebellious youth to conformist maturity. They retain, however, their strong desires for self-identity, and a certain number always continue to reject the accepted norms of society and seek freer life styles.

Among the nonconformists one would probably include everyone in the whole world of entertainment, especially what is called the *mizu-shobai*, or "the water trade." This curious name refers to the precarious nature of enterprises depending on sexual attraction, from the mild flirtations of bar girls to various forms of prostitution, which officially has been illegal since the war. Certain amusement areas have a great number and bewildering variety of bars, including miniature discos and places with floor shows or "sing-along" programs. Facilities for more open sexual activities, from "love hotels," where couples can rent a small room for a few hours, to so-called Turkish baths (a term now avoided because of Turkish objections), exist in almost comparable profusion.

Another group of nonconformists is the criminal element, often organized into powerful gangs known as *yakuza*. These are closely linked with the shadier aspects of the *mizu-shobai*, run protection rackets, and engage in illegal gambling and loan-sharking. The *yakuza* pretend to a romantic heritage from similar groups in feudal times, and they try to imitate, at least in clothes and mannerisms, Hollywood's image of American gangsters. This posturing, grossly exaggerated, has become a genre of films and television shows, but in reality *yakuza* are a far cry from the Mafia or American gangsters. Strict controls make firearms rarities; crime rates are much lower than those in most other industrial countries; and the *yakuza* often cooperate with the police on police terms.

At one time, political wire-pullers, known as *kuromaku*, often based their influence on *yakuza* gangs. A few such men, essentially survivors from prewar days, still attempt to influence political decisions through their connections, their doubtfully acquired wealth, and even the veiled threat of violence by their *yakuza* henchmen, but such efforts are far less common or effective than is commonly supposed. Bureaucrats are beyond their reach, and politicians, though always in need of money, depend on votes from a public that is outraged at the whole concept of wire-pullers. Such figures are a fading feature of Japanese life and may soon disappear entirely.

Still another category of nonconformists are the denizens of occasional skid rows and the residents of a few slum areas, of which Sanya in Tokyo is the best known. These are people who because of adversity or personal shortcomings have been unable to achieve normal Japanese standards of life. Their most remarkable feature is their scarcity. Only a tiny fraction of the population has failed to find a respectable place in society. There are no vast blighted urban areas nor is there any shamefully large underclass, as in the United States.

The nonconformist groups are all vestiges of similar groups from the even more rigidly regulated feudal age. Thus they represent perhaps a natural reverse side of the coin of standard Japanese life. While they are much smaller in number or influence than in most other modern countries, in recent years they have attracted a great deal of attention, particularly among Westerners. This may be because Westerners, surfeited by the homogeneity of Japanese society, the self-satisfaction of most Japanese, and the loud acclaim of foreigners for the Japanese "miracle," are attracted by the seamier side of Japanese life in order to make so much success less cloying.

The great majority of Japanese do adhere to established norms, but even within this firm crust of custom, they are not just human ants. They earnestly cultivate their own individuality, though in ways that are socially acceptable. Many Japanese find a sort of refuge from society and a means of personal fulfillment through identification with the beauties and processes of nature. This is all the more important to them because of their great love of nature.

The press of population and rampant economic growth in recent years have made the Japanese among the worst despoilers of nature, but they retain a passion for it, though often this can be expressed only in miniaturized form. They love outings and hiking, but few can have extensive gardens or wild acres of their own. Instead they cultivate tiny landscape gardens, designed to represent in miniature the grandeur of nature as a whole. They love to paint vignettes of nature and dote on dwarf potted trees (*bonsai*). Some women cultivate the minor arts of tray landscapes made of colored clay (*bonkei*) or sand (*bonseki*), and many more are devoted to the art of flower arranging (*ikebana*), in which a few carefully shaped and placed flowers and sprigs are used, instead of the massed bunches of flowers popular in the West. Some aspects of this cult of the little, such as landscape gardening and flower arrangement, have had a great impact on the West in recent years.

The whole field of literature also provides a broad area for self-expression, or at least for vicarious participation in the individualistic self-expression of others. From the time of its strong resurgence around the turn of the century, Japanese literature has been characterized by the search for self-identity. Much of this has been concerned with the survival of a Japanese identity in the tidal wave of Western cultural influences, but another aspect of this search has been for personal identity within a stiflingly compact society. The Japanese writer has particularly favored what the Japanese call the "I novel"—the introspective, almost embarrassingly frank examination of the writer's personal feelings in a basically hostile environment. Such works usually look at Japanese society from so restricted and individualized an angle as to give only a very incomplete and distorted view of society itself, but they are revealing about the subtleties and vagaries of the individual human spirit, and that is what the Japanese reader is interested in. This same interest probably accounts for the great popularity of prerevolutionary Russian literature in Japan. Although Japanese and Russian personalities and societies are very different, the Russian portrayal of the clash of the individual spirit with an oppressive society and the search for self-expression has obviously struck a deep chord in the Japanese soul.

Not many people can be successful authors, but millions of Japanese find self-expression in writing in one form or another, whether by keeping diaries or by efforts at poetic composition. Both the classical thirty-one-syllable tanka and the more modern seventeen-syllable haiku are very restricted poetic forms, even further limited by countless traditional poetic restraints, but nonetheless huge numbers of Japanese find satisfying self-expression through them. Poetry magazines and study groups abound, and there is an annual national tanka contest on a set theme, with the winning poems read in the presence of the emperor, who himself contributes a poem.

Millions of Japanese also find self-expression through traditional dancing, music, and other art forms. The various types of dance asso-

Preschool children start learning to play musical instruments in large classes. These youngsters performing on the violin according to the Suzuki method are across the moat from the dungeon of the Matsumoto castle. (© *Hiroji Kubota / Magnum Photos*)

ciated with the premodern theater and with geisha are the focus for numerous well-organized schools of instruction, each with its ardent group of devotees. The same is true of all types of traditional music, and many more people acquire skills in the various instruments and forms of Western music. The Suzuki technique of starting young violinists at the age of two or three, often in large groups, is world famous. All the traditional forms of painting and pottery making have their proliferating schools, as do also the various Western art forms and the traditional arts of tea ceremony, flower arrangement, and the like. Judo, *karate,* and the other martial arts are also part of this tradition of the cultivation of individual skills.

Each of these schools of instruction forms a sort of in-group for those who participate in it, but the important point in the present context is that most Japanese do have their own personal literary, artistic, or performing skill, and this is not only a means of emotional self-expression but also a treasured element of self-identity. Only in recent years has the United States begun to see anything like this sort of huge popular artistic endeavor that Japan has had for long, and here too it may in part be the product of the need for self-expression and self-identification in a crowded, constraining social environment.

We tend to dismiss such activities rather lightly as hobbies, but the Japanese value them as *shumi,* or "tastes," which help establish their identity and commonly become of increasing importance to them as they grow old. The individual Japanese takes pleasure in displaying at parties his particular skill—say, chanting in the Nō manner. In fact at such parties each Japanese may perform in turn, while the foreign participant, in embarrassment over his lack of any appropriate ability, settles for trying to sing his half-forgotten college song. The ardent pursuit of a hobby is almost necessary for self-respect in Japan. I know that on many occasions when I have lamely had to explain to interviewers that I lacked hobbies, since my work was also my hobby, I felt that I was making a damaging admission of spiritual incompleteness.

The Japanese cherishes and flaunts his hobby, even if it may be only the traditional one a person in his position is expected to have. The big businessman feels that, as a big businessman, he must make a fetish of his interest in golf and prattle endlessly about handicaps. A more sporting type may perform feats of incredible endurance to cram eight hours on a distant ski slope into a day-and-a-half weekend. All this is somewhat familiar in American life too, and possibly for some of the same reasons. Still, personal skills and hobbies are probably a bigger aspect of self-identity in Japan than in the United States.

A look at the ways Japanese develop personal skills also reveals how the Japanese nurture their individuality. The traditional skills in particular are learned not so much by analysis and verbal explanation as by personal transmission from master to disciple through example and imitation. The teacher-disciple bond is a very important one and accords with the whole group orientation of the Japanese, but of equal importance is the fact that learning is more an intuitive than a rational process. The individual is supposed to learn to merge with the skill until his mastery of it has become effortless. He does not establish intellectual control over it so much as spiritual oneness with it. We are reminded of the original Buddhist concept of losing one's identity by merging with the cosmos through enlightenment. The significant point, however, is that acquiring a skill is essentially an act of will—of self-control and self-discipline. The teacher of archery emphasizes control over one's stomach—that is, the emotions—rather than sharpness of eye or deftness of hand. Mastery of a skill is seen as more a matter of developing one's inner self rather than one's outer muscle. Here is an important area of individual self-development that is not only socially approved but is very much encouraged.

When we look beyond these traditional arts to the art of living, we see that the same approach applies. Ideally the cooperative, relativistic, group-oriented Japanese is not just the bland product of a social conditioning that has worn off all individualistic corners but is rather the product of firm inner self-control that has made him master of his less rational and more antisocial instincts. He is not a weak-willed yes-man but the possessor of great self-discipline. In contrast to normal Western perceptions, social conformity to the Japanese is no sign of weakness but rather the proud, tempered product of inner strength.

No people has been more concerned than the Japanese with self-discipline. Austere practices of mortification of the flesh, such as frigid baths in winter, were and sometimes still are performed not for the reasons of the Western or Indian mystic but to develop will power. Since medieval times Zen meditation has been popular but often less for the original reason of achieving transcendental enlightenment than for the cultivation of self-discipline. This same reason may well explain the re-

Facing page: Elementary school students at a calligraphy contest, writing on scrolls on the floor. Most are composing *Heiwa Nippon* ("Peaceful Japan") in Chinese characters. (© *Richard Kalvar / Magnum Photos*)

cent appeal of such practices to some Western youths, who are uncon-sciously groping for a new form of self-control.

The Japanese commonly make a fetish of self-discipline and the culti-vation of will power. They regard these as essential for the proper per-formance of one's duties in life. They strive for inner calm and the self-less blending of right thought and right action into instantaneous and forceful performance. Their constant preachments show clearly that they do not regard social conformity or the fulfillment of one's role in the world as coming naturally but as being hard learned skills. In earlier days they talked about the heavy burdens incurred from the benevolence (*on*) of parents, feudal lords, or the emperor. Even today they are sharply aware of the need for great effort to live up to the rigid require-ments of society.

Many Japanese seem overburdened by the demands of duty—to fam-ily, to associates, and to society at large. This sense of duty, usually called *gimu,* is so onerous as to have produced the underlying restiveness among the young, but it is a clear continuity from premodern times, when the word used was *giri. Giri* incurred in a thousand ways could not be allowed to be submerged by the personal human feelings, known as *ninjo,* that come spontaneously and can lead to social turmoil and disaster. A favorite theme in traditional literature was the conflict of *ninjo,* in the form of some illicit love, with the *giri* of family responsibil-ities and broader social duties—a conflict that was commonly resolved, at least in literature, by the suicide of the ill-starred lovers.

Something should be said in passing about the role of suicide in Japan, simply because it looms large in the minds of Japanese and others as a very special characteristic of Japanese society. In its traditional form of *seppuku* it was very much part of the cult of *Bushido,* the "Way of the Warrior," and even today suicide is looked on as an acceptable or even honorable way out of a hopeless dilemma, though in actual society, as opposed to popular imagination, suicide is statistically no more preva-lent than in the Occident. *Seppuku* remains a favorite theme in dramas and movies but has virtually disappeared from real life. Except for a rash of such suicides by prominent personages, mostly military, at the end of World War II—and these were perfectly understandable even from a Western point of view—the last notable case of genuine *seppuku* was that of the Russo-Japanese War hero, General Nogi Maresuke, and his wife in 1912 to follow the Meiji emperor in death. The spectacular *seppuku* of the great novelist Mishima Yukio in 1970 was more a matter of dramatic posturing than an act of duty or valid political protest, and it left the Japanese public, though thrilled by the drama, somewhat puzzled and contemptuous. The large number of prominent literary figures who have taken their own lives, though in more prosaic ways, is more a commentary on the introspective nature of modern Japanese literature than a sign of the prevalence of suicide in Japanese society.

Most suicides in contemporary Japan occur for reasons much like those in other countries, and by similar means. As in some other East Asian countries, the rate for women is closer to that for men than it is in the West, perhaps reflecting greater social pressures on women in East Asia; and rates for students are much higher, probably reflecting the greater pressures of the educational system, though in this statistic the West is beginning to approach Japan. What is more significant is that suicide rates in modern times have fluctuated widely with political tensions and economic conditions in society as a whole and today are very close to those of the United States and lower than the rates in several European countries. The Japanese, however, continue to be fascinated by suicides and to make a great deal of them in their news and literature, just as Americans are fascinated by murders.

To return to the theme of self-discipline and ambition, it must be admitted that insistent preaching does not necessarily produce prevailing characteristics in a society. In fact, they sometimes seem almost like mirror contrasts. But in the Japanese case there appears to be considerable correlation between the two. The Japanese on the whole do have a pronounced toughness of character. An extreme example of this is the persistence for a quarter of a century of a Lieutenant Onoda in his solitary war with the United States on a jungle island in the Philippines. The Japanese high command in World War II assumed that greater will power on the part of their people, which they took for granted, would provide the margin of victory over a United States that everyone knew was vastly superior in natural resources. The Japanese often seem convinced that any obstacle can be overcome so long as one has enough will power and tries hard enough. Older Japanese often feel that these characteristics are breaking down in this more affluent and relaxed age, and this may be true to some extent, but beneath their surface shyness and cooperativeness the Japanese on the whole do continue to have a relatively high quotient of firmness of character.

Many observers have noted that the emphasis on hard work, individual drive, and economic achievement, pridefully described as the "Protestant ethic" in the West, is even more characteristic of the Japanese, who have no Christianity, let alone Protestantism, in their background. These traits, in fact, are strongly characteristic of all the peoples of East Asia—the Chinese, Koreans, and Vietnamese as well as the Japanese—who derive their underlying culture from ancient China and its Confucian attitudes. This work ethic is unquestionably associated with the drive for education all these people share, as well as with the cold climate of most of the area. It also seems to have been strengthened by the group orientation of the Japanese. A good group cooperator is also a good worker, and the camaraderie of group work can be a positive pleasure, even when the artisan's pride in individual work has been replaced by more routine machine production in modern times. Diligence (*kimbensei*) is generally recognized by the Japanese themselves as one of their most outstanding virtues. The primary identification of the individual Japanese with his work group and his enthusiastic, even joyous, participation in its activities explain why the Japanese work ethic even today seems far less eroded than in countries of the vaunted Protestant heritage.

A group society made up of self-disciplined, strong-willed individuals can produce sufficient tensions to explain all the drive and ambition the Japanese show. Beneath the surface of harmonious conformity have always seethed great pressures. The premodern Japanese was deeply concerned with honor and face—attitudes that still linger on in the Japanese consciousness. The watchword of the Meiji period was *shusse*, or "success in life." Ambitious personal success was what was meant. William S. Clark, a president of the Massachusetts Agricultural College (later the University of Massachusetts), who was in Japan briefly in 1876 to set up an agricultural school (the future Hokkaido University), is still widely remembered for his parting injunction to his students: "Boys, be ambitious." The dependent child may be compulsively driven by his mother's expectations of him. One hears overtones of the traditional "Jewish mother" in her Japanese counterpart.

All in all, the modern Japanese seems as much motivated by personal ambition and drive as any Westerner. It may puzzle Westerners to find these characteristics in such a group-oriented people, but the Japanese in fact are often quite unrealistically ambitious. It is difficult to measure such traits, but the record of Japanese-Americans affords some comparative data. Though handicapped by a very different cultural and linguistic background and long subjected to severe prejudice and discrimination, Americans of Japanese ancestry have within two or three generations risen to levels of education, income, and status that are at or near the top of all ethnic groups, including WASPs and Jews. Surviving Japanese traits are all that can account for this record.

If there are parallels between Japanese characteristics and the Protestant ethic of the West, they may lie in the fact that the latter appeared in a West still divided by recent feudal conditions into classes or estates, in which merchants and peasants, denied the possibility of feudal political power, made economic achievement a goal in itself. This certainly happened in Tokugawa Japan, where merchants and peasants, completely barred from participation in politics, developed a philosophy justifying economic success as a service to society comparable to the political service of the samurai class. Such attitudes probably help explain why former peasants and merchants moved easily into various types of leadership roles in Meiji times and why samurai shifted with even greater ease to business enterprise as a legitimate and worthy field of endeavor. In countries such as China and Korea, the lesser barriers between functional classes meant that economic success commonly led to an attempt to gain political status and was therefore not justified as an end in itself. If this analysis is correct, the class divisions surviving from feudalism, rather than Protestantism, may be the determining factor behind this aspect of the Protestant ethic. But the main point is that the individual ambition and drive of the Japanese people, instead of being an anomaly in this group society, is an old and basic part of it.

Westerners commonly overlook the hard core of the individual Japanese and his society and instead, struck by the amalgam of what is familiar and what seems exotic, wonder if the Japanese are not a confused people, embodying a sort of schizophrenia between East and West. The same doubts have frequently been expressed by the Japanese themselves. This dichotomy no doubt did exist for many in the past, but for contemporary Japanese it lies more in the eyes of the beholder than in the minds of the Japanese. In any fast-changing society there are curious and sometimes uncomfortable contrasts between traditions inherited from the past and new characteristics produced by new technologies and conditions. Japan, having moved faster and farther than any other country during the past century, may be subject to particularly severe strains of this sort, but they are not different in kind—only in degree—from what the West itself experiences.

Japan has not been Westernized, as is commonly asserted. Nothing is more central to traditional Western culture than Christianity, but less than 2 percent of the Japanese population have embraced this religion. What the Japanese have taken over are the modern aspects of Western culture, which for the most part the West too has only recently developed in response to modern technology—things like railroads, factories, mass education, newspapers, television, and mass democracy. In this sense Japan has become modernized, not Westernized, and the process of modernization has taken place on the foundation of Japan's own traditional culture, just as happened in the West, with the same sort of resulting contrasts and strains.

A head start in the West of four decades in railroading and of a few years in television did not make these features of modern life distinctively Western as opposed to Japanese. Japanese are every bit as much at home with them as are Americans. Tea, an East Asian drink, coffee from the Middle East, kimonolike dressing gowns, or African rhythms in music, lunch in a sushi bar, a workout in the art of karate, or a session of ikebana-style flower arranging have not produced traumas or schizophrenia in the West. Why should Western foods, dress, or music have this effect on Japanese? Brahms and Beethoven now belong as much to Japanese as to Americans or even Germans. "Happy Birthday," sung always in English, and "Auld Lang Syne," sung always in Japanese, are as solid and natural parts of Japanese folk culture as of American. Shakespeare, Goethe, or Dostoevsky are as much a part of literature in their minds and are probably as well known as *The Tale of Genji*. History to them means ancient Greece and Rome and the great dynasties of China as much as the periods of their own past.

Only older ladies and some wealthy women commonly wear Japanese kimonos, while most other women reserve them for only very festive occasions, such as university graduation ceremonies, if they can afford them at all. The Japanese find nothing incongruous in the contrast between the traditional Japanese garb of brides at Shinto wedding ceremonies and the traditional Western white they usually wear at civil ceremonies or Christian weddings, which are popular even for nonbelievers. Grooms are almost always dressed in Western style, specifically in cutaways in more affluent circles, a costume that is much used for formal occasions in Japan and is called *moningu,* from "morning coat." Hardly any men ever wear traditional garb of any sort in public. Neither did

A bride and groom, she in very colorful kimono and he in a white tuxedo. Costumes are often changed in the course of the wedding festivities, but the couple will leave for their honeymoon, very probably in Hawaii or elsewhere abroad, he in an ordinary business suit and she in a chic Western going-away outfit. (© *Dave Bartruff*)

their fathers or many of their grandfathers, and they would feel almost as self-conscious in a traditional Japanese costume as an American dressed as a Pilgrim Father. Cultural schizophrenia, which may seem obvious to the untutored Western eye, simply does not exist for the Japanese, except possibly for some self-conscious intellectuals.

The Japanese live in a society that, despite its rapid changes, is to them a well-ordered, coherent whole. It is remarkable for its homogeneity and strict adherence to patterns of conduct. Though constantly changing, it remains thoroughly and most distinctively Japanese. It is almost monotonously uniform. It is, if anything, more stable than most Western lands, even though they have become modernized at a more leisurely and less stressful rate. Japanese society is rent by no sharp cleavages. There is virtually no great inherited wealth and very little degrading poverty. The social center of gravity is the huge stratum known by the Japanese-English term "salary-man" (*sarariman*)—a more accurate description than our own "white-collar worker." Above these are only a handful of top executives and below them farmers and manual wage laborers, who aspire to and often approach *sarariman* norms of life.

On the surface Japan gives all the appearances of a happy society and probably deserves this evaluation as much as any other country. Children always seem to be bubbling with good spirit. People everywhere seem cheerful and purposeful. The early retirement age for men and the greater confinement of married women to the home may account for the youthfulness of city crowds, as compared to those in the United States, and the consequent impression of greater energy and vitality. The problems of age may be kept more out of sight.

The Japanese are clearly well satisfied with themselves both as individuals and nationally. Until only a few decades ago they tended to be painfully unsure of themselves, fearing that Westerners might be looking down on them, but in recent years such self-doubts have melted fast in the warmth of affluence and international acclaim. They still remain endlessly critical of their society, but behind such attitudes one can discern a deep self-satisfaction in their achievements. They are proud of their economic success, their technological skills, their well-ordered society, their democratic, egalitarian social and political system, and the high quality of life most of them enjoy. As a group the Japanese have proved a resounding success, but for all their group orientation they are also very self-conscious and proud as individuals.

17 Women

The position of women in Japanese society is one of the major differences between it and American society and a subject that is likely to raise indignation in the West. Japanese men are blatantly male chauvinists and women seem shamefully exploited and suppressed. They clearly occupy a better position than in most Islamic nations and many other countries, but there is severe job discrimination against them, and the old Confucian adage that a woman should in youth obey her father, in maturity her husband, and in old age her son still has some validity. In Western eyes, husbands frequently treat their wives coldly and even with disdain. Women are usually meek and long-suffering in their dealings with their menfolk, and girls hide shyly behind a screen of simpering. Social life, insofar as it exists, has little place for the married woman. A double sexual standard, which leaves the man free and the woman restricted, is still common. Thus sexual mores and attitudes toward love, marriage, and the place of women in society contrast sharply in Japan and the United States, though in both countries these are undergoing rapid change, and in Japan many of the changes are headed in the same direction as in the West.

The Japanese do not share Western views about the sinfulness of sexual relations. To them they have always seemed a natural phenomenon, like eating, which is to be enjoyed in its proper place. Promiscuity is in itself no more of a problem than homosexuality. Their attitudes have thus in a sense been permissive. But at the same time, they have a stronger awareness than contemporary Westerners of the necessity for bending the desires of the individual to the surrounding social environment. They abide by social rules that seem to Westerners extremely confining to the individual's emotional life. Japanese may seem to Westerners to be at the same time both licentious and puritanical, with the license applying for the most part to males and the purity to females.

The primitive Japanese revered fertility not just in agriculture but among humans as well, and phallic symbols were common objects of worship in rural Japan until recent times. In the classical period, love became the main literary theme in a court life of astonishingly free sexual ways. Some of this sexual freedom survived into modern times in parts of rural Japan, where premarital sexual relations were condoned and marriages were frequently not registered, and therefore not made permanent, until the bride had proved her ability to bear children. Even today in Japanese society in general there is little condemnation of sexual acts but only anxiety over their social consequences.

Another characteristic of early Japan was a definitely matriarchal substratum in society. The mythical ancestor of the imperial line was a sun goddess; Chinese texts tell us that feminine leadership was common in the third century; and there were ruling empresses as late as the eighth. Women had great freedom in Heian court life and dominated much of its literature. Even in early feudal days women could inherit property and have a role in the feudal system.

Subsequently, however, Confucian philosophy and the long feudal experience combined to restrict the freedom of women and force them into complete subordination to men. Women, who in the age of swordsmanship were obviously less capable of fighting than men, were gradually pushed out of the feudal structure and into a peripheral and supplementary role to men. Confucianism, which was the product of a patriarchal and strongly male-dominated society in China, saw women as important for bearing children and perpetuating the family more than as helpmates or objects of love. Confucianism tended to be puritanical, considering romantic love to be a weakness and sex as merely a mechanism for maintaining family continuity.

Among the peasantry women always retained their importance as coworkers with men in the fields and consequently retained a more earthy independence as individuals, but in polite society women by the Tokugawa period had become the entirely subservient handmaidens and playthings of men. A daughter could, through her marriage, strengthen the family's relations with another family and was therefore raised carefully to be a decorous and unsullied item of value in the marriage market. A wife was expected to devote herself to the well-being of her husband's family under the usually strict or even harsh supervision of her mother-in-law. No extrafamilial social life was considered necessary for her, and in fact any contact with men outside the family was seen as potentially dangerous. Since marriage was determined by family needs and was not the result of attraction between the young couple, who very likely had never seen each other before marriage, conjugal love seemed a secondary matter that might, or might not, develop between the pair.

In this system, sexual looseness or infidelity on the part of women was considered socially very disruptive and was therefore carefully guarded against. Men, however, could develop a broader social and sexual life, so long as they did not let it impinge on family duties. A rich man could maintain secondary wives or mistresses. All those who could afford it could frequent the amusement quarters of the larger towns and cities, where, in a setting of theaters and restaurants, men would be entertained by the sprightly conversation, artistic talents in dance and song, and sexual attractions of professionally trained women. These women themselves ranged from simple prostitutes to famous courtesans who required careful courting before they were likely to enter into a sexual relationship. It is women of this latter type who came to be known in the nineteenth century as geisha and still exist in contemporary Japan, though in very small numbers. To this demimonde of the amusement quarters were relegated the flirtation and courting that were a part of normal social life in the West but were entirely missing from polite society in Japan.

Most of the features of this social system of late feudal Japan existed at one time or another in the West, but in Japan they constitute a more recent tradition, having existed full-blown past the middle of the nineteenth century, and it is therefore not surprising that more of the attitudes and customs derived from this system still persist even in a fast-changing Japan. Dating and courtship, for example, play much lesser roles in social life than in America; conjugal love is little stressed, though in the long run it may be as prevalent throughout the course of a marriage as in the West; and arranged marriages remain part of the system, though ever since the 1920s increasing numbers of young people have insisted on finding their mates through love marriages in the Western manner.

At present the marriage situation is quite mixed. The continuing strictness with which most girls are raised and the Japanese tendency to do things by groups means that there is much less pairing off of couples than in the West, and boys and girls as a result are much shyer in their one-to-one relations. While many do establish bonds that lead to marriage, others feel that family aid in identifying a suitable mate can be helpful. Young people rarely feel obliged to bow to family wishes against their own preferences, but a first meeting between a young man and

Japanese young people tend to do things in groups, and dating by couples is relatively rare though becoming more frequent. This dating couple in Ueno Park in Tokyo would be considered modishly dressed anywhere in the West, but the informal pose the young man has taken is distinctly non-Western. Marriage partners are still often picked in part by the family, though the consent of the pair concerned is now assumed to be necessary. (© *Richard Kalvar / Magnum Photos*)

woman is still commonly arranged by the respective families, and, if the principals are pleased, this will lead to marriage. Moreover, an official go-between couple is likely to play a central role in the marriage ceremony itself, whether or not it has been a partially arranged marriage. One happy result of this system is that almost everyone who would like to get married and is free from serious disabilities can count on finding a spouse.

Conjugal love in such a marriage system is still likely to be something that develops more after marriage than before, and several external circumstances militate against its becoming as central to family life as it is in the West. The long hours devoted to commuting in urban Japan, the relative paucity of vacations, the five-and-a-half-day work week, which is still common, the willingness of Japanese to devote long hours to overtime work, and the limitation of social life largely to men, all combine to make the amount of time a Japanese couple spends together much less than would be customary in the West. The confined living conditions of most homes and the custom of sleeping with the children also cut down on conjugal intimacies. Finally, premodern attitudes of disregard for conjugal love and harsh subordination of women still persist to some extent, especially among the more old-fashioned, and diminish the warmth of the marriage bond.

The double moral standard also remains stronger in Japan than in some Western countries. Many young women, like their contemporaries in the West, now have premarital sexual freedom, but Japanese girls on the whole are still raised much more strictly in such matters than Japanese boys or than most girls in the West. Married women, moreover, are expected to be far more faithful than men. They have virtually no social life outside the family. Except for a very few at the top of society, who may participate stiffly and unhappily in formal banquets, usually those that include foreigners, married women rarely go out with their husbands to dinners and parties or entertain outsiders in their homes, which in any case are usually too small for such activities. Their life is likely to be limited to husband, children, a few close relatives, some old schoolday girlfriends, and possibly the activities of the PTA.

Meanwhile their husbands develop a fuller social life with their work group, which may include a few young unmarried women. Very commonly a group of men from work will stop on their way home at one or more of the myriad bars that are a feature of all cities. Here the bar hostesses, the successors to the geisha tradition, engage them in amusing conversation, skillfully tickle their male egos, and afford an atmosphere of sexual titillation, which can lead to more serious involvements and for some bar girls to a more prosperous and stable life as a mistress or even a wife. The milieu may be very different, but the spirit of the modern Japanese bar is close to that of the amusement quarters of feudal times.

All this is, of course, changing, and the contemporary woman is by no means as browbeaten as she was only a few decades ago or as she sometimes appears to be to Westerners today. Surface appearances can be misleading. Husbands and wives tend not to demonstrate affection for each other in public, and the curtness and derogation some men show their wives—until recently an old-fashioned man might routinely refer to his spouse as "my stupid wife"—are at least partly a convention in speaking to or about a member of one's own family. Most wives for their part would never dream of praising their husbands before somebody else. These are for the most part superficial characteristics inherited from an earlier system. Underneath, great changes are going on, as women win a position of greater equality with men and the assumption grows that there should be a strong bond of love between husband and wife.

Perhaps these tendencies can be best seen through some small but significant examples. I can remember very well that in the 1920s a wife was likely to follow deferentially a pace behind her husband on the street, encumbered with whatever babies or bundles needed to be carried, while he strode ahead in lordly grandeur. Over the years I have seen the wife catch up with her husband, until they now walk side by side, and the babies and bundles are often in his arms. If the family has a car, the wife is likely to drive it as much as the husband. Whereas once no husband would stoop to doing any housework, increasing numbers now help out with the evening dishes. And many a wife has made it clear that she will not tolerate bar hopping or other dalliances on the part of her husband. No one can say how far or how fast these trends will develop, but their direction is unmistakably toward a single standard either of mutual permissiveness at the one end of the spectrum or mutual respect and fidelity at the other.

There is another way in which the position of Japanese women is something more than it has often seemed to be. As we have seen, Japan may originally have had a matriarchal society, and elements of this matriarchy seem to have persisted, despite the heavy overlay of male supremacy resulting from feudalism and Confucianism. There is a hint of this in the expectation in medieval times that women would have as much strength of will and bravery as men. In modern times, it is generally accepted that women have more will power and psychological strength than men, and there can be no doubt that the modern Japanese family centers on and is dominated by the mother, not the father. In fact, the father, though the principal financial support, is otherwise pretty much of a cypher in family affairs. Family finances are run almost exclusively by the mother, with the father often on a sort of allowance provided by her. He is likely to be away from home almost all of the waking hours of his smaller children. Their life is basically with the mother, and it is she who sees to their good performance in school. American comic strips like "Blondie" and family situation comedies on TV and in films, which commonly depict a bumbling, henpecked father, have long been popular in Japan as being entirely understandable despite their unfamiliar social setting.

The domineering father of Freudian psychiatry hardly exists in the Japanese psychological makeup, though another Freudian concern, the male child's excessive attachment to and dependence upon the mother, is a major psychological problem. This is the *amae* syndrome we have already encountered. A husband sometimes seems to be the wife's big grown-up child, requiring tender care and pampering like the other children, or else he shows a need for special feminine attention and flattery from other women—as from geisha in earlier times or bar girls today. Husbands are likely to demonstrate weaknesses of personality and cause family problems. On the other hand, wives are expected to have a strong character, to be always "ladylike," and to hold the family together—and for the most part they live up to these expectations.

The wife may be the dominant member of the family, but women still have an overwhelmingly subservient position in the broader society. With education compulsory through the ninth grade and 94 percent of the age group going through twelve years of schooling, girls receive as much education as boys through secondary school, but they fall off badly at higher levels. Though the majority of junior college students are women, many of these colleges are looked upon, in a sense, as finishing schools, furnishing women with polite accomplishments for marriage. At the four-year university level, women decline sharply in numbers. There are a few women's universities, largely of Christian background, but in the other universities, all of which are now coeducational, women constitute only about a fifth of the student population and a mere 10 percent in the best institutions. An expensive four-year university education seems less worthwhile for girls, who are expected to end up as no more than housewives.

Japanese tend to marry later than Americans—at around age twenty-four for women and twenty-eight for men, which is about three years later than in the United States. Most women thus have from two to six years between the completion of their schooling and their marriages, and during this time they enter the labor market. Those with lesser educations commonly become the labor force in light industries, such as textiles and electronics, or perform menial jobs as waitresses, salesgirls, or elevator attendants. Those with more education are likely to become secretaries and O.L., or "office ladies," as they are known in Japan, but these too are expected to perform menial jobs, such as serving tea to the men in the office. Because of the likelihood of marriage within a few

Women in the labor force. The lunch break at the National Electric Company in Osaka. *(Henri Cartier-Bresson / Magnum Photos)*

years, both groups of women workers are considered to be temporary and for the most part are denied positions on the escalator of lifetime employment at constantly rising wages. Marrying later and being confined longer to motherly supervision of their children than in the United States, Japanese women return later and in smaller numbers to the job market, and once there they are again likely to be excluded from the privileged lifetime employment and seniority system of male workers. On average, women employees earn only about half the pay of men. Despite these conditions more than half of Japanese women are members of the work force, and they constitute more than 40 percent of its total, though most are kept in its lower brackets.

In contrast to urban workers, women in rural areas have always had a large role in agricultural employment, and postwar conditions have made them even more important than before. Since the war, both farm boys and girls have for the most part streamed off after their schooling to more lucrative employment in the cities. Those young men who remained to inherit the family farm have found it very difficult to find brides, and these conditions of scarcity have resulted in a sharp rise in the relative status of farm wives. As we have seen, most men on farms now find their chief employment elsewhere, and though women also commonly find outside employment too, they probably perform more of the farm work than do the men.

The educated career woman does exist in Japan, but in fewer numbers than in most industrialized Western countries. They are prominent in education and research, constituting about a half of the teaching force in elementary education and sizable numbers in secondary schools, junior colleges, women's universities, and research institutes, though extremely few of the professors in four-year universities. They play a large role in literature and the arts and have a role in journalism. Women are often in leadership positions in small businesses, but as executives in big business they are all but unknown. There are many female doctors and occasional female judges, especially in the juvenile courts. Many are petty government workers, but only recently have a few crept into the elite higher bureaucracy. There is about the same small proportion of women in the Diet as in the House of Representatives or the Senate in the United States, but in September 1986 Japanese women pushed ahead of their American counterparts when Miss Doi Takako was elected the secretary general and thereby became the candidate for prime minister of the Socialist Party, Japan's second-largest political party. The chief role of women in politics, however, is in popular citizens' and local residents' movements. More than half of Japanese women belong to organizations such as the ubiquitous Women's Associations *(Fujinkai)*, and it is through these and the influential PTA, which are largely run by mothers, that they have become very active in local politics. Nevertheless most leadership roles in society remain predominantly the preserves of men.

Japan is still definitely a "man's world," with women confined to a secondary position. Their status, however, has changed greatly for the better during the past century, especially since World War II, and it will obviously continue to change. The provisions of the 1947 constitution, which is quite explicit about the equality of the sexes, tip the scales quite definitively toward increased equality and greater prestige for them:

There shall be no discrimination in political, economic or social relations, because of . . . sex. . . . Marriage shall be based only on the mutual consent of both sexes and it shall be maintained through mutual cooperation with the equal rights of husband and wife as a basis. With regard to choice of spouse, property rights, inheritance, choice of domicile, divorce and other matters pertaining to marriage and the family, laws shall be enacted from the standpoint of individual dignity and the essential equality of the sexes.

The laws now give women full legal equality. For example, prewar laws made divorce easy for men and all but impossible for women, but now women constitute the majority of applicants for divorce (a higher percentage by full-time housewives than by women workers), though divorce rates remain far below those current in the United States and much lower even than in Japan a half century ago. The divorce rate is only one eighteenth that of the United States, one reason being that wage discrimination, particularly against older women, makes it more difficult for a divorced wife in Japan to make a decent living; another reason may be that it is usually more difficult for her to remarry.

Despite the great gains made by women in recent decades, social limitations on them and discrimination in employment remain severe. Many Westerners wonder indignantly why Japanese women do not agitate more aggressively against their unequal status. One reason may be that Japanese women in recent decades have made such huge advances that they are still busy digesting them. Labor shortages in the years leading up to and through World War II and then again in the postwar economic surge have given them a much larger economic role and therefore a greater chance for economic independence. The mechanization of housework since the war, through washing machines, vacuum cleaners, and electric cooking utensils, especially electric rice cookers and microwaves, have freed them from much of the drudgery of domestic labor, releasing time for outside work or other activities. These factors, combined with the postwar legal gains and sweeping social changes, have given women much wider opportunities, which are expanding steadily.

Another reason why Japanese women have not taken up the women's liberation movement more aggressively may be that it does not fit their self-image or "ladylike" style. They realize that they dominate the home and tend to be psychologically stronger than men. They may sense that, while the bitter underdog attitude of Western women may fit their traditional role as the "weaker sex," it would not be becoming for Japanese women as actually the stronger sex.

This attitude may tie in with what may well be the most important reason. Japanese women are clearly aware of the satisfactions as well as handicaps of their biological differences from men. They cherish their role as mothers and homemakers who dominate domestic life and supervise the raising of the next generation. The result is that many of them are forced into somewhat empty lives once the children are grown up, but on the whole they seem to find at least as much satisfaction in the balance they have struck as do women in the United States.

Japanese women, however, seem on the verge of a veritable revolution in their status, as was underscored by the enthusiasm that accompanied Miss Doi's election as the head of the Socialist Party and Prime Minister Uno Sosuke's being forced to resign his post on June 2, 1989, in part because of charges of womanizing. Women, who for long had played leadership roles in local politics, began to show their muscle in national politics as well. The LDP countered by selecting two women cabinet members for the first time in 1987 and a woman to a major party post in 1989. This was, of course, only a small beginning, but women appeared to be on the point of breaking through the crust of male domination. It seems improbable that Japanese women will erupt in a stridently assertive female movement, as in the United States, but it appears quite likely that a "women's revolution" will be the next great step in Japanese social and political development.

18 Education

We have seen that the Japanese tendency to divide up into vertical, hierarchical groups naturally weakens horizontal bonds of class or profession. The conflicting pull of a thoroughly feudal system, of course, had the opposite effect, creating strong class lines up until a century and a half ago, but since then Japanese society has changed radically. Class lines were already beginning to blur when the West in the middle of the nineteenth century forced open the doors of Japan to a flood of outside influences, resulting in profound political and social changes. In the process, many class divisions were swept away by the implementation of a uniform nationwide educational system, which has made Japan one of the most thoroughly egalitarian societies in the world. Compulsory education and strict examinations based on it took the place of birth in determining the career and status for which an individual qualified. In short, Japan was transformed from a class-bound society to one controlled by a meritocracy. The new educational system also accounts for the high literacy rate—as high as any in the world—and the excellent educational standards that made it possible for the Japanese to meet the challenge of the technologically more advanced methods of the West and to achieve world leadership in many fields today. Nothing, in short, has been more central in the success of modern Japan than its educational system.

The emphasis on formal schooling in contemporary Japan stems from the very sources of East Asian civilization. From early times the Chinese stressed the importance of literacy and book learning, attributing the authority of the rulers to their greater knowledge and consequent superior moral insights. In time these concepts became institutionalized in an elaborate system of selecting high government officials through a ponderous process of scholastic examinations. The Koreans took over this system whole, and the Japanese, though failing to fit it into their society, imbibed a deep respect for learning. Even in feudal times their warrior leaders were not just literate but often were accomplished in literary skills, in contrast to the untutored leaders of feudal Europe. Buddhist monasteries in Japan became centers of learning comparable to the Christian monasteries of the West.

By the late Tokugawa period the Japanese surpassed the Chinese and Koreans in literacy and educational institutions. Much of Tokugawa education was conducted through private tutoring, but by the middle of the nineteenth century most feudal domains had official domain schools for their samurai, and there were over a thousand private academies enrolling some commoners along with samurai youths. In addition there were tens of thousands of village institutions known as *terakoya,* or "temple schools," because of their usual location in the local Buddhist temple. Here the children of commoners, including some girls, could acquire the three Rs. About 45 percent of the male population was literate by the middle of the nineteenth century and perhaps 15 percent of the female—figures not far below those of the most advanced Western countries at that time.

Because of the traditional emphasis on formal learning, the leaders of the new Meiji government had no difficulty in comprehending the key role of education in acquiring the technology of the West and the necessity of a modern school system if Japan were to catch up to the leading Western powers. In 1871, only the fourth year of the new government's existence, it created a Ministry of Education, which the next year adopted an ambitious plan for a highly centralized and uniform school system, based on the French model and leading to universal literacy. Making this plan a reality was no easy task, for the Japanese lacked sufficient teachers, school buildings, or funds. The plans changed repeatedly, and the realities developed slowly, but a nationwide educational system was finally achieved.

Two points about the new educational system are of special importance. One is that it was an entirely fresh start. None of the domain schools and *terakoya* and hardly any of the private academies survived for long into the new age. Thus Meiji Japan, unlike the nineteenth-century West, was not encumbered with the aristocratic or religious overtones of earlier education but was in a sense already ahead of most of the West in the wholly secular and egalitarian nature of its educational system. The other point is that the Japanese from the start placed their chief emphasis on elementary education, thus laying a firm foundation both for the nation and for higher education. Too many modernizing countries in more recent times have emphasized instead the more prestigious aspects of higher education, which, however good, often produce graduates who find no use for their accomplishments in a society where low educational standards prevail and, their efforts frustrated, they settle in the West as part of the brain drain that has left their countries intellectually impoverished.

It was not until about 1907 that the Japanese managed to get virtually all their children into schools. In that year schooling was made mandatory and entirely free up through the six grades of coeducational primary education. Above the elementary schools a more elite system was forming: a five-year middle school, separate for boys and girls and paralleled by lower technical schools, then a three-year higher school for boys only, comparable to the German *Gymnasium* or the French *lycée* and again paralleled by higher technical schools, and finally a university of three or four years' duration, depending on the subject studied. The higher schools were purely preparatory to the universities, and it was in them, more than in the universities, that the future leadership elite came to know one another and form bonds of close association.

The whole system was rigorously egalitarian, at least for men, opening up the track to the top to any who could complete the necessary preliminary schooling and pass the necessary entrance examinations. Thus it could serve as the chief selector of national leadership, as it already was doing by the early twentieth century. The system was also closely tailored to national needs as the leaders saw them. It created a literate mass of soldiers, workers, and housewives, ample middle-level technical skills—an aspect of education that many of today's modernizing countries have failed adequately to appreciate—and a thin stream of highly talented young men emerging from the universities to occupy the positions of top leadership in government and society. The great bulk of education, including its whole central core, was in the hands of the government. Christian missionary schools and a few Buddhist or other private institutions did exist, especially at the middle school and upper technical school levels, and the Christian schools were important in women's education, but these other schools were merely peripheral to the government system.

At the top of the educational pyramid stood Tokyo University. It grew out of an amalgam of three shogunal schools inherited from the Tokugawa period—a Confucian academy (later dropped), a school of medicine, and a school of foreign learning—which after several reorganizations was named Tokyo University in 1877 and then Tokyo Imperial University in 1886. Its graduates at first qualified without examination for high civil service posts, but in time the supply came to exceed the demand, and graduates of Tokyo University, together with those of other universities, as these were founded, became subject to a uniform examination system for entrance into the high civil bureaucracy.

The government created new imperial universities one after the other—Kyoto in 1897, Tohoku (in Sendai) in 1907, Kyushu (in Fukuoka) in 1910, Hokkaido (in Sapporo) in 1918, and so on. In 1918 a number of private schools were also accorded university status, thus greatly expanding the number of university graduates. The oldest and most prestigious of the private schools were Keio and Waseda. Keio had grown out of an academy founded before the Meiji Restoration by Fukuzawa, the great popularizer of knowledge about the West, and Waseda was founded in 1882 by Okuma, who had been ousted from the ruling oligarchy the year before. There were also other large private universities, such as Meiji, Nihon, and Chuo, which had grown up around the turn of the century, primarily to teach modern law. All five of these private institutions and many others were located in Tokyo.

Following the war the Japanese educational system was restructured by the American occupation to conform to American concepts and to be less elitist and better fitted to the type of mass society Japan was developing. The structural changes may have been largely unnecessary and at first were very confusing, but they have stuck. In place of the prewar six-five-three-three system, as it is called—the numbers corresponding to the respective years of elementary, middle, and higher schools and then university—the American six-three-three-four system was adopted: six years of elementary, three of junior high school, three of senior high school, and four of university. Above the universities are graduate schools, while paralleling the universities are two- or three-year junior colleges. All institutions of higher learning are called universities (*daigaku*), not colleges. This is true even of junior colleges, which are called "short-term universities" (*tanki daigaku*). These are attended largely by women and tend to stress the liberal arts, whereas the full universities, at which on average only about a fifth of the students are women, stress law (including political science), economics and business, engineering, the natural sciences, and medicine.

The American reforms extended compulsory education through the nine years leading through junior high school and made it entirely free. Education was also made coeducational throughout, and, instead of the tangents of the prewar system that led off into terminal technical schools, most education was placed on a single track, with each level leading to the next. The only exceptions, besides the junior colleges, are a few relatively small five-year technical schools started in 1962 at the senior high school and junior college level, and various types of peripheral specialty schools. Within this structure, the Japanese have become one of the most highly educated people in the world. All children go through junior high school, and the number of senior high school students has mounted rapidly until it is now 94 percent. Close to a third of the graduates continue on to higher education, which is somewhat less than the American rate of around a half but appreciably ahead of the countries of Western Europe.

Education is not to be measured merely in terms of years. The intensity of the educational experience counts too, and here Japanese education on average rates well above American, except at the university level. The school day is longer, the school week is five and a half days, and the school year is broken only by a short summer vacation of a little over a month in late July and August, a New Year's holiday, and a break before the start of the school year at the beginning of April. Discipline within schools is firm, and the children devote prodigious efforts to their studies. In addition, they are assigned daily homework from the first grade on. About a third of the age group go to kindergarten to get a running start at the educational process, and about half of all schoolchildren receive outside tutoring or attend private after-class academies (*juku*) for further drill and instruction. Japanese, in their keen desire to get the best possible education, classify schools in their own minds in accordance with the records of their graduates at subsequent levels of education, but Japanese schools actually achieve remarkably uniform levels of excellence, with few of the great discrepancies in quality that are common in the United States among city, rural, and suburban schools.

The net result of all this is that the Japanese are indeed a highly educated people. Despite the somewhat poorer quality of education at the university level than in the United States, the Japanese probably absorb more formal learning on average than the people of any other nation. General levels of educational achievement are usually not susceptible to measurement across language barriers, but where they are, as in the fields of mathematics and science, the Japanese have tended to rank first in the world. It would not be at all unreasonable to conclude that Japan has the best-educated population of any country in the world.

There is no mystery about the vast educational effort in Japan. It not only accords with traditional concepts about the importance of formal education but is a natural product of the key role of education in determining function and status in society. In the looser American system, the self-educated man can more easily make his mark or the late bloomer can make a brilliant finish after a slow start. There is less room for such types in Japan's tighter society. There are, of course, many men who have made great careers in business on the basis of little or inferior educations, and Tanaka Kakuei, who was prime minister from 1972 to 1974, lacked any university education. But the great bulk of Japan's top leadership in every field consists of graduates of the most prestigious universities who qualified for these universities by high scores in their entrance examinations, which were in turn the result of academic excellence throughout their schooling.

The close link between academic achievement and success in life is

A drawing class in a private kindergarten. The *hiragana* phonetic syllabary is on the blackboard in its usual *abc* order, which is *a-i-u-e-o* in Japanese, reading downward from the right. (The second line is *ka-ki-ku-ke-ko*.)(© *Richard Kalvar / Magnum Photos*)

Despite the small size of apartments, children are given ample room for their home-work. Prominent on the desk of this high school girl is her English-Japanese diction-ary. (© *Michal Heron / Woodfin Camp & Associates*)

taken for granted by everyone. Families undergo economic privations so that their children may receive the advantage of kindergarten training or later tutoring. Despite household crowding, children are given adequate space for their school homework, and the mother rides herd on them to see that they perform it and live up to their other scholastic tasks. This special role of the mother is recognized by the common term *kyoiku mama,* or "education mom." It is sometimes thought that the drive for education has been a contributing factor to birth control in Japan, since people, especially in the cities, believe they should have few enough children to be able to afford higher educations for all of them.

The importance of preparing for entrance examinations helps account for the seriousness with which education is taken in Japan and for its high levels of excellence, but it is also responsible for some of its chief flaws. As the child approaches his crucial entrance examinations, the whole life of the family centers around facilitating his studies. These examinations are required not only for entrance into university but before that often for entrance into a particularly distinguished high school that is known for the good records of its graduates in university entrance examinations. The pressures on the examination taker are tremendous, and the whole process is commonly referred to as the "examination hell."

Once students have been accepted into a school, the Japanese very skillfully avoid overt competition among them and downplay differences in ability. In fact, almost no one is ever failed. But the ruthless, one-shot entrance examinations are competition at its worst and cast a shadow far in advance, subjecting the student to severe pressures through most of his schooling and even distorting the content of his education. Much of the training in senior high schools is devoted not to learning as such, but to preparing students to pass university entrance examinations. Thus in an English language course, for example, there is careful preparation for the sort of complex grammar questions that are asked on examinations, but less attention is paid to actually learning to read English and virtually none to speaking it or understanding it by ear. High

A disappointed father and mother looking with dismay at the board that reveals the results of a school entrance examination. Their daughter, who apparently has failed to gain admission, is in tears beside them. (© *Sonia Katchian / Photo Shuttle: Japan*)

school entrance examinations cast a similar though lighter shadow on instruction in junior high schools. The relatively high suicide rates for youth may be in part attributable to the "examination hell," and there can be no doubt that the restlessness and rebellion of university students, once they have achieved the safe haven of the university, come in part as a reaction to the pressures they have been under before then.

There are other problem areas in elementary and secondary education. The American occupation authorities felt that the prewar system had consisted far too much of rote memory work, producing indoctrinated followers rather than thinking citizens. The extreme difficulty of the Japanese writing system and the vast amount of rote memory work it requires may inevitably tip Japanese education in that direction. The American reformers tried to put more emphasis on getting children not just to absorb facts, but to think for themselves. It is hard to say how far their efforts succeeded. Japanese education today is a great deal more lively than it was before the war and calls for much more student initiative. But many Japanese feel that schoolchildren as a result have become excessively unruly, and they commonly place the blame on what they believe was undue relaxation of school discipline by the Americans as well as on the general loosening of moral fiber throughout Japan because of affluence. Most Americans on the other hand see the Japanese school system as quite rigid and somewhat old-fashioned—an evaluation that could be interpreted as criticism or praise depending upon one's point of view.

The control of public education has been a matter of hot political contention ever since the war. Mindful of the role of the prewar educational system in militaristic indoctrination, the American occupation insisted on the dispersal of educational controls to elected prefectural and municipal boards of education, somewhat in the American manner, but subsequently the Japanese in part recentralized the system under the Ministry of Education. Prefectural and municipal education boards remain, but they are appointed by governors and mayors, not elected, and, though they have the right to select the textbooks used and these are produced privately, all textbooks must first receive ministry approval.

Most elementary and secondary teachers are members of the Japan Teachers Union (Nikkyoso), which ever since the war has been dominated by either Communists or other leftists, who have pitted the union in open battle against the Ministry of Education on several issues, including the question of the control of education. This situation has dangerously politicized the school system, but fortunately it has had little effect on the quality of the teaching. While a hot debate rages within the union as to whether, as its leaders claim, it is just an ordinary labor union or its members are part of a "sacred profession," the truth of the matter is that the traditional special aura about learning and the teacher's role lingers on in Japan, and most teachers remain proud and dedicated participants in this heritage. For all its problems, including even the baneful influence of the examination system, elementary and secondary education in Japan has high standards of morale and efficiency, which merit the envy of most other advanced nations.

Higher education is in greater trouble and probably fills less of a role in society than the pressures over entrance examinations would suggest. Actually the entrance examinations themselves perform one of the university's most significant functions, for they, more than a student's work while at the university, help sort Japanese out for their lifetime careers. The university years are usually not as important as they are for many American students. Because of the excellence of education up through senior high school, there is no need for the remedial work that occupies much of college education in the United States. Passing the entrance examinations usually means acceptance to a specific faculty, or branch of the university, such as law, economics, humanities, science, medicine, engineering, or agriculture. There is therefore no need or opportunity to experiment and shop around while at the university for a field of specialization. That has already been determined by the faculty into which the student has won admittance. Graduate schools are relatively unimportant, and the Ph.D. degree is no sine qua non as it so often is in the United States. Both big business and government recruit directly from among university graduates, giving the men they accept further in-service training, which takes the place of much of graduate study as it exists in the United States, or else they subsequently send selected employees abroad for further study or to graduate schools in Japan. For other students, graduate schools are largely limited to preparation for an academic career. The role of the university in research activities, once very important, is also shrinking in comparison with research conducted directly by business or government.

Recruitment into big business and government is normally by examination. What is learned in university is of course vital for the examinations, but at the same time it is clear that those persons who were best at taking the examinations for entrance into university at age eighteen, and thereby got into the most prestigious universities, again prove to be the best at age twenty-two or twenty-three when they take the examinations for business or government. The fact that the pyramid of relative university prestige is almost perfectly mirrored in the results of these professional examinations is probably to be attributed more to the native talent of the students of the prestigious universities than to the excellence of their instruction. A further factor is that many businesses invite only candidates from the more prestigious universities to take their examinations.

This situation makes the pressure to enter the best universities all the greater. Rejection or acceptance by a prestigious university is seen as determining one's whole life. Students who fail will commonly get off the educational track for a year to attend one of the many cram schools (also called *juku*) and try again the next year and possibly the next and the next. Such persons are facetiously called *ronin,* the term for a masterless samurai in feudal times. Some private universities have a system of accepting without examination students from their own affiliated private secondary schools, and in some cases students buy their way into some private universities, but these routes available to wealth lead at best only to second- or third-rate institutions.

The pecking order of universities remains essentially what it was before the war. Tokyo University still ranks far at the top and after it the other former Imperial Universities (the term "Imperial" was dropped after the war) and a few specialized prewar national universities, such as Hitotsubashi for economics. Next come the two most prestigious private universities, Keio and Waseda, and the national universities that were founded in each prefecture after the war by combining former higher schools and higher technical schools and upgrading them. Next come the great mass of private universities, divided into several prestige levels, and at the bottom the junior colleges. The strict correlation between university affiliation and jobs and status in later life is gradually breaking down, but even today the great majority of the higher bureaucracy comes from the most prestigious national universities, particularly Tokyo, while Keio is noted as a source of business executives, Waseda as a producer of politicians and journalists, and the less distinguished private universities pour out the masses of also-rans, who become the lesser businessmen and white-collar workers.

Private universities, being supported mainly by tuition, must charge relatively high fees, while the national universities and the few prefectural and municipal ones, operating as they do on public funds, charge only nominal fees. This means that the best and most prestigious universities cost the least, while the poorest cost the most—a reversal of the traditional American pattern. As a result the prestigious national universities not only draw the best students but also recruit them from all economic strata of society. According to one study, the proportion of students from the wealthiest fifth of the population is a surprisingly small 37 percent and that from the lowest fifth an amazingly high 10 percent, with an almost uniform 17 percent for the three middle fifths. Affluence is more highly represented in some of the less prestigious private schools.

Students who have won admittance to the prestige universities as well as those who have had to settle for lesser institutions often find university life disappointing, and many react to it with apathy or unrest. This is in part a psychological letdown after the years of preparation for the entrance examinations. It is all too clear that performance during a student's university days has less influence on his career than do his entrance examinations and the postgraduate examinations for business or government. The four years at a university are in a sense a long breather between the pressure-cooker atmosphere of the school system and the rat race of office life after graduation.

Lack of interest in university studies is also a natural response to insufficient intellectual stimulation. One reason for this, particularly in national universities, is the rigidity of the Japanese university system and its strong resistance to changing needs. Another reason is the serious underfinancing of universities, particularly private ones, which results in very large classes, a poor student-faculty ratio, and little personal contact with professors.

While Japan devotes to elementary and secondary education about the same percentage of its national income as do the other advanced countries, it provides notably less for higher education, despite the fact that a considerably higher proportion of young people attend university than in the countries of Western Europe. This underinvestment in higher education is seen particularly in the heavy burden the Japanese place on private universities and the great crowding most are subjected to. In other advanced countries, all or most students are in government or government-financed institutions — even in the United States the figure has risen to 75 percent — but in Japan, since the government simply has not met the expanding demand for higher education, some 80 percent of students are in private universities. None of these have any appreciable endowment or can count on substantial outside giving. Under normal circumstances no tax credit is given for this or other charitable giving, and in any case the Japanese do not have much of a tradition of eleemosynary largess. Though tuition fees are much higher than in government universities, they are much less than in the United States. High entrance examination fees, which are milked from the unsuccessful as well as successful examination takers, pay for a large part of their running expenses as well as the special outlays for new buildings. Private universities of relatively low standing are able to entice well-known professors away from prestigious national universities by offering high salaries, since they are not limited by modest government-established pay scales. On the whole, private higher education is a successful financial undertaking in Japan.

The problem of the government universities is not so much finances as rigidity of organization. This may be in part the product of the German pattern copied in the late nineteenth century and in part the result of a fierce fight for academic freedom waged against the oppressive prewar government, which has left a jealously guarded tradition of autonomy in universities and in their various subdivisions. Universities even at the undergraduate level break up into sharply divided faculties, which have only minimal contact with one another. These faculties in turn are usually divided into chairs (*koza*), each made up of a professor, an assistant professor, and one or more lecturers and assistants. Both the faculties and the chairs have almost complete autonomy and tenaciously protect their respective academic domains and budgets. Courses of study for students are rigidly prescribed, new fields of study are hard to start, and the mixing of fields of study is almost impossible. Presidents and deans, being elected by their peers, have extremely little power. On one side the Ministry of Education provides the money but through a rather mechanical budgetary process, and on the other side faculties and chairs have virtual veto power over any change in the use of these funds. Little room remains for innovation, and as a result universities today still operate very much in the patterns established under quite different conditions almost a century ago. Even Tokyo University, for example, does not have facilities for the study of the United States that would match the programs in a score or more American universities for research and teaching about Japan. There is, however, a gradual movement toward innovation in Japanese universities, and many experiments are being tried, especially in such fields as international relations.

Another problem is that the reshuffling of the levels of education decreed by the American occupation meant that the postwar Japanese university is a rather unnatural joining of the last two years of general education of the old higher schools with the first two years of specialization of the old universities. At Tokyo University these two elements still exist in almost total segregation from each other on two far separated campuses.

It is not surprising that students in both private and government schools evince considerable disenchantment, which mounts at times to open rebellion. Some students show little interest in their studies, devoting themselves instead to outside activities, such as sports, hobbies, and radical politics. This is particularly true during the first two years, before students settle down to completing their studies in preparation for the next round of examinations for business or the bureaucracy.

Student government organizations, supported automatically by fees assigned from tuition payments, have for the most part been dominated ever since the war by leftist extremists and have spawned a wide variety of explosively revolutionary splinter groups. These student organizations formerly were known by the name of their national federation, the Zengakuren, but today they are usually referred to by their more abstruse factional names, such as the *Chukakuka* ("the nucleus faction"). Student unrest often focuses on intramural issues, such as increases in tuition or in the cost of student facilities, rather than on genuine academic problems, but the peaks in student unrest have usually coincided with times of political tension in society at large over domestic and, still more, international issues, as at the time of the Security Treaty riots of 1960 and the great upheavals of the late 1960s. At such times, all university life may be paralyzed. Parts of Tokyo University simply did not operate in 1968–69, and no new freshman class was taken in at all. Many other universities were also thrown into prolonged turmoil.

The Japanese are well aware of the problems affecting higher education and since the student troubles of the late 1960s have been making efforts to overcome them, though so far without great success. New experimental faculties and programs have been instituted in many private universities, and the government has even experimented with a new structure of internal university organization, closer to the departmental divisions and strong administrative leadership of American universities. Tsukuba University, near Tokyo, was founded in 1973 on the new model, but so far with disappointing results. A more hopeful experiment may be the international university founded under private auspices near the city of Niigata on the Japan Sea, and many universities are creating new faculties of international studies.

The seriousness of Japan's problems in higher education can be better appreciated in terms of the huge number of students involved. There are about 2 million students, roughly half in the Tokyo area, and another large body in the Kansai region of Kyoto, Osaka, and Kobe. That Japan as a whole continues to operate so successfully despite a flawed university system may seem at first surprising but is probably to be explained by the excellence of its preuniversity schooling and the system of in-service advanced training for new employees in business and government. Efficiently operating universities are obviously less necessary to Japan than to the United States.

The Japanese are often accused of being intellectually not very creative, and this weakness is commonly attributed at least in part to the inadequacies of their university system, though more obvious culprits would be the tendency toward rote memory work in earlier education and the whole conformist nature of their society. No one can doubt that the Japanese have great artistic creativeness, but their achievements in the realms of science and philosophy do seem less impressive. No modern Japanese thinker has appeared noteworthy to the rest of the world—though we should remember that the language barrier is probably in part responsible for this. Japanese have made relatively few contributions to basic science, and only a few have been singled out for Nobel Prizes. Japanese industrial triumphs have been based largely on efficient borrowing or ingenious adaptations of foreign technology rather than on independent scientific discoveries. Political thought, philosophy, and scholarship in the social sciences are to a large extent the reworking or synthesis of ideas derived from abroad, rather than original creative work. When thinkers have drawn more heavily from native Japanese inspiration, as in the case of the philosopher Nishida Kitaro in the first half of the twentieth century, who was strongly influenced by Zen concepts, the rest of the world has not been much impressed.

There is reason to wonder if intellectual creativeness will ever be a special forte of the Japanese. Their past is studded with prominent religious leaders, great poets and writers, outstanding organizers, and even distinguished synthesizers of thought, but not with great creative intellectual figures. Japanese have always seemed to lean more toward intuition rather than toward reason, to subtlety and sensitivity in expression rather than to clarity of analysis, to pragmatism rather than to theory, and to organizational skills rather than to great intellectual concepts. They have never set much store by clarity of verbal analysis and originality of thought. They put great trust in nonverbal understanding and look on oral or written skills and on sharp and clever reasoning as essentially shallow and possibly misleading. Aside from the flat factual statements of newspaper reporting, they value in their literature not clear analysis, but artistic suggestiveness and emotional feeling. The French ideal of simplicity and absolute clarity in writing leaves them unsatisfied. They prefer complexity and indirection as coming closer to the truth than apparently simple verities as defined by fallible men.

All this seems to stand at variance with the strength of theories and ideologies in contemporary Japan. Japanese intellectuals tend to be very theoretical. More of them are distinguished by the ardor of their adherence to their theories than by their ability to derive their theories from the facts or to apply them to reality. Vague, sweeping generalizations have a wide appeal in philosophy and politics. Some Japanese may be so doctrinaire in their political and intellectual beliefs just because they accept them more on faith than on reason. Certainly Japanese Marxists adhere with stubborn blindness to the perceptions and terminology that grew out of a nineteenth-century Europe that differed markedly from contemporary Japan. Scholars hold faithfully to their respective schools of thought and indulge in little cross-fertilization. Intellectuals as a whole tend to be isolated by their hotly defended "isms" from both the unresponsive masses and the pragmatic controllers of government and business. Perhaps forced by their relative weakness as theoreticians into a rigid adherence to whatever theory they have espoused, they may have created, as it were, a reverse mirror image of the pragmatism and relativism of their society as a whole.

Westerners tend to look on the relative lack of intellectual creativity of Japanese as a sign of inferiority, but this may be only a Western cultural bias. Who is to say that truths reached by reason are superior to those attained by intuition or that disputes settled by verbal skills are preferable to a consensus reached through feeling? Hairsplitting analysis and great conceptual schemes, so typical of India and the West, are not obviously better than smooth cooperation and harmony through nonverbal understanding.

Japan, however, seems to be changing in these characteristics as in so much else. It is possible that, standing now among the leaders in the world in knowledge and technical skills, it will be forced to become more intellectually and scientifically creative than it has been in the past. Imitation and adaptation were natural for a country only recently come into close contact with the rest of the world and engrossed in the task of catching up in technology and ideas. Whereas premodern education in

Japan was heavily moral and theoretical, modern Japanese education has been overwhelmingly practical in its aims. It has concentrated on learning about the rest of the world and its technology. Scholarly activity has been largely devoted to absorbing large chunks of information from abroad and synthesizing it with what was already known. Industry has quite wisely stressed the learning and adaptation of already known technologies rather than the creation of new ones. It should be noted, however, that many Japanese adaptations have been so imaginative as to merit being called creative. It should also be pointed out that most other countries in Japan's position have been far less successful in imitation and adaptation, showing that these are by no means easy skills to master. Japan has probably been showing much more creativeness than it has been given credit for.

The traits of relative weakness in theoretical analysis and inventiveness but great skills in practical application were characteristic of the United States too during its period of catching up with Europe. Americans have taken a leading place in science, scholarship, and thought only in recent decades. The same change may well be occurring in Japan as it achieves "the state of the art" in one field after another. We see this trend in a general loosening of the bonds of old theories in the social sciences and in a new spirit of free inquiry. An even clearer sign is the rapid surge in research and development activities in the past few years as Japan, now more or less abreast of the leading Western nations in science and technology, feels the need to forge ahead in its own scientific endeavors. Japan's efforts in research and development, though quite negligible a couple of decades ago, are now surpassed only by those of the United States and Soviet Union. Its devotion of 2 to 3 percent of its GNP to such purposes—mostly through private corporations or research institutes and less through government agencies or universities than in most other countries—does not fall proportionally behind American efforts, especially given the fact that much of the American effort is devoted to economically and scientifically less productive military research.

The concept of the Japanese as lacking in creativeness may well be reaching the end of its usefulness. In any case, there can be no doubt that, with or without an efficient university system, Japanese education as a whole ranks with the best in the world and plays a major role in shaping the whole society.

19 *Religion*

If this book were about a South Asian or Middle Eastern people, it would be unthinkable to have delayed a discussion of religion so long and until after topics such as women and education. Religion in fact might well have been the starting point for these Islamic, Hindu, or Buddhist lands, because of its importance there, but in modern Japan it plays a lesser and more peripheral role. I purposely delayed its presentation to emphasize this point. Before the seventeenth century, religion did play an important role in Japanese society, but the trend toward secularism that has only recently become marked in the West dates back at least three centuries in Japan.

The secularism of Japanese society is the product of the influence of Confucian philosophy, which had the same effect in China beginning in the ninth century and in Korea in the fifteenth. East Asians call this philosophy "the teaching of the scholars" (*jukyo* in Japanese), but in the West it has been named for its first master, Confucius, who lived from approximately 551 to 479 B.C. Confucianism did not take final shape in China until the twelfth century A.D. It stressed a rational natural order, of which man was a harmonious element, and a social order based on strict ethical rules and centering on a unified state, governed by men of education and superior ethical wisdom. It had revered texts but no concept of deity, no priesthood, and very little religious ritual. There was no worship, only right thinking and right living, as shown particularly through loyalty to the ruler, filial piety to one's father, and strict observance of proper social ritual and etiquette.

The Confucian classics, the five basic human relationships, the emphasis on history, and many other features of the Confucian system entered Japan with the first great wave of Chinese influence between the sixth and ninth centuries, but Confucianism tended to be overshadowed by Buddhism until the emergence of the centralized Tokugawa system in the seventeenth century made it seem more relevant than it had before. From then on, Confucian schools of philosophy dominated thought and Confucian attitudes pervaded society, until in the early nineteenth century the Japanese had become almost as thoroughly Confucian as the Chinese or Koreans, despite their very non-Confucian feudal political system.

Confucianism, however, did not survive the great transition of the late nineteenth century as an organized philosophy. Its concepts of the cosmos were seen to be highly inaccurate when compared with the results of modern Western science, and its moral values appeared to be tied to a type of society and government that had to be abandoned in the face of the Western menace. The government, in reorganizing inherited Tokugawa educational institutions into Tokyo University, dropped the old Confucian academy and concentrated only on the Western scientific and medical aspects of these schools. A few Confucian scholars fought a rearguard action, forcing the old terminology and concepts into the new system wherever they could. The outstanding example of this was the Imperial Rescript on Education, issued in 1890 at the time of the adoption of the constitution. It had very little to say about education but was a purely Confucian statement of the Confucian relationships and the duties of citizens to the throne. Thus some Confucian attitudes survived, though Confucianism as an accepted body of thought died out completely with the passing of the older generation.

Contemporary Japanese obviously are not Confucianists in the sense that their Tokugawa ancestors were, but Confucian ethical values continue to permeate their thinking. Confucianism probably has more influence on them than does any other of the traditional religions or philosophies. Behind the wholehearted Japanese acceptance of modern science, modern concepts of progress and growth, universalistic principles of ethics, and democratic ideals and values, strong Confucian traits persist, such as the belief in the moral basis of government, the emphasis on interpersonal relations and loyalties, and faith in education and hard work. Almost no one considers himself a Confucianist today, but in a sense almost all Japanese are.

Buddhism is the Japanese religion that comes closest to paralleling Christianity, for it too is concerned with the afterlife and the salvation of the individual. In this it shows its non–East Asian origin in India, a

On the main approach to Tokyo's most popular Buddhist temple at Asakusa, a grandmother, mother, and three small children stand out in the crowd in their holiday finery. (© *Sonia Katchian / Photo Shuttle: Japan*)

region that in religious and philosophical attitudes is more like the premodern West than like East Asia. The historical Buddha, or "enlightened one," who was roughly contemporary with Confucius, started with the basic Indian idea of a never-ending cycle of lives, each determining the next, and added to this the concepts that life is painful, that its suffering derives from human attachment or desires, but that these desires can be overcome by the Buddha's teaching, thus freeing the individual for painless merging with the cosmos in Nirvana, or "nothingness." As the teaching developed, it came to stress reverence for the "Three Treasures," which were the Buddha, the "law" or teachings embodied in an extensive literature, and the religious community, meaning monastic organizations.

The branch of Buddhism that spread throughout East Asia is called Mahayana, or the "greater vehicle," in contrast to Theravada, or the "doctrine of the elders," which survives in Ceylon and much of Southeast Asia. Mahayana taught salvation into a paradise that is closer to the Western concept of heaven than to the original Buddhist Nirvana. It also emphasized the worship, not just of the historical Buddha, but of myriad Buddhalike figures, including Bodhisattvas, who have stayed back one step short of Nirvana and Buddhahood in order to aid in the salvation of others.

In Japan, Mahayana Buddhism developed three major emphases. The first, appearing in the ninth century, was "esoteric" Buddhism, which stressed magic formulas, rituals, and art. The second emphasis, starting a century later, was on salvation through faith, particularly in Amida, the Buddha of the "pure land" of the Western Paradise, or in the Lotus Sutra, a scripture in which the Buddha promised the salvation of "all sentient beings," that is, of all animal life. This emphasis gave rise to the founding in the twelfth and thirteenth centuries of new sects—the Pure Land Sect (Jodoshu), the True (Pure Land) Sect (Shinshu), and Nichiren—which are today the largest Buddhist sects in Japan. The third emphasis was on self-reliance in seeking salvation through self-discipline and meditation. This became embodied in the two Zen, or "meditation," sects, introduced from China in 1191 and 1227. These developed regimens of "sitting in meditation" (*zazen*) and of intellectual self-discipline through nonsense conundrums (*koan*), which were supposed to lead to salvation through sudden enlightenment (*satori*) and also, incidentally, to character building.

Buddhism first came to Japan in the sixth century and played much the same role as Christianity in northern Europe as the vehicle for the transmission of a whole higher culture. A great part of subsequent esthetic expression in architecture, sculpture, and painting was associated with Buddhism, as it was with Christianity in the West. The monastic establishments became rich landowners, as in the West, and at times exercised considerable military and political power. Even congregations of lay believers were politically active in the fifteenth and sixteenth centuries. Indeed Buddhism permeated the whole intellectual, artistic, social, and political life of Japan from the ninth through the sixteenth centuries.

Not much of this survives in contemporary Japan after the savage destruction of the political power of Buddhist institutions by the unifiers of Japan in the late sixteenth century, the three centuries of the progressive secularization of society that followed, and a ruthless attack by the early Meiji government on Buddhism as an element of the discredited past that stood in the way of the creation of an emperor-centered new political system. Buddhist concepts about such things as paradise and the transmigration of the soul linger on in folklore but serve as guiding principles for few people.

Monasteries and temples, both great and small, dot the Japanese landscape but usually play only a subdued background role in the life of the community. The postwar land reform proved a financially crippling blow to many rural temples because it deprived them of the lands that had helped support them. A few people still come to worship and find solace in the Buddhist message of salvation. Temple grounds are often neighborhood playgrounds for children. Most funerals are conducted by Buddhist priests, and burial grounds attached to temples are the place of interment for most people after cremation, a custom learned from India and adopted by all Japanese, probably because of the scarcity of land. Many people return in midsummer to their ancestral homes in the countryside for the Urabon or Bon Festival ("All Saints Day"), a colorful festival of Buddhist origin. At some places on this day they float miniature lighted boats downstream or out to sea in memory of the souls of deceased relatives. Some families have ancestral tablets, which they place in small Buddhist altars on a shelf in the home. The Tokugawa system of requiring the registry of all persons as parishioners of some Buddhist temple—the purpose of this was to ferret out secret Christians—has given all Japanese families a Buddhist sectarian affiliation, though usually this indicates only the sect of the temple where the family burial plot is located.

Most temples and monasteries today maintain their rituals, though often with pathetically small numbers of monks or priests. Some sects took on new intellectual and religious vigor in modern times, in part in response to the Christian missionary movement. They developed publishing ventures, schools, and even a Buddhist missionary movement in East Asia and America. A few modern Japanese, such as some prewar military men and postwar business executives, have practiced Zen, but their numbers are small and their concern is usually less with Buddhist enlightenment than with the development of their own personalities. Contemporary Japanese life thus is full of traces of Buddhism as a sort of background melody, but it is not for many a leitmotif in either their intellectual or emotional lives.

Shinto, the earliest and most distinctive of the Japanese religions, has also slipped into a background role in modern urbanized Japan. Primitive Shinto centered on the animistic worship of natural phenomena—

the sun, mountains, trees, water, rocks, and the whole process of fertility. Totemistic ancestors were included among the *kami,* or deities, worshiped, and no line was drawn between man and nature. A mythology concerning the deities, reminiscent of early Greek mythology, explained the creation of the Japanese islands and tied the origins of the imperial line to the sun goddess, the supreme *kami.*

Shrines dedicated to the various *kami* are to be found everywhere. The main one for the sun goddess stands at Ise, east of the old capital district, facing the rising sun across the Pacific Ocean. Thousands of lesser shrines, each marked by a *torii* gateway, were dedicated to imperial ancestors, the mythological forebears of other once-powerful local families, the deity of rice, or some remarkable natural phenomenon, such as a great mountain, a beautiful waterfall, or simply an unusual tree or rock. Deities are worshiped through offerings, prayers, the clapping of one's hands to gain their attention, and, at larger shrines, light-hearted festivals. But original Shinto had no theology or even a concept

A Shinto priest performs a ceremony for the ritual purification or blessing of a family. Small sticks with dangling strings of paper signifying prayers are commonly waved by a priest in rites of purification or dedication. In the rear of the picture are small wooden votive plaques (called *ema*), presented by people seeking divine aid in combating a disease or seeking some goal, such as success in school entrance examinations. (© *Richard Kalvar / Magnum Photos*)

of ethics, beyond an abhorrence of death and defilement and an emphasis on ritual purity.

Since Shinto was unconcerned with the problem of the afterlife that dominated Buddhist thought, and Mahayana was no exclusive, jealous religion but throughout its spread easily accommodated itself to local faiths, Buddhism and Shinto settled into a comfortable coexistence, with Shinto shrines often becoming administratively linked with Buddhist monasteries. The Japanese never developed the idea, so prevalent in South and West Asia as well as the West, that a person had to adhere exclusively to one religion or another. Premodern Japanese were usually both Buddhists and Shintoists at the same time and often enough Confucianists as well.

For most of the premodern period, Shinto was definitely subordinate to Buddhism, being thought of as representing the locally valid Japanese variants of universal Buddhist truths and deities. But Buddhist fervor waned after the sixteenth century, while the native origins of Shinto and its association with the foundation myths of Japan and with the cult of the imperial ancestors focused new attention on it in a Japan that was becoming more nationalistic and eventually came to seek a new unity under symbolic imperial rule. A sort of Shinto revival centering on reverence for the emperor became part of the movement that led to the overthrow of the Tokugawa and the founding of the new regime in 1868.

The leaders of the Meiji Restoration, being thoroughly anti-Buddhist, brutally cut Buddhism off from Shinto, and they attempted at first to create a Shinto-centered system of government. Although they soon discovered that this concept could not be mixed successfully with their basically Western political patterns, they did create a system of state support for the great historic Shinto shrines and developed new national ones, such as the beautiful Meiji Shrine in Tokyo, dedicated to the first modern emperor, and the Yasukuni Shrine, also in Tokyo, for the souls of military men who had died in defense of the country. In order to maintain the claim that Japanese enjoyed complete religious freedom, this nationalistic "state Shinto" was officially defined by the government as being not a religion but a manifestation of patriotism. In a sense it was not a religion, because, even though it did impinge, at least in form, on the field of religion in its enforced worship at Shinto shrines and the reverential treatment of pictures of the emperor and empress and copies of the Imperial Rescript on Education that was required of all schools throughout the country, it was essentially an artificial creation, far removed from the basic attitudes of Shinto and deriving more from modern nationalism.

"State Shinto" reached its peak in the frenzy of nationalism preceding World War II. The American occupation naturally attacked it with vigor as a dangerous manifestation of xenophobia, and in the general postwar reaction against militarism and patriotism it disappeared almost completely. The occupation also demanded that a sharp line be drawn between government and religion. The great historical shrines were thrown back on their own individual sources of income, and as a result all but the most popular ones fell into dire financial straits. Although a few had wide support, which has enabled them to generate new sources of income, the ban on public funds for institutions connected with religion hit most of them hard and also, incidentally, contributed to the slowness with which the government came to the aid of private universities, many of which have Christian, Buddhist, or even Shinto affiliations.

With "state Shinto" gone, Shintoism has reverted to a more peripheral role in Japanese life. Shrines of all types are scattered everywhere, often in places of great beauty and charm, though usually with signs of quiet decay. They are visited by a few believers in the efficacy of their rituals and prayers to their deities or, if they are historically famous or are known for their natural beauties, by throngs of eager sightseers. Visits in recent years by prime ministers to the Yasukuni Shrine for the war dead and the enshrinement there in 1978 of some of the men executed by the American occupation as "Class A" war criminals have stirred up great opposition among Christians and other religious groups as well as members of the political left. But on the whole the Yasukuni Shrine is regarded as analogous to the Tomb of the Unknown Soldier, and the Meiji Shrine to the Lincoln Memorial in Washington. Children are often taken to shrines at certain prescribed points in their lives—shortly after birth, at special festivals in their third, fifth, and seventh years, and at annual boys' and girls' festivals. Shrines are also the setting for many marriages, and homes frequently have "god shelves" where offerings are made to Shinto deities.

Traditional Shinto seems most alive today in the spirited shrine festivals held annually on specific dates by all shrines of any importance. At

Facing page: During shrine festivals, local youths often carry around a miniature shrine temporarily housing the local deity. Such festivals are gay occasions and give participants one of their few chances to dress up in traditional garb. (*Courtesy Japan National Tourist Organization*)

these times, scores of booths ply a brisk trade on the shrine grounds, and the shrine deity is boisterously carried about in a portable shrine by somewhat inebriated local youths. These shrine festivals remain a prominent feature of local life, particularly in rural Japan, though some of them are taking on the character of self-conscious, historical pageants, or else are losing out in urbanized areas to more secular community festivals that feature marching bands and drum majorettes.

In these various ways, Shinto continues to be a part of Japanese life, and folklore remains full of Shinto elements. The Japanese love of nature and sense of closeness to it also derive strongly from Shinto concepts. But very few modern Japanese find in traditional Shinto any real focus for their lives or even for their social activities or diversions.

Christianity is usually linked with Shinto and Buddhism as one of the three main religions of Japan, though it is considered a foreign religion in a way Buddhism is not. First introduced by the famous Jesuit missionary, Saint Francis Xavier, in 1549, it spread more rapidly in Japan during the next several decades than in any other Asian country, and Christians came to number close to half a million, a much larger percentage of the population of that time than they are today. But Hideyoshi and the early Tokugawa shoguns came to view Christianity as a threat to political unity and suppressed it ruthlessly, creating in the process a large number of Japanese martyrs but virtually stamping the religion out by 1638. Only a few tiny communities of secret Christians survived, and in time they lost most real knowledge of the tenets of their religion.

The nineteenth-century Japanese remained deeply hostile to Christianity, but they soon learned the strength of Western feelings about the religion and therefore tacitly dropped their prohibition of it in 1873 and subsequently made explicit a policy of complete religious toleration. But Christianity this time spread much more slowly. Even today its adherents number less than 2 percent of the population—divided fairly evenly between Protestants and Catholics.

After the Meiji Restoration, Protestant Christianity, largely brought by American missionaries, was taken up by a number of able young samurai, particularly those from the losing side in the civil war, who sought in Christianity a new ethics and philosophy of life to take the place of discredited Confucianism. These men injected a strong sense of independence into the native church. In fact, under the leadership of Uchimura Kanzo, a leading intellectual of the time, a "No Church" movement was founded in reaction to the sectarian divisions of Protestantism in the West. During World War II the government, for control purposes, forced the various Protestant sects into a United Church, and today some 40 percent of the Protestant movement remains in the United Church of Christ in Japan (Nihon Kirisuto Kyodan).

The influence of Christianity on modern Japanese society is far greater than the small number of its adherents would suggest. Christians are strongly represented among the best-educated, leading elements in society and have therefore exerted a quite disproportionate influence. Another factor is that Christianity, as an important element of Western civilization, has attracted general attention. Most educated Japanese probably have a clearer concept of the history and basic beliefs of Christianity than they do of Buddhism. A superficial example of the general Japanese familiarity with Christianity is the enthusiasm with which Christmas decorations are displayed by department stores and Christmas carols are blared out along the shopping streets at Christmas time.

During the Meiji period, Christians played a major role in education, particularly at the secondary level and in schools for girls. Even today a large percentage of the private secondary schools and women's universities and some of the other private universities are of Christian origin, though the role of Christianity in education is much less important now than it once was. In the early twentieth century Christians also led in the development of social work for underprivileged and handicapped persons, and Protestant Christians were also prominent in the founding of the Socialist movement. In fact, they remained an important element in the movement throughout the prewar period, and they continued even into postwar days as a significant, moderate branch of the Socialist Party. But perhaps the largest area of Christian influence is in ethics. As modern Japanese turned increasingly to universalistic values, they adopted many ethical attitudes that both historically in the West and in the Japanese mind today are associated with Christianity. The Christian influence on contemporary Japanese ethical values is at least more recognizable if not actually greater than the influence of either Buddhism or Shinto. Moreover, many Japanese look upon Christians as people of high moral principles, and they often envy the apparent firmness of Christian beliefs, though they find themselves unable to accept the accompanying theology.

Christianity, though intellectually influential, is numerically only a tiny religion in Japan, and Shinto and Buddhism are for most people more a matter of custom and convention than of meaningful belief. Many if not most Japanese who feel strong religious needs today look elsewhere, turning instead to superstitious folk beliefs, prevalent especially in rural Japan and among the less educated, or to a great variety of popular religious movements, which are normally lumped together under the name of the "new religions." The popular superstitious beliefs are usually an amalgam of concepts derived from Shinto, Buddhism, and Chinese folk superstitions. There are numerous local cults of all sorts, and many people pay serious attention to lucky and unlucky days, astrology, and fortune-tellers.

The new religions have grown in part out of an old Japanese tendency to form special groups for pilgrimages or other religious activities, outside the formal organization of the established religions, but a more important reason for their development is that they have been responsive to the social needs of Japanese, as the movement of people to the cities broke their ties with rural religious bodies or left them without a suitable social group to which to belong. The new religions, thus, do not cater to the common Western religious need for individual strength through the establishment of a personal bond with God, but rather to the typical Japanese need for a supportive social environment.

The new religions tend to be highly syncretic, combining Shinto, Buddhist, and sometimes even Christian or Western philosophic influences. Most, however, are basically Shinto in their leanings, though the largest, Soka Gakkai (the "Value Creating Association"), is a lay association supporting a branch of the Nichiren sect of Buddhism. The new religions usually stress this-worldly values rather than the afterlife, emphasizing the achievement of health, prosperity, self-improvement, and happiness through faith or through magical practices. Some were founded by individuals, particularly women, who felt themselves to be possessed by the deities in a shamanistic way. Other founders merely claimed to have discovered the true way. Leadership in these religions frequently becomes hereditary, and their organization tends to be hierarchical, made up of typically Japanese groups of leaders and followers. This makes them highly susceptible to fissions, and in many there is also a relatively rapid turnover of members.

The officially recognized new religions number in the hundreds, and there are many more small groups lacking official recognition. The total membership is in the tens of millions. Soka Gakkai alone claims 16 million, though 6 million would probably be a better estimate of its actual membership at any one time. Some of these new religions are by now quite old. Tenrikyo ("Teaching of the Heavenly Truth"), which today claims a membership of almost 2 million, was founded by a peasant woman in 1838. Others, like Soka Gakkai, were either founded or had their major growth after World War II. The large new religions tend to have grandiose headquarters and to hold numerous elaborate mass festivals and rallies. Only Soka Gakkai has attempted to play a direct role in politics by founding a party, the Komeito, which later separated at least in theory from Soka Gakkai. All the new religions, however, provide their participants with a tightly organized, protective community, with study groups and social activities that minister perhaps more to their social than their spiritual needs.

All in all, religion in Japan offers a confused and indistinct picture. Shinto shrines and Buddhist temples are found everywhere. The lives of most Japanese are intertwined with religious observances—shrine festivals, "god shelves" and Buddhist altars in the homes, and Shinto or Christian marriages, Buddhist funerals, and other religious rites of passage. But the majority of Japanese—some 70 to 80 percent—even though carried on the rolls of one or more religious body, do not consider themselves believers in any religion. The ethics of the Japanese for the most part are derived from Confucianism, to which none now "belongs," and from Christianity, which is the faith of less than 2 percent. Popular religious customs are derived mostly from traditional Shinto and Buddhism, in which few really believe. And most religious life among the few who are religiously active is devoted to folk religious beliefs or new religions that have little prestige or general influence. Clearly religion in contemporary Japan is not central to society and culture.

20 _Mass Culture_

We started our consideration of Japanese society with its group orientation. We might conclude it with some comment on its mass culture, which epitomizes the group nature of the Japanese today. Japan has its divisions by local community, school, and business enterprise, but these are all surface phenomena, not reaching deeply down into society as ethnic differences, class or caste divisions, or religions do elsewhere. We have just seen how unimportant religious distinctions are to most Japanese. Shinto festivals, Buddhist ceremonies, Confucian ethics, or Christian weddings and Christmas celebrations are normally not acts of religious affirmation but simply customs that everyone takes part in either personally or by way of television. Virtually all Japanese share a very similar mass culture. The mass society that is often hailed or deplored as the worldwide wave of the future and is thought to be most typical of the United States is far more pronounced in contemporary Japan. From the main stem of language out to the latest transient fad, the Japanese are a thoroughly homogeneous people.

Culture, of course, has various levels, from mass customs at the bottom to the most sophisticated fine arts at the top, but even these horizontal layers are not very pronounced in Japan. Ever since the seventh and eighth centuries the Japanese have maintained extraordinarily rich and refined traditions in architecture, sculpture, painting, literature, drama, and the applied arts. This higher culture has always been pervasive in Japanese society; it has not been limited to an elite and talented few. Mass culture correspondingly has been surprisingly refined. Whereas in countries noted for their high culture—say, France or China—the common people display little artistic taste, in Japan the high culture seems to have been absorbed much more fully into mass culture. Neither beauty nor refined manners are limited to the few, and surpris-

216

ingly high levels of artistic appreciation and etiquette reach down to the virtual bottom of society.

Despite the ugliness of overcrowded houses and their constrained environments, most Japanese manage to create in their daily surroundings at least a few small examples of handsome design or islands of beauty—a tiny garden, an artistic arrangement of a few flowers, some tasteful works of art, a striking textile design for a kimono, or merely a pleasingly arranged lunch box. Japanese in general show an amazing deftness in drawing and painting—perhaps the legacy of the calligraphy learned for their complex script. Probably a higher percentage of the population strives with success to write poetry—principally haiku—than in any other industrialized land, and there are literally hundreds of literary and artistic magazines aimed at the interests of such people. Perhaps more of the world's classic literature is available in translation in Japanese than in any other language in the world, including English. Fine music, mostly Western, pervades the country, from great symphony orchestras through college choral societies to recordings for home use on high-quality electronic equipment. High culture does indeed seem to be part of mass culture in a way that is rare elsewhere in the world.

The homogeneity of Japan's mass culture can be attributed to many sources, but two factors stand out in particular. These are the extraordinary uniformity the society already had when the Japanese entered the nineteenth century and the determination of the government in modern times to develop a unified citizenry through political centralization and uniform education. As a consequence, Japan has none of the great regional and ethnic diversity of the United States. It even has much less than the larger countries of Western Europe, despite the fact that it has close to twice the population of any of them and is spread out geographically much more widely. Japan, even excluding Okinawa, extends along its longest axis from northeastern Hokkaido to southern Kyushu almost twice the distance of Italy, France, or the United Kingdom as measured along their longest axes. But only Okinawa, which is farther from Tokyo than Tunis is from London, differs significantly in local dialect, folk culture, historical traditions, and certain contemporary attitudes.

Education has been the chief tool in shaping national uniformity. In prewar Japan one could know that on a certain day every sixth-grade child throughout the land would be learning the same Chinese characters, the same historical facts, and the same arithmetic rules. Education is no longer quite this uniform, since local boards of education make selections from among a variety of textbooks, though all must have Ministry of Education approval. Curricula at the lower levels are closely prescribed, and even in senior high school preparation for the same university entrance examinations produces a great deal of uniformity. Even higher education, swamped as it is by masses of students and inadequate finances, achieves little variation except for its division into a series of disciplinary faculties. All Japanese experience nine years (and 94 percent of them twelve years) of virtually identical education, which is not greatly diversified by the higher education approximately a third of them receive. They emerge into society with a uniformity of information and attitudes that is matched only in a small close-knit primitive society or a modern totalitarian state.

The mass media join education as major shapers of mass society. The role of television in Japan is similar to that in the United States. Nationwide networks, by providing almost identical fare, breed a great deal of uniformity. It is television more than anything else that has smoothed out the contrasts in values and attitudes between rural and urban dwellers, which were so divisive in prewar Japan. Television is present in virtually every home in rural as well as urban areas, and there are in fact more color television sets in Japan than households. Incidentally, the Japanese, though calling television by its English name, have derived from it a different contraction—*terebi,* in place of the "TV" of the United States and the "telly" of England.

Japanese television is organized more like British than American television, but the programs on the whole are more like those of the United States. There are two seminational networks, known as NHK (Nippon Hoso Kyoku), which are supported by public funds from a special tax on television sets. One government network is highly educational, carrying much foreign-language instruction, mathematics courses of amazing complexity, and the like. The other competes with the private networks in general interest, having much the same sort of news, sports, drama, comedy, cartoons, and quiz shows. Five private networks cover large parts of the country and are dependent for support on advertising, which is much like that on American television. The blend between private and government television works well on the whole. The financial resources and high quality of the general network of NHK force the commercial stations to strive for quality to compete, while the challenge of the private channels forces NHK to be lively in a way not characteristic of television that is a government monopoly. For the most part Japanese and American television are very similar in scope, variety, richness, and their pervasive role in society; most other countries have much more limited, less interesting, and more sober fare.

Unlike television, Japanese and American newspapers are quite different from each other. Geographic size has forced American newspapers to remain local and therefore relatively small, and European newspapers tend to divide sharply along political lines, but Japanese newspapers are mostly national and politically neutral, thus fitting the concept of "mass media" even better than do the newspapers of North America or Europe.

With less than a tenth of the number of American newspapers, the Japanese have the largest newspaper circulation per capita among the larger countries of the world—more than twice that of the United States. The three greatest national newspapers are the *Asahi, Mainichi,* and *Yomiuri,* which each have entirely different morning and evening editions of around 4 to 7 million copies in the morning and more than half that number at night, distributed for the most part to individual homes. Each is printed at some four different locations with a hundred or more slight local variations. Two other national papers, *Sankei* and *Nihon Keizai* (comparable to the *Wall Street Journal*), have circulations in the millions, while four regional papers, known collectively as the "bloc"—the *Hokkaido Shimbun* in Sapporo, the *Tokyo Shimbun,* *Chunichi* in Nagoya, and *Nishi Nippon* in Fukuoka in Kyushu—have a combined circulation of around 4 million.

Japanese newspapers are surprisingly uniform in format and content. They tend to be smaller than American papers in number of pages— only about twenty-four pages for the morning editions and less for the evening. Advertising forms a much smaller proportion of their financial support and, except for classified and book and magazine advertisements, takes up relatively little space. Tha main news appears on page one, and more detailed political, foreign, and economic news, editorials, letters, special features, art and theater sections, home news, and the like are to be found on almost the same pages in every paper. The next to the last page—known as "the third-page news" (*sammen kiji*) from an original four-page format—is always reserved for crime, accidents, and other human interest stories, which are called "social news" but never contain the "society news" of American papers.

The material for the papers is collected by armies of newsmen stationed all over Japan and the world. The Japanese, for example, constitute the largest foreign corps of newsmen in both Washington and New

York. The news is then concisely compiled, carefully edited, and meticulously proofread by more such armies of newspapermen in the home office. Bylines are rare, illustrating once again the Japanese propensity for group action. The net result is a high quality product. One can safely say that the Japanese on average are provided with fuller and more accurate newspaper coverage of both national and international news than any other people in the world, and only an occasional newspaper elsewhere surpasses their great national dailies in either quantity or quality of news.

The great weakness of Japanese newspapers is their distressing uniformity in coverage and treatment. They have few individualized interpretive articles and do little investigative reporting. In recent years the most outstanding example of the latter, which was inspired by the Watergate affair in the United States, was the work of a monthly magazine. Commonly newspaper headlines and editorials seem to be almost paraphrases of one another. As a result, tens of millions of Japanese, intellectually armed with the same television and newspaper news and opinions, sally forth to work each day with the same facts, interests, and attitudes.

One reason for the uniformity of Japanese newspapers is the existence of so-called press clubs. Each major paper, wire service, or bloc of papers assigns a reporter to a major news source, such as a political party, leading politician, government bureau, or branch of business. Those reporters assigned to the same source form themselves into a club that acts collectively and is granted semiofficial recognition by the target of their reporting. They are given frequent but always joint interviews, often on a daily basis with politicians. They frequently are assigned a room within a ministry. They pool their questions at interviews and tacitly agree to print only what is agreed upon with their sources of information and among each other. This is a mutually satisfactory backscratching operation in which, so long as both sides conform to the unwritten rules, both profit: the reporters with minimum effort get the latest information without fear of being scooped by their supposed competitors and the source of information has a reliable means of releasing his version of the news to the public. It is not surprising that no one wishes to upset the applecart by digging too deeply into embarrassing facts or extending membership in the clubs to foreign correspondents who lack adequate language skills and cannot be trusted to observe the rules. It takes a news story or scandal of overpowering significance to induce newsmen to scramble without scruples for the news. The net result of the system is reliable, carefully processed news but overall a boring uniformity of the press.

All the major newspapers profess to strict political neutrality, but in reality most of them tend to lean slightly to the left of center and to be critical of the government. This situation is in part the result of their history. Newspapers first grew up in Japan in the Meiji period as organs of protest for men of samurai origin who had failed to become members of the ruling group. From this beginning they developed the attitude that their role in society was to be helpful critics of what, at least before the war, was an overpowering government. Only during the 1930s and World War II were they forced to become the dutiful mouthpieces of the government, and in the postwar period they happily reverted to the role of critics, even though now the government was democratically controlled and very dependent upon public opinion, which the newspapers did much to shape. Another reason for their prevailing leftist slant is that newspapers are produced by "intellectuals" (as the term is used in Japan) living in the great metropolitan centers, where opposition to the conservative government in power runs strongest. (The term "intellectuals," or *interi,* as the Japanese call them for short, is loosely used to include virtually all college graduates who are not engaged in business, politics, or government service.)

The great newspapers, however, see themselves as politically neutral and consciously strive to be so. They are less neutral than television, which tends to be politically bland, but, in any case, the major newspapers are definitely not mouthpieces of governmental indoctrination, as they would be in a totalitarian society, nor are they the tools of owners or of some controlling political party, as might be the case in the United States or Western Europe. Ownership has little influence on editorial policy, which is produced instead by factional struggles among the professional staff and secondarily by pressures from the unionized labor force.

Weekly and monthly publications play less of a national role than do newspapers and add more diversity. There are a handful of monthly magazines—the so-called general magazines (*sogo zasshi*)—that have serious articles on a variety of subjects, but their circulations run at most only in the hundreds of thousands. The size and excellence of the daily press preclude the need for news weeklies like *Time* or *Newsweek*, but there are a huge number and variety of other types of weeklies. At least three claim circulations above a half million, and the top fifty have a combined circulation of about 8 million. The weeklies tend to be more

A shop in the Akihabara district of Tokyo, where there are 250 stores dealing exclusively in electric appliances and electronic equipment. The brand names are often as familiar to Americans as to Japanese. (© *Tadanori Saito* / *Photo Shuttle: Japan*)

sensational and sometimes salacious than the monthlies or the newspapers, and they certainly are far more varied. They include large numbers of specialty magazines on a vast variety of subjects from sports to knitting. Most weekly and monthly magazines make no claim to neutrality and cater quite frankly to particular political biases or other specialized interests.

One distressing aspect of the mass media in recent years has been the vast increase in the reading, or perhaps one should say perusing, of cartoons (*manga*). They have come to occupy large sections of all sorts of magazines and even entire magazines and books. Once Japanese could be seen reading everywhere, on trains, in waiting rooms, and wherever else the situation allowed. They might have been called the "readingest" people in the world. But many of these former readers are now engrossed in the pictures and inarticulate grunts of cartoons. Originally limited to children, their popularity spread to college students, and now sedate businessmen and housewives can be seen devouring them. They run from imaginative adventure stories of all types to equally diverse stories of love or pornographic appeal. What this all means is hard to fathom: a broadening of the public attracted to print, a lessening of the attention span and a lowering of taste produced by television, a revulsion against serious reading by people overburdened by the pressures of school and the workplace, or a sign of the vulgarization of mass society. In any case, cartoons have become a major phenomenon of mass culture in recent years and have had a decidedly adverse effect on the publishing of other magazines and books.

A standardized educational system and the mass media may be basic in giving the Japanese their uniformity as a mass culture, but these are

Children's playgrounds are often set up on the roofs of department stores for the convenience of shopping mothers with children in tow. (© *Richard Kalvar / Magnum Photos*)

underlain by a well-ordered, smoothly functioning society as a whole. It runs in clear-cut, deep channels. Individual careers are more predictable and follow more established courses than in most other countries. News stories, fads, and new ideas sweep the whole land uniformly, inspiring similar reactions throughout. The Japanese are particularly subject to nationwide "moods" (the English word is used). They also turn out by the millions for public events, such as the 1964 Olympics and various expositions. Much the same could be said of Americans and other modernized nations, but these generalizations seem particularly true of the Japanese.

Mass-produced goods flow by the millions into the hands of mass consumers. Name brands in electrical appliances, cameras, and the like are advertised nationally through television and magazines and retailed through tens of thousands of outlets to be bought by millions of people. Almost all households have washing machines and refrigerators and close to two thirds have cars—more in rural areas than in cities because of the lesser problem of parking space. With the postwar economic recovery, a succession of the three treasures of family life—a joke on the "Three Regalia" of the imperial family—gravitated upward in value until by the late 1960s they had become the "three Cs," meaning color television, a car, and a "cooler," the term for an air conditioner. Since then general affluence has made the joke drop out of use.

Huge department stores, or *depato,* some dating from as early as the seventeenth century and others being the creations of commuter railways and located at their terminals, cater to a mass clientele with a bewildering profusion of standardized goods and a series of peripheral services not found in their Western counterparts. They often have, for example, a children's zoo and playground on the roof, restaurants on upper floors, a theater, and a hall for changing art exhibits, usually of high quality. Museums are not very common in Japan, and the average person is likely to see famous works of art either *in situ* in Buddhist temples or else at such department store exhibits.

Japanese are mass participants in sports as either spectators or players. They excel at baseball, volleyball, gymnastics, and a variety of other sports and play almost all games known to man. They climb the highest mountains or sail single-handed across the widest oceans just because they are there. Golf, despite exorbitant costs in land-poor Japan, is a

Facing page: The swimming pool at Korakuen Park in Tokyo on a hot summer day. (*Tadanori Saito / Photo Shuttle: Japan*)

must for any ambitious businessman, and tennis has growing numbers of devotees. Horse racing, professional baseball, college baseball, and even the national high school baseball championships regularly draw tens of thousands of spectators. The professional baseball teams are sponsored by business firms, often commuter railway lines along which their fields are located, and have names, always in English, that are sometimes familiar to Americans—the Yomiuri (Tokyo) Giants—and sometimes strange—the Hiroshima Carps. *Sumo,* which is the traditional form of wrestling between "man mountains" and is vaguely associated with Shinto, has proved to be a fine television spectacular and as a result has gained new popularity. Ski slopes are hazardously crowded in winter. The Shonan beaches near Tokyo attract over a million persons on a hot summer weekend. An endless antlike chain of people on the slopes of Mount Fuji turns mountain climbing in summer into a mass sport.

Sightseeing crowds, mostly organized groups of schoolchildren and village and small-town associations, inundate famous beauty spots in the spring and autumn sightseeing seasons and all but obliterate them from view or even from existence. Shopping streets and popular amusement areas, with their thousands of bars, cafés, and restaurants, always swarm with people. There are hundreds of brightly lighted, bustling local Ginzas, named for the Ginza in downtown Tokyo, which was long the city's most lively shopping and amusement street, until superseded in recent years by flashier night spots like Shinjuku and Roppongi. The usual first reaction of a Japanese visitor to an American town or suburb is surprise at the paucity of people visible in the streets—as if they had been wiped out by some great catastrophe.

Japan's mass society spills over into its finer arts. Japanese girls learn the tea ceremony, flower arrangement, and traditional dancing in large groups and as part of a standardized training for young women. Hundreds of small children saw away together on their violins according to the Suzuki method. Occidental music, whether classical or popular, draws mass audiences, which are always overwhelmingly young.

Sheer numbers or even uniformity, however, are not the main characteristic of Japan's mass culture. Much more significant are its tremendous vitality, creativity, and variety. In the field of Western music, Japan's many symphony orchestras rank with the best in the world, as do individual Japanese musicians and conductors. Japanese architects are world famous. Modern painters and woodblock artists are tremendously prolific. Japanese clothes designers are featured in New York and

Paris. All the traditional arts are more alive today than they have been for many decades. Japanese traditional potters have set the styles that are copied worldwide. Literature is bounding with energy. People of all sorts are sparkling with artistic creativity, and young people are bubbling with new life styles. Japan may have a mass society but it encompasses within its seeming uniformity endless variations and boundless energy.

Much of Japan's mass culture is familiar enough to Americans, who perhaps run neck and neck with the Japanese in the espousal of mass society. But in some ways Japan is ahead. No sight in the world seems more characteristic of modern mass society than the hordes of commuters—actually in the millions—who each day surge like the tide through the great commuting terminals of Tokyo and Osaka. To the foreigner, these vast throngs, clad alike and looking very similar to an outsider and all moving determinedly but in orderly fashion to their destinations, seem to be a vision of a robotlike future that may await us all. But if one looks more closely and can penetrate the veil of the language barrier, one can see that, however crowded and uniform this future may seem in some of its patterns, it is still a distinctly human future, teeming with energetic and creative individuals.

Part Four ————————————————

Government and Politics

Businessmen watching the incomplete results of the July 6, 1986, election as posted by the Asahi newspaper. Returns on the 252-seat House of Councillors are on the left; those for the more powerful 512-seat House of Representatives on the right. The five columns on the right give the numbers of already elected and predissolution strength of the various parties, showing from left to right the five largest ones: the Liberal Democrats (LDP), the Socialists, Komeito, the Democratic Socialists, and the Communists. As of this posting, the LDP had already elected 257 Representatives, and it ended up with a recordbreaking 300. The row of television monitors below gives rapidly changing details on the vote of individual election districts; below them are election pictures and handwritten announcements of noteworthy election developments. (AP/Wide World Photos)

21 The Political Heritage

When people speak of the Japanese "miracle," they usually have in mind the rapid industrialization of the country and its rise to undreamed-of prosperity and economic power. As we have seen, "miracle" is not the right word for a perfectly natural even if remarkable growth on the basis of a long preparatory background and certain deeply ingrained characteristics. But in any case, there is another often overlooked aspect of modern Japan that is even more deserving of wonderment and admiration. This is Japan's transformation in less than a century and a half from a full-fledged feudal land into a firmly based, functioning democracy. To the historian this is more surprising and praiseworthy than Japan's spectacular economic success.

The Japanese political heritage includes no experience with the concepts and practices of democracy. There is little real basis to the idea of a basic Asian village democracy. At the village level almost anywhere there is likely to be a certain degree of egalitarianism among persons in daily contact with one another and frequently engaged in communal tasks. Group decisions may be the rule, as they were in the traditional Japanese village. But the member families of these villages differed sharply in status and authority. In any case, village communalism is a far cry from modern political democracy, which depends on individual rights and representative institutions among large groups of people not in daily face-to-face contact.

In the West, both the concept of individual rights and the practices of representation grew in part out of the feudal experience, which had stressed the legal nature and the mutuality of feudal rights and obligations. In Japan, feudal bonds were seen as basically moral. At the height of feudalism in the fifteenth and sixteenth centuries there was a certain degree of mutuality and bargaining in feudal relations, and in the late feudalism of the Tokugawa period there was a well-established and highly complex system of interrelationships between lord and follower, but throughout the Japanese ideally saw the feudal bond as committing the inferior to absolute obedience and loyalty and granting the superior unlimited authority. There were no inalienable rights, no concepts that might have underlain a Magna Carta, and no experience of any sort with representative bodies. In these terms, one could scarcely imagine a system less congenial to democratic ideas and institutions than the Japanese polity on the eve of the opening to the West.

The Japanese leaders of the mid-nineteenth century also did not have any desire to create a democratic system. Unlike so-called modernizing nations in the twentieth century, they did not find democracy an appealing concept, nor did they see any need to attempt to create a democratic system. What seemed imperative was to build as rapidly as possible a strong, centralized Japan capable of meeting the military and economic menace of the West. As they experimented with ways to do this, they came to realize that elements of the Western democratic system might be of use to them, but these were seen as means to an end and in no sense as primary objectives in themselves.

Despite the lack of democratic experience or leanings, the nineteenth-century Japanese did derive from their heritage many great assets for building a strong, centralized nation, and some of these qualities facilitated and in cases encouraged later democratic developments. The single most important aspect of the Japanese political heritage was the strong sense of unity. This contrasted greatly with the situation today in many developing countries, which often had little sense of political unity until after undergoing colonialism. In Japan, feudal divisions might have obscured this unity but it was firmly based on Japan's relative isolation, its exceptional homogeneity, its ancient traditions of political centralization, and the whole Chinese, or East Asian, emphasis on the centralized state as the highest embodiment of civilization. The contrast was sharp with most other non-Western lands, which traditionally were either religiously oriented or else tribally or linguistically divided.

The Japanese shared the tradition of political unity with the other countries of East Asia, but four factors distinguished them from their near neighbors. One was their self-conscious distinction from China. The Chinese themselves saw all other lands as subordinate to China, and the Koreans accepted this world view. But the Japanese sense of nationalism was strengthened by their keen awareness of an overwhelmingly large and prestigious China, which, for all its cultural influence on Japan, they still felt to be essentially alien. This attitude proved to be better fitted than those of the Chinese and Koreans to the Western concept of international relations, to which all three nations had to accommodate themselves.

The second difference was that in Japan the ideal of uniform, centralized political rule conflicted sharply with the feudal realities of local autonomy and class divisions. This contrast created internal tensions in nineteenth-century Japan that, by opening cracks in society, made change easier than in the more monolithic and long-established systems of China and Korea. One of the changes made possible by this situation was the introduction and development of democratic concepts and practices.

The third distinguishing feature from the rest of East Asia was that the nineteenth-century Japanese could find adequate native justification for the great political, economic, and social revolution being forced on them by the menace of the West. They found this justification in the "restoration" of imperial rule, which could satisfactorily explain the necessity of eliminating feudal political and social divisions and modernizing the economy. The Chinese, in contrast, had no native justification for major change, except for a dynastic transfer that would have brought no change in the system. They therefore had to look to foreign ideologies, such as republicanism, democracy, and eventually communism, to explain basic changes, but to do this was a traumatic and time-consuming process. Though challenged by the West earlier than the Japanese, the Chinese found it difficult to carry through basic reforms, and, when a republican revolution did finally come in 1912, it succeeded only in destroying the old political order but not in creating a functioning republic to take its place. Democracy, though honored in theory, was never established in practice. China instead degenerated first into warlordism and then into the one-party dictatorship of Chiang Kai-shek's Nationalist government. Not until 1949, over a century after its first war with the West, was China at last fully reunited through a foreign ideology—this time communism.

The Japanese went through no such traumatic spiritual shifts. The great transformation of the nineteenth century was seen as a "restoration" of an old native institution, to which the other great changes were subordinate. Thus they too seemed justified, even though in fact they led to sweeping modifications of Japanese society. Among these were social freedom and universal education, which made representative institutions and democratic concepts both comprehensible and attractive. Democracy grew naturally in Japan, and, though it faltered in the 1930s, its strong postwar revival has been basically a continuity from prewar days, particularly the 1920s, and not an incomprehensible or uncongenial borrowing from abroad.

A fourth way in which the nineteenth-century Japanese differed from their near neighbors—and in this case from most of the rest of the non-Western world as well—was that they were willing to learn from the West even though their original objective was to repel the West and restore their own antique institutions. The Chinese felt that there was little to learn from any other country, and the Koreans were ready to learn only from China. But the Japanese not only knew that they had always learned much from China, but also were not unaware of their borrowing of Buddhism from India, of guns and other technology from the Portuguese in the sixteenth century, and of the "Dutch learning," which was currently bringing new elements of Western science into Japan. They also seem to have had a more realistic appraisal of Western military and economic power than did the Chinese or Koreans. As a consequence, they felt no compunction about borrowing what they deemed necessary from the West to achieve their objectives of self-defense and imperial restoration. The Chinese and Koreans, in contrast, stubbornly resisted all Western innovations.

Another great political asset the Japanese derived from their past was a strong sense of the ethical basis for government, drawn from their Confucian heritage. Closely associated with this were their relatively high standards of honesty and efficiency in political administration. There were, of course, some cruel, inefficient, and even dishonest government officials. Gift giving to superiors was rampant, but, though this would be viewed today as corruption, it was regarded at the time as part of the system and was usually limited by fixed custom. Within the limits of the system, almost all administrators were absolutely loyal to their superiors, scrupulously honest, meticulous in the performance of their duties, and efficient, at least by premodern standards. For example, the maintenance of order and the collection of agricultural taxes in the shogun's vast personal domain were performed by a handful of relatively low-ranking intendants with a thoroughness and at a cost that would have been the envy of any regime in the world in the eighteenth century.

These high standards of administrative efficiency continued without break into the modern period, accounting for the relative smoothness of the transfer of power and change of systems following the Meiji Restoration. Despite the tremendous confusion at the time, there was no general breakdown of law and order or any prolonged slump in the collection of taxes, which by the early 1870s had been successfully transferred from more than 260 autonomous feudal domains to the new central government.

The new government also had surprisingly little difficulty in reorganizing the bureaucratized samurai officials of the old system into a new prefectural and central government bureaucracy, a modernized police force, and the officers of a modern army and navy. The division of the central civil bureaucracy into ministries like those of the Western political pattern was for the Japanese a relatively simple change, and was perfectly understandable because of the ministerial divisions of the system borrowed in ancient times from China and the incipient ministries of the Tokugawa period. There was not even any difficulty in making the shift by the end of the nineteenth century in the method of selecting the bureaucracy from the hereditary system of Tokugawa times or the reliance on personal association in the early Meiji period to a mechanical use of the new educational system and formal examinations. This was because the new system was consonant with late Tokugawa demands for more emphasis on individual merit and was reminiscent of the old Chinese concept of choosing the top administrators through examinations. Thus, there was throughout a great continuity in the spirit of bureaucratic loyalty, efficiency, and honesty, which even today is largely responsible for the continuing high standards of government service in Japan. The presence of such a reliable bureaucracy provided a strong foundation for any form of government, including democracy.

Another important political heritage was the long tradition of group rather than personalized leadership. As early as the Kamakura period, in the thirteenth century, there was a tendency to share power, as through the various councils in Kamakura, paired deputies in Kyoto, and the system of having a "co-signer" who paralleled the shogunal Hojo "regent" in Kamakura. In Tokugawa times this sharing of power was even more marked. The councils of "elders" and of "junior elders" were the two highest decision-making bodies, and most of the chief administrative positions below them were either paired or held by groups of four men, who, like the members of the top councils, rotated as officers in charge.

The Meiji leaders continued the same general pattern of group leadership. Unlike the situation in most countries undergoing rapid change, there was never any one dictatorial leader, nor did any person ever attempt to gain such powers. The leaders, who, as we have seen, came to be known informally as the *genro,* or "elder statesmen," always formed a group, taking turns at the various administrative tasks and in the position of prime minister after this post was created in 1885 but yielding willingly to each other when they ran into difficulty or tired of the responsibility. One of the early leaders, Okubo Toshimichi, before his assassination in 1878, and Ito while shaping the constitution in the 1880s, enjoyed a certain predominance, but even they operated basically as team players.

In time power became even more widely shared, and the ultimate expansion of the number of power sharers into a full democratic system was in that sense not an unnatural development. As the government grew in size and the original leaders of the Meiji Restoration passed from the scene, the sharing of power between individuals became more the sharing of power among institutions. Under the constitution of 1889 there was a steady shift in the balance of power among a number of groups: at first the *genro* and later their successors as high officials surrounding the throne, the various ministerial branches of the civil bureaucracy, the military, the Diet and its contending parties, big business, and the general public. At first, the *genro* were in ultimate control, though not as fully as they had expected to be. By the 1920s the Diet and the parties were at the center of the balance, and both big business and the general public had increased in power through their influence over the parties. In the 1930s the military, particularly the army, achieved the leading role in the balance and on the eve of the attack on the United States in 1941 concentrated greater power in the hands of General Tojo than any individual had enjoyed for a half century. But even Tojo's authority was that of a group leader, not a dictator, and, when in 1944 the war was seen to be going badly, he meekly left office. Thus an aversion to dictatorial power or even to charismatic leadership and a strong tendency toward group cooperation were pronounced features of Japan's political heritage, helping to open the door to the eventual triumph of a fully democratic system.

Another heritage from the past was the strong orientation of society to formal education and the relatively high levels of literacy in the middle of the nineteenth century. The achievement of universal literacy was a practical immediate goal for a society of this sort, and it in turn made possible much of the technological and economic success of the new Japan. It also underlay the development of a successful mass democracy. The contrast is marked with many modernizing countries today, in which literacy is low to begin with and education must battle countercurrents of apathy or even hostility.

Still another important heritage of the nineteenth-century Japanese was the strong entrepreneurial spirit, which, though basically associated with economic development, also had political implications. Entrepreneurship is not characteristic of feudal societies or most other premodern social systems, but it was marked in Japan by late Tokugawa times. The concentration of the samurai in the capital of the shogun and the castle towns of the lords had freed the countryside from close feudal control and had made the village a largely autonomous entity. The unification of the country into a single economic unit had also given wide scope for commercial activities. The big city merchants, who took advantage of this situation in the seventeenth century, had reached a sort of plateau by the eighteenth, but subsequently rural entrepreneurs developed the main push, processing local agricultural products and then marketing these in other areas. When Japan was opened to foreign trade and the new political system removed most social and economic barriers, great numbers of peasant entrepreneurs were prepared to seize the new opportunities. It was this responsiveness of the Japanese people as much as the efforts of the government that accounted for the economic modernization of Japan.

Successful peasant entrepreneurs as well as affluent peasant landholders also played a large part in the development of demands for popular participation in government. They had enjoyed much actual autonomy in running affairs in their own communities and had also built up a considerable degree of experience, often operating virtually as the lower ranks of the government bureaucracy. Just as they responded in the economic field to the new freedoms of the Meiji reforms, they responded in the political field with demands for a role in political decisions, especially on taxation. The concept of "rights" did not exist in Japan, but the autonomous functions of the peasant leaders came close to being such rights, and they were not prepared to relinquish them. Many members of the samurai class who had lost their feudal privileges and been frozen out of power in the new system naturally were eager to regain their old position or win back a share in power by other means. Their agitation and occasional revolts are not surprising, but more noteworthy is the fact that already in the 1870s peasants were joining them in a demand for a share of political power. Thus the concepts of popular rights and political participation were not just strange foreign ideas but grew spontaneously out of conditions within Japan. The terminology used was indeed borrowed from the West, but "the freedom and people's rights movement" that suddenly sprang up grew from Japanese soil and formed the basis for what was eventually to become Japan's sturdy democratic system.

Thus Japan's modern political development has not been marked by the psychic discontinuities that have characterized the development of most of the non-Western world in recent times. Despite some periods of very rapid change, its development has been basically evolutionary rather than revolutionary, giving it a certain degree of stability and suggesting that further changes, whatever they may be, are likely to grow naturally out of conditions within Japan. In any case, there can be no doubt that the Japanese of the nineteenth century, though lacking any background in democracy, did derive from their heritage many qualities and attitudes that contributed directly to the subsequent development of democracy in Japan.

22 *The Emperor*

Japanese have often claimed that the distinctiveness of their nation derives from its unique history in having had only a single reigning family ever since its shadowy protohistoric beginnings. To be sure, the emperors lost actual control of the country around the ninth century, and, after the failure of Go-Daigo to reestablish imperial leadership in 1333, no effort was ever again made to restore actual rule to the emperors. Still, reverence for the imperial line always remained high, and no one before contemporary times ever challenged the concept that all legitimate political authority derived ultimately from the imperial line.

The first great step in the modernization of Japan in the nineteenth century, as we have seen, was justified as being necessary for the "restoration" of imperial rule. For a century and a half there had been growing interest in and respect for the imperial institution, and the groups that overthrew the Tokugawa found the slogan "Honor the emperor and expel the barbarians" a powerful battle cry. Subsequently their control of the emperor proved their strongest weapon. The "restoration" thus brought the emperor back to the center of the political stage, and everything was done in his name, but it never occurred to the new leaders that the emperor should actually rule. A thousand years of reigning but not ruling emperors made this all but unthinkable. And in any case, the Meiji Emperor was only a boy of fifteen in 1868. In time, as he matured, his views and preferences did come to have some weight, but his ministers simply took for granted that they would not only carry out the "imperial will" but would also decide for him what it was. Following Meiji came Taisho (1912–1926), whose mental incapacities made any participation in decision making quite out of the question. All the way up to the end of World War II the Japanese leadership was able to combine an extreme reverence for the emperor with a complete willingness to force decisions on him regardless of his own wishes. The one great concern of the Japanese leaders at the time of surrender in 1945 was the future status of the emperor. This combination of awed respect for the emperor and callous manipulation of his person is hard for non-Japanese to comprehend.

This curious dual attitude toward the emperor was embodied in the 1889 constitution. In drawing up this document, Ito quite frankly sought in the imperial institution the underlying spiritual force that he believed Christianity provided for constitutional government in the West. Lacking Christianity or any other suitable religion, Japan, Ito felt, would have to find its spiritual unity through reverence for the throne. The constitution thus called the emperor "sacred and inviolable" and emphasized the continuity of the imperial line "unbroken for ages eternal." Sovereignty and all powers of government were assigned to the emperor, but under conditions that ensured that others would make the actual decisions. His powers seem unlimited when we read that "the Emperor determines the organization of the different branches of the administration . . . has the supreme command of the Army and Navy . . . [and] declares war, makes peace, and concludes treaties." But then we also learn that he "exercises the legislative power with the consent of the Imperial Diet" and only "gives sanction to laws and orders them to be promulgated and executed." "All Laws, Imperial Ordinances, and Imperial Rescripts . . . require the countersignature of a Minister of State," and judicial powers are to "be exercised by the Courts of Law, according to law" and only "in the name of the Emperor."

The ambiguity regarding the powers of the emperor led to no misunderstandings. None of the three modern emperors made any real effort to assert his own will against the decisions of his ministers. Emperor Showa (Hirohito) is known to have chafed at the actions of the military in his early years and to have attempted to get reconsideration of the steps leading to war, but the only political decision he himself made, though at the urging of his closest advisers, was when his ministers in August 1945 pointedly presented him with a tied vote on surrender and he opted for accepting the Allied ultimatum.

The framers of the Meiji system were entirely successful in making the imperial institution into an effective symbol of national unity. A fervent reverence for the emperor was inculcated in the whole nation. This attitude, backed up by the cult of "state Shinto," reemphasized the aura of divinity that had always surrounded the throne. Common people were not supposed to look at the emperor directly. His pictures in all the schools of the nation were treated as holy icons and were housed if possible in separate little shrines, constructed in later years of concrete in order to prevent their being burned in some conflagration. All Japanese in theory lived merely to repay the emperor's "benevolence," and millions of soldiers were willing to die abroad in his name. One is reminded of the cult of the national flag that is to be found in other modern countries, but the devotion of the prewar Japanese to the emperor as their symbol of national unity was probably the most extreme example of this modern nationalistic phenomenon.

The shapers of the Meiji system were less successful in achieving through the imperial cult the spiritual unity Ito had sought. Except for a few radicals in the twentieth century, no one, not even the party men in the Diet, disputed the duty of the government to put into effect the "imperial will," but there was little agreement over what the "imperial will" actually was. High officials around the throne felt that they were best able to interpret it, and at first they were able to override opposition by claiming imperial support for their views, but as early as 1913, in the so-called Taisho political change, they discovered that the Diet would no longer knuckle under to this sort of pressure. The politicians felt that the "imperial will" was to be discovered through the voice of the people as shown in elections. Militarists and extreme nationalists believed that only they understood the "imperial will." No one thought of asking the emperor himself. As we have seen, Professor Minobe's liberal interpretation that the emperor was an "organ" of the constitution, which was accepted by most well-educated people in the 1920s, was declared lese majesty in 1935. The military, by then in the saddle, repeatedly tried to clarify the *kokutai,* or "national polity," by which was meant the emperor-centered Japanese system, but the results were always mystical and vague.

The basic ambiguity of the constitution on the role of the emperor also left a dangerous vacuum at the center of the government. All power stemmed from the emperor, but he exercised no power. It was not clear how the chief ministers who acted in place of the emperor were to be chosen. The system for their selection, in fact, varied over time and was never clearly defined. At first, the choice was largely the decision of the "elder statesmen"; then it became a consensual decision among leadership elites, in which party power in the Diet was the biggest factor; and finally the consensual decision came to be swayed basically by the military. The emperor's "supreme command of the Army and Navy" was in time reversed to signify the independence of the military from the civil government and, ultimately, their control over the emperor. The disastrous consequence of this particular ambiguity we have already seen.

The postwar constitution of 1947 has cleared up all these problems. The emperor is defined as "the symbol of the State and of the unity of the people, deriving his position from the will of the people with whom resides sovereign power." The emperor's functions are described as purely symbolic, and it is expressly stated that the emperor "shall not have powers related to government." To make the point still clearer the constitution adds that "the advice and approval of the Cabinet shall be required for all acts of the Emperor in matters of state, and the Cabinet shall be responsible therefor." "State Shinto" was abolished, and the emperor, on January 1, 1946, issued a statement denying his own divinity—largely to please the American occupation authorities, to whom "divinity" meant a great deal more than it did to most Japanese. The emperor continues to perform certain traditional Shinto ceremonies but these are officially defined as having no religious significance. The Imperial Household Ministry, which handled the affairs of the imperial family, was reduced to the rank of an agency in the prime minister's office, imperial finances were drastically cut and put with the rest of the budget under the control of the Diet, imperial properties were transferred to the state, and the imperial family was limited to the emperor's immediate family and those of his three brothers. Even Emperor Showa's married daughters were classed as commoners.

The emperor who himself underwent this great change in roles was Hirohito, now posthumously known as Showa (reigned 1926–1989), who occupied the throne longer than any of his forebears in historical times. He adjusted to his newly defined role with an apparent sense of relief, obviously being more at ease in civilian clothes, playing a symbolic role for his civil government and its people, than he had ever been before the war, dressed in military uniform astride his white charger reviewing his conquering armies. The role better fit his personality as a shy but friendly and sincere individual, a model family man, and an enthusiastic marine biologist.

Much more important than the emperor's personal reaction is the response of the Japanese people to this great theoretical change in the imperial institution. They appear to have accepted it with ease and approval, for it finally brought theory into line with reality. A tiny fringe

The Imperial Family in June 1993. Standing behind Emperor Akihito and Empress Michiko are, from left to right, Princess Sayoko, a 1992 graduate in Japanese Literature from Gakushuin University, Prince Naruhito, invested as crown prince after his return from Oxford University in 1991, and Crown Princess Masako, a graduate of Harvard who also studied at Oxford, and Prince and Princess Akishino. *(Courtesy Japan Information Center)*

of old-fashioned nationalists still call for a restoration of the old *koku-tai,* whatever that was, and for a couple of decades after the war the more conservative politicians advocated the restoration of theoretical "sovereignty" to the emperor, but neither issue has any meaning for the great majority of Japanese. Older Japanese continue to have a sense of reverence for the emperor, and large numbers of rural folk showed their devotion by contributing their services to the upkeep of the extensive imperial palace grounds in Tokyo. Most people, however, have only rather vague feelings of respect or affection for the emperor, and many, particularly young people, are quite indifferent. But there is no substantial antiemperor movement either. At present not even the Communist Party calls for the abolition of the throne. Favorable interest in the imperial family was revived even among younger Japanese when the crown prince in 1959 married a charming daughter of a businessman, who was a commoner even by prewar standards. The fact that the young couple had met on the tennis courts and fallen in love was appealingly modern and democratic. She was a graduate of Seishin ("Sacred Heart") University. Akihito's son continued the tradition of love marriages to commoners when the crown prince married the daughter of a diplomat in 1993. Emperor Showa had visited England when crown prince, something quite unprecedented at the time; his son, Emperor Akihito, visited many countries as crown prince, but Crown Prince Naruhito had studied at Oxford and his bride was a graduate of Harvard. Thus the imperial family, like the rest of Japan, was becoming steadily more international.

All in all, the postwar imperial institution had come to parallel closely the pattern for modern kingship already established by the mature democracies of northern Europe. Entirely divorced from politics, the imperial family serves as a symbol of national unity, a token of stability, and a comforting emotional link with the past. Any use of the throne that could in any way be interpreted as bearing on politics meets with vigorous protest, but otherwise the imperial institution seems to be generally accepted as a permanent, noncontroversial embellishment of the national scene. This form of monarchy appears to be a congenial pattern for countries like Japan and those of northern Europe, which are monarchies that have achieved their democratic systems largely through evolutionary rather than revolutionary means.

23 *The Diet*

The 1947 constitution not only stripped the emperor of all claim to political power but also made clear where actual power did lie—in the hands of the Diet, or parliament. The Diet had already evolved a long way before World War II. In the 1889 constitution, the Meiji leaders had set it up to be a partially elected national assembly that was expected to win the respect of the Western nations, solidify the support of the common people, and serve as a harmless safety valve for discontent. They had preceded this daring innovation with various local experiments in elected bodies, starting with prefectural assemblies in 1878 and following these with village, town, and city ward assemblies in 1880 and then city-wide assemblies in 1888. These local assemblies as well as the new national Diet had only very limited powers and were elected by an extremely restricted electorate. Only adult males over twenty-five years of age and paying fifteen yen or more in taxes had the franchise in Diet elections. This amounted in 1890 to merely 1.26 percent of the population. Only about 6 percent of the population belonged to enfranchised families, about the same percentage as the old samurai class; but this enfranchised elite was made up largely of peasant landowners and businessmen.

Although imperial ordinances could be issued between sessions of the Diet, the "consent" of that body was necessary for a law to remain permanently on the books, and the budget and all taxes specifically required action by the Diet. Many acts of the government, as in foreign affairs, were not felt to require laws and therefore Diet approval, but financial matters were considered its special prerogative, because the money, after all, came as taxes from the people. But even here, the government sought to protect itself from popular control by the constitutional provision that, if the Diet failed to act on the new budget, "the government shall carry out the Budget of the preceding year." This supposed trump card to prevent Diet control over the purse strings was borrowed from the Germans and was agreed upon for the new constitution as early as 1881.

The powers of the popularly elected House of Representatives in the Diet were also restricted by a House of Peers, modeled on the British House of Lords and given power equal to that of the lower house. To man this House of Peers, as we have seen, the government in 1884 created a new peerage, made up of the old court nobility, the former feudal lords, and some of the new leaders. The upper ranks of this nobility were all members of the House of Peers, but the lower three ranks elected a limited number of members, and there were in addition imperial appointees, mostly of a scholarly nature, and one member elected from each prefecture by those paying the highest taxes. A body so constituted was obviously an extremely conservative check on any action by the lower house.

Despite all these precautions, the Diet proved extremely unruly and succeeded in rapidly expanding its powers and broadening the electorate. Starting with the experience gained in local elections after 1878, the popular parties swept every national election from the inception of the Diet in 1890 up until World War II. Even in the infamous second election of 1892, when the government leaders freely resorted to bribery and police suppression, their parliamentary supporters fell far short of winning a majority. And the prized budgetary trump card proved almost valueless. In a rapidly growing economy, last year's budget was never enough. The annual battle to get the budget through the Diet became so disagreeable and difficult that some of the government leaders even suggested that the Diet should be abolished, but they were overruled by the others, who feared that such an admission of defeat in attempted modernization would humiliate Japan before the West and endanger the prospects for getting rid of the unequal treaties.

A compromise was worked out, at first tentatively in the latter half of the 1890s and then more permanently after 1900, between the government leaders and the Seiyukai, the party Ito himself founded in 1900 by uniting his own bureaucratic following with the political stream deriving from Itagaki. In return for support in the Diet, the Seiyukai would get some say on national policies and a few cabinet posts and other plums. The balance shifted over time. The Seiyukai, and after 1913 a second rival party as well, gained steadily in power, until finally in 1918 Hara, a pure party leader, was selected as prime minister basically because of the plurality of his Seiyukai party in the House of Representatives. For the next fourteen years, except for a brief period from 1922 to 1924, all the prime ministers were party leaders, selected on the basis of their party support in the Diet, and the cabinets, except for the army and navy ministers, consisted mostly of party men.

Meanwhile, as education spread and Japan modernized itself in other ways, the franchise too was steadily broadened. In 1900 the ballot was made secret and the tax qualification was dropped to ten yen, almost doubling the electorate. In 1919 the qualification was reduced to three yen, this time more than doubling the electorate. About a quarter of the families of Japan now had a member who had the vote. Finally, in 1925 tax qualifications were eliminated entirely, and all adult males were enfranchised.

Thus the Japanese political system in a mere three and a half decades evolved from almost complete authoritarianism to a fair approximation of British parliamentary democracy as that institution existed after the achievement of universal male suffrage in 1867. Of course, in Japan the system was much less securely established than in Britain, as the reversion to military domination was to show in the 1930s. The prime minister might be the president of the majority party in the lower house, but

The Diet building, paradoxically erected in the 1930s during the temporary eclipse of the Diet's powers. (© *Sonia Katchian / Photo Shuttle: Japan*)

his selection as prime minister was not automatic, nor was it made by the Diet itself but by persons acting in the name of the emperor. Moreover, he and the Diet did not have firm control over the army and navy nor even over certain elements in the high bureaucracy. Still, it should be noted that the growth of this parliamentary system, imperfect though it was, had resulted largely from internal evolutionary developments, albeit with an awareness of the British system. It had taken only a small fraction of the time that the growth of British parliamentarianism had required, and the system was to prove strong enough to serve as the basis for a vigorous revival of parliamentary rule after the war.

The Parliamentary system as established under the 1947 constitution is essentially a clarification and improvement of the system that had evolved in Japan by the 1920s. As such it has been easily comprehended by all Japanese and has worked with reasonable efficiency. The chief innovations have been to make the Diet clearly "the highest organ of state power" and "the sole law-making organ" and to give it the power to select the prime minister. He is elected from among the members of the Diet, by the lower house in the event of disagreement with the upper house, and he in turn selects the ministers of his cabinet and the other appointed officials. The lower house of the Diet always has the right to a vote of nonconfidence in the cabinet, in which case the prime minister must resign or else dissolve the lower house and hold new elections in an effort to gain majority support.

Two other important postwar changes in the parliamentary system were the extension of the suffrage to all women as well as men above the age of twenty and the transformation of the nature of the upper house. An entirely elected House of Councillors was substituted for the House of Peers. It is chosen in a different way from the House of Representatives, in the hope of giving it a less narrowly partisan membership. Its 252 members are elected for six-year terms, half every three years. Of these, 152 (increased from 150 in 1972, when Okinawa reverted to Japan) are elected from Japan's forty-seven prefectures. Each prefecture has at least 2 seats in order to have at least one seat contested at each election, and the more populous prefectures have more—Tokyo has 8. The remaining 100 seats are elected by the nation at large. At first this was done on an individual basis, resulting in the election of many show-business celebrities and famous authors, known as *tarento* from the English word "talent," but more recently they have been chosen proportionately from slates put forward by the parties.

The upper house no longer serves as much of a check on the lower house, as it did before the war, and, being entirely elected, it has in any case the same general makeup as the House of Representatives. For all practical purposes, the lower house chooses the prime minister, so far always from among its own members. The budget must be presented first to it, and its action on the budget becomes final in thirty days even if the upper house does not concur but remains in session. This same provision applies also to the ratification of treaties. On all other legislation, the lower house can override a negative vote in the House of Councillors by a two-thirds majority. The only crucial power of the upper house is that a two-thirds vote is required in both houses for an amendment to the constitution, but so far none has been made, just as none was ever made to the 1889 constitution, until a so-called amendment changed it into an entirely new constitution in 1947.

The House of Representatives is very much like its prewar predecessor and functions in much the same way as in the 1920s. In fact, it builds its practices on both prewar and postwar precedents. As before, it is elected

Formal opening session of the Diet, held in the chamber of the House of Councillors in the presence of the emperor, who is seated in the elevated alcove behind the speaker's rostrum. (© *Kaku Kurita / Photo Shuttle: Japan*)

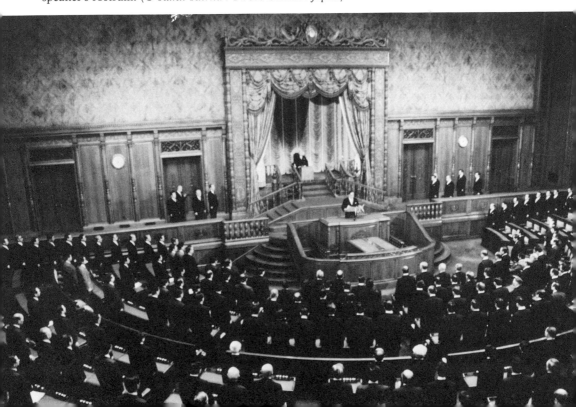

for a four-year term, though commonly it is dissolved by the prime minister before the four years are up at a time politically advantageous to him or his party. The system of elections (see Chapter 25) is also the same unusual one established in the 1925 Diet reform. Even the size of the lower house in the early years after the war was the same 466 members established in 1925, but subsequently it was gradually increased to adjust to shifts in the population, reaching 512 in 1986.

The Diet normally starts serious work in late January and completes action on the budget before the start of the fiscal year in April—a practice that contrasts sharply with the usual failure of the American Congress to vote the budget until the fiscal year is almost half over. Both houses elect their own presiding officers, who have very broad powers, including the right to limit debate in order to avoid filibusters. They also have the right to make committee assignments—each member in both houses can expect at least one such appointment—though in reality these assignments are made by the respective parties, which traditionally are given a number of assignments on each committee corresponding to their strength in that house. In the House of Councillors, committee chairmanships are also given to the various parties in proportion to their strength in that house, but in the lower house all regular committee chairmanships were held by the majority party, until the thinness of its majority in 1977 forced it to share some of them with the opposition. Each house has the same sixteen permanent committees and creates special committees as needed for what are regarded as special issues. The two committees of greatest significance, however, are the Audit Committee, in which wrangles over past government actions draw the close attention of the mass media, and the Budget Committee, which has become the traditional venue for interpellations—that is, the questioning of cabinet members on almost any problem of government.

The whole committee setup is a clear departure from the British parliamentary system and from Japan's own prewar Diet. It originally reflected an effort to bring Japanese parliamentary procedures more in line with American congressional practices, but as such it has not succeeded. The two systems of democracy, presidential and parliamentary, simply do not mix. Since the prime minister and his cabinet, as in the British system, are the creatures of the parliamentary majority and therefore serve as a sort of executive committee for the Diet, the legislature and the executive are not balanced as conflicting political forces, as they are in the American system. The result is that most laws, including all important bills, are drafted not by the Diet but by the bureaucracy in behalf of the cabinet. They are presented by the cabinet to the Diet and are then passed by the same Diet majority that has chosen the prime minister in the first place.

Thus the Diet committees do not carry out the detailed study of proposed legislation or negotiate over it as happens in the United States, but leave these functions to other bodies, primarily committees of the party in power. Instead they perform other functions. The opposition parties can use any of them as well as plenary sessions of the two houses to slow down and attempt to block legislation, thus putting pressure on the majority party to make compromises. The interpellations in the Budget Committee, or in any other committee, also have a major role in politics. Interpellations developed before the war as a feature of Diet activity and correspond to the famous "question time" of the British House of Commons. Members of the opposition pose questions which are meant to embarrass the government and which the cabinet ministers or their bureaucratic representatives do their best to sidestep. Members of the party in power may ask questions designed to allow the cabinet ministers to bring out points they wish to emphasize. Neither sort of question and answer is expected to change a single vote either in the committee or later in the two houses of the Diet. Instead they are all aimed at the mass media and the general public in an effort to build up support and a record for use in the next election. Thus the committee system, designed by Americans for one purpose, has been turned to a very different use that better fits the parliamentary system.

24 Other Organs of Government

The prime minister, as we have seen, is elected by his peers in the lower house of the Diet and is always replaceable by them. As a result, he is incomparably less powerful than an American president, acting more like a chairman of a committee and usually lacking the personal charisma of a man elected by the nation as a whole in the American way. The only postwar prime minister who can be considered autocratic or even strong was "one man" Yoshida Shigeru, who held the post during two periods between 1946 and 1954. The secret of his strength, however, was the absolute authority of the American occupation under which he operated for five of his seven years in office.

Though the prime minister is elected by the lower house, he is in fact chosen by the party convention of the party in power. This has been the Liberal Democratic Party ever since its formation in 1955. Most of the delegates to this convention are party members in the Diet. They elect a party president who then is inevitably elected prime minister by the party's Diet majority. Because of various political contingencies and changing rules for electing party presidents, the terms of office of prime ministers have varied widely: Kishi Nobusuke (1957–1960), Ikeda Hayato (1960–1964), and Sato Eisaku (1964–1972) held the post for relatively long periods. In fact, Sato's seven and a half years were the longest single stretch of any prime minister in Japanese history. The next five men averaged only two years apiece. Two lacked strong support in the Diet; Tanaka Kakuei (1972–1974), who was for many years the most powerful man in the Diet, became implicated in a financial scandal and had to resign; Fukuda Takeo (1976–1978) ran foul of a new regulation (since abandoned) that candidates for party president must first contend in popular primaries and was replaced by the winner in the primaries, Ohira Masayoshi (1978–1980), who unexpectedly died in office.

Nakasone Yasuhiro, who became prime minister in 1982 with Tanaka's strong backing, fulfilled the two two-year terms at present allowed by the party rules and then, because of the party's strong showing in the election of July 6, 1986, was permitted an additional year in office.

The prime minister chooses the members of his cabinet, a majority of whom must be members of the Diet. In practice virtually all are, as in the British system. The only notable exceptions have been Fujiyama Aiichiro, a prominent businessman who was appointed foreign minister in 1957 before being elected a year later to the Diet; Nagai Michio, a university professor turned newspaperman, who was appointed minister of education in 1974; Ushiba Nobuhiko, a former foreign ministry bureaucrat and ambassador to the United States, who was made a special cabinet minister in charge of foreign trade in 1977; and Okita Saburo, a leading economist who became foreign minister in 1979.

Twelve of the cabinet ministers serve as heads of the twelve ministries, of which Finance, International Trade and Industry (MITI), and Foreign Affairs are perhaps the most important. The others, who are ministers without portfolio, normally are the directors of some of the more important subministry organs of government. One is the chief cabinet secretary (*kambo chokan*), who serves as a sort of chief of staff for the prime minister. Another is the director of the Prime Minister's Office (Sorifu), which corresponds to the White House Executive Office. The directors of the Economic Planning Agency, the Defense Agency, and the Science and Technology Agency are also members of the cabinet.

Most cabinet members tend to have much shorter tenures than the prime ministers, frequently being in office for only a year. During this time they can at best establish only a very general policy control over their respective ministries or agencies. The one or two parliamentary vice-ministers or vice-directors assigned from the Diet to the various ministries or agencies are also brief appointees and have no significant functions, though these posts are coveted as building the prestige of their occupants for future Diet elections.

Weak Diet leadership by the ministers leaves the ministries and agencies fairly autonomous and influential. Each is made up basically of a solidly organized, elite corps of career bureaucrats, headed by an administrative vice-minister or vice-director (*jimu-jikan*). He is facetiously called the head of the organization and the minister or agency director is the hat he wears. The situation is much like that found in the various parliamentary systems of Western Europe and contrasts sharply with the

American executive departments, in which secretaries, under secretaries, and many assistant secretaries and lesser officials are presidential appointees who attempt to exercise a strict control in his behalf. The Japanese ministries and agencies thus have a much greater self-identity and political voice than do most American departments or agencies. The chief exceptions to this general rule are the armed services in the United States, which have more self-identity and influence than do other administrative branches of government, and the Defense Agency in Japan, which has notably less than other comparable government organs. Since the ministry bureaucrats serve their whole careers in a single ministry, or else occasionally on loan from it to another ministry or agency or to local governments, each ministry constitutes a sharply defined, permanent group of officials that fiercely defends its prerogatives and powers. While there may be policy conflicts between subdivisions or factional groups within a ministry, each ministry develops its own policies on controversial issues and fights for these in competition with other ministries and even with the party in power.

The contemporary bureaucracy is clearly the inheritor of the high levels of honesty, efficiency, and prestige established by the prewar bureaucracy. The higher civil service is a truly elite corps, which is the cream of the Japanese educational system, drawn from the most prestigious universities, especially Tokyo University, by a selection process of rigorous examinations. Professionally very competent and enjoying security in their positions, these higher civil servants display a self-confidence in their dealings with politicians that would rarely be found in the United States. They are also very dynamic, because the system of early retirement around the age of fifty-five means that the holders of the top positions in all ministries are vigorous men in their early fifties who have had at least two decades of experience in the ministry. Despite their prestige and political power, however, the higher civil servants receive only modest salaries.

At the bottom of the bureaucratic pyramid are the great mass of lesser functionaries in the central administration and local governments and the various categories of specialists, such as professors and teachers in government schools, the police, and workers in the national railways and a few government monopolies, such as tobacco. Some of these categories are selected through examinations, but most achieve their positions on the basis of educational qualifications and past achievements, as is the case in most other modern countries.

The prewar bureaucracy tended to be haughty and to treat the common people with condescension or even contempt. This was particularly true of the police, who were greatly feared as well as respected, but even railway officials tended to strut around in their uniforms. These attitudes were probably survivals of feudal times, when the ruling samurai class monopolized all political power and functions and the phrase *kanson minpi*—"the officials honored, the people despised"—prevailed.

The breakdown in respect for all authority that came with defeat and the postwar collapse, however, seems to have swept such attitudes away. The higher bureaucracy does continue to enjoy considerable prestige, but this is because of its high standards and its very obvious political power. The lower bureaucracy certainly evokes no particular respect and is actually looked upon with the same mixture of exasperation and contempt that Americans and Western Europeans show for the seeming pettifoggery of their own lesser officials. In reality, the minor functionaries of Japan are usually polite and businesslike, drawing on the same fine traditions as the higher bureaucracy, and both groups see themselves and are seen by others not as "officials" in the old sense but as modern public servants.

Japan is divided for purposes of local government into prefectures and these into cities, towns, and villages, with the largest cities being further subdivided into wards. The prefectures, which continue from the prewar system unchanged in size, are actually of four theoretically distinct categories. There are one metropolis (*to*), Tokyo; one circuit (*do*), Hokkaido; two municipal prefectures (*fu*), Osaka and Kyoto; and forty-three regular prefectures (*ken*). To refer to them all together, the Japanese have to use the rather clumsy term *to-do-fu-ken*. Below the prefectural level, local jurisdictions are the product of a long process of amalgamation forced by the central government. Villages are those areas with populations of less than 30,000, towns are areas with populations of less than 50,000, while cities have more than 50,000. All villages are made up of a large number of small natural villages, known as hamlets (*buraku*), and so-called towns and smaller cities usually contain large stretches of countryside and hamlets as well as one or more urban center.

Before the war the powerful Home Ministry appointed the prefectural governors, controlled the police, and exercised close supervision over all local government, in a manner common among the countries of Western Europe. During the occupation, the American authorities were determined to break up this extreme centralization of power and foster greater local autonomy in the American manner. Even before the war, prefectures, cities, city wards, towns, and villages all had elected assemblies, and mayors of cities, towns, and villages were elected officials. After the war these assemblies were all continued and their powers considerably expanded, while governors as well as mayors are now elected. (Postwar Tokyo has no mayor, only a governor.) The Home Ministry was abolished, and its remaining functions were assigned to an Autonomy Agency (later made a ministry), which was comparatively small and weak. Control over the police was assigned to local jurisdictions, and much of the control over education was also transferred from the Ministry of Education to locally elected boards of education.

This effort to develop broad local autonomy, however, was on the whole unsuccessful. The old system of centralized national control was too deeply entrenched and probably fitted better the small size and intense crowding of Japan. Even greater centralization of power, after all, is the pattern in democracies such as the United Kingdom or France. Municipally divided police forces proved impractical in so compact a land, and therefore, after the occupation ended, powers of coordination were restored to the central Police Agency. Fearing that unqualified persons might gain control of elected boards of education, the Japanese also made these bodies appointive and restored much of the supervisory control to the Ministry of Education. Still, many powers remain in the hands of local bodies, and the election of governors, mayors, and prefectural and municipal assemblies breathes life into local Japanese politics, which makes it a strong foundation for national politics.

One serious flaw in the effort to foster greater local autonomy was the failure to provide local governments with an adequate tax base to carry out all the functions permitted them. Since they collect in taxes only 30 percent of the money they need, they have to look to the central government for 70 percent of their budgets. With this money, of course, comes control. It has been estimated that four fifths of the work of local government is actually performed in behalf of ministries of the central government, and many key figures among the local officials are in fact members of the central ministries on temporary loan. There are a number of signs indicating how completely the central government dominates the local ones: much local legislation is based on model legislation suggested by the central government; each prefectural government maintains a large liaison office in Tokyo; and governors and mayors spend a considerable part of their time at the capital, negotiating with the central government. As political interest has shifted somewhat in recent years from international relations and national economic growth to the environment and the quality of life, local issues have gained in relative weight and have enhanced the importance of local government, but even on these issues national policies take precedence over local ones.

The contemporary Japanese judicial system also derives in large part from the prewar judiciary, which despite the authoritarian trends of the time maintained high standards of efficiency, honesty, and independence. The chief innovation of the new constitution in the judicial field was the creation of a Supreme Court in which all judicial power is vested and which nominates the judges for lesser courts and has the right to determine the constitutionality of all laws, in the American manner. The justices of the Supreme Court are appointed by the prime minister, but once appointed they and the judges of lower courts cannot be removed except by formal impeachment procedures or, in the case of Supreme Court justices, by popular vote, since their names appear on the ballot at the first general election following their appointment and then every ten years thereafter. This last provision, however, has proved a dead letter, because Supreme Court justices are not well enough known to stir up more than a trifling opposition vote.

Judicial review by the courts of the constitutionality of legislation is an American innovation that has been inserted into an otherwise purely parliamentary system with somewhat uncertain results. In the British system, nothing can override Parliament, and the Japanese Supreme Court for its part has tended to show a reluctance to go against political decisions of the Diet. It has not sought the vigorous role played by the American Supreme Court in shaping social and political developments but has tended instead to stick to narrow legal decisions and to defer to what the Diet majority has voted.

Though inferior courts, staffed by younger, more liberal judges, sometimes declare laws unconstitutional, the Supreme Court usually overrides them. In 1952 it established that it would not rule on abstract constitutional issues, only on specific problems, and it has tended to take the stand that important political considerations or public welfare interests are paramount. It is on these grounds that the Supreme Court has uniformly ruled against lower courts when they have challenged the constitutionality of the Self-Defense Forces or the Security Treaty with the

United States because article 9 of the constitution renounces forever "war as a sovereign right" and the maintenance of "land, sea and air forces." The effect of such rulings has been to accept the Diet's right to reinterpret the seemingly uncompromising language of the constitution to permit self-defense and the military forces and alliances needed for them. The general public, as seen through popular polls, seems largely to have gone along with this reinterpretation.

The Supreme Court and the lesser courts, however, have proved vigilant watchdogs guarding individual rights as defined in the constitution. No fewer than thirty articles list these "fundamental human rights," which are not restricted by phrases such as "within the limit of the law," as was the case in the 1889 constitution. When in the early 1970s pollution, or rather the broader Japanese concept of public injury (kogai), became a popular issue and doubts grew concerning the validity of the policy of economic growth at any price, it was the courts that, through a number of landmark decisions, established the principle that the pollutor must pay the individuals who are damaged. The most famous of the cases was that of mercury poisoning through marine products at the Kyushu coastal town of Minamata, where the source of the pollution was identified as early as 1959 but a final Supreme Court decision was not handed down until 1978.

Japanese law since the 1890s has been based on the codified law system of continental Europe, rather than the Anglo-American common law system, but it has been greatly liberalized since the war and most of the constitutional safeguards familiar in American law have been introduced. The American adversary system of trial, however, is not followed in the courts. Instead, judges attempt to seek out the facts, and lawyers merely serve as counsel to the parties involved. The use of juries was optional for a period before the war, but, because their verdicts were unpredictable, choosing a jury trial was usually considered tantamount to admitting that one had a poor case. The jury system, therefore, was dropped without objection after the war.

In criminal cases, public prosecutors, or procurators, who correspond to American district attorneys as the representatives of the state's interests, will not bring charges unless they have strong evidence, and, since the reactions of the judge can be predicted with fair accuracy, they have a stunning record of over 99 percent convictions. Plea bargaining is not part of the system, and knowledgeable Japanese are appalled by the American judicial system, which seems to them more a matter of plea bargaining than of justice. Punishments imposed by Japanese courts are on the whole lenient, and judges take into consideration the criminal's attitude of repentance after his crime. A sincere expression of remorse is considered an important first step toward rehabilitation.

Special family courts handle most domestic and juvenile matters, and great efforts are made to settle civil cases through conciliation rather than through formal court procedures. The Japanese, in fact, are not very litigious and prefer arbitration and compromise, turning to the courts only as a last resort. Thus their system does include a large measure of bargaining, but between individuals, not with the court. This approach accords well with Japanese concepts of interpersonal and group relations. Only in cases of traffic accidents, which bring entirely unrelated persons into conflict, has there been a sharp increase in litigation in recent years.

Politically sensitive cases, such as those based on charges of the unconstitutionality of the Self-Defense Forces, on complex issues of damage from pollution, and on the delicate line between rightful political action by demonstrators or strikers and the maintenance of law and order, may drag out for years of complicated trials and appeals, but on the whole the Japanese feel that their courts operate adequately, and there is little of the perception, so common in the United States, that justice is inordinately slow and uncertain. Judges are assumed to be honest and fair. The police are well respected, and the special riot police in particular turn in a magnificent performance in their skillful containment of violence. Most people are law abiding and approve of stringent and strictly enforced regulations that keep both guns and drugs out of the hands of the populace. There is virtually no drug problem, and the number of crimes of violence is markedly lower than it is in the United States. Nowhere in the world is one safer from crime than on the streets of Japan, regardless of the time of day or night. All in all, the Japanese legal and judicial system would rate near the top by any criteria.

With litigation relatively infrequent, the role of lawyers in Japan is much smaller than in the United States. There are fewer than one fifteenth as many lawyers in Japan per capita as in the United States. Lawyers are produced by the same state-operated system that turns out judges and public prosecutors. Graduates of university law faculties are eligible for the government legal examinations that select some hundreds each year for about two years of further training by the Japanese Legal Training and Research Institute, which operates under the direction of the Supreme Court. Successful graduates of this program are then free to choose careers as judges, public prosecutors, or lawyers. In the first two categories they receive prestige as distinguished government officials. As lawyers they may achieve greater financial rewards but, unlike lawyers in the United States, no great social recognition. Lawyers are not only relatively few in number but are largely concentrated in Tokyo and other large cities, where a surprisingly high proportion of their work concerns foreign economic relations. Whereas some two thirds of the members of the American Congress have backgrounds as lawyers, there are few lawyers among the members of the Diet—actually no more than doctors.

Although the Japanese are not very litigious, they are extremely legalistic. They are accustomed to a highly centralized system, overseen by a powerful bureaucracy and carefully regulated according to detailed law codes and myriad bureaucratic rulings. Many of their leaders in the bureaucracy, in business, and in politics are graduates of the law faculties of the universities. Japanese tend to be meticulous in observing the letter of the law. But the central figures in this Japanese legalism are not the lawyers or even the judges but the higher bureaucrats, who are largely the product of legal training, and the masses of petty functionaries who must enforce the law codes and regulations.

25 Elections

Elections, as in any other democracy, are at the heart of the political process in Japan. The Japanese electoral system is a unique one that creates some special problems but also has definite advantages. Governors, mayors, and a few of the members of the House of Councillors are elected in the American fashion, and the 100 members of the upper house who are elected at large are chosen through party slates in a manner common in continental Europe; but the lower house, which is by far the most important political body, the remaining members of the upper house, and the members of the local assemblies are elected by the unique Japanese system in which there are multiple-seat electoral districts but each voter has only a single vote. This system produces a loose sort of proportional representation that is not subject to the sudden large shifts in seats that occur in the Anglo-American system and is also free of the extreme divisiveness of splinter parties found in some of the democracies of continental Europe.

Like so much else in the Japanese government, this system has been inherited from prewar days. There had been a long dispute over the respective merits of the one-man American-type constituency, called in Japan the small electoral district system, and the large electoral district system, in which as many as sixteen persons (in the case of Tokyo) were chosen from a single district. Finally in 1925 the present middle-sized electoral district system was adopted. In accordance with it, the members of the lower house are elected from three- to five-seat districts and about half of the members of the upper house from two- to four-seat districts. The same system is used for prefectural assemblies and those of larger cities, but in villages, towns, and small cities candidates run at large.

In the key lower house elections, close to 20 percent of the vote in a

261

five-seat district will elect a member. This permits a certain degree of proportional representation for minority parties but squeezes out most small splinter groups. It also necessitates a shift of more than 20 percent of the vote to alter a party's strength by more than one seat in a district, making improbable a sudden great change in party strength, as happens all too frequently in the Anglo-American system, in which a political landslide can result from a shift of only a few percentage points in a large number of one-seat, winner-take-all districts. As a consequence, the Japanese Diet is much more stable in makeup than its Anglo-American counterparts and much less fragmented than many of the continental parliaments.

Another strong feature of the Japanese electoral system is that it strikes a healthy balance between party discipline and a close relationship between the members of the Diet and their constituencies. Since in the larger parties candidates contend for votes more with other members of their own party than with those of other parties, whose votes they probably could not attract in any case, they must have strong personal local appeal. They cannot be some worthy of the central party assigned a safe seat, as in the English system, nor are they simply faceless names on a national list, as in some continental systems. They must be, in the American manner, genuine native sons—bona fide local residents or at least hometown products who have made good in the big city. They also need their own local political machines to support them. But this does not mean that they can flaunt party discipline, as is almost the rule in the United States. To have much hope of being elected, they normally require party endorsement, which cannot be achieved independently through local primaries but can be granted only by central party headquarters. This situation ensures party discipline over Diet members despite their individual local power base. Even when a particularly self-confident local candidate bucks the system and is elected as an independent, he normally returns at once to the party and its discipline.

There is a weakness in the system, however, in that it poses special problems for major parties. A small party naturally runs only one candidate in a district, but a large party can hope for more than one seat. However, if it runs three candidates in a district where it has the votes to elect only two, it may so dilute its vote as to end up with only one elected. Similarly, if one of its candidates is too popular and draws an excessive share of the votes, other party candidates will fail of election, though they might have won if the party vote had been more evenly divided.

An even greater weakness of the Japanese electoral system is that there is no automatic method for bringing electoral districts and numbers of seats in line with population changes. After World War II the traditional 466 seats were quite equitably assigned, but since then rural areas have lost population and bigger urban areas gained vastly. Occasional additions of a few seats for urban areas ameliorated the situation only slightly, and a 1976 Supreme Court ruling that the system was unconstitutional as being unequal had no immediate effect. But the subtraction for the first time in 1986 of 7 seats from rural areas and the addition of 8 in urban areas for a total of 512 seats made the situation a little more balanced. Before, the ratio of seats was five to one between the most overrepresented rural district and the most underrepresented urban area, but the reform reduced the discrepancy to three to one. Discrepancies of close to five to one also exist in the value of votes for the members of the House of Councillors elected by prefectures. But, of course, this is trifling compared to the discrepancy of seventy-five to one for members of the powerful American Senate.

The underrepresentation of urban areas, combined with Japan's political history, has given politics a strong rural flavor, which has persisted to some extent to the present day. Japan was a predominantly agrarian society when the electoral system first developed during the 1880s and 1890s, and the tax limitations on the suffrage excluded most city dwellers until after 1925. As a result, rural Japanese have had more experience with elections than their urban compatriots, and even today they vote in higher proportions than do city people. Local elections, at least in rural areas, also draw more interest than national elections, and local issues more attention than national ones. Voting rates in all parts of Japan, however, are far above those for the United States.

Another characteristic of Japanese electoral politics is its intensely personal nature, much like that of the United States and contrasting with the ideological basis for politics in most of Western Europe. This feature is tied in with the closeness of candidates to their constituencies and the group orientation of Japanese society as a whole. Electoral politics started in the nineteenth century with relatively small leader-follower groups, largely rural in makeup and typically Japanese in style. Village groups, led by local "men of power" (*yuryokusha*), tended to vote as blocs on the old assumption of village solidarity and for the sound reason that split votes would cancel each other out and thus weaken local political leverage. Congeries of such blocs would be put together to elect local assemblymen, and pyramids of such groupings to elect a member to the House of Representatives.

A strong political figure might create from these blocs a solid base, called a *jiban*, that would return him to the Diet election after election and might be passed on to a political heir, possibly his son. In return he was expected to produce benefits for the area, such as favorable locations for schools, bridges, railways, and the like. A *jiban* was usually concentrated in one part of an electoral district, which would vote overwhelmingly for its favorite son, leaving other parts of the district as *jiban* for other candidates of the same party.

The system of electoral *jiban* was never very effective in cities, and it has eroded seriously even in rural Japan, especially since the war. Even farming communities no longer vote as blocs. The great numbers of farm residents who work as industrial laborers and the ever-growing presence of outside influences in an age of mass communications have made rural Japanese much more diverse in their political interests and loyalties. Candidates can no longer count on a relatively solid bloc of votes from one particular area and therefore have had to spread their electoral net more widely throughout the district. As the Japanese put it, the old vertical political base has had to become steadily more horizontal. One result of this has been the development by most politicians of large and complex personal support organizations, known as *koenkai*, which attempt to appeal to women, young people, and various interest groups throughout the electoral district.

The activities of the *koenkai* are influenced by severe restrictions on the financing and conduct of elections. Ostensibly designed to discourage corruption and inequities of competition among candidates with differing financial resources, the restrictions are at least in part survivals of prewar rules designed by men unsympathetic to democracy who wished to make it difficult to operate. Electioneering is permitted only during the three to five weeks before the announced date for an election—always on a Sunday. There can be no house-to-house soliciting of votes or any parades or dinners. Only a limited number of posters, advertisements, and brief radio statements and television appearances are allowed. A blaring sound truck is the only overt campaigning freely permitted—with disastrous results for peace and quiet. Campaign funds are limited to entirely unrealistic levels, which are always greatly exceeded by one means or another.

As a result of all these regulations, petty infractions of the rules are frequent, and the *koenkai,* which are actually quite active the year round, are forced to pose as "cultural" groups instead of election organizations. They hold "educational" meetings for their various groups at which the Diet candidate or a supporter appears to give an "educational" speech. The politicians themselves are also endlessly busy cultivating the goodwill of their constituents. They greet them warmly at their offices in Tokyo, make themselves available for public appearances back home, minister as best they can to their personal needs, and drop them endless postcards when traveling abroad. All these activities are very familiar to their American counterparts.

The larger cities do not lend themselves to personalized political relations of this sort. This was true even before the war and has become markedly more so since then. Even in the smaller cities, towns, and rural areas personalized politics has been eroding. It does not fit well with modern ways of life. The *koenkai* no longer can operate very effectively as competing associations increase and neighbors know each other less well. Many persons are likely to reside in one district but have most of their economic and social contacts in another. Since their inception in the 1920s the parties of the left have made their appeal more through ideologies than through personal contacts, and now all the parties are working increasingly through such groups as labor unions, agricultural cooperatives, women's organizations, youth groups, and various pressure groups. The nature of the *koenkai* has gradually shifted with the times, but it is still an important feature of the political process, and personal contacts do remain more important in Japan than in most other industrialized democracies.

26 _Political Parties_

The Japanese political system, as in other democracies, operates through parties. This is true despite the fact that the very concept of a political party was regarded with stern disapproval in premodern Japan. It suggested disharmony or even subversion. Commoners were supposed to have no role in politics and samurai to serve their lords without question. Rival bureaucratic factions, however, had come to be a feature of the politics of both the shogunate and the daimyo domains by late Tokugawa times, and the Meiji Japanese took quickly to the concept of popular parties, though misgivings about their legitimacy did remain strong in some quarters all the way up to World War II.

As we have seen, Itagaki in 1874 started the first political party, which quickly burgeoned into the "freedom and people's rights movement," and Okuma followed with a second party movement in 1882. From these two sources stemmed the two major traditional party currents. That of Itagaki dominated the early Diets under the name of the Liberal Party (Jiyuto, which literally means Freedom Party) and then in 1900 joined with Ito's bureaucratic following to form the Seiyukai (Political Friends Society). It continued to dominate Diet politics and produced in 1918 the first full party prime minister in Hara. After the war it was revived under the name of the Liberal Party.

The other party had more frequent changes of name, becoming in 1927 the Minseito (People's Government Party). It first won a plurality in 1915 and thereafter alternated in power with the Seiyukai, producing Kato as its first party prime minister in 1924. It was revived after the war as the Democratic Party (sometimes called the Progressives). In 1955 it and the Liberals merged to form the Liberal Democratic Party (LDP), or Jiminto, a name that reveals its double origin.

In 1901 an effort was made, largely by Christian idealists, to found a

266

socialist party, but it was immediately suppressed by the authorities. The Communist Party in 1922 was the first of the so-called proletarian parties to be successfully launched, but two years later it was banned, and police pressure on its supporters steadily mounted. Starting in 1925, several short-lived socialist parties were founded, and these groups, insofar as they were tolerated by the police, consolidated into the Social Mass Party in 1932. Both it and the more conservative parties, however, were forced to dissolve in 1940 and enter the officially sponsored Imperial Rule Assistance Association.

Shortly after the end of the war the Communist Party was revived by its few remaining members, who were released from prison or returned from exile in China or the Soviet Union. The Social Mass Party was also resurrected as the Socialist Party, and its popular vote of 19 percent in the 1946 election and 26 percent in 1947 showed a clear extension of its rising popularity before the war, when it won 5 percent of the vote in 1936 and almost 10 percent in 1937. It also showed its prewar divisiveness over ideology, which might be described in simplified terms as the division between those who emphasized socialism over democracy and those who had the reverse priorities. The party split into left and right wings between 1951 and 1955 and then split again in 1960, with the seceding moderates forming the Democratic Socialist Party. Most of Japan's present parties thus have clear prewar antecedents, despite a welter of new parties that flourished briefly after the war. As we have seen, among important existing parties only the Komeito, which was founded by the Soka Gakkai religious group in 1964 after a decade of dabbling in elections, is a purely postwar phenomenon.

In prewar elections, which were dominated by rival voters less concerned with national politics than with local issues, personal knowledge of a candidate usually meant much more than his party label. In fact, most local politicians ran simply as independents. There is a strong though dwindling carryover of these conditions even today in local politics. The smaller and more rural the electoral unit, the more likely it is that a candidate will run as an independent, but in larger urban units a party label is more necessary. Governors and mayors offer a special case. In the larger urban areas, where the conservative LDP is not likely to have a majority and no opposition party is big enough to elect its candidates by itself, governors and mayors are commonly the nominees of a coalition of parties and call themselves independents.

The rural background of the LDP and its diverse origins have left it somewhat amorphous in composition and vague in ideology, but this has served on the whole as an asset rather than a liability. The parties of the left, particularly the Communists and Socialists, have restricted their appeal by their clear-cut party platforms, but, bowing to this fact, they have tended in recent years to back away from their original doctrinaire Marxist stands. The Socialists depend heavily on the more radical Sohyo federation of labor unions, made up largely of white-collar workers and government employees. The Democratic Socialists depend on the more moderate Domei federation of blue-collar unions. The Komeito has its own solid core of Soka Gakkai believers. But all three of these bases tend to detract from their respective appeals to other voters.

Despite an amazing continuity of voting trends in Japan, most voters prefer to consider themselves political independents. For them, the diversity and personal approach of the LDP are more effective than firm ideologies. The resulting loose mix of moderates and conservatives that constitutes the party gives it a desirable flexibility of action and an ability to win votes from many different types of voters. In its comprehensiveness and amorphousness the LDP resembles the two major American parties more than any others among the advanced democracies.

Except for the Communists and possibly the Komeito, none of the parties has a grass-roots membership at all commensurate with its voting strength. As organizations, they are largely made up of Diet members, members of local assemblies, and professional party workers. This situation has given rise to the joke that the LDP is a ghost party with a head but no feet. In fact, it has a very strong grass-roots base through the *koenkai* of its Diet members and the local rural politicians, who are often stalwart LDP supporters even though some may call themselves independents.

Despite the tremendous upheaval in Japanese society resulting from the disastrous war, the American occupation, and the years of dire poverty following the war, Japanese voters have remained surprisingly constant in their loyalties. The two traditional parties that had dominated politics before the war continued to do so after it. Their rural backbone gave them a conservative coloration according to modern standards. This phenomenon is not surprising given that rural populations everywhere tend to be conservative. They did less well in the big cities, which grew enormously following the war. The two traditional parties were forced to merge as the LDP in 1955 to offset the rising vote of the parties of the left. The shift from right to left was basically demographic and only incidentally ideological.

In its first election for the lower house in 1958, the LDP won 59 percent of the votes and 61.5 percent of the seats, but thereafter its vote slowly declined to 42 percent by 1976. Because the splitting of the opposition vote could be counted on to give the LDP a slightly higher percentage of seats than votes and a few independents always joined the party immediately after an election, it maintained its absolute majority in the lower house of the Diet, and on the few occasions when it did not, the tacit or formal support of some centrist party, for a while the New Liberal Club, which broke away from the LDP from 1976 to 1986 as a splinter group, kept it in power.

Since 1976 the LDP has recovered somewhat. In 1986 it won 49.4 percent of the votes and a resounding majority of 300 seats out of 512. Its particularly good showings in 1980 and 1986 were widely attributed to the scheduling together of "double" elections for the lower house and half of the upper house, but this was probably not the reason. The LDP victories were probably due more to the fading attraction of Marxism even in the cities, the public's general satisfaction with LDP policies, and, in 1986, to the charismatic appeal of the prime minister, Nakasone, who cut a more impressive figure than did other politicians both abroad and on television at home. The influence of this last factor, if indeed it exists, suggests the appearance of a new and not necessarily desirable feature in Japanese politics. In the past the prime ministers have been the politicians' rather than the people's choice, and this may well be preferable to choosing prime ministers through "beauty contests" by television.

The second largest party since the founding of the LDP has been the Socialists. They garnered 33 percent of the vote in 1958 and were commonly expected one day to supersede or to alternate in power with the LDP. They have failed, however, to live up to expectations. Their popular vote declined slowly to 22 percent in 1972 and then plunged to 13.4 and 17 percent in 1980 and 1986 respectively. The Democratic Socialists, while accounting for some of the decline of the Socialists, have themselves had a lackluster record, slipping slowly from 9 percent in 1960 to 6.4 percent in 1986. The Communists have had a more erratic record. They reached a low point of 1 percent in 1955 but rose to 11 percent in 1976 before declining to 8.8 percent in 1986. The Komeito, in its shorter history since 1967, reached a high point of 11 percent of the vote in 1969 but tapered off to 9.4 percent in 1986.

Taken together, the four main opposition parties could balance the

LDP; they actually outvoted it in every election from 1971 to 1983. But the historical and ideological divisions between the Communists and Socialists and between the two of them and the centrist parties—the Democratic Socialists and the Komeito—run too deep to make an effective coalition among them a possibility.

Since the LDP has been in power for more than three decades, it deserves special attention. Its heart is its Diet membership, which makes up the majority of the delegates at its national convention, where they elect the party president, who then is inevitably chosen by the party's Diet majority as the prime minister. To exercise strong control in the Diet, however, the party must maintain strict discipline over its members. Judging from American experience, this might seem difficult to do, since all the members, as in the United States, are elected on their own personal appeal with the aid of their own *koenkai* support organizations. But despite this situation the Japanese succeed very well in maintaining strict party discipline. Their skill in acting in groups is probably one reason for this achievement. Another is the history of the two traditional parties that formed the LDP. Before the war they were united in their fight to achieve parliamentary government against the antidemocratic forces and since the war by their defense of traditional political democracy and economic free enterprise against the largely Marxist opposition, collectively known as the "progressive" parties. Another factor is the individual Diet candidates' need for official endorsement from party headquarters and also for financial aid to have much chance of being elected. Once in the Diet, members also have little hope of political plums unless they adhere strictly to party discipline. Such plums, which might improve their chances for reelection, are assignments to cabinet or subcabinet posts, committee chairmanships, and influential positions in the party organization. The ultimate prize of the prime ministership, of course, would be unattainable for anyone who had not been strictly faithful to the party. In the United States, where the whole system works quite differently, a congressman who on occasion flaunts party policy is almost the rule; in Japan such a person is virtually unknown.

Until the end of Sato's term as prime minister in 1972, most prime ministers were former long-term ministry bureaucrats, and Fukuda and Ohira were later men of the same stripe. Such persons, who had the advantage of extensive government experience, managed to take the party leadership away from the professional politicians after the war. But starting with Tanaka in 1972, there have been more faction leaders and prime ministers with little or no apprenticeship in the bureaucracy before entering politics, and given the present membership of the Diet this will increasingly become the case.

Despite the strong solidarity of the LDP, one of its outstanding features is its division into a number of factions—usually some four or five major ones at any given time, ranging in size between 40 and 100 members in the two houses together. These factions are typically Japanese leader-follower groups, centering on some particularly powerful Diet member who hopes to use his faction as the base for his bid for the party presidency and prime ministership. A grouping of two or more factions is usually necessary to achieve this goal, giving rise to "mainstream" and "antimainstream" divisions within the party.

The lesser members of the Diet are happy to join factions for a number of reasons. It fits their propensity for operating in relatively small groups. Factional backing at party headquarters is also helpful in winning designation as one of the restricted number of party candidates, and extra financial aid for elections is likely to be forthcoming from the head of a faction. Once in the Diet, the new member finds the informal factional club a good schoolroom for learning the ways of the Diet, and factional support is needed to win any of the Diet or party plums of office. Only a few Diet members refuse to join factions, and they usually have little personal success, especially in the lower house.

The factions are almost universally condemned, and announcements of their imminent dissolution are periodically made, but nothing of the sort ever happens. They are simply too natural and useful a device for running the party to be done away with. Charges that they are a divisive element in the LDP, making the party in reality merely an association of miniparties, simply are not true. Even though their leaders may lean politically in differing directions, the membership of all the factions is likely to hold views that cover the whole broad spectrum of attitudes within the party. For important controversial issues, not factions but special study groups drawn from all the factions are likely to serve as the main pressure groups.

Personal rivalries over high positions and controversial policies are of course inevitable, but factions are not the source of such divisiveness. Instead they are considered as good a way as any—and one particularly suited to Japanese methods of operation—for reaching a party consensus on a prime minister or controversial legislation. Junior party members can air their opinions better in such smaller groups than in a caucus of the party as a whole; the faction leaders can more easily achieve a consensus on the basis of the views of their respective faction members than could a meeting of the whole party; and the multiplicity of factions allows for a greater flexibility in policy and, incidentally, more breadth of voter appeal than would a tightly knit party. It may not be an exaggeration to assert that the factional structure of the LDP is probably a major reason why the party has remained in power for more than three decades, and there is good reason to believe that factions will continue to play their present role for some time to come.

The organization of the other parties is in general much like that of the LDP. Their Diet members play a key role, and a national convention made up of them and the local party leaders chooses the head of the party, usually called a secretary general. Only the Socialists are large enough to have factions, but these are divided more by ideology than by personality. In fact, the division within the Socialist Party between leftist ideologues and more pragmatic moderates is probably the deepest cleavage in Japanese politics. The national conventions of both the Communist and Socialist parties tend to the extreme left under the leadership of ideological intellectuals and labor leaders, but the parties swing back toward the center when faced with the realities of an election. Labor union men have a disproportionate influence in the Socialist and Democratic Socialist parties, constituting a large part of their leadership and Diet membership. The Communists and Komeito exert an even stricter control over their Diet members than do the LDP and the other parties.

None of the opposition parties shows any promise of replacing the LDP, and only the Democratic Socialists and Komeito seem capable of a constructive association with each other or with the LDP. If the LDP were to lose its preponderance, the most likely result would be the incorporation of one or both of these parties into a partnership with the LDP.

27 The Decision-Making Process

The legislative process in Japan is much like that of the United Kingdom and most other parliamentary democracies, differing considerably from that of the United States because of the concept of the division of powers in the American presidential system. The prime minister and his cabinet act as a sort of executive committee for the Diet, not as a balancing power with Congress. They oversee the preparation of most bills, which they present to the Diet for virtually certain passage. The Diet subjects the proposed legislation to scrutiny and votes on it both in committees and in plenary sessions, but rarely makes major changes.

This system means that most political decisions are made, not in the Diet, but within the party in power, where a great deal of preliminary work goes into a bill before it is presented to the Diet. As a consequence, the party organization must represent the whole party fairly and have a structure more or less parallel to that of the Diet. When an LDP president is chosen at a regular convention or following the resignation or death of a prime minister, his selection is usually accompanied by agreements on several other key party and cabinet positions, carefully balanced to give each faction a fair share of posts, held by either the faction leaders themselves or their leading henchmen.

Next in importance to the president (and prime minister) in the LDP hierarchy is the secretary general (*kanjicho*), who supervises the party organs. The chief of these are an Executive Council, an Election Policy Committee, which has the important task of designating candidates for Diet elections, and the Policy Research Committee (known in Japanese by its shortened name, Seichokai). All these groups are made up in such a way as to represent the balance of factions in the Diet.

The drafting of legislation normally starts with proposals by various groupings in the bureaucracy and negotiations by them with the sub-committees of the Policy Research Committee that have responsibility for the problems concerned. Each Diet member of the party is a voting member of one such subcommittee, but all Diet members can attend the meetings of any subcommittee and speak their minds freely. The proposed legislation produced by the various subcommittees together with the bureaucrats is then submitted first to the Policy Research Committee as a whole and then to the Executive Council for emendations and approval, after which it is submitted to the cabinet. There it is passed to the Council of Administrative Vice-Ministers for a final vetting by the bureaucracy to avoid conflicts or inconsistencies with other legislation. The cabinet then makes its final judgment on the bill before presenting it to the Diet for action. After this careful preparation, most legislation naturally is passed without significant change by the LDP's Diet majority. When insoluble difficulties are encountered down the line, the decision may be referred to the Executive Council, to informal negotiations among the faction leaders or chief party officers, or even to the prime minister himself, but this is rarely required. The whole process is reminiscent of the normal decision-making process throughout Japanese society, in which consensus is sought throughout and the initiative often starts in the lower echelons of the leadership group. Given such a procedure, strongly unified support is to be expected when the Diet finally votes a bill into law.

While the party in power is the key actor in the legislative process, other elements of society do have a role in political decisions. As we have seen, the various elements of the bureaucracy do most of the original drafting of bills, and 70 percent of their drafts receive eventual enactment, compared to 30 percent of those offered by individual members of the Diet, and almost none by opposition parties. An example of the power of the bureaucracy can be seen in the way in which the budget is drawn up. Each ministry or agency prepares its own budget, usually somewhat higher than that for the previous year but apportioned among its various branches in much the same way as the year before. The Finance Ministry in making the final budget proposal attempts to maintain the old balance among the ministries and agencies, though of course with some deference to the current views of the prime minister and other members of the LDP as well as to public opinion.

Other important forces in the decision-making process are outside pressure groups. Many political commentators have thought of these primarily in terms of big business, which was extremely influential during Japan's rapid rise to economic power and also happens to be the chief source of funding for the LDP. A picture has been built up of a country run by a tightly knit triumvirate: the LDP, which is financially under the control of big business; big business, which in turn is under the control and patronage of the bureaucracy; and the bureaucracy, which in turn depends on the legislative power of the party in order to operate. This symbiotic relationship was seen as being strengthened by the Japanese practice facetiously called *amakudari,* or "descent from heaven," in which after their retirement influential ex-bureaucrats and sometimes ex-politicians are given respectable, relatively lucrative, but not very taxing positions in business, often in the very industries over which they exercised control while in office.

The concept of an establishment triumvirate had some validity at an earlier time, when all three groups were chiefly concerned with Japan's economic growth and therefore concentrated on helping one another promote it. But this alliance has faded considerably in recent years. Economic growth is no longer the only priority concern of the LDP and bureaucracy, and as a consequence big business looms less overwhelmingly in their policies. Other conflicting interests, such as pollution and foreign affairs, have become rival concerns. Moreover, big business now supports the LDP's finances less exclusively; it also contributes to some of the other parties, though these derive their main incomes from other sources—the Socialist, Democratic Socialist, and Communist parties from labor unions, the Komeito from the Soka Gakkai religious movement, and the Communists from their very successful party newspaper, *Akahata* (Red Flag). The bureaucracy has relinquished much of its detailed control over big business. As a result of these changes, big business has become freer of bureaucratic controls but has also lost much of its political influence and is now simply one among many external forces that play a role in political decisions.

The Japanese political process, however, can still be viewed as three-sided. The bureaucracy supplies the expertise and administrative continuity; the party in power makes the final political decisions; and the general voting public and a mass of pressure groups bring influences to bear upon the party's decisions and the bureaucracy's attitudes.

Among the outside forces the voting public is the most important because it determines the party or parties in control of the Diet. Among the pressure groups big business is undoubtedly still the most powerful, but there are also many other strong groups, such as the farmers' cooperatives, the Japan Medical Association and many other professional and business groups, the Teachers Union and various federations of labor, women's organizations, and, in recent years, a great number of single-issue "citizens' movements" and "local residents' movements." These bring pressure directly on the bureaucrats concerned, the subcommittees of the Policy Research Committee, the various political parties as a whole, and, through the mass media, on Diet proceedings when these finally take place. The great newspapers also must be recognized as important shapers of public opinion. The government for its part attempts to draw on the knowledge and views of the public and to communicate its viewpoints in return through a great number of advisory boards (*shingikai*) attached to the various ministries and agencies.

The role of the opposition also should not be overlooked. The general desire in Japan for consensus agreements and the resulting popular dissatisfaction with narrow majority decisions on important matters give the opposition parties more influence than in most other democracies, where their minority position leaves them quite helpless. Debate in the Diet offers them a final opportunity to block undesirable legislation through delaying tactics or even the boycotting of sessions, and such disruptive tactics find support in the mass media and mass demonstrations in the streets. If the LDP were to use its perennial majority to ram through many hotly contested bills without allowing time for full debate, its action would be seen as undemocratic and would run the risk of stirring up public demonstrations to the point of civil disorder, as happened in 1960. At the least it would cut into the LDP's vote at the next election. As a result, the LDP limits the number of important controversial bills presented in any one session. Three or four such bills tend to be seen as the maximum advisable. A good case in point is the proposal that the Defense Agency be raised to a Defense Ministry. The LDP has long wished to do this and, of course, has the votes, but year after year the bill is shelved as being more symbolic than substantive and therefore to be sacrificed for some more meaningful legislation.

Severe clashes over legislation were characteristic of the politics of the 1950s, but since then they have become noticeably less frequent and less bitter. One reason for this is that the LDP politicians have learned to confer both with the opposition parties and with concerned pressure groups in drawing up proposed legislation in an effort to make it as acceptable to them as possible. As a result, close to two thirds of the bills voted by the Diet are passed unanimously. If meaningful changes are going to be made in legislation by the opposition, they are much more likely to occur in advance through quiet negotiations with the LDP rather than through Diet debates and votes. Somewhat the same situation exists in the British Parliament, but the British put great store on forensic skills and love to display them in Parliament even in essentially meaningless debates. The Japanese, having less respect for verbal skills, tend to limit their Diet debates to embarrassing questions and evasive answers, with the effect on the next election chiefly in mind.

In summary, we can conclude that the political process in Japan, though extremely complex, is reasonably effective and seems well adapted to Japanese styles of interpersonal relations. It is flexible and thorough but inevitably slow. It probably accords more veto power to minority opposition groups and therefore produces more compromises than most other democratic systems. Its most basic procedures are conducted largely out of sight in negotiations and informal consultations among bureaucrats, party organs, opposition parties, and pressure groups. What is most clearly visible may not be very attractive to Westerners' ideas of how a democratic government should conduct itself. There is little enlightening Diet debate but instead considerable disruptive activity in the Diet and a certain amount of mass confrontation in the streets. Concentrating only on these visible portions of the process, foreigners have often come to uncomplimentary conclusions about the quality and effectiveness of the Japanese political process. But when compared with the wild scramble every four years in the United States to choose presidential nominees and the continuous jockeying for votes in the American Congress, the Japanese system is in fact very orderly and efficient. It is unlike the other advanced democracies in certain respects, but it operates quite smoothly and appears to be as efficient as any other system in translating the will of the electorate into political actions by the government.

28 *Issues*

Japanese politics ever since the war have been character-ized by a sharp division between the Liberal Democratic Party and its predecessors on the one side and the "progressive" parties, largely of Marxist background, on the other. This cleavage grew out of prewar and wartime conditions. At that time the predecessors of the LDP, though representing the democratic elements in government, were none-theless part of the establishment and were heavily based on rural and small-town Japan. The predecessors of the "progressive" parties, on the other hand, represented urban intellectuals and labor, who espoused in various degrees fundamental social and political change along Marxist lines and were as a result severely suppressed by the government. The whole prewar and wartime experience left these people and their sym-pathizers extremely suspicious of all authority and deeply resentful of anything that might indicate government insensitivity to the rights and interests of ordinary citizens. They were convinced that the LDP was seeking to restore prewar conditions. After all, one LDP prime minister, Kishi, had actually been a member of Tojo's wartime cabinet. The LDP in turn feared that the "progressive" parties would attempt revolution-ary reforms that would sweep away free enterprise and democracy and bring the country to chaos.

The dichotomy in postwar Japanese politics was sharpest in the early years and diminished only as the country became increasingly stable and prosperous, the new system fostered by the American reforms became accepted by both sides, and both gradually learned that they had less to fear from each other than they had thought. At first, when mutual ani-mosities were greatest, armed conflict and chaos were definite possibili-ties, but the overwhelming presence of the American army and Mac-Arthur's dictatorial power fortunately prevented this from happening.

278

Members of the special riot police (Kidotai, or "Mobile Unit"), protectively outfitted with shields and medieval-looking helmets, confront rioters in hard hats and armed with staves. (*Kyodo News International*)

Large-scale demonstrations and occasional violence did occur, and the opposition became accustomed to challenging vehemently almost anything the party in power proposed. Even seemingly small or technical issues were fought over with a fury that baffled the outside observer. This bitter political divisiveness, which still lingers on to some extent today, stood out strangely in a society characterized by consensus and harmony. But the period of greatest danger passed without any widespread disorders, and gradually the situation settled down to a prolonged political battle within the bounds of the new constitution.

Since the LDP had the support of big business and the relatively conservative rural voters while the opposition parties based themselves largely on Marxist ideology, one might imagine that basic Marxist concepts would be the main area of controversy, but this has not been the case. The Marxist appeal to class divisions never really caught on in Japan and in time became meaningless in its virtually classless society. A slogan such as "the dictatorship of the proletariat" merely had the distasteful ring of authoritarian systems of the past. In the field of economics, too, the opposition parties were never able to formulate a clear challenge to the conservatives. By the time Japan recovered its independence in 1952, economic recovery had begun, and soon it was racing at such a speed that the opposition could offer no plausible substitute for what the conservatives were already doing. All it could do was take a weak "me too" attitude.

In the early postwar years the left made a bid for the control of industry through the unions, but the occupation stopped them, and the effort was never revived. With the conservatives in complete control of the government, the opposition parties made no concentrated effort to extend the government's control over the means of production but instead tended to fight small battles over specific issues, usually in support of the rights of small business against the large corporations. In agriculture, the occupation's land reforms proved so successful that the opposition, far from advocating collectivization, joined the LDP in championing the small individual farmer. Ideological purists, of course, still exist in the hard cores of the Communist and Socialist parties, and Marxism retains considerable vigor among some intellectuals, especially in the universities, and thus ironically affects the thinking patterns and rhetoric of conservative businessmen; but Marxist concepts have not proved a framework on which a rational, cohesive opposition could be built in Japan. In fact, instead of being an asset to the opposition, it has served more as an albatross hanging around its neck, pointing the attention of the opposition in unproductive directions and discouraging the adherence of centrist voters.

Under these circumstances, it is not surprising that Marxist tenets and radical reforms, such as the abolition of the monarchy, have been gradually sloughed off by the opposition parties, and they all have slowly drifted toward the center. The Komeito, which at first used Marxist rhetoric to indicate its opposition status, has come to stand perhaps to the right of center on many issues. The Democratic Socialists, who have never wavered in their devotion to democracy, have become virtually indistinguishable from the more liberal elements in the LDP. The Socialists have remained divided between leftist ideologues and centrist pragmatists. When Eda Saburo, a right-wing Socialist leader, championed his "vision" of a combination of British parliamentarianism, Soviet social welfare, American affluence, and the Japanese peace constitution, he lost out in 1962 in the race for the party leadership, but more recently the party has definitely drifted in the direction of his ideas. The Communists swung for a while between militant ideas derived from abroad and more moderate domestic leadership. When they broke with Soviet control in 1949 and declared themselves a "lovable" Communist party, their vote suddenly soared to 10 percent. When subsequently they returned first to Soviet and then to Chinese guidance, they fell to as low as 1 percent in the polls. They returned to around 10 percent only after they established their independence of both the Soviet and Chinese parties and declared themselves in 1970 to be in favor of a "multiparty political system under socialism designed to defend parliamentary government," which, though confusing, sounds more democratic than Communist.

The LDP for its part has also dropped some of its more extreme positions, such as the revision of the new constitution in order to restore theoretical sovereignty to the emperor. The opposition parties and the majority of the public simply would not have stood for this, clinging determinedly to the constitution as their anchor to windward against any drift back toward prewar conditions. They are adamantly opposed to any change in the constitution, however innocuous or even desirable it might be, for fear that permitting even a single small change might open the gate to more important alterations. The LDP, though still including elements desirous of revising the American inspired document, has had to accept the realities of popular attitudes. Thus the LDP too has joined in the drift toward the center, and the constitution, despite its curious provenance, has become virtually sacrosanct and a solid foundation for the whole Japanese democratic system.

Having little effect on basic economic policies and the other chief areas of traditional Marxist interest, the opposition parties have concentrated more on foreign policy, social problems, and the championing of the individual rights guaranteed in the constitution, but with only mixed results. One area of conflict has been the powers and prerogatives of labor unions. As we have seen, the American occupation during the early postwar years blocked the left from taking control of industry through the unions, and it repeatedly supported less radical workers in their efforts to free themselves from control by tightly organized minority Communist groups. The labor movement was weakened from the start by its divisiveness, and it has steadily lost strength. The Sohyo federation backs the Socialists, Domei supports the Democratic Socialists, many individual unions champion the Communists, and other federations and unions take a neutral stand. None is able to deliver the undivided vote of its members, because unionized workers, like other Japanese, often prefer to consider themselves independents and vote accordingly.

Still, many fierce political battles have raged in the field of organized labor. Since its inception the militant Teachers Union has fought the Ministry of Education over the control of education and the curriculum, from the choice of individual textbooks to the issue of whether moral training should be included. A major dispute with the Sohyo federation, which is heavily made up of government workers, has involved the right of public workers to strike. Strikes, however, whether they concern such broad policy issues or merely wages, can be a two-edged political sword. An inconvenienced public may react against the unions, as happened with the general strike by communication workers in the late autumn of 1975. Taken on the whole, the labor movement, which started with a great show of union power, has gradually subsided in zeal and importance as workers, like other Japanese, have become increasingly satisfied with the way things are going in Japan.

Students have played a less significant and more tangential role than labor in the clash between the opposition and the LDP. For the first decade and a half after the war they were sometimes spectacularly prominent, as when the Zengakuren, the national student organization, led the mass confrontation with the government over the ratification of the Security Treaty with the United States in 1960. But subsequently the students broke up into various splinter sects of Trotskyites and various obscure ideologies, such as the Red Army (Sekigun) and the Nucleus Faction (Chukakuha). Groups of this sort, armed with staves and workingmen's hard hats, engaged in lethal combat with each other and sometimes committed atrocities against the public.

When the causes of the students happened to coincide with concerns of the public, as over Vietnam, the entrance into Japanese ports of American nuclear-powered submarines, the return of Okinawa, and the extension of the Security Treaty in the late 1960s and early 1970s, the student groups surfaced to temporary public attention, and they managed to close down Tokyo University and some other universities in 1968. They still figure sporadically in the prolonged fight between the government and the farmers whose land was expropriated for the Narita International Airport near Tokyo. This fight started in 1966 and still produces occasional incidents. But no party wishes to have anything to do with the student activists because of their acts of violence. In short, the organized student movement has simply marched itself off the main stage of public affairs and into the obscurity of political irrelevance.

While opposition to the existing political system has shrunk on both the right and the left to insignificant "lunatic" fringes, dissatisfaction with the way the system operates is widespread and is naturally focused primarily on the party in power. Desiring harmony and consensus, the public is disgusted that the most visible parts of the decision-making process are demonstrations in the streets and confrontations in the Diet over unresolved issues. Those who support the opposition parties are frustrated and indignant over the seeming permanence of LDP rule, which they mistakenly interpret to mean the denial of any role to them. Some are distressed that the electoral process and party organizations are closely tied up with personal relationships and do not seem to be determined by issues. Most are unhappy that the strict electoral rules are constantly flouted or at least circumvented by strategies of dubious legality. There are always charges of corruption and a strong feeling that politics is dirty.

The cries of corruption are often misunderstood by foreigners. Political corruption is less widespread in Japan than in many other countries and is probably much less than in local government in the United States. There is little vote buying in Japan because the secret ballot and a huge electorate—it normally takes upward of 50,000 votes to win a lower house seat—make it impractical. The national bureaucracy is entirely untarnished by scandal, though politicians and local bureaucrats are sometimes suspected, not of stealing public funds, but of receiving bribes for political favors. In the case of politicians, such payments are probably taken not so much for personal gain as for campaign purposes.

A major problem in Japan, as elsewhere, is the vagueness of the line between legal and illegal political contributions. The lavish entertainment of politicians and bureaucrats by businessmen well provided with expense accounts can seem unsavory, as can also the Japanese propensity for giving gifts, even though these are considered merely customary. More serious is the fact that almost all politicians receive and expend vastly greater funds for elections than they are allowed to by law. Both business firms and labor unions are permitted to make political contributions, but the line between legal political contributions and payoffs remains indistinct, leaving much room for suspicions of corruption.

Concern over financial corruption has been building up for some time. Two famous cases have involved Tanaka, who was prime minister from 1972 to 1974. He was a self-made business magnate, quite different from

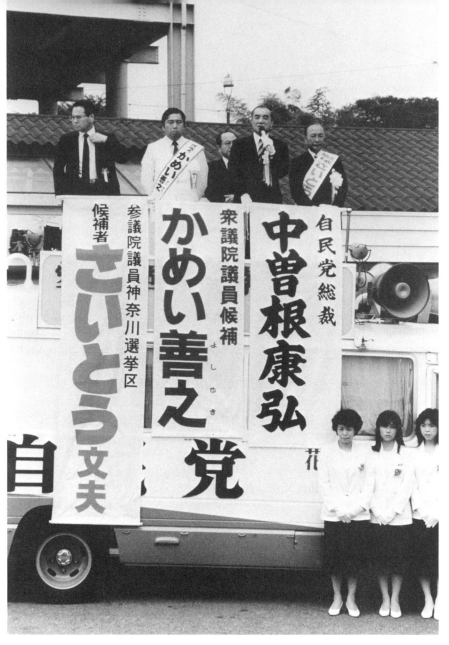

Electioneering from the top of a sound truck. Prime Minister Nakasone is speaking in support of two LDP candidates, one each for the two houses of the Diet. The names of all three men are prominently displayed on the side of the truck, and the two candidates wear distinguishing paper rosettes and sashes with their names. Their family names are written for absolute clarity in phonetic *hiragana*, their given names in more difficult Chinese characters. Nakasone is wearing white gloves, which seem to be *de rigueur* for such occasions. (© *Kaku Kurita / Photo Shuttle: Japan*)

the usual university graduate prime minister, and he was felt to be too free and easy in his acceptance of political contributions and the use of his own money to exert political influence. A magazine exposé of this "money politics," inspired by the Watergate scandal in the United States, led to his resignation as prime minister in December 1974.

The other case started with allegations made in Senate hearings in Washington in February 1976 that high Japanese officials had received huge bribes from the Lockheed Corporation to influence their decisions on plane purchases. The scandal, the worst in Japan's postwar history, produced a prolonged crisis in the operation of the Diet. Tanaka and some other politicians as well as a number of businessmen were indicted and eventually convicted. Tanaka and the other politicians resigned from the LDP to save it embarrassment, but all but one were reelected to the Diet, and Tanaka remained the most powerful figure in LDP Diet circles until he became seriously ill in 1985.

Major corruption cases are rare, but the public distaste for politics and politicians remains strong. The political situation is more confused now than for many years. Takeshita Noboru succeeded Nakasone on November 7, 1987, in orderly fashion but was forced by the Recruit scandal to give way to Uno Sosuke on June 2, 1989. Then on August 8 Uno, because of womanizing and other political gaffes, had to relinquish the prime ministership to Kaifu Toshiki, who was not expected to last long. Meanwhile the LDP lost heavily in local elections and those for the Upper House. It seemed dubious that it would maintain its Diet majority through the next general election. A brief coalition of the opposition parties seemed possible, but a more lasting result might be a coalition of the LDP with some centrist groups.

The largest and clearest area of controversy between left and right ever since the middle years of the occupation has been foreign policy, which because of the occupation and close Japanese-American relations since then have always centered on relations with the United States. This political issue, reflecting as it does Japan's relations with the outside world, is discussed more fully in Part Six of this book.

In the areas of social problems and basic human rights, the opportunities for dynamic, imaginative policies have been great, but the record of the opposition parties has been spotty. The increasing imbalance between industrial growth and social welfare, the rush of rural people to the cities, and the lagging investment in public facilities such as housing, roads, sewage systems, parks, and higher education, all created serious problems. The blessing of improved health care and the achievement of the highest longevity in the world produced new problems of care for the aged. The policy of economic growth at any price, which had been at least tacitly accepted by all the parties, led to tremendous crowding and pollution. In addition to air and water pollution, the Japanese became concerned about sound pollution from aircraft around airports and traffic on high-speed highways. The shadows cast on neighboring residences and apartments by high-rise buildings led to demands for the "right to sunshine," sunshine being especially important to the quality of life in Japan because of the heat it provides in winter and its usefulness for drying clothes. (Most Japanese households have small washing machines but lack the space for dryers.) All these threats to the quality of life the Japanese lumped together under the useful term *kogai* ("public injury").

Many of the social problems, such as those of old age and the funding of universities, elicited criticism from the opposition parties but no clear solutions. The threats to the environment and to the quality of life produced more positive reactions but no well-coordinated policies. Being concentrated in the cities, these problems contributed to a rising urban protest vote, most of which went not to the Socialists but to the Communists and Komeito, which the public felt were better organized and therefore more likely to take effective action. But as a result the urban vote tended to be spread more thinly among the opposition parties, weakening their challenge to the LDP. The shift in the urban vote, however, did help the opposition during the late 1960s and early 1970s to win control from the LDP over most local governments in the metropolitan areas.

Public injury issues were by their very nature essentially local. There were numerous cases, but only a few drew much national attention, such as the mercury poisoning of the waters off the coastal town of Minamata, in Kyushu. Since most cases were treated as local issues, they greatly increased interest in both local governments and their powers. For the most part, local ad hoc organizations, usually called "local residents' movements," took the lead rather than national parties. These

Facing page: To improve "the quality of life" certain downtown streets have in recent years been closed to traffic on Sundays and opened to the enjoyment of the public. Note the elevated high-speed highway in the background. (© *Ben Simmons / The Stock Market of NY*)

groups concerned themselves with only a single issue, such as a polluting factory, a plan for a local nuclear plant or industrial zone, or the noise of a local airport. Unlike the various "citizens' movements" of the 1950s and 1960s, which had normally been concerned with national problems such as American bases and the Vietnam War and had as a result often been manipulated by the national parties, the local residents' movements tried to avoid becoming involved with the parties, knowing that to do so might lose them some local support and that in any case they would have to deal with LDP politicians and apolitical bureaucrats. Actually the LDP responded to these new local issues almost as quickly as the opposition parties, thus stealing a march on the opposition and neutralizing the problems as issues the opposition could use against them.

On the whole Japan responded very rapidly and effectively to the problems of pollution. An Environment Agency was created with cabinet rank in 1971 and over the next two years a series of court rulings established the principle that polluters must pay for the damage they do. The final Minamata judgment in 1979 and other landmark decisions strengthened this principle. Meanwhile strong laws against various forms of public injury had been passed and were being strictly enforced. As a consequence, conditions improved markedly. For example, sulphur dioxide in the atmosphere was reduced by more than half by 1975, so that Mount Fuji, which had always been clearly visible from Tokyo in good weather but had disappeared almost completely from sight because of the smog generated by cars and factories, once again became visible. The Japanese record in dealing with the problems of public injury is as good as any in the world, and the LDP has minimized this whole area of dispute as a political issue.

29 *Political Style*

Foreign critics of the Japanese democratic system often fail to appreciate the extraordinary achievement it represents and the strength of the democracy it embodies. They do not realize that contemporary Japan is the one great extension of democracy the world has witnessed since the end of World War II. Elsewhere once-democratic nations, such as West Germany and Italy, have been regained; the tiny democracy of Israel has established itself in the Middle East; the city state of Singapore has become a democracy, albeit under an iron-fisted leader; and a welter of countries both large and small are trying to operate as democracies with varying degrees of success. Japan, however, is something quite different. Here before the war a shallowly rooted, incomplete democratic system withered under the hot sun of militaristic nationalism, but now this new world giant is a flourishing, smoothly operating democratic system ardently supported by virtually the whole nation.

A major reason why outside observers often fail to appreciate what has happened in Japan is that its democracy operates in ways unfamiliar to Westerners. Many elements elsewhere considered essential to democracy, such as public debate in electioneering and in the Diet, are almost entirely absent. Few Japanese rally around party labels. Many prominent features of the Japanese political system, such as mass demonstrations of protest, inflamed public rhetoric, and confrontations in the Diet, are unattractive. Yet outside observers do not realize that these distasteful features are offset by extensive personalized electioneering, vast amounts of behind-the-scenes negotiations among political allies and with opponents, and reams of political commentary in the mass media, which most foreigners cannot read. Nor are most observers aware that, despite the popular skepticism shown toward political parties, Japanese in fact turn out to vote in far greater numbers than Americans and are personally as active in local political issues as people anywhere. All these factors make the Japanese democratic political process a very lively one, however obscure or deficient it may seem to foreign observers.

It must be admitted, however, that Japanese democracy still has relatively shallow roots when compared to democracy in the English-speaking nations. It is not unreasonable to fear that their "gut" feelings about democracy are less strong. But it should not be forgotten that Japanese experience with voting does date back more than a century and that for close to half a century Japan has operated very successfully as a fully democratic country. The commitment of all but the lunatic fringe to democracy and specifically to the 1947 constitution is extremely strong. Though some of its American-inspired wording once sounded slightly strange and foreign, it has become familiar through use, and almost all Japanese are now extremely proud of it as their "peace constitution." Ironically, the somewhat anti-American left is probably strongest in its support.

A foreign observer might feel that less group orientation in Japanese society and more individualism would provide a stronger basis for democracy, but this point has by no means been proved and may not apply very well in comparisons between Japan and the West. Japan lacks the social fissures of race, language, religion, region, and class, which are such complicating factors in many Western countries. Far fewer Japanese are caught up in divisive political ideologies than in many of the nations of the West. Most voters for the opposition parties are not true believers in the ideologies being touted but instead represent a floating protest vote against current government policies. As such they are free to move from party to party, including the party in power. Similarly, the personal contacts that form the core of the LDP's rural vote are relatively flexible and in any case are a fading feature of Japanese politics.

For many years after the war, there was little faith, particularly among the Japanese themselves, in the stability of democracy in Japan. It had faltered once before, and the gap in trust and objectives between right and left appeared quite unbridgeable. The LDP's loss of a majority seemed inevitable, and to some imminent. People envisaged a sudden shift to a Socialist majority or to a coalition of leftist parties, bringing chaos through the quickness of change or internal divisions among the new leadership. Some people even imagined a rightist coup d'état in such a situation.

But all this has changed. The parties have all drifted toward the center, with the result that any plausible change in the parties in power would bring surprisingly few important shifts of fundamental policy. The revival of the LDP during the 1980s made many think that it would retain power for some time to come. When it does lose power, as no doubt it will someday, it seems likely that alliances with centrist parties will be the outcome, entailing very little change indeed. Sharp shifts of direction seem possible in even the most firmly established democracies of the West, but in Japan a moderate, centrist public has in a sense triumphed over the divisiveness of party leaders, creating a democracy with extraordinarily stable political prospects.

All in all, democracy in Japan seems as flexible, rational, efficient, and stable as in any Western country. The system does not lend itself to sudden major shifts in leadership or policies. There is a strong prejudice against the sort of charismatic leadership commonly sought in a president of the United States or provided by a Churchill in wartime England. By comparison the Japanese system may seem colorless and ponderously slow, but on the whole a slow consistent change in policies seems safer for a democracy than sudden fits and starts in rapidly shifting directions. And when necessary the Japanese system can move swiftly, as it brilliantly demonstrated in its astounding rise to become an industrial superpower and its rapid and thorough handling of the problems of pollution. The efficiency of the Japanese government in providing its people with services and the effectiveness of the political system in converting the popular will into political action probably stand up well in comparison with other countries anywhere in the world. In short, Japanese democracy must be adjudged a great success. It is only when we look beyond Japan itself at its economic and political relations with the outside world that we have reason for concern.

Part Five _____

Business

Robots welding parts of cars at the Nissan plant at Oppama, on the outskirts of Yokohama. Many Japanese factories are largely automated, with huge areas of machines monitored by only a handful of workers. (© Richard Kalvar/Magnum Photos)

30 *The Premodern Background*

Japan's political success in creating an efficient and solid democracy may be its most remarkable achievement in recent times, but it is the extraordinary record of the Japanese in modernizing their economy and becoming one of the top two or three industrial powers and trading nations in the world that has drawn the most attention and inspired wide acclaim for "the Japanese miracle." Whereas the Japanese artist and later the fanatic soldier once seemed to typify the nation, everyone would now recognize the Japanese businessman as the national symbol. Instead of Mount Fuji and Hiroshige prints or the Rising Sun flag and *banzai* charges, the name Japan now conjures up factories, robots, endless streams of automobiles pouring off ships onto American roads, and the ubiquitous Japanese businessman with his attaché case rushing through airports all over the world.

The Japanese have displayed since early times many of the characteristics that have contributed to their modern economic success. One was their tendency to work hard. Another was their drive for formal education. Others were the painstaking effort they displayed in their workmanship and their skill in mastering difficult technologies. Although they were introduced to agriculture and the casting of bronze and iron relatively late, they quickly caught up with the continental lands that had known agriculture for millennia and metalworking for centuries. The Japanese soon mastered the intricate water control systems and the transplanting of rice shoots for paddy-field cultivation. The two Great Buddhas of Nara and Kamakura of the eighth and thirteenth centuries are still among the largest bronze figures ever cast. The steel of Japanese swords had become the finest in the world by the twelfth century. The Japanese mastered the weaving and embroidery techniques of the Chinese in the seventh and eighth centuries and also their beautiful architecture in wood. They acquired dozens of other skills, such as papermaking, still unknown at that time in Europe, and in the eighth century printed with woodblocks a million Buddhist talismans. With the wave of new technology from China came Chinese painting and the other fine arts, which the Japanese absorbed with amazing speed and skill. Thus in the course of only a few centuries Japan changed from a technologically backward land into a nation of fine artisans. It also remade its institutions, at first on a borrowed Chinese model, to accommodate the rapid development of its technology.

In the sixteenth century the Portuguese were astounded by the skills of Japanese craftsmen, while the Japanese rapidly adopted what interested them most in Western technology. In an age of constant warfare, the guns of the Portuguese drew their special attention. First seen by the Japanese in 1542 or 1543, muskets were being produced in great numbers and sometimes with slight technical improvements within two decades and were used successfully in battle by massed bodies of musketeers as early as 1575.

Subsequently, more than two centuries of self-imposed isolation caused the Japanese to lag technologically behind the West, which just at this point was entering the age of science and the early phases of the industrial revolution. Nevertheless, Westerners in the middle of the nineteenth century were struck by the high quality of Japanese technical skills in metalwork, porcelainmaking, multicolored woodblock prints, which were triumphs of technical skills as well as art, and a number of other crafts. It should have been obvious to Westerners, though it was not to most of them, that the Japanese, if given the opportunity, could readily master the technology of the West and learn to produce machine-made goods of comparable quality to those of the Occident.

The Japanese entered the modern age not only with the work skills and habits needed for economic success but also with many of the necessary institutions, at least in partially developed form. They had a highly monetized economy and a single nationwide market. Under the Tokugawa all the feudal lords were forced to spend a large part of their incomes outside their domains for the maintenance of their large establishments at the feudal capital, Edo, and in annual trips to and from Edo. This required them to produce within their domains for sale to consumers elsewhere either sizable surpluses of staple commodities, such as rice, or some special local products, such as sugar, as in the case of the Satsuma domain in southern Kyushu and the Ryukyu Islands. Surplus commodities were shipped either directly to Edo or, in western Japan, to the great entrepôt of Osaka at the eastern end of the Inland Sea. These two cities became the twin economic capitals of Japan, as they still are today, one for East Japan and the other for West Japan. Already in the seventeenth century fluctuating prices on futures in rice in the one city would be raced to the other, where they would immediately affect prices there.

Commercial, banking, and, to a lesser extent, manufacturing activities of nationwide importance centered in these two cities and also in the old imperial capital of Kyoto, not far from Osaka. Already in the early seventeenth century, some family businesses that were centered in one or another of these cities spread into a number of regions in a variety of fields of activity, such as sake brewing, dry-goods retailing, and banking. Financial institutions were well developed (though the currency system remained extremely diverse), and major retail stores developed fixed prices, with none of the haggling that is still to be found in most parts of the world. Such advanced retail outlets developed smoothly into the great department stores of today.

The ownership of large family enterprises remained in the hands of the original family, but management was gradually transferred to head clerks, who stayed with the company for life. In fact, the whole business firm was a sort of extended family, with a strong sense of mutual loyalty between employers and employees. Only a few of the large firms of the premodern period, such as Mitsui, which established dry-goods stores and moneylending enterprises in Kyoto, Edo, and Osaka in the seventeenth century, survived the troubled times of the mid-nineteenth century, but the spirit of the old Tokugawa companies is still very much alive in their contemporary successors.

The commercial drive of the big city merchants and a surge of peasant entrepreneurs in the late eighteenth and early nineteenth centuries prepared the Japanese well for the modern age of international business. So also did the attitudes of many members of the samurai class. They desperately sought new ways to make a living after the Meiji reforms swept away the feudal system and with it their hereditary stipends. The new government encouraged them to go into manufacturing, banking, and trade, which many of them did, some with great success. Even under the old regime, some of these samurai had become semibusinessmen through their service in the economic branches of their domain, managing its warehouses, the transportation and sale of its surpluses in the centers of trade and consumption, and the operation of its monopolies.

A premodern woodblock print of the Echigoya dry-goods store, which was established in Edo (Tokyo) in 1673 and became the foundation of the fortune of the Mitsui family. Renamed Mitsukoshi in 1928, it is the largest department store company in Japan. (*Shashinka Photo Library*)

An outstanding example of a samurai entrepreneur is Iwasaki Yataro of the Tosa domain in Shikoku, who managed to become the domain's economic agent in Nagasaki, acquired its remaining ships, and with this start built up the Mitsubishi Company, which grew to be second only to Mitsui among the great economic enterprises of modern Japan. Not all samurai turned businessmen were as successful, and many failed miserably, but probably because of the connections they had with their colleagues in government, more of the new captains of industry came from the samurai class than from either the peasantry or the old merchant class.

As we have seen, some of Japan's neighbors, such as China and Korea, had many of the same talents as the Japanese, including a capacity for hard work and skills in craftsmanship and commercial organization. They also had the same esteem for formal education, which unquestionably was one of the chief reasons for Japan's subsequent economic success. But they lacked some of the attitudes that helped the Japanese rapidly modernize their economy and start catching up with the West. The Chinese and Koreans were relatively oblivious to the outside world and as a consequence were not as able as the Japanese to discern the magnitude of the political and economic menace the West posed for them. In addition, they lacked the historic consciousness the Japanese had of having learned from abroad in the past. For these reasons they neither perceived the necessity or comprehended the possibility of learning much from the West. They sought to continue in their traditional ways, avoiding all changes they could. They felt little of the urgency to catch up to the Occident that the Japanese felt so keenly.

Because of these differences Japan got off to a faster start in closing the gap in technology and institutions between itself and the West. This fact has profoundly affected its history ever since. Although both China and Korea eventually stirred into action, Japan's head start put it well in advance of all other non-Western nations and has enabled it to come abreast of the frontrunners in the world today.

31 The Prewar Economy

Japan faced a huge task in the second half of the nineteenth century just to defend its economy from the predatory foreigners, to say nothing of catching up with the West in technology. The treaties forced on the Tokugawa regime in its final years robbed the Japanese of control of their own import tariffs, which were set on average around 5 percent, far too low to give their textiles and other handmade goods protection from the cheap machine-made wares of the West. A different exchange rate between gold and silver in Japan and the outside world also produced a serious drain of gold and disrupted prices. Japan was saved from complete economic disaster only by the general lack of appeal of Western goods to the Japanese public—a significant parallel to conditions today—and a blight that struck European silkworms and produced a strong temporary demand for Japanese silk and silkworm eggs.

After coming to power in 1868 the Meiji government at once sought means to save the economy. It established modern economic institutions—a nationwide monetary system, modern banking institutions, Western types of taxes, and a national budget. It hired Western experts at great expense to build railroads, improve port facilities, set up factories, and teach Japanese disciples their technical skills and Western science in general. It dispatched promising youths abroad, again at great expense, to learn the skills of the West. It did away with the class restrictions of feudalism, making it possible for ambitious young men from all social backgrounds to achieve success in the business world. The response was tremendous, especially from the sons of lower-ranking samurai and wealthy farmers, who saw opportunities opening up to them that they never could have aspired to under the old regime. They crowded into schools to learn Western business techniques, new technology, and the English language, the chief gateway to Western knowledge and international business activities.

Despite these vigorous beginnings in the 1870s, Japan had virtually bankrupted itself by the end of the decade because of the very ambitiousness of its attempts at reform and the costs of liquidating the ancien régime against armed opposition. A serious financial retrenchment became necessary, but just at this point Japan's arduous efforts at economic modernization began to pay off. Agriculture production increased significantly as the technology of the more advanced parts of the country spread to all regions in a now thoroughly unified nation. The privately financed Osaka Spinning Mill was built in 1882 on a large enough scale to be competitive in the world market, and its success was followed by a rush of private capital into spinning and then weaving. Except for factories in militarily strategic industries, the government had sold off the many pilot plants it had built, and these, now under private management and capitalized at the low levels their purchasers had been able to pay, began to show a profit, leading to industrial booms in one field after another.

Japan took off at a relatively rapid rate of industrial growth, which was soon stimulated by the Sino-Japanese War of 1894–95, the large indemnity it brought from China, and the Russo-Japanese War of 1904–05. World War I left the Asian empires of the European powers open to Japanese industrial exports. The worldwide economic slowdown of the 1920s and the stock market crash at the end of the decade affected Japan along with the rest of the world, but, stimulated by renewed military expansion in the 1930s, the Japanese economy returned rapidly to its upward industrial surge.

Japan's modern economic growth followed the classic patterns already established in the West. Increased agricultural production, improved communications, and efficient centralized government set the stage for industrial success, which came first in cotton spinning and weaving, expanded into other light industries, and then spread into heavy industries and chemicals. Early exports were often shoddy, and the label "made in Japan" became almost synonymous with second-rate goods. The Japanese still could not equal the longer-established industries of the West and had to seek their chief markets in the impoverished lands of Asia. But gradually the gap in quality was narrowed, and by the 1930s Japan had become one of the major industrial nations of the world.

By the beginning of World War II Japan had established certain characteristics in its economy that distinguished it from most other industrialized nations and still persist to some degree today. At one time these distinctive characteristics were looked upon as survivals from the feudal past that indicated an economic immaturity Japan would in time outgrow, but, following Japan's tremendous postwar success, they came to be looked on as part of a sinister plot through which the Japanese sought to gain unfair advantages over their Western competitors. In actuality, however, Japan's unusual economic characteristics were the result of natural evolutionary developments from earlier Japanese patterns of organization or in some cases ingenious inventions to meet new problems. They are more deserving of study and, where appropriate, of emulation than of disdain or condemnation.

One characteristic of Japan's modern economy is common to most newly industrialized nations but has been especially marked in Japan because of the speed of its industrialization. This is the "dual structure" of the economy, as the Japanese call it. Many of Japan's economic activities, including agriculture, small handicraft industries, many service industries, and most retailing, continued little changed from Tokugawa times, becoming a lower level of the Japanese economy. It was joined by new machine production that could be performed in small units by family members or pseudo-family apprentices in tiny machine shops supplying parts for larger enterprises. Meanwhile, large-scale new industrial undertakings were built on top of this foundation as an upper level of highly mechanized production. The two levels contrasted in scale of operations, productivity, wages, and profitability. Although at first the upper level employed very few people, it grew rapidly and absorbed increasing numbers of workers from the lower level. But the sharp differences between the two levels spawned many economic and social problems. Before World War II the surplus of underemployed, low-productivity workers in the lower level depressed wages in the upper level as well.

Eventually this situation turned around. With the great success of Japanese industrial production after World War II, a general shortage of labor developed, and wages in the lower level were pulled up by the great productivity of the upper level. But this situation saddled the upper level with the cost of paying for higher wages for the low-productivity workers. Agriculture is an extreme case in point. Despite its present high mechanization, the smallness of farms makes agriculture still an extremely labor-intensive operation. Generous government price supports help maintain Japanese rice prices that are five to ten times those of the world market. Economically it makes no sense for Japanese to grow

Floor of the Tokyo stock exchange. (© *Richard Kalvar / Magnum Photos*)

rice, but lingering sentimental feelings about the small family farm as the foundation of the nation and outmoded strategic worries about the need to produce one's own staple food (even though Japan is already dependent on foreign lands for about half its total food supply) make the Japanese determined to maintain their agricultural sector, however heavy a drain it may be on the economy as a whole.

Japan has less choice in regard to its inefficient retailing system. The Japanese have cars, but there is little room for parking lots to service supermarkets and shopping centers, which are relatively small and rare in Japan. Narrow roads further complicate the problem of cheap distribution through large retail outlets. Lack of space simply rules out the supermarket, shopping-center approach to retailing that prevails in most of the United States and binds the Japanese to greater reliance on "mom and pop" size stores and a bewildering complexity in wholesale distribution. Lack of space is a serious handicap to the Japanese economy, for it will continue to necessitate the maintenance of a relatively large lower level of the economy in the form of costly small-scale enterprises.

Another characteristic of Japan's prewar and postwar economy is the close-knit bond between most employers and employees. This reflects the family-based organization of Japan's premodern business enterprises and also the national tendency to organize by groups. This close employer-employee tie was natural in the small units of the lower half of Japan's dual economy, but, as will be discussed more fully later, it has gradually been adopted in the large-scale upper half as well, giving a paternalistic and humanistic feel to Japanese industry that is usually lacking in big business enterprises in other countries.

A third distinctive feature of the Japanese economy both before and after the war has been the close cooperation between government and business. In the United States, as in many other countries, the two have been seen as rivals, with business continually seeking to escape the taxation and control of government; but in Japan industry grew up and throve under the eager encouragement of the government. As a result, it learned to look to the government for patronage and guidance. Only as it became strong during the early twentieth century did it begin to chafe at government interference, but by that time it had itself become influential in government decisions by means of the Diet and political parties. The destruction of the Japanese economy in World War II put business again under the sponsorship and guidance of the government, and, despite considerable erosion of this situation in recent years, habits of close cooperation persist between the two. In contrast to the hostility between them that we find in America, government and business remain essentially partners in Japan.

In prewar times the distinctive Japanese economic institution that most caught the attention of the outside world was the so-called *zaibatsu* system. The term zaibatsu is pejorative, literally meaning "financial clique." It is specifically applied to certain giant financial, commercial, and industrial combines but is loosely used for prewar Japanese big business in general. The four greatest zaibatsu in the 1920s were, in order of size, Mitsui and Mitsubishi, which have already been mentioned; Sumitomo, dating back to an early seventeenth-century copper mining and smelting company; and Yasuda, founded as a banking institution in the 1880s. Some of the late entrants into the category, known as the "new zaibatsu," were particularly involved in military-related industries and the exploitation of Manchuria, which had recently been conquered by Japan.

The zaibatsu came to control a very large part of the upper level of the Japanese economy. This concentration of wealth and economic power was greatly aided by the sale of the government enterprises in the early 1880s to the relatively small number of individuals who could pay even the low prices demanded and who appeared to the government leaders to be capable of managing them well. Marxist historians charge that this sale of government property at bargain rates was motivated by a desire to create a strong capitalist class, but, as we have seen, it was necessitated by the government's desperate financial plight, and before long the government became suspicious of the growing political influence of big business. By the 1920s and 1930s there was wide condemnation of the zaibatsu, particularly by the supporters of the military, as being elements of Western decadence in Japanese society, corrupters of the parliamentary system, and moneygrubbing betrayers of Japan's imperial destiny.

It is ironic that after the war the American occupation in turn attacked the zaibatsu for being the root cause of Japanese imperialism and on these grounds singled them out for destruction. Their ownership was removed from the controlling families virtually without compensation, and the great combines were broken up into their component parts. Before they could be further atomized in a traditional American "trust-busting" operation, the occupation's reform program was halted, leaving the larger corporate subunits of the original zaibatsu intact. Since the occupation, these have gradually reassumed their old names (except for the Yasuda Bank, which became the Fuji Bank) and have drawn together in loose, informal associations, now known in Japan as *keiretsu*.

Because of the existence of these keiretsu groupings, many observers have asserted that the zaibatsu system has been restored, but this is not correct. The keiretsu form something like clubs, whose members may look first to each other for aid or cooperation before trying other sources. There is thus a certain degree of mutual back scratching. But their relations are by no means exclusive, and there is no central ownership and none of the rigid controls once exercised within a zaibatsu organization. Other relations have become much more significant, such as the groups of firms in the same line of business and the overall grouping of the Federation of Economic Organizations (Keidanren). There are many nostalgic survivals of the feelings of closeness of the old zaibatsu system, but the system itself has disappeared entirely.

In their heyday before the war, the zaibatsu were typically under the control of a central holding company, largely owned by the original family. The holding company controlled several major affiliates and these in turn a series of smaller affiliates. This sort of pyramiding of control is common enough in the West, but what made the Japanese case unique was the fact that the controlling company often lacked majority ownership, sometimes having as little as 10 percent of the stocks of some minor affiliate. Control, however, was exercised through other means. The affiliate would probably be completely dependent on the banking, shipping, and trading facilities of the combine; interlocking directors were common; executives were switched around among the component firms as though they were members of a unified bureaucracy; the advantages and prestige of belonging to a large zaibatsu combine were great; and a strong sense of personal loyalty to the combine permeated the leadership, much as in a premodern feudal domain. Young executives joined a zaibatsu enterprise for a lifetime career. This was the feature of the zaibatsu system that was most like earlier Japanese society and is still most characteristic of contemporary Japan.

A typical zaibatsu organization was not like the contemporary American conglomerates, which bring together entirely unrelated corporations under the same ownership. Instead they were rational outgrowths of evolving economic activity and therefore are better described as combines. They tended to cluster around a central bank that financed the various activities of the combine. These functions often stood in a vertical relationship. For example, a series of separate companies might mine a certain ore, fashion it into manufactured products, transport these abroad on the combine's shipping line, and sell them abroad and purchase needed raw materials for the whole process through the combine's "general trading company" (*sogo shosha*), while all of these different stages of the operation would be financed by the combine's bank.

The extent and nature of a zaibatsu combine's activities are illustrated by the names of the many major companies that still use the Mitsubishi name today. There are the Mitsubishi Bank, the Mitsubishi Corporation (the general trading company), Mitsubishi Chemical Industries, Mitsubishi Electric Corporation, Mitsubishi Estate Company, Mitsubishi Gas Chemical Company, Mitsubishi Heavy Industries, Mitsubishi Metal Corporation, Mitsubishi Mining and Cement Company, Mitsubishi Motors Corporation, Mitsubishi Oil Company, Mitsubishi Paper Mills, Mitsubishi Petrochemical Company, Mitsubishi Rayon Company, Mitsubishi Steel Manufacturing Company, Mitsubishi Trust and Banking Corporation, and Mitsubishi Warehouse and Transportation Company. The Mitsubishi combine started in shipping, but the shipping company never bore the Mitsubishi name, being known as Nippon Yusen Kaisha (NYK).

A particularly interesting component of the zaibatsu system and of the postwar Japanese economic system as a whole is the general trading company, an ingenious innovation that developed to meet specific Japanese needs. From the start the upper level of the Japanese economy depended heavily on the importation of raw materials and on foreign markets, but Japanese companies were still small and lacked much knowledge of economic conditions abroad. They also lacked capital. It made sense to concentrate capital, knowledge of the outside world, and skills in trading abroad in specialized institutions that could then service many companies unable to maintain their own independent purchasing and sales forces overseas. The general trading companies of the various zaibatsu did this primarily for the member companies of their combines, while other trading companies serviced all the companies in some particular field.

The trading companies built up excellent worldwide services, which individual companies could not hope to match and which helped fund much of the trade they carried on. They conducted a huge amount of business, on which they charged only a very slim margin of profit. At first their activities were almost exclusively in Japan's foreign trade, but they later extended them to domestic business, and since World War II, because of their unique services, they have come to do considerable trade between other countries not involving Japan at all. At one point more than a third of Japan's total GNP passed through the hands of the ten largest trading companies, but in more recent years the development of a number of giant firms fully able to conduct their own foreign contacts has cut into the role of the general trading companies.

The overall influence of the zaibatsu system has long been a hotly debated subject in Japan. The great concentrations of power and wealth it produced were undoubtedly unhealthy in many ways for Japanese social and political development. But it did not have the unfocused gigantism of the modern conglomerates, nor did it produce the stultifying economic effects of a monopolistic system. No zaibatsu ever held a monopoly in any important field of activity. In fact, they developed rival enterprises that usually operated in stimulating competition with each other. At times a few zaibatsu or other large firms formed virtual oligopolies in certain fields, but these could be transformed into temporarily useful cartels in times of stress. The concentration of capital the zaibatsu system made possible helped channel funds into particularly promising though risky fields in which the returns could be realized only over a long period, and thus made possible important long-term investments that otherwise might not have been made. Finally, the narrowness of the ownership group, combined with traditional Japanese frugality, permitted a high rate of reinvestment and growth. Despite government interference under the military leaders in the 1930s and their squandering of much of Japan's economic power in fruitless foreign conquests, Japan under the zaibatsu system did lay a solid industrial base for the country's spectacular growth in recent decades.

32 _The Postwar Economy_

Japan had not fully closed the economic and technological gap between itself and the West before World War II, and the conflict and its aftermath once again widened it greatly. The Japanese had been absorbed in military adventures since 1931; full-scale war came with China in 1937 and with the United States and Britain in 1941; Japan's merchant marine and industrial cities, both of which were essential to its livelihood, were all but wiped out; the country emerged from the war a pariah nation, shunned by most of the nations with which it had to trade if it were to live; it lacked most natural resources, not even being able to feed itself; and, finally, the drastic American reform program caused such disruption and uncertainties that long-term investments even by the few who still had some resources were unattractive. Only the black market flourished. Most Japanese were reduced to grim subsistence living, and the economy as a whole remained moribund. Japan seemed more hopelessly behind the West than in the desperate days at the beginning of the Meiji period.

Recovery was much slower than in any of the war-devastated lands of the West and did not start until the United States had carried out its stringent retrenchment policies of 1949, stopped further American reforms of the economy, and then started heavy purchases in Japan of supplies for use in the Korean War, which broke out in 1950. At first recovery went slowly, but it gradually picked up speed, having the strong underpinnings of Japan's high educational levels, the good working habits of a populace familiar with industrial labor, a large reservoir of experienced technicians, industrialists, and businessmen, and a superb government bureaucracy intent on rebuilding the economy. The government targeted certain basic industries, such as shipbuilding, coal mining, and production of steel, electric power, fertilizers, and chemicals for ini-

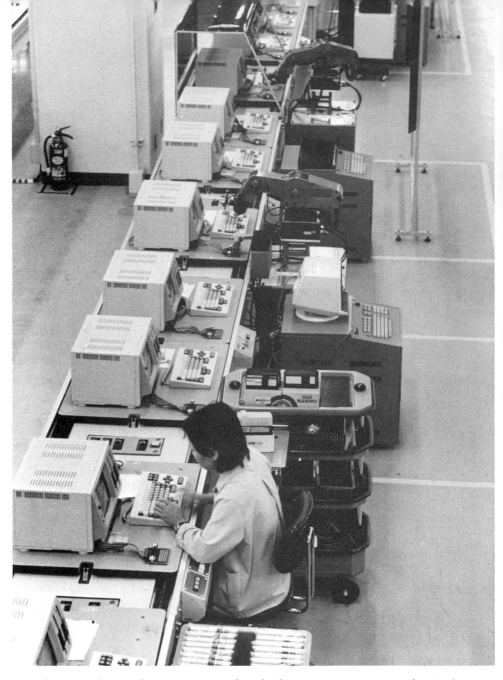

The two robots and one woman worker checking computers on a production line illustrate the growing need for high technology and the shrinking demand for labor. (© *Tadanori Saito* / *Photo Shuttle: Japan*)

Workers displaced by new technologies are being retrained in new skills. (© *Richard Kalvar / Magnum Photos*)

Two workers at the control center of a steel plant illustrate the shift from intensive labor to high technological skills. (© *Abbas / Magnum Photos*)

tial concentration of investment and effort, and business cooperated smoothly with it. By 1955 per capita levels of wealth had regained prewar levels, and economic growth was accelerating. Prime Minister Ikeda's proposal in 1960 of a ten-year income-doubling plan proved a gross underestimate. The Japanese miracle was well under way.

Japan's first postwar successes in exports were in industries that had been stimulated by the recent war. Binoculars, cameras, buses, and trucks had all benefited from technology developed during the war. Shipbuilding had also progressed to meet wartime needs. Japan had built the world's largest battleship, so it is not surprising that in the 1960s it began to construct the world's largest oil tankers to haul this primary source of energy all the way from the Persian Gulf around Singapore to Japanese ports especially designed to receive these behemoths of the sea.

On the whole, however, the Japanese once again followed the classic line of industrial development, though this time at a much faster pace. Textiles were the first major postwar exports. Then, as newly industrializing areas such as Taiwan and India entered the textile field, the Japanese shifted their main export emphasis to steel and machines, such as motorcycles, cars, and tractors. From these they progressed into the electronic industries, gradually emerging as the only major competitor with the United States in computers and some other high-technology products and the leader in some fields, such as robotics. They also began to show signs of displacing the United States as the world's financial center. They became the world's greatest creditor nation just as the United States sank to the status of being the world's largest debtor nation. By the late 1980s the Japanese had more than closed the gap with the countries of the West and appeared ready to push ahead of them.

The brilliant success of the Japanese economy since 1950 must be attributed primarily to the nature of Japanese society, Japan's prewar economic experience, and certain distinctive characteristics of Japanese business organization, which we shall discuss later. It is frequently explained, however, as being basically the product of lower wage scales than in the West. At first Japanese wages were indeed quite low, but this fact primarily reflected the low productivity of labor in early postwar Japan. Actually low wages, by limiting the domestic market, were as

Rolls of sheet steel. During the 1960s Japan laid emphasis on steel and some other heavy industries, becoming one of the leading steel producers. (*Courtesy Japan Information Center*)

much of a drag as an asset to the economy as a whole. As the economy recovered and productivity soared, wages kept pace, rising to half, then two thirds, and eventually equality with those in the United States. With the recent rise in the value of the yen relative to the dollar, they may well be higher now. But in any case labor costs have all along represented a shrinking share of the costs of production, and Japan's economic success must be attributed basically to other factors.

The very destruction of the prewar economic machine proved in some ways a stimulus to the growth of the postwar economy. Old factories had either been destroyed by bombing or allowed to rust into obsolescence because of the lack of replacement parts and labor. As a result they were not worth restoring and were replaced by brand-new plants, often quite superior to the aging factories of the United States and Europe. The destruction of the zaibatsu system shook Japanese businessmen out of their traditional patterns of operation, which were beginning to become too rigid, and forced them to innovate. Even more important, the removal of the zaibatsu giants gave room for growth to a whole new generation of entrepreneurs, and the unsettled conditions of the time rewarded innovation and daring. Small prewar enterprises and a great number of entirely new ones flourished, and some blossomed into leading companies of worldwide prominence. Matsushita, Canon, Sharp, and YKK, the largest producer of zippers in the world, are examples of the first category and Honda, Sony, and Sanyo of the second.

Despite the primary role of the Japanese in their own economic recovery, it cannot be denied that fortuitous external influences also played a major role. One relatively small factor, already noted, was the Korean War. A much greater influence was the American occupation itself. Although its radical reforms impeded early recovery and caused uncertainties in business circles, its many basic economic and social measures had an extremely helpful long-range impact and probably could not have been carried out by the Japanese themselves through normal democratic procedures in the turmoil of the early postwar years. The economic retrenchment of 1949 and the shaking up of business practices through the destruction of the zaibatsu system are cases in point. Far more important were the clear and unchallenged democratic reforms of the new constitution, the liberation of women to a status of equality with men,

Facing page: The plant of the Mitsui Petro-Chemical Company at Iwakuni, on the Inland Sea. Petrochemicals was one of Japan's key industries of the 1960s. (*Courtesy Japan Information Center*)

and the thoroughgoing land reforms, which, though of little or no economic benefit, gave Japan a stable social base for its democratic system.

The American involvement in Japan was helpful in another way. It removed the costly burdens of military defense. After the war the Japanese shunned any type of militarism, and the United States and Japan's other erstwhile adversaries as well as its neighbors, remembering how formidable and cruel the Japanese military had been, were all happy to see Japan without arms. World conditions, however, did not permit an entirely defenseless Japan, and the United States, as the occupying force, naturally stepped in to fill the vacuum. Japan supplied the United States with bases, but Americans bore the cost of maintaining a large military establishment in and around Japan. As a result, while other large countries were devoting between 4 and 7 percent of their GNP, and sometimes much more, to military expenditures, the Japanese were paying

A giant tanker being painted before launching at the Mitsubishi Shipyard at Nagasaki, in Kyushu. Japan became the world's leading shipbuilder in 1956. The industry was ideal for Japan at the time, demanding high technology and skills and a large labor force. It also met Japan's own great need for ships for imports and exports. (*Courtesy Japan Information Center*)

next to nothing. Even after they subsequently created a modest Self-Defense Force, they made it a rule to restrict expenditures for it to no more than 1 percent of GNP. This arrangement permitted them to keep taxes considerably lower than in other countries and to devote research and development activities exclusively to economically beneficial undertakings.

Japan had been so thoroughly defeated and its economy so badly injured that Americans could not imagine it rising to become a serious economic competitor. They worried more about Japan's economic viability and its domestic stability in the face of serious poverty and political confusion. Under these circumstances the United States did all it could to get the Japanese back on their feet, treating them with surprising generosity. At first it supplied emergency economic aid to prevent starvation, and subsequently it opened its markets wide to Japanese exports while permitting the Japanese to maintain tight import restrictions to protect their supposedly "infant" industries. The Americans also provided the Japanese with useful technology. Private companies who sold obsolescent technology to Japanese firms at a small profit regarded this as an unexpected windfall and never considered that the sharing of this technology might someday come back to haunt them. In this way the Japanese were able to narrow rapidly the technological gap. With their new industrial plant and their often superior business organization and marketing techniques, they developed quickly into formidable economic competitors.

The most important external influence on Japan's renascent industrial economy was the world trading environment the Americans and their allies fashioned after the war. They made strong efforts to reduce barriers to trade between nations everywhere, and worldwide commerce flourished. This was an environment in which Japan, poor in national resources and heavily dependent on foreign markets and sources of supply, could thrive without resorting to the old technique of attempting to conquer its own economic empire.

Many countries were at first reluctant to permit Japan to join the world trading community. Except for Americans, who had developed a paternalistic pride in Japan because of their role there as occupiers and reformers, the peoples of the West, still feeling the bitterness of the recent war, were not ready to welcome the Japanese into their group, and Japan's neighbors remembered the Japanese conquerors and feared a revival of Japanese military power. Only the Americans championed Japan's full membership in the world community, winning for the Japanese

Oil pipelines and wharfs at Yokkaichi, a city near Nagoya and a center of the petro-chemical industry. Japan has become the largest importer of crude oil in the world. (*Courtesy Japan Information Center*)

membership in the General Agreement on Tariffs and Trade (GATT) in 1955 and in the Organization for Economic Cooperation and Development (OECD) in 1964. In 1975 Japan was one of the six (later seven) major democratic countries that started holding annual summit meetings.

European hostility toward Japan still has not disappeared entirely, but Australia, which was among the most bitter in the early postwar years, suddenly woke up in the 1960s to the fact that Japan was becoming its chief market and adopted an attitude of warm interest comparable to that of the United States. At the same time the less developed countries of the world increasingly turned to Japan as the best source of the industrial goods and technology they needed. The quality of Japanese manufactures had improved greatly over those of prewar days, until by the 1980s "made in Japan" signified excellence in every field. Japan was universally recognized as being not only a genuine economic giant but also a world leader in every type of industrial production. It had more than drawn abreast of the West. In the eyes of many people it was a model of economic success and a harbinger of the future.

33 The Employment System

Japan's economic success has caused a veritable mystique to grow up around it in the West. Many nations see Japan as the master of some secret and probably unfair business practices that should be changed to permit others to meet Japanese business on a level economic playing field. A more generous view is that the Japanese have developed mysterious skills that others would do well to learn about and emulate. Neither attitude is quite correct. Japan does have some special economic characteristics that are little understood abroad and on the whole are advantageous to the Japanese. These, however, are evolutionary developments from within Japanese society and, though surprising to Westerners, are in no way mysterious. They also are not set in concrete but keep evolving as conditions change.

One of the most outstanding characteristics of the Japanese economy is the lifetime employment system. For executives this is a carry-over from premodern days. Big companies select their future executives through examinations administered to fresh university graduates, often limited to a few prestigious universities. Successful candidates are enlisted for lifetime careers with the firm. In their early years they are all trained thoroughly, often through advanced study in Japan or abroad and through a variety of jobs in order to broaden their knowledge of the company's activities, though the most promising are likely to be given the most challenging assignments.

The members of the annual cohort keep in step with one another throughout most of their careers in both salary and rank. Normally no one is asked to serve under either a member of his own age group or a younger person. Only when the group nears the top are the ablest selected for the chief executive posts and the remainder retire—a common age is fifty-five—though many receive peripheral positions as executives

320

in smaller affiliated enterprises that may supply parts for the main company.

This general system of selection, training, promotion, and retirement is also used by the various ministries and agencies of the central government. Bureaucrats when they retire usually take advisory positions in the government or more frequently in business, where their income remains much the same but the duties are much lighter.

The whole Japanese employment system has certain drawbacks but also some major virtues. It tends to ameliorate if not eliminate corrosive competition and friction within the age cohort and across age and status lines. Because a subordinate cannot leapfrog an incompetent superior, the superior has nothing to fear from an able or ambitious subordinate. No one tries to demonstrate individual brilliance or aggressive leadership for fear of being considered a misfit. All office workers see themselves as members of office teams. The leader consults fully with his subordinates and encourages them to show initiative and special abilities, because their achievement redound to the credit of the whole office team. The subordinate dares to speak up without fear of drawing disapproval. At the same time, he gives his superior full support, regardless of the latter's ability or lack of it. The result is a system of easy consultation that brings out the best in all members of the office team. Full cooperation is counted on among all levels of management, and initiative is expected to be displayed at any level.

This brings us to the Japanese decision-making process in business and the bureaucracy, which foreigners often find puzzling. Americans, accustomed to a relatively dictatorial top-to-bottom style of decision making, are surprised to see in Japan decisions that appear to come from the bottom up. This phenomenon is related to a system called the *ringisei,* in which documents are widely circulated, usually from the lower echelons to higher ones, and officers at each level affix their seals as a sign that they have seen the document and are not actively opposed to it. This is not unlike the clearance system in American bureaucracies or the distribution of memoranda for information. Many routine matters can be settled in this way, but the system is not peculiar to Japan nor is it a way to make difficult high-level decisions.

What is indeed special in the Japanese decision-making process is the system of careful and thorough consultations before a decision is arrived at by general consensus. This is called *nemawashi,* a term literally denoting cutting around the roots of a plant before it is transplanted. Instead of an individual making a decision at the top, yanking out a plant

Lower-level executives confer about a problem over a cup of coffee. Such discussions could be considered the lower level of the *nemawashi* (consultation) process. (© *Richard Kalvar / Magnum Photos*)

by its stem, as it were, the Japanese conduct wide informal discussions involving concerned subordinates. From this may emerge a consensus that can be embodied in a *ringisei* document drafted by some subordinate. Or the final decision may still have to be made by a small group or one man at the top. In any case, all persons concerned are made fully familiar with the decision in advance and are in a position to carry it out much more effectively than if they were suddenly handed it without previous warning.

This corporate decision-making process and the tight cohesiveness of the age cohort and the office team do have some serious drawbacks. They slow up the decision-making process and also make it difficult for outsiders, especially foreigners, to fit in. Foreigners tend to lack not only fluency in Japanese but also sufficient knowledge of Japanese styles of personal relations and long enough associations with their office mates to perform effectively. As the Japanese economy rapidly becomes more international, the difficulty of incorporating foreigners at the highest levels of leadership will become a growing problem.

On the other hand, Japan's system of lifetime employment for executives has the advantage of reducing internal frictions and building up great loyalty to the company or branch of government a person joins. He tends to identify himself not by his specialized function as an engineer, electronics expert, sales executive, economist, or the like so much as by his firm or branch of government as a Toyota, Nippon Steel, Hitachi, or Finance Ministry man. He proudly wears his company logo in his buttonhole, and his "name cards" (*meishi*), which are ubiquitously exchanged, will always feature this professional affiliation. The value of such intense loyalty is incalculable.

Lifetime employment for persons in executive positions is by no means limited to Japan. It is common in most military organizations and in many civilian branches of government, such as the American foreign service. But the extension of this system to labor is a unique feature of the Japanese system. This is commonly assumed to be a survival from premodern Japanese society, but it is in fact a more modern development. Early Japanese machine production, as in the West, was mostly in textiles and, again as in the West, was largely staffed by transient young female workers. In Japan most of these were girls attempting to build up dowries, who lived in dormitories under close company control and chaperonage.

Workers in the technically more demanding metal industries were men who wandered from job to job, selling their labor to the highest bidder as in the West. Around the turn of the century Japanese employers began to realize that such skilled workers were a relatively rare commodity worth holding onto through various special privileges, the chief of which was job security. The hold on this labor could be made more secure by a wage system that rewarded length of service, making it progressively less attractive for workers to leave. Promising young men with adequate educational records would be recruited at relatively low wages determined by the abundance of unskilled labor, trained for specialized jobs at company expense, and retained by promises of steadily rising wages in accordance with seniority.

The lifetime employment system is essentially the same for executives and workers, though it started earlier with executives. It began to be important for labor only after World War I and became the dominant system in big business only after World War II. It succeeds in building almost as much loyalty to the company among workers as among executives. The office groups of executives and white-collar workers are paralleled by work groups or quality control circles on the floor of the factory. Together with their supervisors, workers form small close-knit units that take pride in the achievements of their particular group, policing the quality of the work they produce and collectively seeking means to improve their performance or suggesting innovations for the manufacturing process.

No clear line is drawn between executives and workers, though executives are clearly on a higher track from the start. They usually wear the same work jackets and hats in the plant and eat in the same company restaurants. Cheap company housing may be provided both groups, and a great deal of company indoctrination is included in the initial in-service training for both. In some companies all employees start the day by singing the company song together. The company takes a paternalistic interest in both young workers and executives. Warm relations of trust are encouraged between superiors and subordinates, and the former often function as personal counselors to those below them. A big firm may have a vacation resort for groups from the company, and sports teams, field days, and other activities are sponsored to strengthen the feeling of company solidarity. The lives of young workers and executives are focused on the company as much as possible, usually with considerable success in building a sense of personal identification with the company.

Although the whole system of lifetime employment and pay in accordance with seniority grew out of labor needs, it fits well into basic Japanese group attitudes and produces a number of important side benefits. It makes for a loyal and even enthusiastic work force that takes pride in its products and is happy to work overtime. Many workers, particularly junior executives, make a point of not taking full advantage of the vacation time allotted them, perhaps wishing to impress others with their loyalty and the importance of their work. Workers are diligent and police their own output so carefully that, in contrast to most countries, outside inspections are not needed for quality control.

The worker finds that his close identification with his company satisfies his need for membership in a group, and the steady rise of his wages with age fits his economic requirements as he progresses through the various stages of life—marriage, having children, paying for their education, and, finally, preparing for his retirement. The system is much more modernized and humane than that of industrialism in the nineteenth century, when wages were determined primarily by skills and energy, which often tapered off as a person grew older. It is similar to the pay system of modern armies and bureaucracies and can be considered more the pattern for the future than are the old-fashioned wage practices still found in many other industrial countries.

The Japanese lifetime employment system also acts as an ameliorating counterforce against the waves of unemployment that have buffeted the industrialized world in modern times. If a company no longer needs workers for some particular line of activity, it will always seek to train those displaced for some other form of work in the company, and even when it faces an overall surplus of labor, it may seek to keep workers occupied in make-work activities until natural attrition has eliminated the surplus.

This approach, of course, is socially as well as economically beneficial to the workers, saving them from loss of self-respect as well as the economic strains of unemployment. For the economy of the nation and society as a whole, and even for the individual companies, it also has its benefits. The system assures the companies of the loyalty of its workers and of public goodwill. It also may not increase its long-term economic burdens. Unemployed workers must be supported in some way, probably out of taxes, and these in the last analysis are borne by the companies themselves. The costs of unemployment ultimately must be paid.

Japan seems to have done very well with its lifetime employment system. Unemployment figures have for some time been only a small fraction of what they are in other industrialized countries and have not risen appreciably even at times of economic crisis, as in the oil shocks of the 1970s. Of course, the chief reason for this has been the thriving of the Japanese economy. Another factor is that Japanese unemployment figures are in some cases deceptively low because of the tendency of unemployed female workers not to register as part of the work force. But the Japanese employment system has unquestionably been an important part of Japan's economic success.

The seniority system of pay also acts as a built-in spur to economic growth. A dynamic, rapidly growing company will have a disproportionately large number of newly hired young workers who are underpaid in terms of their productivity, while a stagnant company will on average have an older, more costly work force. There are thus strong economic incentives for rapid expansion. Growth in Japanese business breeds more growth. And the fact that wages are a fixed cost not easily reducible by dismissals militates strongly against any reduction of production, regardless of demand or price. The natural pressures are all for expansion and against contraction.

As described above, the Japanese employment system sounds almost idyllic, but it has severe limitations. It has never applied to the bulk of the workers in the lower level of the dual economy or to most women, who have always been considered temporary employees outside the system. Workers in petty retailing and small industrial plants have no assurance of lifetime employment or steadily rising wages geared to seniority. Around each of the great manufacturing corporations are gathered scores of small subcontracting firms that serve as feeder plants, supplying small elements to the manufacturing process but affording their workers none of the privileges of the system. Even within the big corporations there are whole categories of workers who are considered temporary labor outside the system, however permanent their employment may actually be. These various peripheral workers receive fewer financial benefits and run the risk of unemployment, while only the elite workers of the big companies enjoy the full privileges of the system.

Changes are taking place even among them. During the period of most rapid economic growth, from the late 1950s to the 1970s, labor was plentiful, and companies could grow quickly by hiring relatively inexpensive young workers, especially those from the postwar baby-boom period. Rapid growth thus was definitely advantageous for a firm, since it lowered average labor costs. The increase in population, however, subsequently slowed down. As young workers became less numerous and older ones became a larger percentage of the work force, the so-called graying of the population made labor more expensive on average and the rapid growth of firms less easy or advantageous.

Younger workers also are beginning to find the Japanese employment system less attractive than did their predecessors. Distant economic rewards for present hard work do not have as much appeal. They find the paternalistic attitudes of the company a little stifling and crave more freedom in their personal lives. As a result they show less loyalty to the company, and more of them, including young executives, are inclined to shift jobs, to the horror of their elders. The whole wage system, which is highly complex, is moving toward more emphasis on skills and production results and away from an overwhelming reliance on seniority. In other words, the system is showing signs of erosion.

The Japanese employment and wage system, however, still seems on the whole to be firmly entrenched and will probably remain basically intact for some time. The poorer wages of the lower level are being pulled upward toward the better wages of the upper level because of the general scarcity of labor. Although it seems clear that the whole system will continue to erode to some extent, and conditions in Japan will grav-

Dockyard workers huddle, possibly on some work-related problem, during a lunch-time break. (© *Henri Cartier-Bresson* / *Magnum Photos*)

itate closer to those in the West, it is even more probable that the Western system of employment and wages will move even further toward the obviously successful Japanese pattern.

The employment and wage system in Japan has clearly influenced the development of labor unions there. As we have seen, immediately after World War II the labor movement flourished on the foundations of a determined though oppressed prewar labor movement and with the strong encouragement of the American occupation. For a while it even made a bid to take over control of industry. Subsequently, however, because of American opposition to such activities and the satisfaction of Japanese workers with their rapidly rising wages, the labor movement settled down into a less militant stance, which has been maintained ever since.

Only a third or less of Japanese workers are unionized—a figure comparable to much of Western Europe and definitely higher than in the

United States. Since the workers think of themselves primarily as lifetime members of some specific company rather than as pliers of specific skills and their lives are heavily bound up in the activities of that company, most unions are not craft unions spread throughout several companies, like those of the West, but are limited to a single company, in which they embrace all workers, including often even the lower echelons of management. Such unions might be called enterprise unions to distinguish them from "company unions," a term that implies an artificial creation dominated by the company. Japanese enterprise unions are entirely independent organizations designed to defend the workers against management and engaging the company in an annual nationwide "spring offensive" over wages.

Enterprise unions commonly are banded together in larger groups to include all the unions in a certain line of economic activity, and these in turn are sometimes formed into nationwide federations that are likely to be focused more on national issues than on local ones. As we have seen, Sohyo, the largest, is primarily made up of government employees and white-collar workers, whose wages are more likely to depend on political action than on the marketplace. As a consequence, its unions tend to retain the early emphasis on political activity, particularly through support of the Socialist Party or even the Communists. The second-largest federation, Domei, made up mostly of blue-collar workers in private industry, emphasizes wages and working conditions for its members and gives its political support to the Democratic Socialist Party. The lesser federations and independent unions tend to remain politically neutral.

The average worker in most of private industry is fundamentally interested in his own enterprise union, not in the national federations. Both he and his union realize that his own well-being depends on the success of his company. Knowing that the company will retrain him for a new job if his old one becomes outmoded, he and his union put up no opposition to technological advances, which sometimes cause costly losses in the West. They also realize that the company can scarcely increase its wages and benefits for its workers without increased productivity and profits. Though bargaining stubbornly for their share, they remain reasonable in their demands, tailoring them to fit the financial conditions of their company. When the Japanese economy was growing very rapidly, Japanese workers could expect annual wage increases of around 15 percent, which made everyone happy, but in more recent years of slowed growth or even setbacks the workers and their unions have proved to be equally reasonable.

Demonstration by the Automobile Transport Workers Union (Jiko Soren in Japanese abbreviation; ATU according to a logo on a banner). The signs say "Opposition to the 'Liberalization' of Haitaku." From the context *haitaku* must mean *haiya* and *takushi,* derived from the English words "hire" (which means "limousine") and "taxi." (© *Richard Kalvar / Magnum Photos*)

Workers and their unions are about as unhappy to see strikes and other work stoppages as management itself, because they realize that they too must pay for the profits lost. For this reason many strikes are purely symbolic, set for short periods before the commencement of work in the morning, allowing workers to demonstrate their muscle without impairing production. Real strikes are normally brief. Prolonged strikes are likely to occur only when a whole industry is going under and workers must be shifted out of it. The last such strike was the Miike coal strike in 1960, when the strikers inevitably had to give way in their demands. In recent years, man-days lost to strikes have been far fewer than in the West—a mere third or quarter as many as in the United States and the United Kingdom.

In these and other ways the Japanese labor unions have contributed to the rapid growth of the Japanese economy while satisfying the needs of the workers. They are one of the significant ways in which the whole Japanese employment and wage system has been an important asset to the Japanese economy. Of course, the system works more smoothly when Japan's economy is steeply rising, but it still seems to run very well even when the economy slows down, as it now has. It is obviously one of the reasons for the extraordinary success of the modern Japanese economy.

34 Business Organization

Japanese business organization at its higher levels has been another major reason for the country's economic success. This aspect of Japan's economy in particular is little understood in the West. One question often asked is who owns Japanese business, since most remaining industrial wealth was virtually confiscated in the capital levy by the American occupation at the end of the war. The answer basically is the nation itself, that is, the people in general.

Successful new entrepreneurs, farmers owning land near cities, and people with desirable nonagricultural land have built up considerable fortunes, but stockholders typically do not own or control most of the big companies. Instead, they are run though not owned by their own executives, who operate under the watchful eye of the financial institutions that provide them with most of their capital. Ownership exists, if anywhere, with banks and other lending institutions. Debt-equity ratios sometimes run as high as 80 to 20 percent, which would be considered a very dangerous situation in the West. Behind the banks, insurance companies, and other sources of capital stands the central Bank of Japan, which in turn is supported by the credit of the government and the taxes and savings of the population as a whole. The net result is a sort of national ownership.

Because of this situation, most Japanese businesses do not have to worry much about the quarterly bottom line, as their American counterparts do. They can concentrate on long-range stability and growth in market share, which are of primary interest to the lifetime employees who are the executives of the company and to the lending institutions, which look for security and long-term returns on their loans. As a result, the Japanese businessman pays more attention to a good growth record, which will entitle him to more bank loans, than to immediate profits, which would be helpful in raising equity capital. Whereas the American executive must keep his eye on stock prices and the quarterly bottom line, his Japanese counterpart can take a more Olympian view, seeking to maintain a sound company and to lay the basis for growth that may not pay off for a decade, long after he himself has retired. This longer time horizon for Japanese business permits a wiser strategy for growth and is probably the single greatest advantage it has over business in the West.

The role financial institutions play in providing adequate capital for Japan's spectacular growth raises the question of where they obtain so much money. The answer starts with the credit of the national government, which stands behind these institutions. Then comes Japan's huge economic success, which has added vastly to its financial resources. But a third and vital factor has been the strong propensity of the Japanese people to save under diverse circumstances, including even the early postwar years of economic want and the subsequent period of exuberant consumer spending. Unlike Americans, who have become accustomed to living in debt through home mortgages, credit-card buying, and other forms of borrowing, the Japanese have a firm tradition of saving. In part this has been necessitated by fewer social security programs and lower retirement pay, but it seems to be fundamentally a survival from a long history of penurious living. Japanese savings rates actually approached 40 percent of GNP in the 1960s, and even today personal savings is roughly 15 percent, as compared with around 7 percent in Europe and only 3 percent in the United States. Corporations, freed from the need to bow to demanding stockholders, tend to reinvest a much larger share of profits in further expansion than is normally possible in the West.

The tax and wage systems are also set up in such a way as to encourage savings. Tax benefits accrue to companies reinvesting their profits rather than distributing them as dividends, and for the small saver postal savings, though paying low interest rates, have been tax free. The higher wages of older workers are specifically designed to be saved for retirement, and the whole wage system has a special quirk that encourages savings at all age levels. Twice a year, at New Year's and midsummer, employees receive a bonus, usually running from one to three months' salary, depending upon the company's profits. Since most employees are accustomed to living on their monthly pay, these bonuses are easily squirreled away as savings.

An advertisement for a family savings plan through salary withholding, hanging in a Mitsubishi Bank. Below is a sign for a water outlet for fire fighting. (© *Michal Heron / Woodfin Camp & Associates*)

As we have already seen, another major feature of Japanese business organization is the close cooperation that has existed in modern times between business and government. Some Americans, exaggerating the situation, have viewed Japanese business and government as secretly united into a single entity, which they call "Japan, Inc." This greatly overstates the case, because government controls are limited and business is eager to be entirely free of them. But there is enough truth to the picture of government-business cooperation to form a sharp contrast with the United States, where the two have traditionally been considered to be enemies.

In premodern Japan, business was seen as an undesirable reality that disrupted the ideal patterns of the feudal system, but in the mid-nineteenth century the new Meiji government became the sponsor of business in order to catch up with the West, while businessmen gratefully accepted government leadership and assistance. Business, however, grew so rapidly that in the eyes of some the tail began to wag the dog. Eventually military leadership in the 1930s forced most businesses to become dissatisfied but obedient handmaidens of government.

During the American occupation, the concept of free business activity was introduced through the dissolution of the zaibatsu, passage of the Anti-Monopoly Law, and the establishment of a Fair Trade Commission and other institutions borrowed from United States models. In reality, however, government control over business was never more thorough. This was because the desperate economic situation called for such controls, as did the sweeping social and political reforms the Americans were carrying out.

The occupation reformers thought of their innovations as temporary measures, but many became a permanent new starting point for government-business relations. Much of the government control was exercised through the powerful Ministry of International Trade and Industry (Tsusansho)—commonly known in the West as MITI (pronounced *mee-tee*)—which replaced the prewar Ministry of Commerce. While an Economic Planning Agency formulated broad economic objectives, the various branches of MITI set goals for specific industries and guided much of Japan's actual growth. Through control of foreign exchange and the licensing of foreign technology, the bureaucrats carefully supervised the acquisition of new technology, seeking to obtain the best on the most favorable terms for those best able to make optimum use of it.

At the same time they avoided creating monopolies within Japan and encouraged competition by ensuring that two or more strong companies would get similar technology. MITI also helped in the formation of depression cartels when production had to be curtailed and export cartels when "voluntary" restrictions on exports were demanded by foreign countries, especially the United States. It also encouraged mergers of weak, small companies with larger, stronger ones in order to improve the overall performance of the economy.

As has been mentioned, tax strategies were designed to encourage industries that had good prospects for growth, and the Bank of Japan adopted policies that assured the ample flow of funds into such fields. Both MITI and other ministries also gave "administrative guidance" with a view to steering companies into the most productive lines of activity. This "guidance" did not have the force of law, but businessmen voluntarily accepted it, because they realized that MITI and the other ministries had many administrative means of rewarding or punishing them.

In these various ways, the government played a major role in guiding Japan's postwar economic recovery. As we have seen, it first encouraged a few selected basic areas of industrial activity and then, as the economy prospered, moved on to other more advanced fields. It has had a steadily shifting strategy as economic conditions have changed. Already by the 1960s it was moving away from labor-intensive industries, as the newly industrializing countries, the so-called NICs, such as South Korea, Taiwan, Hong Kong, and Singapore, appeared on the world industrial scene with their decidedly lower wage scales. Subsequently it began to shift from heavy industries, which required huge imports of raw material and energy resources, such as oil, and were likely to cause heavy pollution, to high technology that could be characterized as knowledge and information industries, where Japan's high educational levels and scientific skills gave it an advantage over the NICs and parity with the best in the West.

Another important role of the government has been to ease the difficulties caused by declining industries. With the exception of agriculture, it frankly accepted the necessity of shifting workers from these sunset industries to growing ones, and it aided in the process. It adopted policies of retraining workers for other fields and reducing production in planned stages to which companies could accommodate. Its role has been diametrically opposed to that of the American government, which, yielding to the pressures of congressional representatives of areas with declining industries, has sought to prop up these unhealthy elements in the economy at the expense of higher prices for consumers and higher taxes on the stronger parts of the economy. Thus the Japanese government helps to channel resources to the most productive industries, while the American government seeks to retain them for the least productive industries. The Japanese strategy naturally produces faster growth and a healthier economy.

Not all Japanese postwar industrial growth resulted from government guidance. The bureaucrats were as fallible as others in predicting the future. For example, Japan's great success in the automotive field was achieved without any particular government aid or realization of what was happening. The government in its economic guidance, however, was wise enough to leave actual business initiatives up to private industry. Thus, unlike the countries with fully planned economies, it permitted free enterprise to escape from governmental miscalculations and to exploit fields that the government had overlooked. The balance between private initiative and government aid and guidance seems to have been a happy one—perhaps the best such balance struck anywhere in the world.

The government-business relationship has by no means been all one way. Big business, or the *zaikai* ("financial world") as it is known in Japan, is no mere puppet of government but more of an equal partner exerting a reciprocal influence. The government has given big business guidance and aid, but it has also sought its advice. The powerful Keidanren (Federation of Economic Organizations) has played a major role in determining the government's economic policies and sometimes even its leadership, especially in the 1950s and early 1960s. The Keizai Doyukai (called in English the Committee for Economic Development), whose members initially were somewhat younger business executives than those who headed Keidanren, has also played an important advisory role. The Japan Chamber of Commerce (Nissho), which represents slightly smaller companies, and Nikkeiren (the Federation of Employers Associations), which operates as a central strategy board in labor relations, have served more parochial business interests.

In recent years both the role of government in providing guidance to industry and government-business cooperation seem to have been waning. As Japanese industry has become stronger, it has had less need or tolerance for government controls of any sort, and the demands by foreign countries for reciprocal treatment in Japan to balance the openness of their own economies to Japanese economic penetration have required the government to abandon many of the controls it once exercised. Exchange controls have had to be dropped as well as most tariff limitations on imports and MITI's supervision of the importation of technology. The one area in which government leadership has actually expanded is pollution controls. Aroused by the Japanese public, the government vigorously took up pollution controls in the early 1970s. These, unlike earlier measures, were not welcomed by business and were designed not to foster economic growth but to meet social demands. The concerns that once gave priority to economic growth and made government and business congenial partners in achieving this goal are disintegrating. The government, responding to popular emphasis on the quality of life over mere quantity of production, is being pulled in one direction, while businessmen, with their unchanging drive for economic success, are losing their position as the heroes of Japan's postwar economy and are increasingly being regarded as the villains, as the chief pollutors and creators of overcrowding. The basic cooperation between an efficient government and a dynamic, competitive business world will probably continue, but the old warm partnership as the twin engines of Japan's postwar economic success is not likely to be restored.

Another major feature of Japanese business is the strength of group ties, which pervade it as they do the rest of Japanese society. Members of management regard their superiors, peers, and subordinates all as members of the same club, with whom they must do their best to cooperate during their whole careers. They are not likely to be lured away by higher pay in other companies, and those who may be are looked on askance as misfits or persons with a serious character flaw. This system minimizes disruptive changes in leadership and also damaging interpersonal competition. The company benefits greatly from lessened frictions and stronger cohesion among its leaders.

The resulting sense of solidarity may be one reason for lower overhead management costs in Japan than in the United States. Salaries for management are decidedly more modest than in the United States, and there is much less ownership of company stock by executives. The only exceptions are the relatively new family companies, but even in these not much of the ownership can be passed on in the face of extremely steep inheritance taxes. Success is measured less by money than by the symbols of prestige—large company residences, cars, chauffeurs, sumptuous offices, liberal expense accounts, and, most of all, the holding of a high office in a company of national importance. In any case, we do not find the bloated salaries or large competing bureaucracies common in American corporations.

Since the executive officers of a Japanese company form a lifetime club sharing similar objectives, they operate smoothly together. Unless a company runs into serious financial difficulties and comes under the control of its creditor banks, the leadership is chosen from the most successful members of the club. Engineers or scientists who are thoroughly familiar with the whole process of manufacturing the company's products are likely to be in charge rather than sales managers or financiers from some larger company that has taken it over to milk its immediate profitability, not to develop its long-term strength. One result of this sort of leadership is that a Japanese company usually stays in the field of production or business it knows best and keeps its eye on further growth in that field, rather than proliferating into a conglomerate seeking short-term profits.

Japanese business executives are less concerned with quick profits to please stockholders than with long-term growth to increase the company's market share and win national and international prestige. This is the best way to achieve both personal and company goals. The two cannot be entirely disentangled from each other, since personal rewards clearly can only come if the company is successful, but management is united in taking the long-term view of the company's success. Such attitudes contrast with American concentration on personal success in whatever company pays best and immediate profits to demonstrate personal effectiveness. They fit in well, however, with the long horizon of Japanese economic planning and the national drive for economic success.

The tendency toward group cooperation spreads into the relations between companies. As we have seen, those in the same line of activity often form associations, which in turn make up the components of the overall Keidanren federation. Businesses in one of the keiretsu groups inherited from the time of the zaibatsu combines also often have closer relations with each other than with other companies, and long association and personal friendship and trust are likely to play an important role in determining a company's corporate partners. The importance of personal respect and trust cannot be overemphasized in any explanation of how Japanese big business works. Friendships are strengthened by the exchange of gifts, intermarriage, and recreation together on the golf course and at geisha parties—or bars in the case of less exalted executives. Such personal ties play a major role in business relations, preceding legally binding agreements, which merely spell out the details. Businessmen shy away from cold legal relationships, preferring warm personal contacts. If possible, litigation is avoided and problems are decided by compromises based on personal trust. This is one reason why Japanese business employs only a small fraction of the number of lawyers per capita that the United States requires. The result is a tremendous saving in lawyers' fees and a much lower intensity of friction in business.

The emphasis on personal friendship reaches beyond relationships between companies and into their cooperation with government. One of the reasons this cooperation was so successful at a crucial time in Japan's postwar development was that the bureaucrats and the business leaders, except for some of the new self-made men, came mostly from the same prestigious universities. They were friends already or at least symbolically wore the same old school tie.

In many ways, Japan's postwar industrial system is the best in the world, as it has clearly demonstrated. It might be called postcapitalist because of its leadership by salaried "business bureaucrats" and its orientation to national service and growth rather than merely to personal salaries and immediate company profits. Monetary recompense is relatively equal, and the welfare of the nation as a whole is seen as the main objective.

In a sense the Japanese economy is a blend of the best aspects of capitalism and socialism. It does not submit itself entirely to the unseen hand of the market, but accepts government guidance. At the same time, the government does not stifle economic growth, as it does wherever it attempts to plan and control the whole economy. There is ample room for free enterprise and stiff competition. The economy operates harmoniously and effectively; it brings to positions of leadership men of proven intellectual talent and practical skills drawn through open competition in school and business from the whole country; and it brims over with a drive for growth, which is kept alive by vigorous competition between rival companies. Undoubtedly the Japanese economy is an outstanding success, worthy of study and, where appropriate, emulation, though it should be noted that part of its strength lies in characteristics that other people might not be able or willing to imitate.

In conclusion, however, we should remember that, for all its success, Japanese business is not without serious problems and weaknesses. There is no guarantee that it will operate as smoothly in the future as it has in the recent past. Many of its greatest strengths are clearly starting to erode. Young people have less of the unquestioning loyalty to their companies than their predecessors had. The whole wage force is aging and as a result becoming more costly and less productive. The Japanese are unwilling to see labor shortages filled by immigrants or "guest workers," as happens in the United States and in northern Europe. This attitude makes it more difficult to fill low-paying jobs but also saves the Japanese from having to cope with some of the difficult social problems of ethnic diversity.

The greatest problem area for the Japanese is foreign trade. They see themselves as precariously perched on a narrow economic ledge, depending on huge imports of food, energy resources, and other raw materials and therefore as equally dependent on large exports of industrial goods to pay for their imports. When Japan was still a relatively small economic unit recovering from the war and the world economy as a whole was rebounding vigorously from its recent devastation, there was plenty of room for rapid Japanese growth; but now Japan has become an economic giant, and although it has no problem obtaining raw material imports, since the world appears to be heading into a period of surpluses in raw materials, Japan is now encountering serious difficulties in finding markets for its exports. The newly industrializing nations with lower labor costs are pushing Japan out of labor-intensive fields, such as textiles and electronics, and into the high-technology, capital-intensive areas. But the markets in those fields are largely in the richer, highly industrialized countries like the United States and those of Western Europe, which are themselves desperately clinging to this sort of production. They are not likely to permit directly competitive Japanese imports to continue to grow at the same rate as in the past at the expense of their own industries. For example, America's current annual deficit of fifty or more billion dollars with Japan simply cannot be tolerated over an extended period and must be curbed by negotiation before it brings some more drastic and dangerous reaction.

Japan's tariffs on trade are no higher and in many cases are lower than those of most of its rivals, but other countries feel that Japan has maintained nontariff barriers through trickery, creating an economic playing field that is tilted against foreigners. They also believe that the Japanese can maintain their economic vigor and bring greater benefit to their

Businessmen visitors at a "Software Show '86" exhibit held on October 1–3 in Sunshine City, the largest skyscraper in Ikebukuro, one of Tokyo's satellite downtowns and commuting centers. The woodblock print in the style of Sharaku (active 1794–95) on the poster announcing the show indicates how easily tradition and modernity mix in Japan. (© *Sonia Katchian / Photo Shuttle: Japan*)

country by devoting more of their production to enriching their own land, especially in improving housing, roadways, sewerage, and other social needs, and putting less effort into exports.

The Japanese perceive the situation quite differently. They are perilously dependent on massive foreign trade. They remember that the world oil shortage and subsequent worldwide runaway inflation over which Japan had little control forced the inflation rate in Japan to soar for a while in the 1970s as high as 26 percent. They also remember America's sudden embargo in 1973 of soybeans, which are so necessary in the Japanese diet. Such incidents give them a strong sense of vulnerability. They are keenly aware of their inability to produce their own food. They feel that they must maintain a rapid rate of growth to build up a cushion between themselves and some unforeseen disaster. They attribute the favorable balance in their trade to the unwillingness of other countries to reform their economic systems and their failure to learn the Japanese language and how to exploit the Japanese economy in the way that Japanese businessmen mastered foreign languages, the economic requirements of the countries to which they wished to export, and their methods of doing business.

There is some validity to both points of view, but the important point is that Japan's economic problems lie primarily in its relations with other countries. In fact, this is true of almost all of Japan's serious problems. Japan left to itself is an extraordinarily successful and happy land. Obviously, however, at this stage in history Japan cannot live by itself; it is inevitably one of the central foci of world events. It is to Japan's relations with the outside world that we must now turn.

Part Six

Japan
and the
World

Dockside cranes and cars lined up for export epitomize Japan's current relations with the outside world. (© Sonia Katchian/ Photo Shuttle: Japan)

35　The Prewar Record

The importance of Japan's relations—or lack of them—
with the outside world has been a recurring theme throughout our story,
sometimes just as a background melody but becoming a crashingly dominant leitmotif in recent times. Some 122 million Japanese—or even half
that number—can live in their narrow islands only if there is a huge
flow of natural resources into Japan, a corresponding outward flow of
manufactures to pay for these imports, and the conditions of world
peace and global trade that permit this vast exchange of goods. The
Japanese must also be able to cooperate effectively with the other
peoples of the globe on the multitudinous and increasingly complex
problems that beset mankind. All other skills and accomplishments will
avail them little if these conditions are not met. A suitable world environment and satisfactory relations with other peoples are overwhelming
necessities.

International relations, however, are perceived both by the Japanese
themselves and by foreigners as the area of Japan's greatest weakness.
Here lie the rocks on which Japan may founder. The past experience of
the Japanese has not prepared them well for foreign contacts. Their very
assets, such as their strong self-identity, extraordinary homogeneity, and
close-knit society, are sometimes handicaps when they face the world
today. Their language, so radically different from all others, is a barrier
of monumental size between them and other peoples. We might compare
them to an incomparably skilled baseball player who suddenly finds
himself called on to play in a tennis tournament.

The shift in priorities to foreign relations has come quite unexpectedly
to the Japanese. While they were dealing brilliantly with their own postwar domestic problems, they suddenly found that their chief difficulties
lay in a different direction. Only during the two past decades have they

become aware of this fact, and they are still far from comprehending its full import. Throughout most of Japanese history foreign relations have either not been very important for them or else have proved manageable with the skills they possessed. We might start with a brief review of the record.

Up until the sixth century, there had been large influxes into Japan of people from Korea and, probably connected with this, Japanese military involvement in the Korean Peninsula. But thereafter for almost a thousand years the Japanese had only minimal contacts with outsiders. The peaceful importation of elements of Chinese culture was a major theme of Japanese history, but not foreign wars or the migration of people. Trade gradually increased and with it some Japanese piratical activities, starting in the fourteenth century on the coasts of the nearby continent and spreading later as far as Southeast Asia. The Portuguese and other Europeans appeared in Japan as traders and Christian missionaries in the sixteenth century, but they were forced out in the seventeenth, and their religion was obliterated from the islands. Japan then settled into two centuries of artificially enforced isolation, except for tiny and closely regulated trade contacts with the Chinese, Koreans, and Dutch. During this whole great sweep of history from the sixth to the nineteenth century, the only foreign wars the Japanese experienced were the two attempted invasions of Japan by the Mongol rulers of China in the thirteenth century and Hideyoshi's attempted conquest of Korea from 1592 to 1598. No other major nation has a record remotely this free of invasions and foreign military adventures.

Foreign relations first posed a truly serious problem for the Japanese in the middle of the nineteenth century, when the Western world beat on Japan's closed doors, demanding entry and trade. The Japanese were forced to open up and to scramble hard to protect themselves from superior Western military and economic technology by acquiring it for themselves. In the process, they found it necessary to make revolutionary changes in their society and political system, but, drawing on their traditional characteristics of homogeneity, hard work, and skill in cooperative enterprise, they succeeded in this task in a way no other people did when first confronted by Western technological superiority.

It was a dangerous and rapacious world, however, that Japan had been forced to join. The late nineteenth century witnessed the height of the age of imperialism. The strong devoured the weak and contended with one another for strategic advantages. Military strength appeared to the Japanese as essential as industrial power to win security and full independence. Accordingly, they put great emphasis on developing a strong army and navy and embarked on expansion abroad. Korea was perceived as a dagger pointed at the heart of Japan if it were in the hands of a hostile power. Japan fought two wars over its control and won both, the first with China in 1894–95 and the next with Russia in 1904–05. Out of these wars, a Japanese Empire emerged, embracing Taiwan, Korea, the southern tip of Manchuria, and the southern half of Sakhalin. By World War I Japan was the paramount military as well as economic power in East Asia, and during that war it extended its economic predominance over large parts of China. Through the war settlement it also acquired the German islands of the North Pacific and the German holdings in the coastal Chinese province of Shantung.

A subtle change came over Japanese perceptions of foreign relations at about this time. Military strength and expansion had in one way brought Japan security, but in another it had brought a new vulnerability. The industrial base and increased population on which Japan's military might stood had made Japan dependent for the first time in its history on foreign sources of supply. Iron ore and other key minerals came from abroad; oil, on which the army and navy ran, largely from Indonesia (then the Dutch East Indies) and the west coast of the United States; soybeans, which were important as a source of protein for humans and fertilizer for agriculture, from Manchuria; and some rice from Korea and Taiwan. As industry and population grew further so also would Japan's dependence on the outside world.

World conditions, however, had become less favorable to imperial expansion. The Western powers, exhausted by World War I, had called a halt to foreign conquest and sought security in international cooperation. Any Japanese expansion would henceforth draw the condemnation of the world rather than its admiration. The spirit of nationalism also was growing in the less developed countries, particularly China, where Japan's best hopes for future expansion lay. Trade boycotts and popular resistance threatened to make imperialist expansion more costly and uncertain than it had been in the past.

In these circumstances it is not surprising that the party cabinets of the 1920s, under strong pressure from businessmen, who disliked high taxes and feared damage to their international trade, turned away from military expansion, withdrew from Shantung and a military adventure in Siberia, reduced military expenditures greatly as a proportion of the national budget, and agreed at the Washington Conference in 1921–22 to a limitation on capital ships that would give the more concentrated Japanese navy a ratio of three to five with the two-ocean fleet of the Americans and the worldwide fleet of the British. While maintaining their military dominance in the Western Pacific, the Japanese sought security for their expanding economy through reliance on international trade and a peaceful world order, as symbolized by the ideals of President Wilson and the League of Nations.

We have already seen how elements of the Japanese army reversed this policy in 1931 by starting the conquest of Manchuria and returning Japan to a course of imperial expansion. We need not reexamine here in detail the reasons for this rapid about-face. Certainly internal dissatisfaction, especially within the military, with the foreign policies of the party governments was a major factor. So also was the world depression that struck in 1929, greatly heightening political and social tensions within the country and frightening the Japanese with the prospect of being shut out of most of the world by restrictive trade policies. Some felt that the Western powers, satiated with imperial expansion and relatively secure from world depression because of the size of their holdings, had tricked Japan into giving up its expansion before it had acquired an adequate base to maintain its economic and military power. In addition, they saw the white race as having seized for its own use the attractive open lands of the world, such as North America and Australia, and as excluding the Japanese from them on arrogant racial grounds, thus bottling the Japanese up, as it were, in their own narrow islands.

The Manchurian Incident led to further expansion into China, more clashes with Chinese troops, and eventually the China War, when in 1937 the Nationalist Government of Chiang Kai-shek, under pressure from the Chinese Communist regime in the northwest, finally stood up against further Japanese encroachments. While the Japanese army won an almost uninterrupted string of battles and campaigns, seizing control of much of China, both the Nationalists and Communists continued to resist from their bases in the deep interior of the huge land, and the Japanese war machine bogged down in the quagmire of Chinese nationalism. Japan kept expanding the war in the hope of finding a way to knock out Chinese resistance, but its alignment with Germany and Italy and the association in American minds of Japan's bid for hegemony over East Asia with the Nazi attempt to establish hegemony over Europe aroused the United States to increase its economic pressures against Japan. A virtual ban on oil shipments in the summer of 1941 forced the Japanese government to choose between going to war with the United States or backing down. It elected to attack, winning spectacularly at first but ending in 1945 in total collapse, as Japan for the first time in its history came under the rule of a foreign conqueror.

36 *Neutrality versus Alignment*

The postwar Japanese found themselves in an unprecedented position. They were international outcasts, destitute, and demoralized. They had no economic or military power. Their chief concern was simple survival as individuals and as a nation. When they finally did regain their independence and gradually grew prosperous and economically strong again, they discovered that their increased numbers and greater reliance on industry had made them far more dependent than ever before on the resources and trade of the world. But they no longer had any options in seeking to solve this problem. Imperial expansion was clearly out of the question; only peaceful trade could ensure Japan a viable future.

Japan had been stripped of its small empire in Korea, Taiwan, Manchuria, and Sakhalin, and even of some of its integral parts—the Kuril Islands and, for a while, the Ryukyu Islands, or Okinawa. Moreover, the spirit of nationalism had become still more powerful everywhere in the world and imperial conquests entirely impossible. The remaining imperial powers soon found that they could not hold on to the colonies they already had, even those they had ruled for centuries. While great land powers such as the Soviet Union and China were able to maintain their grip on contiguous territories inhabited by subject peoples, all maritime empires melted rapidly away. Some colonial powers fought to keep their empires, as the Dutch did in Indonesia and the French in Indochina and Algeria, but most were given up voluntarily in recognition of the new realities. Under these circumstances, no Japanese, no matter how old-fashioned, could think in terms of imperial conquest.

It was obvious that the only possibility for Japan was a peaceful world of relatively open trade. At first the bitter antimilitarism and enthusiastic pacifism of the Japanese were largely an emotional reaction to the horrors of war and the tribulations it had brought them, but gradually these attitudes became a matter of rational conviction as well. As postwar emotions faded and a new generation grew up with no memory of the war, the strong intellectual conviction remained that world peace was a necessity for Japan. Today no people surpass the Japanese in their devotion to pacifism. It is their great ideal, supported by both their emotions and their intellects.

As long as Japan was powerless and under foreign occupation, it had no foreign relations problems, and most Japanese could agree simply on the need for world peace. But as the country regained its independence and gradually increased in economic power, questions arose as to what position it should take for its own safety and in behalf of global peace in a world that was divided into bickering nations and hostile military camps. No one doubted that Japan should stay out of any sort of war and seek to avoid involvement in international disputes. Accordingly the government, with general approval, sought to adopt a "low posture," as the Japanese described it, and to concentrate on Japan's economic recovery and growth. But the deep divisions of the Cold War soon made it clear that Japan would either have to seek security through close alignment with the United States or else cut itself free and hope to maintain strict though unprotected neutrality in world affairs. As we have seen, this became the chief area of controversy in Japanese politics for the next two decades. The party in power saw the need for close dependence on and cooperation with the United States, but Marxist ideologues in the opposition parties argued in all seriousness for many years that both "capitalist imperialism," meaning the United States, and "monopoly capitalism" were the chief enemies of the Japanese people.

The issue of alignment versus neutrality was forced on the Japanese by the United States when it decided to go ahead with a separate peace treaty with Japan in 1951, without the participation of the Soviet Union or China, and to parallel the peace treaty with a Security Treaty between Japan and the United States, permitting the retention of American military bases in an independent Japan and committing the United States to Japan's defense. From the point of view of the United States, both decisions seemed necessary. The occupation had already outlived its usefulness, and its further continuation threatened to do harm to the accomplishments already achieved. But a peace treaty including all parties seemed impossible. It was difficult to invite China because there was disagreement between the United States and its allies as to which Chinese regime really represented China. The United States recognized the

Nationalists and the United Kingdom and some of the other allies the People's Republic in Peking, with which the United States was then at war in Korea. It also seemed clear that neither Moscow nor Peking would agree to the peace terms the United States felt to be necessary. This was particularly true of the maintenance of American bases in Japan, which to Americans appeared essential both for support of the American military position in Korea and for the defense of an otherwise unprotected Japan, situated in a dangerously exposed position.

Japan's conservative political leadership understood this reasoning and shared it. Prime Minister Ashida Hitoshi first advocated a continuing defense relationship with the United States, and Yoshida, who succeeded him, supported this policy. Even the more moderate Socialists accepted the necessity of a "separate peace treaty" and split with the left wing over this issue. The remainder of the opposition groups, however, fought bitterly against the treaty. In their eyes the Americans had shifted from liberators to enemies by stopping further reforms in Japan in their wish to foster economic recovery and had thus ruled out the possibility of socializing the Japanese economy. Their sympathies lay more with the Communist nations, which they felt were the real "peace camp," resisting the capitalist aggressors. They felt that the Security Treaty and the American bases it permitted endangered Japan rather than giving it security, for these bases, they feared, would inevitably involve Japan in America's wars and would serve as targets for retaliation from the other side. The Security Treaty and the bases, they also felt, trampled on Japan's constitutional renunciation of war, in which most Japanese took great pride, and on their ardent desire to remain neutral in international conflicts.

Such attitudes had great popular appeal and were shared at least in part by many supporters of the conservative parties. While the economic record of the Liberal Democratic Party was to prove its chief strength, its foreign policy of alignment with the United States long remained its greatest weakness. Neutrality appeared far more attractive to Japanese than even a passive alliance with either side. Extensive American bases, particularly the many around Tokyo, were a constant social irritant and affront to Japanese pride. Inevitably unpleasant incidents and crimes occurred involving American military personnel, who at first were subject only to American military courts in a system reminiscent of the hated extraterritoriality of the nineteenth century. The bases occupied choice land desired for other purposes, and proposals for extending their runways, as at Sunakawa at the American airbase in Tachikawa near Tokyo in 1954, provoked violent and protracted demonstrations. The rest of the world might be distressed by Soviet military actions or political pressures in Czechoslovakia, Hungary, or Berlin, but such matters seemed far away to Japanese, to whom American bases and men in uniform in their own land were the chief reminders of the hated militarism of the past.

There was a particular sensitivity in Japan to the nuclear weapons of the Americans. Japanese had been the victims of the two atomic bombs that helped bring World War II to an end. When in 1954 fallout from an American atomic test at Bikini in the mid-Pacific showered down on a Japanese fishing boat, the *Fukuryu-maru,* resulting in the death of one crewman, there was a vast public uproar over what was called with some hyperbole the third atomic bombing of humanity. Mass memorial meetings, held each year in Hiroshima on August 6, the anniversary of the first bombing, became huge demonstrations of protest against the United States and the Security Treaty, though in 1961 these demonstrations began to divide between the various opposition parties and then to lose their anti-American focus as concern rose in Japan over Soviet and Chinese nuclear armaments.

The nuclear sensitivity of the Japanese, sometimes called their "nuclear allergy," was not limited to weapons but included nuclear power and propulsion. During the 1960s Japan cautiously moved into the commercial production of electricity through nuclear power. Such a development appeared particularly necessary for this energy-poor nation, but there was always intense opposition, at first largely political in motivation but in time more from local residents who simply did not welcome nuclear power plants as neighbors. Nuclear-powered vessels of the American navy were also a special target for protests. Only after years of careful negotiations to ensure their safety were nuclear-powered submarines finally allowed in 1964 into naval bases in Japan, at first in the face of massive demonstrations. These in time died down, but in 1968, when excitement over the Vietnam War was running high, the visit by a nuclear-powered aircraft carrier occasioned even greater protests. Japan also experimented with building its own nuclear-powered vessel, the *Mutsu,* but the effort was plagued with political strife and mishaps and ended in fiasco in 1974 when no Japanese port community would agree to serve as the home port for the ship.

Throughout the 1950s and into the 1960s much of Japanese politics focused on military base problems, antinuclear demonstrations, and opposition to the Security Treaty. The revision of the treaty in 1960 led, as we have seen, to Japan's greatest postwar crisis. The revision was necessary because the original treaty had certain features that did not befit a fully independent nation of Japan's stature. It permitted the use of American troops in Japan to quell civil disturbances, if requested by the Japanese government; it provided for no Japanese control over American nuclear weapons, which were such a sore point to the Japanese public; and it had no terminal date or means of termination. The 1960 revision dropped the possible use of American troops in Japan and set a ten-year limit on the treaty, after which either side could renounce it on one year's notice. On the nuclear problem, the new treaty and some attached agreements established that the United States would not make major changes in armaments in Japan without first consulting with the Japanese government. This in more direct language meant that the United States would not mount or stockpile nuclear weapons or even bring them into Japan without formal Japanese approval, which most people felt would never be given. The same stipulations about prior consultation, which implied a Japanese veto, were also applied to the use of American bases in Japan for direct military action abroad, as in Korea.

These changes were naturally to the liking of the Japanese leadership, but the opposition forces, with the exception of some Socialists who split off to form the Democratic Socialist Party, decided to fight the ratification of the treaty on the grounds that the earlier treaty, though worse, had been forced on a Japan that was not yet free, while a new treaty, even though an improvement, was being voluntarily agreed to by a now independent Japan. Various extraneous factors stirred up public excitement—the U-2 incident in which an American spy plane was shot down over the Soviet Union, the resulting cancellation of a summit meeting between Eisenhower and Khrushchev, and Kishi's forcing through of the treaty's ratification in the lower house so that it would go into effect by the time of a planned visit to Japan by President Eisenhower on June 19. The opposition maintained that this amounted to antidemocratic acts by the prime minister and American intervention in Japanese domestic politics. The result was a tremendous popular outburst.

Once the new Security Treaty went into effect, however, the political situation calmed down, and for the next few years the debate over neutrality or alignment was less violent, as the new prime minister, Ikeda Hayato, adopted a "low posture" in domestic politics and drew attention to Japan's growing prosperity through his ten-year "income-doubling" plan.

Another defense issue also began to lose its edge at this time. This was the clash over the creation by the government, in seeming violation of article 9 of the constitution, of an army, navy, and air force under the name of the Self-Defense Forces. When in 1950 the remaining American ground troops in Japan were hastily dumped into Korea to stem the North Korean advance, MacArthur ordered the Japanese to create a national police reserve to take their place in Japan. This the government reorganized and expanded at the end of the occupation and in 1954 further expanded and renamed the Land, Sea, and Air Self-Defense Forces, placing them under a Defense Agency.

The conservative politicians clearly felt that Japan should have some defense capabilities of its own, but they wished to keep these small for financial and political reasons. Yoshida and his successors stubbornly resisted American pressures for a more rapid military buildup or a wider regional role for the Self-Defense Forces, on the grounds of the constitution and popular attitudes. Eventually the American government came to accept the Japanese view that, given the political climate in Japan, a very limited military posture for Japan was all that could be expected and probably was the wisest course in any case, because of the fears of Japan's neighbors about restored Japanese military power. The total size of the Self-Defense Forces had been set at 250,000 persons in 1954 and has grown only very little since then.

Since the occupation, Japan has kept to a very modest defense budget in relative terms. From slightly over 1 percent of GNP, it declined proportionately as GNP grew to a trifle below 1 percent and then rose slightly to 1.004 percent under Nakasone amidst loud cries of protest. Compared to the 3 to 6 percent usually spent by the major industrialized democracies and the 6 to 7 percent spent by the United States in the 1980s, this amounts to a great saving for Japan. On the other hand, the present huge size of the Japanese economy means that the military budget is in reality the sixth largest in the world, supporting well-paid, well-equipped, and excellently trained land, sea, and air forces, which would loom large in some parts of the world. Its air force, in fact, is one of the best in Asia. But Japan's military power is completely outclassed by that of the United States and Russia, and it has under arms scarcely more than a twentieth as many men as China and far less than half as many as Taiwan or either of the two Koreas.

The opposition parties in Japan from the start bitterly challenged the

Tanks of the Self Defense Forces pass in review before Prime Minister Nakasone. (*AP / Wide World Photos*)

creation of the Self-Defense Forces, fearing a restoration of prewar militarism and pointing out that they clearly transgressed the constitution. Public opinion at first also ran strongly against them. They outraged the antimilitarist and pacifist feelings of most Japanese, who yearned for an unarmed neutrality in which other nations would respect Japan's high pacifist ideals and not attack it. MacArthur had somewhat anachronistically held out the ideal of Japan's becoming "the Switzerland of Asia," and many Japanese aspired to being a nation whose neutrality, like Switzerland's, would be honored by others. They seemed to be quite unaware that the Swiss maintained a heavy military burden in order to help produce this result. Unarmed neutrality was always a slogan of the Socialists, though the Communists more realistically believed in national military power, so long as it was under the control of their party.

For several years public attitudes toward the Self-Defense Forces remained quite hostile, and the strength of antimilitarist sentiment and pacifism still prevents the Defense Agency from being upgraded to a ministry. Facing the competition in salaries of a booming economy, the Self-Defense Forces also find it difficult to fill their ranks, and conscription is, of course, entirely out of the question. But popular attitudes toward the Self-Defense Forces have mellowed greatly in the past two decades. Few people now fear that they might lead to the revival of the militarism of prewar days. The Self-Defense Forces for their part have conducted themselves throughout in exemplary fashion, maintaining a low profile, avoiding all involvement in politics, and doing their best to be of service to the public in times of natural calamities, such as typhoons and earthquakes. Beginning in 1959, Supreme Court decisions accepted the obvious reinterpretation of the constitution by the Diet that is implicit in the concept of self-defense. The public too seems to have accepted this reinterpretation. For some years now, public opinion polls, while strongly rejecting any expansion of the Self-Defense Forces and any role for them abroad, have given overwhelming support to their maintenance at current levels.

Despite the relative calm of the early 1960s, the dispute over neutrality versus alignment came to a boil a second time in the latter half of the decade. The heightened American involvement in Vietnam after 1965 raised again the specter of Japan's becoming embroiled in war because of its association with the United States. Detailed television and newspaper reporting made vivid the horrors of the war. The sympathies of the Japanese, as of most other people in the world, were with those Vietnamese who were fighting on their own soil against the alien American interlopers. The Japanese equated the war with their own misguided efforts in China, and as recent victims of American bombing they identified with the North Vietnamese who were experiencing American air attacks. Citizens' movements against the Vietnam War and organized student demonstrations intensified, and some local authorities with opposition leanings, such as the mayor of Yokohama, took actions to block the use of American bases in Japan for the supplying of the American forces in Vietnam.

At much the same time excitement arose over continued American military rule over Okinawa, which began to loom as a Japanese irredenta. Okinawa prefecture, named for its largest island, had been before the war the southernmost Japanese prefecture, occupying the southern two thirds of the Ryukyu chain of islands. The Ryukyus are inhabited by a branch of the Japanese people who speak a very distinct form of the language and show some cultural differences deriving from long and close trade contacts with China. They had had their own kings but in 1609 were conquered by Satsuma, the great southern Kyushu feudal domain, and thereafter were a tightly held subfief of Satsuma, although their "kings" were allowed to continue to pay "tribute" to China as a means of maintaining a clandestine foreign trade with the outside world in Satsuma's behalf. This anomalous position led in the nineteenth century to controversy between China and Japan over their conflicting claims to the islands. This was settled in Japan's favor when China agreed in 1874 to pay an indemnity to Japan for the killing of some Okinawan seamen by aborigines on Taiwan and for the Japanese military expedition sent to chastise the aborigines.

The United States, which seized Okinawa in bloody fighting in the closing months of World War II, decided to keep the whole of the Ryukyu chain to serve as its chief military base in the Western Pacific but soon discovered that the frequency of typhoons reduced its value as a naval base. In 1954 the United States returned to Japan the northern islands of the chain but continued to hold on to Okinawa prefecture, which took on increased military significance as the Vietnam War led to a buildup of American military power in the Western Pacific and mass demonstrations interfered with the free use of American bases in the main islands of Japan. It became American military dogma that, since Japan had put restrictions on the use of American bases in Japan and a victory of the opposition parties there might lead to their total elimination, American bases in Okinawa must be maintained at all costs.

At the end of World War II, the attitude of the Okinawans had been at first somewhat ambivalent toward both Japan and the United States. They were full of resentments toward other Japanese because they had been treated by them as inferior country bumpkins. Okinawa was also the only part of Japan in which fighting had actually occurred during the war, and therefore its inhabitants had suffered more than other Japanese. But American military rule, which only grudgingly opened the way to local autonomy, gradually persuaded the Okinawans by its alienness and arrogance that they were Japanese after all. A movement for the restoration of Okinawa to Japan developed in the islands and in the late 1960s began to draw an ardent response from other Japanese, whose affluence and pride had revived enough for them to become exercised over the plight of close to a million compatriots in Okinawa still living under foreign rule. Such sentiments tugged at the hearts of both nationalistic conservatives and anti-American leftists. Okinawa thus became a major new issue in Japanese-American relations, threatening to impair, if not destroy, Japan's alignment with the United States.

A third issue joined Okinawa and the Vietnam War to create a crescendo of political excitement as the 1960s drew to a close. This was the approaching date of June 19, 1970, when the new Security Treaty would complete its first decade and thereafter be open to change or renunciation. Remembering the 1960 treaty crisis, the various opposition groups looked to 1970 as the year for the next great effort to terminate the Japanese alignment with the United States.

The expected crisis never materialized. Neither government proposed any change and thus there never was any need for the Diet to ratify a new treaty, which would have provided a specific target for the opposition. In fact, it was because they realized how difficult winning ratification would be that the two governments sought no changes, though both probably would have preferred to have seen some made.

The Okinawa issue also melted away before reaching crisis proportions. Aware of the strength of nationalistic sentiments over Okinawa and the significance of 1970 in the minds of the opposition, the United States yielded on this issue and promised to return the islands within a few years. This decision was announced in a communiqué issued by President Nixon and Prime Minister Sato Eisaku on November 21, 1969. It was also agreed that, once the islands had reverted to Japan, the extensive American bases there would fall under the same restrictions that applied to the bases in the main islands. The United States made these concessions because it could see that the Okinawan situation endangered general Japanese-American relations and that, if these turned sour, irredentist feelings in Okinawa would probably undermine the utility of the bases there as well. The islands were finally returned to Japan on May 15, 1972, and political tensions in Okinawa soon shifted from the United States and its bases to the treatment by the Japanese national government of this most remote and economically backward of its forty-seven prefectures.

Even the Vietnam War faded as an issue as the United States stopped increasing its forces in Vietnam in 1968 and then started a slow withdrawal, which was completed in 1972. Thus all three issues that had threatened a crisis in Japanese-American relations in the late 1960s disappeared in the early 1970s.

The whole question of neutrality versus alignment, in fact, began to lose much of its original force. It remained as a major formal issue dividing the opposition parties from the Liberal Democrats, and occasionally some special problem would arise to heat up the old feelings. For example, in October 1974, a statement by a retired American admiral revived excitement over the old issue of whether or not American naval vessels putting into Japanese ports or transiting Japanese waters had nuclear weapons on board and thus were violating the agreement not to introduce nuclear weapons into Japan. The problem hung on the precise meaning of "introduce," translated in Japanese as *mochikomi*. The American government interpreted it to mean something much more permanent than "transit," while the Japanese public put a very restrictive interpretation on it.

Such incidents, however, no longer led to large demonstrations or threatened violence. The whole American relationship was coming to be taken for granted. In the 1975 elections the Social Democrats openly came out in support of the Security Treaty under existing conditions, and gradually most of the other opposition parties came to accept it at least tacitly. In the election of 1976 for the first time none of the parties chose to make it a major campaign issue.

Changing international conditions and new problems caused the question of neutrality versus alignment to lose its central place in Japanese politics in the 1970s and 1980s. Several decades of experience with the American alliance had not involved Japan in American wars, and further American military adventures in East or Southeast Asia seemed improbable. The alliance had also drawn nothing more than verbal attacks from the Communist powers, and even these gradually diminished and eventually stopped. The rift between China and the Soviet Union increased, and both wooed Japanese as well as American support in their rivalry. In the 1970s the Soviets initiated what the Japanese have called a "smiling diplomacy." Both the Soviet Union and China now fear that a Japan without the Security Treaty with the United States might drift into the other's orbit or else build up its own military power to major proportions. Leftist critics of the Security Treaty found the ground completely cut from under their feet, especially when Peking began to praise rather than condemn it.

A definite turning point in the situation in East Asia came when President Nixon suddenly announced in 1971 that he would visit China. In February 1972 he established informal relations with the People's Republic, which later were upgraded to full diplomatic recognition of Peking in place of the Nationalist government on Taiwan. These steps permitted the Japanese government to eliminate one of the hottest of all domestic issues and a major source of friction with the United States.

Yoshida had been forced by the United States in 1952 to recognize the Nationalist government as the real China. Representatives of the American government had made it clear that otherwise ratification of the peace treaty with Japan would encounter difficulties in the Senate. The opposition parties pushed for recognition of Peking, and most Japanese sympathized with them. But the Liberal Democrats hung back even when most other countries switched their recognition to the People's Republic. The government was motivated in part by respect for Chiang Kai-shek, who had treated Japan generously at the end of the war, in part by interest in Taiwan as a former colony with which Japan had important trading relations, but mostly by fear that recognition of Peking would endanger Japanese relations with the United States. With the American shift of position in 1972, Japan happily formalized its relations with Peking, according it full diplomatic recognition in place of Taiwan, but maintained informal relations with the latter. The planes of the two national airlines were kept apart at separate airfields in Japan. Although new frictions arose in relations between Taiwan and Japan, the substantial trade between the two and their other contacts were little affected, and a major source of tension between Japan and the United States was removed.

In both the American and Japanese communiqués with China in 1972, the problem of Taiwan was set aside for future solution. The Americans and Japanese stated their recognition that Chinese on both sides of the Taiwan Straits felt that Taiwan was part of a unitary China. The Chinese, by not objecting to the American defense commitment to and continued (though temporary) recognition of Taiwan and by accepting Japanese trade and other contacts with the island, tacitly agreed to let the actual separation of Taiwan from China continue for the time being. But Chinese feelings on the mainland about unity remain strong, and the 20 million people on Taiwan, particularly the native Taiwanese five sixths of this population, remain determined not to be incorporated into a Communist China. Since Taiwan has proved to be a very successful economic unit and has strong military forces as well as an American military commitment, while China is absorbed in its own revolutionary changes under the leadership of Deng Xiaoping, resolution of the problem seems quite remote. The whole problem also appears much less menacing to peace in East Asia in the 1980s than it once did. Basically similar Japanese and American interests in and attitudes toward the matter also make it a reason for increased solidarity rather than divisiveness between them. Their joint though uncoordinated support of what amounts to a carefully unstated "one China one Taiwan" policy will probably help this situation to continue well into the future.

The chief military danger to Japan lies in its closest neighbor, Korea. The peninsula, which had been closely unified both politically and culturally for well over a thousand years, was left bitterly divided by World War II and still more by the Korean War. The 20 million people in the North lived under an extremely repressive, secretive, totalitarian Communist regime, which had the backing of China and the Soviet Union but insisted on its independence from both. The 42 million in the South lived under a basically dictatorial military regime that brutally suppressed human rights but nonetheless enjoyed the military safeguards of American air bases and ground troops. For four decades the peninsula was one of the potentially most explosive sectors in the Cold War front line between East and West.

Unlike the North, South Korea brilliantly followed Japan's lead in industrializing itself and became a relatively affluent and rapidly rising industrial power, carrying on a thriving trade with the rest of the world. The boom was led by great conglomerates, the Chaebol, which profited from government loans and favoritism. They were strongly export-oriented, family owned and run, and driven by determination to raise production and GNP. Before long their hard-working labor force was joining with the increasingly affluent and educated urban population to demand more civil, political, and economic rights. By 1987, when the stability of the regime was clearly in question, the military dictator stepped aside to permit presidential elections. Worker demand remained explosive, but as the new regime worked to improve conditions protests gradually subsided. South Korea's ability to host the 1988 Olympics brought the sense of achievement Japan itself had experienced in 1964. Strategically conscious Japanese were aware that the American military presence in South Korea was Japan's best guarantee of safety.

Despite this trade, public attitudes between Koreans and Japanese remain poor. The Koreans resent past Japanese colonialism and the denial of equal treatment to long-term Korean residents in Japan. Resulting acts of protest and defiance produce Japanese reactions against Koreans as troublemakers, which blend with unconscious Japanese attitudes of contempt for their former colonial subjects. The Japanese government has made halfhearted, and thus far largely unsuccessful, efforts to improve this situation, but on the whole Japanese and Korean attitudes toward each other have been slowly improving on both sides in recent years, probably because the older attitudes no longer seem of much relevance to younger people.

The sharp clash in Japan over attitudes toward the division of Korea has also lessened since the early postwar years. At that time the Japanese government supported South Korea, and the majority of Korean residents in Japan backed the North, largely to show opposition to the Japanese government. Now this issue seems less important, and the Japanese government joins the United States in advocating the cross-recognition of both Korean regimes—that is, the recognition of North Korea by Japan and America and the recognition of the South by China and the Soviet Union. In any case, the American military presence in South Korea effectively reduces anxiety among the Japanese over political or military conditions there.

The one country that inspires strong Japanese fear and animosity is Russia. Hostility between the two dates back to their rival explorations of the islands north of Japan in the late eighteenth century and was greatly heightened by the Russo-Japanese War of 1904–05. These feelings were further strengthened in Japanese minds by the Soviet Union's entrance into World War II in its closing days in 1945 and the incarceration for many years of hundreds of thousands of Japanese prisoners in Siberia and the death of many of them under conditions of slave labor. In the early postwar years the determined friendliness of the Socialist and Communist parties in Japan for the Soviet Union as the supposed champion of peace muted the expression of anti-Soviet feelings in Japan, but eventually the Communist Party itself turned nationalistic and anti-Soviet, and the Socialists were embarrassed by Soviet nuclear armaments and the brutal suppression of its satellite states in Europe.

For some time now public opinion polls have shown that Russia is the country that Japanese like the least and fear the most. China, on the contrary, remains relatively popular with Japanese. A sense of historical respect and cultural kinship helps account for this difference in attitude toward China and Russia, though it should be noted that even closer kinship does nothing to make South Korea more popular with Japanese.

During the 1970s Japanese views of the Soviet Union were softened for a while by dreams of large-scale exploitation of gas, oil, and lumber in Siberia, but such plans came to little, running foul of the hard realities of distance, terrain, and the inflexibility of Soviet organization. Meanwhile anti-Soviet attitudes mounted and began to focus on two issues.

One was the tremendous buildup of Soviet naval power in East Asia. Soviet ships could reach the open sea only through straits wholly or in part controlled by Japan, but they had the Okhotsk Sea, north of Hokkaido, as a safe preserve for their activities. Japanese now saw their Self-Defense Forces almost completely as a means of short-term protection for the islands against Soviet attack—until American aid could arrive, they hoped—or as protection for Japanese sea lanes for a thousand nautical miles from Japan—again presumably against Soviet attack.

The other focus of animosity against the Soviet Union was the issue of the "Northern Territories." In 1875 Russia and Japan agreed that Russia would give up its claims to the Kuril Islands and that Japan in exchange would relinquish its claims to any part of the large island of Sakhalin, but in 1945 the Soviet Union seized the Kuril Islands and has held them ever since. At first only the few Japanese expelled from these barren pieces of land and fishermen and seaweed gatherers from nearby Hokkaido showed much interest in this irredenta, but in the late 1960s most Japanese became aroused. This was largely the result of reviving Japanese self-confidence but may have been stimulated by the government's desire to shift some of the attention away from what was then the embarrassing issue of Okinawa at the other end of the Japanese archipelago. The Japanese have made no claim to the whole of the Kuril chain but only to its southernmost part, which is visible from Hokkaido. The Northern Territories consist of the two relatively large islands of Kunashiri and Etorofu, the smaller island of Shikotan, and a group of islets known as Habomai. Japanese feelings became intense, but the Soviet Union, and then Russia, remained adamant, refusing even to consider the return of these islands. To do so would open territorial issues all along the long Soviet frontier. The economic and strategic stakes were insignificant in the dispute, but it became a major stumbling block to the improvement of Japanese-Russian relations and generated enormous ill will in Japan.

By the 1980s the once hot issue of neutrality versus alignment in Japanese foreign policy had cooled to ashes which the winds of other problems have all but blown away. It still lurks in the rhetoric of the Socialist and Communist parties but is not taken seriously by anyone. Although politicians timidly avoid references to it, and euphemisms such as "partnership" are preferred to firmer words like "alliance," it is obvious that Japan has become a central member of the "first world" of industrialized democracies, ranking only behind the United States in this group of nations. Whereas people for a while spoke carefully of "North America, Western Europe, *and* Japan," it is no longer felt necessary to mention Japan separately, and it is quite unselfconsciously included in the minds of those who speak of "the West."

When leaders of the six main industrialized democracies met at Rambouillet in France in November 1975 for the first of their annual summit meetings, the Japanese prime minister quite naturally was included with the leaders of the United States, West Germany, France, the United Kingdom, and Italy. It was Canada that, because of its somewhat smaller economic size, was not added to the group until later. Except in connection with defense matters, a major meeting of the first world countries that did not include Japan would be quite unthinkable both in Japan and in the other countries. These obvious signs of alignment cause no protest in Japan even among the opposition parties. The Japanese are clearly living in a different age from the early postwar years.

Japan's membership in the first world is fundamentally the outgrowth of its economic, intellectual, and social integration into the group. Its life styles and social problems approximate those of the other first world countries, and the vast majority of its scientific and intellectual contacts are with them. Its dynamic economy has made it in many ways a central focus for the activities of the group. Eight of the ten largest banks in the world are Japanese. Close to half Japan's trade is with first world nations. The remainder is largely with the exporters of oil in the Middle East and countries such as South Korea and Taiwan, which seek to follow Japan's path into the industrialized world, or else, like Indonesia, Thailand, the Philippines, and much of Latin America, are in a way economic client states of the first world. In 1988 the only significant exception was China, which took about 6 percent of Japan's trade. Only a little over 1 percent was with the Soviet Union.

Many Japanese are unhappy about the close social and intellectual identification of their country with the rest of the first world, wishing that Japan somehow maintained more of its former differences from other industrialized countries or that it was less "Western" and more "Asian." But realities simply belie these nostalgic yearnings. If anything, Japan is drifting further from most Asian lands and closer to Western norms, and this is likely to continue to be the situation as far ahead as one can see. Young people do not feel the emotional pull of "Asia," which, in fact, usually means "China," that their elders are subject to. They see nothing wrong in being like Westerners, or, as they might see it, having Westerners like them. As a Japanese school child recently exclaimed, "Oh, do they have McDonald's in America too?"

The once very heated debate over Japanese neutrality versus alignment has narrowed to the question of what Japan's defense role should be. Because of their wartime and postwar experiences, the great majority of Japanese remain adamantly opposed to nuclear weapons, hostile to military power of any kind, proud of their no-war constitution, and opposed to the use of Japanese forces anywhere overseas. As we have seen, most of them support the Japanese Self-Defense Forces but only at present levels, even though it is hard to conceive of circumstances under which a force of that size would be of any use. They could ward off for a short time a conventional invasion of Japan, but such an attack is virtually unimaginable under present strategic conditions, and the Japanese forces would soon run out of ammunition in any case. They could defend shipping in nearby seas, but this limited capability would be meaningless for a nation dependent for its very existence on lifelines of commerce that stretch many thousands of miles to all parts of the globe.

Public opinion prevents the Self-Defense Forces from performing either of two functions of which it would be capable. One would be to serve as a major element of a NATO-like defense grouping in East Asia, an abhorrent thought to most Japanese. Nor would Japan be welcomed by some of its neighbors, such as South Korea and the Philippines, who would presumably be part of such a league but remember vividly the harshness of past Japanese rule. The other function would be to provide forces for United Nations peacekeeping missions, but the Japanese themselves are still too sensitive about their past misadventures abroad to consider even such useful activities.

Japan's huge economic resources, its high technological skills, and the efficiency of its military forces combine to suggest to others the possibility that the country might develop nuclear armaments. Japan certainly has the capacity to do this, and in a sense it has left its nuclear options open. A relatively high proportion of its electric power is produced by nuclear plants. It is also well advanced in rocketry, the most difficult aspect of producing deliverable nuclear weapons. For the Japanese it would be only a short and easy step to full membership in the nuclear club. Many foreigners, especially among Japan's neighbors, remembering the fanaticism of its warriors in World War II, fully expect them to take this step one day.

The Japanese themselves, however, remain firm in their opposition to nuclear weapons. On this point their thinking has changed little since the end of World War II, and it is the rest of the world that has moved closer to them in its attitudes. Anything to do with nuclear matters continues to be a sensitive issue in their dealings with the United States or their own domestic politics. There is good reason for their attitude on this subject. No role, except precarious blackmail, exists for a minor nuclear power. Even nuclear superpowers need vast territorial extent to have any chance of surviving a major nuclear exchange. Japan's small land area assures its utter annihilation, no matter how strong its nuclear arsenal might be, leaving it only the hollow satisfaction of knowing that it could strike back from submarines at sea after it itself had been obliterated. The existence of one more nuclear superpower would add nothing to its own or the world's security. Japan is certainly better off eschewing nuclear weapons and saving its resources for other more constructive purposes. There is little doubt that this is the way most Japanese will continue to think.

This analysis leaves the quite sizable and efficient Japanese Self-Defense Forces with no clear mission except as a backup to the police and other agencies in the case of a natural catastrophe within Japan. Actually their most important function is psychological rather than military. They give the Japanese a vague sense of security and in some cases pride. They are a sort of security blanket that affords some comfort though not much real protection. More significantly, the Self-Defense Forces do provide a substantial supplement to American military power in the Western Pacific. They already operate in this capacity though without any treaty provision or publicity. Japanese naval units regularly hold joint operations with American vessels, and the two air forces have for many years operated in close coordination.

Curiously enough, there has been much more talk in recent years, not about the coordination of Japanese and American military units, but about the reliability of the United States as an ally. How meaningful, people ask, is the American nuclear umbrella? Critics say that the United States might risk New York in a nuclear war for the sake of London, but not for Tokyo. Racial feelings quite clearly enter into such judgments. The skeptics are probably wrong, but they have memories of a still fairly recent time when American concern over Japan was not very keen. They remember Nixon's totally unexpected announcement in 1971 of his proposed trip to the People's Republic, after years of assuring a nervous Japanese government that America would make no sudden shift on China without first informing Tokyo. The Japanese government felt betrayed, and two years later it was outraged when Washington suddenly placed an embargo on the export of soybeans to Japan, which are critical to the Japanese diet. Japanese assume that American attitudes are influenced by racial prejudice and remain somewhat dubious about the reliability of American commitments to them.

In the more than four decades since the end of World War II, the once central issue of neutrality versus alignment has dwindled greatly in importance and has in a way been turned on its head. Virtually no Japanese now believes that the Communist nations are the "peace camp" and that alignment with either China or the Soviet Union would be in any way desirable. Neutrality still has great appeal, but completely disarmed neutrality and simple dependence for security on the United Nations are now seen only as distant dreams. A sizable Self-Defense Force, close working relations with American defense forces in the Western Pacific, and a tacit American nuclear umbrella are taken for granted though they usually receive little public attention. Friction over American bases in Japan has become only a minor issue. The United States periodically urges Japan to build up its military forces, grumbling about Japan's "free ride" in defense at the American taxpayer's expense, and the Japanese continue to proceed at their own slow pace, but the dispute never reaches serious proportions. In place of earlier Japanese worries that the United States would embroil Japan in American military adventures, the Japanese now are more afraid that American defense commitments to Japan are not strong enough. The whole neutrality-alignment issue has become almost a mirror image of what it once was.

37 Trade and Economic Dependence

During the first quarter century after World War II, Japan's foreign relations seemed to focus on its military relations with the United States, but even at that time a more important theme looming in the background was the nation's economic recovery through foreign trade. In actuality, economic growth took primacy over all other matters. But there was such universal agreement on this point that it did not stand out as a foreign policy problem until the wilting of the neutrality-alignment debate and the immense growth of trade made it suddenly overshadow everything else. Today if Japan's foreign relations are mentioned, the first things that leap to mind for Japanese and foreigners alike are the problems of trade and the frictions they stir up.

After the war foreign trade went hand in hand with economic growth because of Japan's heavy dependence on foreign sources of raw materials and markets. At first, trade was largely with the United States, but Japan gradually restored its economic contacts with its neighbors. It established full relations with Taiwan as early as 1952 and it made reparation settlements with its other neighbors, starting with an agreement with Burma in 1954, paid largely in Japanese manufactured goods. The normalization of relations with South Korea in 1965 opened the way for a rapid growth of trade with that country. By the late 1960s Japan had become the largest or second largest trading partner of almost every country in its part of the world. Trade with Australia, Canada, and the United States grew by leaps and bounds, and great quantities of Japanese manufactured goods began to penetrate to almost all non-Communist countries in the world.

Japan was assisted in its economic surge by a favorable turn in the terms of trade. The raw materials it was forced to import came to be in

370

Giant tankers, bulk carriers, and container ships have revolutionized the economic geography of the world, putting once-isolated Japan into close contact with all parts of the world. (*Kyodo News International*)

plentiful supply, and the world's demand for the manufactured goods it could supply proved insatiable. Japan also benefited from certain chance advantages. The war necessitated the replacement of destroyed factories with efficient new plants that had advantages over the older industrial establishments of the West. New factories using bulk raw materials were located at sea level, often on newly filled-in land, so that raw materials like iron ore could be unloaded directly from ships at one end of the factory and the finished products, say steel and machinery, could be loaded directly onto ships for export at the other end. Meanwhile giant tankers and bulk carriers had made oceanic transport costs plummet in comparison with the costs of land transportation, giving the island nation an advantage in foreign trade over countries more dependent on inland transportation.

These factors, combined with Japan's strong work ethic, high educational standards, orderly society, and determination to catch up with the leading countries of the West, produced sustained rates of national growth of around 10 percent in real terms—levels never before achieved in world history. Despite a sharp slowdown in the increase of its population, Japan's rate of economic growth for many years was roughly twice that of the rest of the world. From the late 1940s, when it was a half-starved nation of dubious economic viability, it grew by the 1980s into one of the three industrial giants of the world, ranking with the United States and the Soviet Union.

Vast industrial expansion brought Japan difficulties as well as benefits. The problems of pollution reached their height in the late 1960s, and the curse of crowding and inadequate housing seems all but insoluble. Japan also faces increasing dependence on the outside world for economic survival. Already in the 1920s and 1930s this had loomed in Japanese eyes as a dangerous situation and helped to bring on the militarists' efforts to create through conquest Japan's own Greater East Asia Co-Prosperity Sphere. This adventure led to the disaster of World War II, but even if it had proved successful, Japan would find its Greater East Asia empire today quite inadequate to supply the raw materials and markets its present economy demands.

Many people think that the bulk of Japanese GNP is involved in foreign trade, but actually only about a tenth is. This, however, is a crucial tenth, supplying most of Japan's energy resources in the form of oil from the Middle East and over half of Japan's food and feed grain from the United States, Australia, Canada, and other distant regions. Without these imports and a number of crucial metals and other materials, Japan's whole economy would wither away. Many smaller countries have a much higher percentage of their economy involved in foreign trade. Small countries such as New Zealand or Denmark, for example, do not have an adequate domestic market for many types of production, such as automobiles, and therefore must import and export more of their goods. To be a major industrial nation, Japan must have a large domestic market, as it does with its 122 million people. But it is less generously supplied with raw materials than are the other economic giants, which as a result are less dependent on foreign trade. The United States, for example, despite a symbiotic economic relationship with its huge neighbor, Canada, is only about half as dependent on foreign trade as is Japan, and more of its trade happens to be with countries close at hand. Japan depends largely on distant markets and countries as its chief trading partners. Only about a quarter of its trade is conducted with coun-

Prime Minister Nakasone (next to President Reagan in the center) hosts the 1986 summit conference of the seven leading industrialized nations. (© *Sonia Katshian / Photo Shuttle: Japan*)

tries that lie within 3,000 miles of it. Its lifelines of commerce lead far beyond any area it could itself protect and into troubled regions, such as the Middle East, over which it can exercise no control. The precariousness of Japan's economic situation was brought home with traumatic force in 1973 by the first OPEC oil crisis.

As Japan grew rich and economically powerful, it also discovered that more was expected of it. To other countries Japan seemed selfishly concerned only with its own economic growth and reluctant to contribute to the economic or political well-being of the world as a whole. It was contemptuously called an "economic animal." Americans, as we have seen, complained of the "free ride" in defense it was taking at American expense, and President De Gaulle of France is said to have referred to Prime Minister Ikeda as nothing more than a transistor salesman.

Some of Japan's neighbors viewed it with renewed hostility, fearing that it was establishing through economic means the Greater East Asia Co-Prosperity Sphere it had failed to attain by arms. All expected Japan to show more generosity in its treatment of its poorer neighbors. The early reparations settlements had been shaped to bring more long-range trade benefits to Japan than to the recipient nations. Japan gained a reputation for being selfishly exploitative of others and stingy in providing aid. The Japanese were shocked when a goodwill trip by Prime Minister Tanaka to Southeast Asia in 1974 sparked anti-Japanese rioting. Asians resented the social exclusiveness and offishness of the Japanese as fellow Asians, expecting more sympathy and greater help from them than from the clearly alien Westerners.

The Japanese leaders gradually came to recognize the expectations created by their position of economic world leadership and attempted to meet them. They realized that Japan's lesser military burdens should give it more leeway for greater aid of other sorts. The government became more generous, providing volunteer workers of the Peace Corps type, establishing fellowships for students to come to Japan, and funding economic aid on a scale comparable to the United States and the countries of Europe. But it has proved difficult in a democratic nation to translate good intentions into budgetary outlays, particularly against the deeply ingrained insularity of the Japanese people. The Japanese government has achieved less than it had hoped, and considerable resentment against Japan persists among its developing neighbors.

Meanwhile an even larger problem area has developed in Japan's economic relations with its closest partners, the other industrialized democracies of the first world. Japan's much more rapid rate of growth has constantly upset the balance between it and them. Aside from the first world, Japan faces a huge deficit in its trade. It must import great quantities of oil from the Middle East; many underdeveloped countries that are too poor to buy many of Japan's high-quality products are unwilling to purchase more than they sell; and the Communist nations by their very nature tend to have only very restricted foreign trade. Less than 10 percent of Japan's trade is with the Communist second world, most of it with China. This leaves the industrialized democracies as the only market for close to half of Japan's high-quality goods. But these countries for the most part are competitors with Japan in the production of sophisticated manufactures, and their agricultural exports to Japan, which once offset their imports, have tended to shrink in recent years in the face of world surpluses.

The less developed countries will certainly expand their exports of simpler manufactured products to the advanced countries in the years ahead, but growth in their populations is likely to continue to leave their people poor and unable to purchase appreciable quantities of the sophisticated, high-priced products of the first world countries. This means that the latter will continue to be each other's chief markets, contending for market share with one another. They will be living, as it were, by taking in one another's laundry. There will be intense pressure to prevent any one of them from increasing its share too rapidly, as Japan has been doing. Without significant worldwide economic growth well beyond the rise in population, long-term economic prospects for the world and especially for a resource-poor country like Japan appear quite dim, and economic frictions between the highly industrialized nations are likely to increase.

As we have seen, the United States during the early postwar years could not imagine Japan's ever becoming a serious economic competitor. It therefore allowed the transfer of advanced American technology to Japan at bargain rates and accepted Japanese goods quite freely, while permitting Japanese restraints on imports to protect its "infant industries." Already by the late 1950s, however, there were signs of trouble. First because of lower Japanese wages, as in textiles, and later because of superior Japanese workmanship, better economic organization, and higher rates of saving and reinvestment in production, Japanese goods found their way into the United States in an increasing flow, until they

Honda automobiles stand in vast numbers awaiting loading on a special Honda-owned ship for export. Names of Japanese cars, such as Toyota, Nissan, Honda, and Subaru, are now as familiar to Americans as to Japanese. (© *Tadanori Saito / Photo Shuttle: Japan*)

constituted a serious threat to some American fields of industry, though a boon to American consumers. Certain American industries, such as shipbuilding, some textile production, steel, electronics, and areas in the automotive industries, were severely hurt and in some cases all but destroyed. The "rust belt" of heavy industry was particularly hard hit, and unemployed American workers came to complain bitterly that their jobs were being exported to Japan.

The countries of Europe were less affected, having maintained many of the restrictions on trade with Japan inherited from the early postwar years, but they contributed to the problem by joining the Japanese in putting pressure on the more open American market. And in areas in which rapidly rising Japanese wages made Japan no longer competitive, other Asian countries quickly took Japan's place, putting pressure on Japanese as well as American producers. Among the newly industrializing countries, the "four little tigers" stood out: South Korea, Taiwan, and the city states of Hong Kong and Singapore. All shared the same Chinese Confucian background as the Japanese, and the two larger ones had actually got their industrial and educational starts as former parts of the Japanese Empire. Behind them, especially in the simpler fields such as textiles, came the population giants of India, China, and Indonesia as well as Malaysia, Thailand, and possibly the Philippines and Vietnam. There was no doubt that East Asia, led by Japan, had become the most economically dynamic part of the world and the source of the greatest economic friction. By the 1980s more American trade was flowing westward across the Pacific than eastward across the Atlantic.

The imbalance in trade between Japan and the rest of the world, particularly the United States, has become so great that it threatens to destabilize the world economically and possibly politically as well. Whereas Japanese after the war worried first about keeping alive and subsequently about becoming involved in American military adventures in East Asia, they now see their chief danger as being economic ruin through the collapse of world trade or their own economic isolation. It seems all too possible that a resentful United States and Japan's other first world allies might box it in with restrictive trade measures or that Japan's neighbors might turn on it in fear and enmity. The Japanese find themselves torn between self-satisfaction over their remarkable achievements and nervousness that they will be unfairly singled out for discriminatory treatment by the outside world.

Efforts naturally have been made for many years to correct the upsetting imbalances in trade between Japan and the rest of the world, but without appreciable success. Already in the late 1950s the United States persuaded Japan to adopt "voluntary" restraints on textile exports to the United States by cartel agreements that would have been illegal in the United States, but other East Asian countries simply filled the void, to the irritation of the Japanese. Similar measures were tried in other fields such as electronics, steel, and automobiles but with no significant results. In time, the worried Japanese even adopted restrictions not after American arm-twisting but of their own volition, though with no better results, and Japanese government drives to increase foreign purchases in Japan also failed.

Foreigners insisted that the scarcity of Japanese imports from abroad was the result of Japanese government restrictions of various sorts. At first this was the case, but it became progressively less so. The Japanese gave up tariff restrictions and various other controls much more slowly than their trading partners demanded. Commonly they waited until a new industry was securely established before lifting the restrictions that protected it. But today tariff and nontariff barriers stand at levels on a par with or below those of most other first world countries, and yet the imbalance is greater than ever. In the mid-1980s the United States' annual deficit in trade with Japan ran around an almost unbelievable 50 billion dollars.

For a while inappropriate exchange rates were blamed for a major share of the imbalance of trade. The rate had been 360 yen to the dollar from 1949 to 1971, by which time the yen was clearly undervalued, but a series of major adjustments since 1971 has appeared to do no good. By 1987, when the dollar stood at about 40 percent of the value it had had in relation to the yen in 1971, no great effects were yet visible, and experts explained that these would appear only slowly and even then would be slight.

Much of the Japanese surplus has been invested in the United States in the building of large factories, the establishing of joint enterprises with automotive and other firms, the purchase of hotels, office buildings, and other real estate, and the establishment of banks and other credit institutions. The economies of the two countries have become blended to an amazing extent. While some parts of the United States are bitterly anti-Japanese because of lost industries, the governors of other states beat a path to Tokyo and enthusiastically welcome Japanese business delegations in their desire to attract Japanese investments.

The imbalance in trade relations not only with the United States but with many other parts of the industrialized world is basically unhealthy and a possible source of serious frictions or even trade wars. Both sides recognize that some corrections must be made, but just what they are is not clear. The Japanese see themselves as squeezed from below by low-wage Asian nations, which will eventually force Japan out of the simpler, more labor-intensive industries, and threatened from above by trade restrictions imposed by countries such as the United States that also specialize in high-technology production. In the event of a showdown, they feel that a country such as the United States, which has great natural resources as well as skills, is bound to win out over resource-poor Japan, mercilessly squeezed from both sides. They therefore feel that they must maintain if not expand whatever competitive advantages they have.

The Japanese also believe that the United States is basically more at fault than Japan for having lost out in its competition with the Japanese. They are in part correct in this judgment. They point out that Americans allowed their industrial enterprises to stagnate, let shortsighted concern over quick profits eclipse concern for healthy long-term growth, developed a less well-educated, less diligent, and less loyal work force and an overpaid, top-heavy managerial superstructure, and paid little attention to foreign markets until they found themselves hopelessly behind in them. Americans became so confident in their days of strength after World War II that they believed the rest of the world would continue to hunger for American goods and therefore could be taken for granted as safe overseas markets. They failed to develop goods designed for overseas purchasers, did not study foreign business practices, and did not learn foreign languages. A simple example is that they did not produce righthand-drive cars for Japan, where, as in England, cars drive on the left. Similarly, they made refrigerators that would not fit into Japanese apartments. Up until a few years ago, virtually no foreign businessmen spoke Japanese. As Japanese love to point out, if they had approached the American market the way Americans approached Japan's, their trade with America would consist primarily of things like paper fans.

Most knowledgeable Americans would accept most of these Japanese criticisms, but they see the fundamental problem quite differently. They blame Japanese nontariff restrictions for a much larger share of the imbalance and claim that, though most of these are now ostensibly removed, endless petty Japanese regulations and rulings persist that militate strongly against foreign imports into Japan. Such charges, involving as they do many complicated technicalities, can be studied only on a case-by-case basis, but they probably are in large part correct, though the Japanese, accustomed to such petty obfuscations by a powerful bureaucracy, are largely unaware of the cumulative seriousness of their effect. This is an area that calls for more meticulous and thoroughgoing action by the Japanese government.

American accusations that the Japanese have engineered insidious plots to keep out foreign goods and are prejudiced against buying them are probably not correct. Japanese not unnaturally find most Japanese goods superior to imports and more to their own tastes, but the general public actually has long been prejudiced in favor of imports as being intriguing or even stylish, in much the same way Americans might prefer French wines or perfumes. The common use of English names for Japanese products is a superficial example of this attitude.

The most important barrier to foreign imports probably lies in the organization of Japanese business and the tendency of companies to buy from old established contacts and to do business particularly with firms belonging to the same keiretsu grouping. This situation is only imperfectly perceived by the Japanese themselves and, being deeply ingrained, is not likely to change rapidly, because its origins are more sociological and psychological than economic. When American companies have learned to operate in a Japanese fashion in Japan and establish close business affiliations and warm personal ties, some of them have been spectacularly successful.

A nation's security was once measured in terms of its ability to preserve order at home and fend off military attack from abroad. Under present conditions Japan appears remarkably stable domestically and faces little likelihood of an attack by any other country. Aside from a worldwide nuclear holocaust, over which Japan would have little control, all it needs to fear is a general breakdown of world order or trade. In short, the traditional concepts of security no longer have much relevance for Japan.

The only foreign policy areas in which Japan can take meaningful action are its economic relations with the rest of the world and its economic contributions to the maintenance of world peace and order. Here its tremendous economic power gives it great potential influence. As the most dynamic economy in the world, it has become a major source of upsetting economic imbalances, especially among its fellow industrialized democracies. It can certainly contribute to solving these problems by helping to smooth out areas of dangerous friction, establishing a more workable monetary system, achieving orderly marketing procedures to head off trade restrictions and possible trade wars, and creating a more balanced process of growth for this group of nations as a whole. If the result were a cut in Japan's rapid rate of growth, this would still be a sounder investment than the great military expenditures Japan made in the past for the sake of its security.

Japan's gigantic economy could also be used to help the growth of less developed countries so that they could ultimately participate fully in the economy of the first world. To achieve this is probably the largest, most intractable, but most necessary task the world faces over the long run. Japan's wealth and technology can also be used to help solve threatening problems of global ecology and world population growth, which otherwise might someday destroy mankind.

A Japan that finds a way to contribute significantly to the solution of these problems would also find itself in a position to help solve the political problems that keep arising in the world and threaten its stability. What these will be in the future no one can say, but an economically strong and respected Japan that has established good cooperative relations with the other countries of the world will certainly be able to do more for its own security and that of the whole world than a rich but mistrusted and psychologically isolated nation. It will take bold and determined action on the part of the Japanese to play the role of which they are capable in helping to establish and maintain world peace and prosperity, but such a course is their only hope for survival.

Japan internally is a very strong and healthy nation, but it faces grave external problems. These are clearly not military but are basically economic or even psychological. Japan's international economic problems are as threatening as they are because of failures in mutual understanding and communication between Japan and other countries that produce suspicions and fears of Japan. Faulty understanding is in part a technical problem based on inadequacies in the mechanics of communication, but its more serious psychological basis arises from deep differences in perceptions and habits of thought. Here lie the truly grave problems Japan faces. The isolation and resulting uniqueness Japan has experienced throughout its history turns out to be the main problem it must contend with today.

38 *Language*

Language may seem a side issue, perhaps best considered as an element in "The Setting" or "Society" earlier in this book. In the case of Japan, however, language plays a central role as one of Japan's most distinctive features and as a determinant in its relationship with the outside world that helps shape the country's whole future.

Our chief interest is not in the Japanese language itself, fascinating though it may be, but in the ability of the Japanese to communicate through it with the outside world. Still, certain myths about it need to be corrected. One myth is that Japanese is imprecise, leading easily to misunderstandings. It is true that it can be vague, but only when the speaker wishes it to be. One can be equally imprecise in English, but the Japanese, who commonly seek a cautious approach to consensus rather than a sharp clarification of differences of opinion—"Let's get down to brass tacks"—are more likely to cultivate vagueness of expression. When they want to be clear, as in drafting laws or explaining technological processes, Japanese can be used as precisely as English. In literary writing, on the other hand, most Japanese prefer a suggestive, sometimes ambiguous style to the crystal clarity favored in some Western countries, but this is a difference fostered by literary preferences, not by the nature of the language.

Another myth is that there is a multiplicity of Japanese languages. This is an absurdity in a country that through education in recent times has all but wiped out most dialectical variants and strong regional pronunciations. Even in earlier days, Japanese were no more divided by these than were Germans or French. A source of the multiple language myth is probably the sharp differences in levels of politeness and formality in Japanese. All languages have such differences—"I wonder if you would be so kind as to tell me the time, sir" and "Hey, Bud, what's the time?"—but these differences are particularly marked in Japan, for two reasons. One is the importance of social and age differences that lie not far back in Japan's feudal past. The other is the tendency of Japanese to omit from a sentence elements, especially the subject, that are already clear from the context or the level of politeness.

This stands in sharp contrast to the Indo-European languages, which insist on the inclusion of elements that may be entirely superfluous or even absurd. In English it is impossible to use the generic term "house," only the more specific terms "a house," "the house," "the houses," or "houses." Even English speakers, who have sloughed off the gender of other Indo-European languages, find it silly to designate a chair as feminine—"la chaise"—or a pencil as masculine—"le crayon"—and to take care that the two take appropriately feminine and masculine modifiers. At the other extreme, Japanese see no need to specify "I," "you," or "they" when the context or the level of politeness makes the subject clear. In age- and group-conscious Japan, polite, humble, or neutral forms often indicate the subject. Thus, *irassharu* would be "you go," *mairu* "I go," and *iku* "they go." This may be confusing to foreigners but is not in the least vague to Japanese, nor does it involve different languages.

Perhaps the chief source of the myth about multiple languages is a confusion between writing and language. Japanese is written in a mixture of well over 2,000 Chinese characters (*kanji*), most read in a variety of ways, and two different phonetic systems derived from *kanji*, which are called *hiragana* and *katakana* and are collectively known as *kana*. This multiple writing system produces what is possibly the world's most difficult system in common use today anywhere in the world, but this does not affect the unity of the Japanese language. As a writing system, the closest rival of Japanese in difficulty is probably the wildly erratic spelling of English, but this does not influence the unity of the English language, either.

In Japanese, nouns and the uninflected stems of verbs and adjectives are usually written in *kanji*, pronounced either according to the native Japanese words to which they correspond or the modern forms in Japanese to which the ancient pronunciations of the Chinese characters have evolved. Most characters have at least two different pronunciations, and some have ten or more. Deciding which is the right reading is often quite a puzzle. Prepositions (which are actually "postpositions" in Japanese) and the inflected parts of verbs and adjectives are usually written in *hiragana*, while *katakana* is largely reserved for the transcription of foreign names and words that are neither Chinese nor Korean in origin and therefore are not written in characters. The *kana* syllabaries (each symbol represents a whole syllable) are relatively simple though actually not very well suited to modern Japanese as it has evolved over the centuries. The real problem comes with the *kanji*. No less than 1,945 are taught in the nine years of compulsory education and many more are needed for higher levels of education.

Foreigners often wonder why Japanese tolerate this tremendously difficult writing system, which demands such an intellectually deadening burden of rote memory work. Other peoples have seen fit to change their writing systems. The Vietnamese have jettisoned Chinese characters during the past century, and the Turks adopted Latin letters in place of their traditional writing in the aftermath of World War I. *Romaji* ("Roman letters"), as the Japanese call the Latin alphabet, is an extremely efficient system of writing Japanese, and a shift to it might have been possible, but only if it had been vigorously pressed in the traumatic days at the end of World War II. Now such a change would be quite unthinkable. *Kanji* have far too strong an esthetic hold on the Japanese and are much too strongly linked with Japan's history and culture to be easily abandoned. They are also very useful in forming abbreviated names, pithy slogans, and short but meaty headlines.

One other reason for holding onto Chinese characters, however, is fading. This is the role they once played in binding East Asia culturally together. They were the common basis for a shared Confucian vocabulary, somewhat like Latin in medieval Europe. Many Chinese, Japanese, Korean, and Vietnamese words and phrases were identical in writing, even though they were pronounced entirely differently in the four countries. Now the old unity is gone. Vietnamese do not use the characters at all; Koreans are allowing their independently invented and truly excellent phonetic system, *hangul*, to displace characters more and more; and the Chinese and Japanese have developed usually different abbreviations for many of the original characters. Only in Taiwan and the various overseas Chinese communities are all the old characters still written in their traditional form. In addition, written communication through Chinese, which once was effective among Korea, Vietnam, and Japan when much of the education in these countries was in Chinese, has virtually disappeared, and characters are of no help in speaking. For example, the Yellow River of China, though written with the same characters in Chinese and Japanese, is pronounced Huang-ho in China and Kōka in Japanese. Mao Zedong to the Japanese is Mō Takutō, and the Japanese cities of Osaka and Yokohama are Da-fan and Heng-bin to Chinese.

The great days of the culturally unifying force of Chinese characters are gone, and their role within Japan is also beginning to erode. *Kana* increasingly substitutes for *kanji* in almost all types of Japanese writing, particularly in popular forms such as comic books, novels, and advertising. Products are commonly given English names or are pseudo-Western creations. Sony and Datsun, for example, have no genuine counterparts in Japanese itself. *Kanji* will no doubt continue to remain preeminent in Japanese writing for many years to come, but it is likely to fade slowly into primarily scholarly and official use. In the meantime, however, the multiplicity of writing systems in Japan will continue to be a definite handicap, creating serious difficulties for typewriters, word processors, computers, and electronic transmission of messages as well as for the foreign learner of Japanese but causing no problem for the unity of the language itself.

The Japanese have always taken pride in the supposed native purity of their culture and especially its language, but in actuality the language ever since it was first committed to writing has been decidedly a bastard tongue like English. This would be a distressing thought to most Frenchmen and some others who futilely wage a losing battle against foreign linguistic influences, but most Japanese are quite unconcerned. They could, if they wished, point to English, which has brilliantly proved that the bar sinister is a mark of vigor and flexibility for any language. The ease with which Japanese borrows, modifies, and adopts foreign words and idioms is perhaps its greatest asset and in no way detracts from the strength of Japanese culture or its fundamental homogeneity.

Primitive Japanese was probably already an amalgam of various dialects of Korean type with admixtures of Chinese and other words even before the language started to be inundated with Chinese and its writing system in the sixth century. The Chinese linguistic influx was thoroughly modified and absorbed, but by the ninth century it left a mixed language, natively Japanese in structure but heavily Sinified in vocabulary. After further additions of vocabulary from China over the next several centuries, Japanese emerged as a language in which more words, especially in the learned vocabulary, were of Chinese than Japanese origin.

More recently a second great linguistic wave, this time from the West, swept the country. It started with a sprinkling of Portuguese words in the sixteenth century and subsequently of Dutch, but it became a tidal wave in the nineteenth century. The pseudo-classic Greek and Latin terminology of modern science was adopted, and German contributed especially in the field of medicine and French in the arts, but most of the words came straight out of English, the rising new international language of trade, brought by American and English teachers and merchants. Hundreds of English words were in common use by the time the militarists tried to turn back the tide in the 1930s, and thousands more entered the language with the American occupation and the subsequent emergence of Japan into the world market. English words have become so prevalent that the conversation of a contemporary intellectual, the advertisements on television, or even much household chitchat would be quite incomprehensible to persons who knew only the Japanese of a century ago.

One would imagine that, after such massive linguistic borrowings from the world's two most widespread languages, the Japanese would be well prepared for verbal communication with the outside world and many foreigners would find an open door to fluency in Japanese, but this is not the case. The basic structure of the Japanese language has remained almost unaffected by either Chinese or English. By sheer accident Chinese and English have become languages in which word order determines meaning ("The cat sees the dog" or "The dog sees the cat"), but Japanese has remained a strictly agglutinative language in which the concluding word, which is a verb or adjective, ties onto itself subsidiary elements that specify such things as tense, mood, politeness, and whether the sentence is causative, passive, negative, or a question. Chinese and English are structurally so alike that a person speaking in English words with Chinese word order can produce perfectly understandable pidgin English. A similar combination of Japanese word order with either Chinese or English words would make only gibberish. For example, the simple verb *kaku*, "to write," can be expanded through agglutination into *kakaserarenakattaraba*, "If (he) had not been caused to write," or dozens of other forms that would defy direct translation into Chinese or English.

Even the individual words borrowed from Chinese and English do not help very much. The Chinese words as used in Japanese were borrowed in now outdated ancient pronunciation and so distorted to fit the limitations of the Japanese phonetic system as to be quite incomprehensible to Chinese. Only a very occasional name or word, such as Taiwan, leaps out as being mutually intelligible. In the case of English, more words may be identifiable but certainly not most. Many curious mispronunciations arise from the Japanese inability to pronounce *l* and several other sounds used in English, and in the ending of all syllables with a vowel, except in the case of *n*. Thus we have *raion* for "lion" and *hōmu* for "home" and also as an abbreviation of *purattohōmu*, "railway platform." The Japanese also cannot pronounce most groupings of consonants, and thus break them up into multiple syllables, as in Sarutoru, the Japanese form for the name of the French philosopher and novelist Jean-Paul Sartre.

A further complication is the changed meanings Japanese give to many borrowed words. *Handoru*, from "handle," is a steering wheel, and *kurakushon*, from the outmoded word "klaxon," is the horn on a car. Even more mystifying are Japanese inventions from English words. *Kūrā*, from "cooler," is an air conditioner, a *naita* ("nighter") is a night game in *bēsu-bōru* ("baseball"), a *Gurīn-kā* ("Green Car") is a first-class coach on a train, and a *sarariman* ("salary man"), as we have seen, is an office worker. Abbreviations of English words, which tend to become annoyingly polysyllabic in Japanese, are still more baffling but often ingenious. *Zene-suto* for *zeneraru-sutoraiki* is a general strike, and *pan-suto* means "panty stockings," more usually called panty hose in America. *Bēsu-appu*, or "base up," means an across-the-board raise in base pay, an important concept for which we have no convenient term, and special honors should be paid to the delightful *sayonara hōmu-ran*, which quite reasonably is a home run that wins the game in the last half of the ninth inning. Such terms are, of course, incomprehensible to English speakers, and Japanese are dismayed to discover that hundreds of the English words they habitually use are so much Greek, or Japanese, to speakers of English. The common witticism that the United States and England are two countries divided by a common language might better be applied to "Japanese English."

Except for its overly cumbersome writing system, the Japanese language is an admirably efficient medium for Japanese who live in Japan and who deal with other Japanese. The literature and thought of the whole world is as available to the Japanese in translation as to any other people in the world. But this is no longer enough. Japan is not an isolated country or one chiefly concerned with absorbing new knowledge from the West. It has become a world leader deeply involved in the economy and life of the whole world. Verbal communication between Japanese and speakers of other languages has become vastly important. Japanese must now be able to talk and write with ease in a foreign language.

One could wish that the rest of the world would meet the Japanese linguistically half way, but this is not likely to happen. Japanese is spoken by too few people and is grammatically too different from most other languages to become a world language. It is of course true that many more foreigners are learning Japanese today than a few years ago. The number of Chinese, Koreans, Americans, and Australians studying Japanese has increased dramatically, but the total remains small. There is really only one world language, English, with French a poor second. Russian and Chinese are world languages merely by courtesy or, more accurately, by politics. Japanese is even less in the running. This means that it is largely up to the Japanese to surmount their surrounding linguistic wall.

Unfortunately the Japanese have proved notably inept at learning to speak foreign languages or to comprehend them aurally. Throughout the world one hears this commented upon with surprise and contrasted to the skill Japanese show at almost everything else. Only the English-speaking peoples seem to do as poorly as the Japanese, and this is probably because many of them live far removed from speakers of other tongues, as in the United States, Australia, and New Zealand, and all suffer the handicap of speaking *the* world language. Before an English-speaking person has managed to utter a few halting phrases, the other person has come forth with a fluent stream of English.

The Japanese suffer from the same handicap of geographic isolation, and they also have several other serious handicaps. One is that, because of the phonetic poverty of Japanese, they find most other languages a nightmare of sounds that are difficult for them to recognize or reproduce. It is as if an English speaker were to encounter the confusing French *u* or German umlaut multiplied many times over.

In contrast, there are relatively few phonetic problems in Japanese serious enough to obscure meaning for an English-speaking person. The English tendency to accent heavily certain syllables can be confusing to Japanese, who have virtually no stress accent in their language. A more serious problem is the English ignoring of differences between long and short vowels and consonants. *Koko*, "here," means "senior high school" when the vowels are lengthened to *kōkō*. Similarly, *kita*, "north," becomes "cut" when the *t* is lengthened to *kitta*. But Japanese often prove surprisingly good at understanding foreigners, even when both of these rules are transgressed, as in the almost universal foreign mispronunciation of Japan's second largest city as Osáka instead of Ōsaka.

A much more important obstacle to Japanese learning foreign languages and foreigners learning Japanese is the fact that very few people speak an agglutinative type of language like Japanese. Indo-European languages prevail in most of Europe, the whole Western Hemisphere, the Soviet Union, and much of West and South Asia, including most of the Indian subcontinent, and they have been adopted as the official language in many former colonial countries that are linguistically too divided to have their own national languages. Much of the rest of the world speaks Chinese or Semitic tongues, which bear resemblances to Indo-European. This leaves the Japanese among the relatively few people who have no special advantages in learning English or any other important world language. Korean, Mongol, and Turkish are the only languages that are clearly linked to Japanese in structure, and few Japanese choose to study Korean (though more Koreans learn Japanese), and practically none learn either Mongol or Turkish. The linguistic barriers to establishing intellectual contact with the rest of the world are indeed high for the Japanese.

One might assume that the Japanese, who have been so successful in most of their efforts to modernize their country, would have tackled this problem too with dazzling success. Instead their failure has been notable. This has not always been true. Perhaps the best way to understand Japan's poor showing in recent years in the learning of foreign languages is to consider the record since the 1860s.

When the Japanese faced a life-and-death confrontation with the West in the middle of the nineteenth century, they rapidly mastered sufficient English to survive the crisis and start their climb to technological equality. Careful use of American and English teachers, a rash of American missionary schools, textbooks imported largely from the United States, a strong flow of promising students abroad, and dogged determination saw them through these crucial years. Many young Japanese leaders came to speak adequate even if sometimes quaint English and wrote elegant letters in a beautiful Spencerian hand.

By the turn of the century, however, a command of spoken English was no longer so necessary. The Japanese had trained their own teachers and created their own educational system up through the university level. It had become possible to learn all that seemed necessary about science and the outside world through Japanese books and translations. Japan and its empire became the only part of the world where students could receive a full modern higher education in a non-European language, and many Chinese flocked to nearby Japan for educational purposes. The Japanese school system became recognized as the road to success in Japan. Most foreign teachers were dropped as too expensive; the best Japanese students stopped going abroad; and foreign travel was postponed to more superficial tours of observation at an age when foreign languages were no longer easy to learn. Skill in speaking foreign languages actually came to be looked down on as suggesting the speaker had no more important abilities. The word *Eigo-zukai,* "English user," became a pejorative.

The study of foreign languages lost most of its significance except for scientists and scholars who wished to puzzle out original foreign texts instead of depending on often very unreliable translations. The teaching of foreign languages froze into an antiquated system that students found boring in its emphasis on recondite points of grammar and classical texts. Conversation and possibly useful contemporary written English were all but ignored. English together with mathematics was also found to be easy to grade in examinations and therefore was stressed in the crucial entrance examinations. The result for mathematics was to help push Japanese standards to the highest in the world, but for English the outcome was disastrous, pushing instruction still further toward grammar and classical texts and away from conversation and contemporary English. Classes in English tended to become preparations for the passing of examinations, not the learning of a living tongue.

It is not surprising that Japanese skills in English gradually withered, reaching a nadir in the xenophobia of World War II. It was from this low base that they had to start their rise after the war, when it became clear that the Japanese would have to master a language of international communication. A great deal of progress has been made since then, particularly in the areas of most urgent need. Many Japanese scientists are now quite proficient in English in order to participate in the world scientific community. Thousands of Japanese businessmen engaged in foreign commerce have developed the fluency they need for commercial success abroad. Bureaucrats in areas involved in foreign relations have acquired the language skills they need. Translations, which before World War II frequently relied on direct word-by-word transcriptions (*chokuyaku*) and frequently distorted the meaning drastically, have now been largely superseded by more adequate versions. Interpreters once were notoriously unreliable. I have witnessed cases in which one translator made a slight mistake that produced an answer aimed at a question differing from the one asked, and this answer in turn was mistranslated, leaving the original questioner feeling that Japanese and American minds must operate differently. Such blunders are now rare, and some interpreters are even proficient at simultaneous translation (*doji tsuyaku*), which is almost a miraculous feat between Japanese and English because of the radical differences in syntax between the two.

Significant progress has indeed been made in recent years, but this is only a small part of the picture. Almost no Japanese politicians, except for a few younger ones, speak any foreign language beyond some trifling social phrases in English; most scholars, writers, and other intellectuals, except for those concerned with science and foreign trade, read a foreign language only with difficulty; and the general public makes no pretense of speaking English except for some catchphrases. Only a handful of men and women speak for Japan to the outside world or learn directly what others may say or write about Japan. One sees the same few faces time after time at international conferences. This certainly is not a tolerable situation for a leading nation in the world. Most Japanese live basically behind their high linguistic walls, largely unheard by others and listening only to what they wish to hear from abroad. There is no easy give-and-take that would put them into real intellectual contact with the rest of the world.

Since most Japanese have had at least six years of formal classes in English in junior and senior high school and much continuing contact with the language after that, their dismal record in mastering the language must be viewed as a flagrant case of wasted brainpower. Of course, there are, as we have seen, some special reasons for their difficulties. Japan is still a very isolated country, and Westerners are almost never seen except in certain areas of a few cities and along the beaten tourist trails. Most Japanese go for years or even their whole lives without having any significant contact with a foreigner. There is little chance to practice a foreign language. As a result, droves of students may descend on an isolated Westerner to try out their rudimentary English—*Harō. Howatto izu yuā nēmu?*

The situation, of course, is much better than it was before World War II, when Westerners were rare enough to seem like goblins to small Japanese. The postwar inundation of American soldiers and later the influx of sizable numbers of businessmen and students has changed all this, but English speakers are still a rare commodity. Thousands of English academies have sprung up all over Japan, not just to help students pass the crucial English examinations but also to teach them to understand and speak idiomatic modern English. Hundreds of young Westerners survive economically in Japan by teaching in such schools or on their own. Many young Japanese have developed quite competent pronunciations through listening faithfully to the Far East Network, an American military radio station, which unintentionally serves this useful purpose while promoting a lot of culturally less desirable programming. Young Japanese have shown themselves eager to learn English and reasonably competent when given an opportunity. The problem does not lie with them but rather with the official English teaching establishment, which blocks effective approaches to a solution.

A key stumbling block consists of the roughly 50,000 teachers of English in the government school system, who for the most part cannot really speak English themselves. They feel threatened by any reform of the system. In addition the whole school system finds useful the present utilization of English for examination purposes, despite the fact that it teaches very little usable English. And behind the school system sit the bureaucrats of the Ministry of Education, who, like bureaucrats everywhere, have little desire for any change. The whole system is deeply entrenched against reform, and unfortunately the politicians perceive little personal gain for themselves by championing it. Children do not vote; their parents see nothing wrong with the system they once suffered through themselves; and the whole school system is aligned against change. Many people realize something should be done, but few have the interest or energy to initiate reforms.

The irony of the situation is that Japan has ready at hand all the necessary tools for language reform. Foreign teachers are no longer costly for them; young native speakers of English are available in large numbers and ready to work for very modest salaries; Japanese are rich enough to afford travel and periods of study abroad; the country is bursting with the electronic gadgetry that other countries have found helpful in teaching foreign languages; efficient new methods of foreign-language instruction have been pioneered abroad; and the students themselves are eager to learn. English Speaking Societies, which perform English language plays and hold speech contests, are popular on most university campuses and in many schools. Business firms and government ministries and agencies are accustomed to sending promising candidates abroad at considerable expense for a few years of study aimed mostly at perfecting their foreign-language skills—which could have been achieved at no extra expense by a reformed educational system. All that is lacking are some people in positions of authority who are ready to organize the various parts of the solution into a rational system.

The meager results in language learning despite all these possibilities make one suspect that the real problem is a lack of interest on the part of the Japanese leadership and public. Ridiculous though this may seem, there appears to be a genuine reluctance to have English very well known by many Japanese. Knowing a foreign language too well, it is feared, would erode the uniqueness of the Japanese people. Young Japanese, some claim, would lose their skills in their own language. Though ambiguously expressed, such feelings are widespread. To Westerners, they seem absurd. The Japanese language seems extraordinarily distinctive, and the uniqueness of the Japanese people a handicap rather than an asset. Young Netherlanders, they know, learn two closely related foreign languages, English and German, with no impairment whatsoever to their ability to speak and write Dutch. That Japanese would lose their skills in the Japanese language or their distinctiveness as Japanese simply because they learned English seems laughable.

This attitude, however, is symptomatic of the contrasting Japanese desires to be unique and to be international. The language problem is one of the most glaring examples of this dichotomy that looms so large in contemporary Japan. It must be met head on if Japan is to surmount its language barriers and play the international role in the world that other factors force on it.

Many correctives to the situation suggest themselves, but some are particularly obvious and simple. In view of the particular difficulties of pronunciation for Japanese, the sounds of English or other foreign languages should be learned at an early age, when children can absorb them with ease. The use of native speakers among the teachers, songs and games in kindergarten, and amusing children's programs on television and radio could largely eliminate the pronunciation problem before it arises. Taking advantage of children's superior language-learning abilities, many of the hours of English instruction in school could be shifted from senior high school down to elementary school, where the study of English would be perceived as fun rather than a chore. At the same time, class time would be freed in the upper grades for other more sophisticated studies. The learning of a foreign language at an earlier age would also make it an available tool at higher levels of education and thus turn it into a more interesting and meaningful subject of study. Naturally, the emphasis throughout should be shifted from classical texts and grammar for the sake of examinations to useful contemporary English and conversation. Changes of this sort could multiply the value of English-language instruction in school many times over without increasing the burden on classroom time or cutting into the study of Japanese subject matter.

Another aspect of the language problem is the potential role of the thousands of Japanese children now being raised in part abroad because their fathers have been assigned to foreign posts. One can sympathize with the Japanese desire to prevent these children from losing their native language and its extremely difficult writing skills. The present system of special weekend schools and after-hour classes seems desirable. But at the same time, the often almost perfect command of a foreign language these children acquire is a rare asset that Japan greatly needs. It is in fact a potential national treasure, but instead of being treated as such it is often looked on as a bothersome problem and embarrassment. Since the experiences of the children abroad and their foreign-language skills make them somewhat different from other young Japanese, they are usually hustled back home at an early age to ensure that they do not turn out differently from their peers. They are often virtually brainwashed of traces of foreign-language skills. This is particularly true for boys, who, it is felt, will have to surmount the usual examination hurdles. Girls may be treated more leniently; because they are not expected to have real careers, their foreign-language skills are more acceptable as possibly useful polite accomplishments.

A more rational approach would be to encourage both boys and girls to acquire as complete a mastery of foreign languages as possible while living abroad. Special schools back in Japan should be created to ensure that they maintain these skills while catching up on what they may have missed in normal Japanese education while living abroad. A second, international track might well be created for them in the most prestigious schools, including Tokyo University. Government bureaus and big businesses would probably find the products of such international track schools at least as useful as those using the regular track. They certainly would prove themselves more suited to the world leadership role that Japan now must fill.

A second, international track would also have another value. If foreign students, especially those from the developing countries, could receive their higher education in Japan in schools utilizing English as their chief language of instruction, they would flock to Japan in great numbers, and Japan would begin to play the educational leadership role of which it is capable except for its incapacities in language. The presence of these foreign students in Japan would also help to internationalize the Japanese themselves and spread Japanese influence much further abroad than it now goes.

There are many promising beginnings now under way for surmounting the language barrier and injecting a significant international element into Japanese education, but they are still very small, peripheral, and tentative. As with foreign-language instruction in the schools, there are not enough persons of influence who care. Japan is a startlingly international country on the surface but an isolated, inward-looking country beneath its cosmopolitan sheen. This is primarily a psychological problem and is probably the most significant fact about the Japanese today. This fundamental underlying factor is the focus of the final chapter of this book. Is Japan indeed unique? Is it destined always to be a separate, isolated country—an international odd man out? Or is it on the way to becoming internationalized in the manner of most other important countries? In other words, does it have a future as a true world leader?

39 Uniqueness and Internationalism

The language barrier between Japan and the rest of the world is relatively easy to define and therefore perhaps to deal with, but underlying it is a much more ambiguous and insidious problem. This is the dichotomy between the actual Japanese position of being among the world leaders and their perception of themselves as being so distinct from the rest of humanity as to be unique. They are both self-satisfied almost to the point of arrogance and at the same time somewhat ill at ease with others. They are simultaneously world leaders and world loners. This situation is confusing not only to others but also to the Japanese themselves. It gave rise to the great *Nihonjin-ron* debate in the 1970s over what it meant to be a Japanese. Today it has made the word *kokusai-ka,* "internationalization," virtually a buzzword. Almost every organization seems to wish to include "International" in its title. "Internationalization" is on everyone's lips even when the speaker has no real concept of what it means.

The origins of Japan's sense of uniqueness are easily found in its long history of isolation, at first natural but later self-imposed, its distinctive culture, its unusual type of language, its unique and very difficult writing system, and its strong patterns of group organization. Above the close-knit family stood the local community, above it the feudal domain or modern company, and at the top the nation, which was geographically, linguistically, and culturally very distinct from all others. To the Japanese the world seemed quite obviously divided between Japan and the rest of the world. Other categories were not important, such as the lands of East Asian culture, Christendom, or even the human race. The important thing was that one was either Japanese or one was not.

Nation, language, race, and culture are all related but distinct concepts to most modern peoples, but in Japan they all seem virtually synonymous. Until recently all the people in the world who spoke the distinctive Japanese language and lived in the distinctive Japanese way resided in Japan, and there was virtually no one else in the country. The only exceptions were a handful of aboriginal Ainu in the north of Japan and a few Chinese, Koreans, and Dutch traders in Kyushu, but all of these were obviously outsiders. The line between *uchi* and *soto*—between "inside" and "outside"—was clear. A person was by race, language, culture, and nation either fully Japanese or not a Japanese at all. The Japanese formed a sort of gigantic modern tribe. Even the use of foreign models and the heavy borrowings from China and the West of political institutions, culture, and language did not change the situation. These borrowings became part of Japanese culture and therefore part of the amalgam all Japanese shared, but they did not change the uniqueness of Japan.

If one were to ask people throughout the world what they are, their initial answers might be quite diverse: a student, a Muslim, a woman, a farmer, or even a human being. A Japanese even today would almost certainly reply "a Japanese." Anyone who goes abroad for the first time is likely to be surprised by the strength of his own nationalistic feelings, but Japanese are less able than most to lose consciousness even momentarily of their national origins. They always see themselves as being not just themselves but as representatives of the whole Japanese nation from whom others will form their judgments of Japan. A Japanese who distinguishes himself in the world is much less likely to think of himself or be thought of by his friends as little Yamamoto Hiroshi, who made a name for himself in the world, but as a Japanese who brought glory to Japan. Despite the nationalistic fervor that has developed around the Olympic Games, contenders from Western nations feel the pride of personal achievement much more than Japanese, who are overwhelmed by the sense of representing the national honor of Japan.

Race looms large in the self-image of the Japanese, who pride themselves on the "purity" of their blood, despite the obvious mixture that went into the forming of the Japanese people as late as early historic times. We often think of racial prejudice as being a special problem of the white race in relations with other races, but it actually pervades the world. Nowhere is it greater than in Japan and the other lands of East Asia. Because the Japanese have merged their feelings about race, culture, and nation together, they have probably made their attitudes toward race all the stronger. It is almost as if they regarded themselves as a different species from the rest of humanity.

Before World War II few Japanese had ever had any significant contacts with Westerners, and they still reacted with some of the shock they felt when they first encountered the Portuguese in the sixteenth century and the more numerous Englishmen and Americans in the nineteenth century. They found them positively revolting with their blue eyes and "red" hair—the attributes of goblins in Japan—and their sweaty bodies clothed in hot woolen clothes and inadequately bathed according to more fastidious Japanese standards. A strong body odor resulting from a diet richer in animal fats made them still smellier. *Bata-kusai,* "stinking of butter," is still a term used for obnoxiously Western things. Styles in clothes, food, and bathing have changed since then, but the hairy bodies of Caucasian men are still somewhat revolting to Japanese, and the sense of racial difference still runs deep in Japan. In the many cases of interracial marriages I have known, if family objections were raised, it was almost always the Japanese family that protested the most.

Japanese attitudes toward the black or darkly colored races are worse than toward Caucasians, whose blue eyes and "red" hair are now much admired. Having had almost no contacts with blacks before the coming of the American army of occupation, Japanese still tend to view them with some wonderment and revulsion. During the civil rights movement of the 1960s in the United States, most Japanese unconsciously looked at the problem from the point of view of the majority whites. The long injustices that the blacks had undergone impressed them less than the difficulty the whites faced in dealing with such a large and very distinct minority.

One would assume that Koreans and Chinese, who in physical characteristics are usually indistinguishable from Japanese, would be racially more accepted than Westerners, but this is not the case. Probably more Japanese parents today would tolerate an American son-in-law or even a daughter-in-law than they would a Korean or Chinese. "Racial" prejudice is severe against the roughly 700,000 Koreans who remain in Japan from among those imported for forced labor there during World War II. Despite the fact that more than forty years have passed and most of these so-called Koreans have become Japanese in language and living style, they are prevented as much as the laws permit from acquiring Japanese citizenship. Most Japanese still feel that marriage with the child of a Korean or Chinese immigrant, as with the surviving 2 percent of Japanese irrationally designated as outcasts (*burakumin*), would sully their "pure" Japanese blood. Prejudice against darker-skinned Southeast and South Asians is even stronger. During the past two decades of disturbances in Southeast Asia, only a few hundred Southeast Asians have been granted permanent domicile in nearby Japan—a shameful contrast to the white countries that, half a world away, took them by the thousands.

Attitudes in Japan toward racially similar peoples contrast sharply with those of Europe, where international marriages have always been common, particularly among the aristocracy, and where class has been more important than nationality or minor physical differences. The British royal family is predominantly German, even though family names have been changed from Hannover to Windsor and Battenberg to Mountbatten. Wilhelm II, the last of the kaisers, and Nicholas II, the last of the czars, were both grandchildren of Queen Victoria and spoke to each other in English. In East Asia mixed marriages occurred only between the social scum of port cities.

The racist attitudes of East Asia are clearest in the treatment of children of mixed marriages. In Korea and Vietnam the offspring of American soldiers and native women, usually of low social status, have normally been rejected by the local society or subjected to severe discrimination. The situation has been worse for the half-blacks than for the half-whites. The best hope for either group was to be adopted into so-called racist America. Somewhat the same situation existed in postwar Japan. A worthy Japanese lady, who was much praised for her orphanage for such children, could only hold out the hope that they might in time find a new life for themselves on the frontiers of civilization in the Amazon. Biracial children of better family background have commonly achieved normal careers, but most of them have done so not in Japanese society but in the United States.

The strength of the "we-they" dichotomy among the Japanese has created special problems for those who have gone for prolonged periods to foreign countries. We have seen how this affects the education of children of Japanese living temporarily abroad. In the case of emigrants to the United States, the first-generation *issei* fitted themselves quietly into the lower strata of American society and accepted denial of the right to become American citizens. When war broke out between Japan and the United States in 1941, they meekly acceded to expulsion at great financial loss from their West Coast farms and homes and incarceration in virtual concentration camps, euphemistically called "relocation centers." Their *nisei*, or second-generation, children reacted with more anger but usually with unequivocal loyalty to America. Since they could not accept the insistence upon an all-or-nothing loyalty to Japan, they gave their total allegiance to a less demanding United States. The young Japanese of Hawaii formed the most renowned and decorated unit in the American military forces in World War II. The third-generation *sansei* have shown themselves to be even more typically American by trying to learn the Japanese language, which few of them know, loudly insisting on their minority rights, and outdistancing in achievements almost every other ethnic group in the country. Three Americans of Japanese descent once served simultaneously in the United States Senate, constituting 3 percent of that body in contrast to the half percent of the American population they form. When people of Japanese descent visit Japan as successful citizens of their new countries, it is all too clear to both themselves and the Japanese that they are not "insider" Japanese but "outsider" foreigners.

If it is extremely difficult for other East Asians living in Japan to cross over the imaginary "racial line" and actual "culture line" into full membership in Japanese society, it is all but impossible for a Westerner. Occidentals are treated with amazing kindness and hospitality, though rarely invited to a Japanese home simply because of the embarrassing lack of space. Only in a few specialized situations are Westerners subjected to unpleasant discrimination, as, for example, when they are excluded from certain bars because of fear of their rowdiness or the uneasiness they would cause other patrons. Usually the treatment they receive is so generous as to make them seriously embarrassed when it comes to reciprocating.

But such kind treatment is based on the assumption that they will remain merely visitors or at least outsiders. It is very difficult for a Westerner to be accepted as truly one of the group. As an external adornment he or she may be lionized, but no one wants him as a full member. A Westerner who becomes very well informed about Japan may even be resented. To the extent that he becomes accustomed to Japanese habits of thought and ways of life he may come to be considered a *hen na gaijin*, a "foreigner with a screw loose," who makes the Japanese feel ill at ease. True fluency in Japanese may raise feelings bordering on hostility, though a few outrageously mispronounced phrases will produce enthusiastic praise. The Japanese feel that foreigners should never forget that they are foreigners.

The contrast with the United States is marked. Americans commonly assume that any foreigner in their midst is eager to become an American and probably will in time. Japanese regard foreigners as irrevocably on the other side of the great dividing line between "us" and "them." I remember an official cultural conference between Japanese and Americans that illustrated the difference in attitudes. On one side of the table sat the "Americans," including Americans working in Japan, Americans of Japanese descent, and even one Japanese citizen who taught permanently in the United States. On the other side sat only Japanese permanently resident in Japan.

Many Americans living in Japan are infuriated by their ultimate rejection and irritated by the unconsciously pejorative overtones of words used for foreigners. In my childhood clearly insulting words, such as *ijin,* "strange people," or *keto,* "hairy barbarian," were sometimes heard, but neutral terms won out, such as *Seiyojin,* "Westerner," for all Caucasians and the official word *gaikokujin* for all foreigners. *Gaikokujin* still remains in official use but has been shortened for informal use to *gaijin,* "outsiders." This term emphasizes the exclusiveness of Japanese attitudes and has picked up pejorative overtones that many Westerners resent. Interestingly, it is not used for Koreans, Chinese, and some of Japan's other near neighbors, who are differentiated by their national origins. But such more specific names usually carry even more derogatory overtones than *gaijin.*

The feeling of national distinctiveness in Japan has probably been strengthened by its history of two periods of massive borrowing from abroad. In early times and then again in the nineteenth and twentieth centuries the Japanese found themselves inundated by more advanced technologies and their accompanying cultures, first from China and then from the West. Each time they had to work hard to catch up with the more advanced area, and the consciousness of their own national identity was strengthened in the process. In both cases they eventually swung back to a defiant reassertion of their own uniqueness. In most other countries people have been less aware of the coming of foreign influences, which seeped in by trade, osmosis, or in small short bursts. But the Japanese have interpreted their whole history in terms of foreign borrowings and native reactions. They make a fetish of distinguishing carefully between what is known to have come from China or the West and what they regard as natively Japanese. This they feel to be uniquely their own, placing on it a higher value.

The Japanese have historically swung like a pendulum between an inferiority complex and a superiority complex in their attitude toward other countries. This trait has been strengthened by the nature of their whole society, in which conformity to the group and the acceptance of the judgments of others take precedence over individual preferences. The opinions of Westerners, many of them too ignorant to have an opinion worth listening to, are constantly sought by newsmen or private citizens. One is reminded of self-conscious Americans not so long ago asking visiting British notables as they descended the gangplank in New York what they thought about American women. Japanese are extremely self-conscious if they think others are observing them. When going abroad or taking up a new foreign sport or activity, they are likely to be meticulous about having the correct garb and displaying the approved form, whether it be golf, tennis, or cocktail sipping. Their very insistence on appearing to do things correctly often gets in the way of their doing them well. Certainly their self-consciousness has been no aid in learning to speak foreign languages, which requires a certain degree of reckless abandon rather than tongue-tied perfectionism.

Feelings of inferiority seem to have been a natural breeding ground for nationalism throughout the world. The first stirrings of modern nationalism in northern Europe were probably inspired by feelings of backwardness relative to the older lands of the Mediterranean. Early American spread-eagle patriotism was obviously linked to the country's position as a raw and weak frontier land on the edges of the Western world. Nationalism throughout the non-Western world seems clearly to have been a reaction to Western domination.

The Japanese experience is particularly reminiscent of the British, whose early and strong sense of nationalism may derive from the same sources as those of Japan. Overrun repeatedly by foreign military and cultural invasions, the British developed the same irrational pride and sense of distinctiveness. Their island position probably contributed to the similarities. The Japanese often refer to their distinctive attitudes as *shimaguni-konjo,* "the feelings of an island people." In time, as people began to realize the undesirability of such attitudes, the term developed the same negative overtone as "insularity" for the British.

In Japan the early expressions of nationalism were largely made in response to a Japanese sense of inferiority to China. China might be huge, old, and the home of the Confucian sages, but only Japan was "the home of the gods." The long period of intensive learning from China from the sixth to the ninth centuries left a deeply ingrained sense of inferiority in Japan that only slowly wore away as the Japanese assimilated what they had borrowed and turned it into their own distinctive civilization. Not until the nineteenth century did Japanese attitudes toward China change to a sense of superiority because of their newly developed power, wealth, and greater success in handling modern problems, and even then Japan's superiority complex was tempered by a lingering respect for what China once had been.

Modern Japanese nationalism has been couched largely in terms of catching up with the West. Because of the need to win Western legal and social acceptance, the Japanese not unnaturally were determined to achieve Western norms and win Western approval of themselves, both individually and as a nation. This determination, combined with their traditional desires to enjoy group approval, made them somewhat stiff and awkward in their dealings with foreigners, causing others to be ill at ease with them. Their formality, offishness, and noncommittal approach in their dealings with others have often been contrasted by Westerners with the apparent relaxed heartiness of Chinese and Koreans. This image of the Japanese, whether true or false, is just one more barrier that stands between them and the world role of which they are capable.

Japan has gone through two brief but very intense periods of borrowing from the West. The initial phase of uncritical imitation has each time been sufficiently successful to permit a swing back in which the less essential borrowings were sloughed off and many natively Japanese traits reemerged. Japan ran through one such cycle from the 1860s to the 1930s. At first the West seemed to have all the answers for Japan's national survival and future development, but once the essential lessons had been mastered the Japanese turned back nostalgically to their own culture with a feeling that it provided the true roots of Japanese superiority, for which Western technology was merely a stimulating fertilizer. They came to emphasize their superiority to others as much as they had openly accepted their inferiority only a few decades earlier.

A second such cycle is now just concluding. America seemed to have all the answers when a backward-looking Japan was crushed in World War II, but hard effort and brilliant improvisation soon brought Japan back to new levels of prosperity and social well-being. It began to surpass the United States and other Western countries in many fields. It even started to feel some condescension for its erstwhile mentor, and a little contempt for those who fell behind. The poor productivity and labor disputes of the United Kingdom came to be known as "the English disease."

Such attitudes of inferiority and superiority are scarcely unique to Japan. Inferiority and superiority complexes seem to be closely related: one flips easily into the other. This may be particularly true of Japan because of the intensity of its experiences in modern times. To have had to scramble desperately to catch up with the West twice in the past century and a half has left a deep mark on the Japanese psyche and made the people all the prouder of their achievements. It is quite understandable that some of them now cannot resist feelings of arrogance and condescension.

Japanese sometimes claim that their sense of distinctiveness from the rest of the world has nothing to do with feelings of superiority or inferiority, but this is difficult to accept in a society that has always been so conscious of hierarchic order. The Japanese among themselves are an extraordinarily egalitarian people today, but the terms *Nihon-ichi,* "first in Japan," and *sekai-ichi,* "first in the world," are constantly heard. One of the most popular T-shirt symbols written in *kanji* that Americans have imported from Japan is *ichiban,* "number one." As has been mentioned, most Japanese have clearly in mind the hierarchy of prestige among universities, corporations, or almost everything else. It would be extraordinary if they did not apply this same perception of the superior and inferior to countries as well.

Japanese, like Americans, love public opinion polls, but so many factors go into decisions on national rankings and answers are so greatly dependent on how questions are phrased and what specific problems a respondent may have in mind that no clear national pecking order can be constructed. Still, the general tenor of Japanese attitudes is clear. Japan itself comes clearly first, primarily because it is Japan and therefore in a class by itself and secondarily because it has so successfully blended modern technology with traditional Japanese virtues. Next to Japan come the United States and a wide assortment of Western democracies, such as France, the United Kingdom, Germany, Switzerland, the Scandinavian countries, Canada, and Australia, all of which are perceived to be more or less like America. Then would come China, which, however distasteful its present political and social system may be, carries with it the aura of a great past. A vote for it would be somewhat like a vote in the West for the Greco-Roman-Renaissance tradition. Next would come a vast blur of developing countries, with those of Latin America and Southeast Asia—both important trading areas for Japan—coming at the upper end, India near the middle, and the states of the Middle East and Africa—the furthest from Japan culturally—at the lower end. This leaves the contest for last place between the two Koreas and the Soviet Union, for all three of which the Japanese feel positive dislike.

One point emerges clearly from such an international popularity contest. The nations that stand highest are all Western democracies with life styles most like those of contemporary Japan, while the countries close in race and historical experience rank relatively low. Some Japanese have fought this tendency but with little popular success. Around the turn of the century Okakura Kakuzo, the art historian and philosopher, declared sententiously but quite mistakenly, "Asia is one." Other philosophers took up the cry, but the common people showed little response. In the 1930s the militarists claimed to be liberating Asia from Western political imperialism, economic exploitation, and moral corruption, but their call for a Greater East Asia Co-Prosperity Sphere fell on unresponsive ears in the rest of Asia and aroused little interest even in Japan. Pan-Asian sentiments have surfaced in one form or another for over a century, but the average Japanese have stuck unconcernedly to their preference for the Western democracies and lack of interest in the less developed parts of the world.

The strong Japanese sense of nationalism has at times been of great benefit to Japan. In the middle of the nineteenth century, though gripped by a severe struggle for power among themselves, no Japanese dreamed of making common cause with the foreigners against the best interests of Japan as a whole. Unlike the leaders of many more recently created states, Japanese leaders did not attempt to stash away personal riches in foreign lands. Every one of them remained entirely committed to Japan and its national fortunes. As the country began to surmount the crisis and achieve its objectives, individual Japanese were not averse to harvesting riches and honors for themselves, but they all continued to put national interests first.

Nationalism again came to the aid of the Japanese in the catastrophe of World War II and its aftermath. Most Japanese were forced to struggle desperately to survive, but few of them tried to do this at the expense of national interests. Again many in time became affluent, but they prospered as part of a bigger effort to bring prosperity back to Japan. Again none of them sought to sequester their own riches abroad to escape some possible future national calamity at home. In much of the developing world today, such unsullied nationalism is more the exception than the rule.

Nationalism, however, has not always been a boon for Japan. It has at times carried the Japanese in swings from an inferiority complex to the dangerously euphoric excesses of a superiority complex, as happened in the disaster of World War II. It has also strengthened Japanese feelings of being separate from the rest of the world and encouraged fears that too much borrowing from other countries or even contact with them might somehow rob Japanese of their Japaneseness. The problem of English-language teaching is a good case in point, for such attitudes, as we have seen, underlie the failures in this area. Some experts advocate quite rationally that foreign languages should be taught less rather than more. Their argument is that it would be more efficient to have fewer Japanese trained better in English and to save the time and energy spent on teaching many Japanese to speak and read English inadequately. This is a good point, but it misses the need for great numbers of Japanese to communicate effectively in a foreign language if Japan is to play the role it should in the world. Latent in the argument is also the feeling that knowing much English would weaken the Japaneseness of the people. This is an argument for stepping back toward psychological isolation, which is still one of Japan's major shortcomings. The danger for a now powerful Japan is that it will be too Japanese, not that it will not be Japanese enough.

The pendulumlike swings between feelings of inferiority and superiority in Japan may be gradually diminishing. The latest postwar cycle from an abject inferiority complex through renascent pride to arrogant self-satisfaction and even some xenophobia has developed with surprising slowness and moderation. It seems much less emotion packed than the earlier cycle between the 1860s and the 1930s. Perhaps the Japanese are growing past the inferiority-superiority phase of their history. If so, this is a good sign of increasing stability in Japanese foreign relations and an indication of its growing capacity to fulfill its role as a true world leader.

One reason why the Japanese may be overcoming their fears of inferiority to the West and the resulting counterbursts of a superiority complex may be a growing realization that they had set up a false dichotomy for themselves between Western technology and native virtues. In time the same realization will probably come to the rest of the non-Western world, relaxing the whole inferiority-superiority problem. At first all modern technology was defined as being Western, leaving very little untouched by it that could be defined as Japanese or Eastern. But in actuality modern technology is Western not by nature but only by time sequence. There is very little in the contemporary West that has not been profoundly changed by modern technology. We are about as far from our seventeenth-century forebears as the Japanese are from theirs. Modern technology started in the West, to be sure, but technology by its nature belongs to all people. The spread of agriculture and the use of iron and bronze did not make all cultures part of the ones where these innovations started. The spread of Chinese inventions such as paper, printing, gunpowder, porcelain, and even the bureaucratic system did not make other lands culturally Chinese. Modern technology and industrial society belong as much to the Japanese as to the peoples of the West. The Japanese have operated steam engines two thirds as long as Westerners, and the time gap in later technological innovation has become steadily shorter until it has now disappeared entirely. Subtract technological change, and the Japanese are still every bit as much Japanese as Americans are American.

Cultural differences often remain as sharp as ever. Nothing is more central to historical Western culture than Christianity, but less than 2 percent of Japanese are professing Christians today—probably a smaller percentage, as we have seen, than in 1600. In institutions influenced by technology, both Japan and the West have gravitated in the same direction. Educational systems, political institutions, industrial organization, and a myriad other things are remarkably similar. For contemporary Japanese, particularly younger ones, there is no longer any sharp sense of differences, and those that exist lose their significance except to give each country an intriguing sense of identity.

Since World War II both the Japanese government and people have sought to minimize nationalism in every way they could. Most of them, not without reason, see themselves as being one of the most internationalized people in the world. Japanese schools probably teach more about the world than do those of any other nation. The history and culture of the West and Chinese antiquity form major elements of Japanese education together with ample teaching about Japan itself. Does the educational system of any other country embrace so fully three different cultures? In the West, the content of most education usually gets little beyond the confines of the Occident, and in former colonial lands, what is taught about the former colonial masters is likely to be offset by inadequacies in education about the country itself. Education in Japan does ignore vast areas of the world, but not as egregiously so as elsewhere.

Life in Japan is as international as in any other country. Newspapers and television keep the people as well informed on international affairs as any other people. Japanese scientists are on all the frontiers of science, and Japanese scholars are fully aware of the intellectual trends of the West. World fads, styles, and fashions probably sweep Japan faster and more fully than in most Western countries. The music of the West is available in as great quantity and high quality as in the West itself. Performances of Beethoven's Ninth Symphony have become a nationwide mania at the New Year season. The art of the whole world is well known and appreciated. The cuisine of the West, China, and much of the rest of the world is available in rare excellence in the cities of Japan. As a practical mixture of native traditions and Western norms, Japanese life styles are perhaps more international than those of any other people.

No people have committed themselves more enthusiastically to the concept of internationalism or have so specifically repudiated nationalism for themselves. In the early postwar years, the Japanese shunned all symbols of nationalism, such as the national flag and anthem. Even today the flag is displayed much less often than in most other countries, and the anthem, the "Kimigayo," was once so little used that small children, hearing it only on television at the start of sporting events, in the way "The Star-Spangled Banner" is used in the United States, made the wrong connection and called it the *sumo* song. "Patriotism" is virtually a dirty word in Japan, carefully eschewed by all but the extreme right. *Kokka-shugi,* the traditional word for nationalism, was felt to be too "feudalistic" in its composition from Chinese characters that mean "country-family-ism," but one common substitute for it, *minzoku-shugi,* "race-ism," has an even more sinister ring to my ears. The most neutral and safest substitute has turned out to be *nashonarizumu,* from English.

As we have seen, official visits by high government functionaries to national shrines, such as those at Ise for the Sun Goddess, the mythological progenitress of the imperial line, or the Yasukuni Shrine in Tokyo to those killed in battle for the country, have raised bitter public controversy. These visits stirred debate not only over nationalism but also over the problem of official relations between religion and the state, which were banned by the new constitution. At first officials carefully avoided these shrines, but this was unnatural. The shrines were too closely linked with Japan's long history, and the dividing line was too vague between them and places of historical interest and beauty. It was as if American political leaders were self-consciously to stay away from Mount Vernon and the Lincoln Memorial. Gradually government leaders began to make official visits to these shrines, though Christians and some other religious groups still protest these acts.

Japan's renunciation of war in its "peace constitution" and its very modest defense force and complete avoidance of offensive power put it in a special position in the world for a major nation. It has steadfastly attempted to avoid military alliances and embroilment in any sort of military or political controversy abroad. It has repeatedly proclaimed its devotion to the United Nations and given it consistent support. These national policies all have the overwhelming support of the Japanese people.

In the late 1980s Japan stands out in some ways as the most international major country in the world. Economically it is prominent almost everywhere. It depends for its livelihood on its economic relations with distant parts of the world, and its products are valued everywhere. It has blended with unparalleled success its own native culture with elements from the West. Japan seems almost the model of what a modern international country should be.

And yet the greatest single problem the Japanese face today is their relationship with other peoples. During the past century and a half they have overcome truly mountainous problems, but they now find themselves struggling with the largely self-created psychological problem of their own self-image and the attitude of other nations toward them.

Japan naturally is much admired, but it is not widely liked or trusted. It is feared both for its past military record and for its current unprecedented economic success. Its low political posture in world politics is looked on with suspicion as an attempt to avoid responsibilities and concentrate on its own narrow advantages. To others Japan's low posture seems a form of trickery rather than a positive effort to promote peace, as it is seen in Japanese eyes. Most non-Western peoples perceive the Japanese to be more Western than Asian, while to Occidentals they appear to be the epitome of the mysterious and menacing "East." Less-developed countries feel Japan should be more sympathetic and generous, while the other advanced countries see it as uncooperative in facing world problems. On both sides it is recognized as an economically dominant power, but it is not well understood and is felt to be uncommunicative and to hold itself self-consciously apart.

Lingering feelings of separateness and uniqueness are still serious problems for the Japanese themselves. Once the problems Japan faced were quite different. They centered on technological backwardness, strategic defense, and massive reforms of society and government. Now they concern successful communication and cooperation with the other peoples of the world. If world peace crumbles, Japan will collapse with it. If the world trading system stagnates, Japan's future will be at risk. Even continued brilliant economic success, such as Japan has enjoyed during the past few decades, could bring on catastrophe if it is not balanced by worldwide growth and understanding. It could produce retaliatory trade restrictions and possibly a trade war, which could plunge the world into a descending spiral toward economic collapse. It certainly would concentrate the ill will of other nations on Japan. The country's narrow emphasis on its own economic growth, which has been its chief policy ever since World War II, has become positively dangerous. Japan as a world leader must adopt broader aims, which embrace the other nations of the world. International understanding is not just a pleasantly innocuous catchphrase for Japanese policy but has become a practical necessity.

The Japanese are intellectually aware of this situation, but they find their own sense of uniqueness difficult to shake off. It is not easy for them to give up their past cozy life, safely insulated by their language barrier and thriving economy, for a more adventurous life dealing with the problems of world peace and the global economy. To put it in dramatic terms, they find it hard to join the human race. For one thing, they still have inadequate skills of communication. More seriously, they have a strong sense of separateness.

A good illustration of the latter point was provided by Prime Minister Nakasone in October 1986 when he made slighting references to certain American ethnic groups as lowering overall American intellectual standards. He unquestionably expressed attitudes taken for granted by most Japanese, but he also revealed an appalling lack of understanding that Japanese leaders, now that they are world leaders as well, will have to be more circumspect in their public utterances, since the whole world now pays attention to what they say. It is to be hoped that the resulting outcry to this incident in the United States taught the Japanese a needed lesson.

Much depends on Japan's choice between continued separateness and a genuine internationalization of its attitudes. Its own stable democracy, smoothly operating social system, and commitment to peace, when combined with its tremendous economic power, can do much to help solve the problems the world faces. However, if it continues to be resented by the less-developed countries and to be seen as uncooperative by the advanced ones, economic frictions could escalate and bring on a general decline in international relations. In these days of growing complexity in world affairs such a decline could all too easily end in catastrophe.

Only time will reveal the outcome, but there are good reasons for optimism. The Japanese have already fitted themselves with remarkable success into the dominant "first world" of the industrialized democracies. Their history shows that for the past century and a half they have risen to meet whatever challenge Japan faced as soon as they could clearly see the problem. When superior Western military and economic technology threatened Japan's future in the nineteenth century, the Japanese proved themselves equal to the situation, fundamentally transforming their political, social, and economic systems in order to achieve technological equality. When the age of rampant imperialism threatened Japan's future, the country concentrated on building sufficient military power to become one of the five great powers of the world, though its failure to perceive in time the ending of this age led to Japan's one great disaster in modern times. When it found itself at the end of World War II a devastated land living under greatly changed global conditions, it concentrated with unprecedented success on economic growth, once again reforming its whole political, social, and economic systems.

Today the great problem for Japan is to become a fully cooperative member of world society, serving as a leader in helping to develop a peaceful world order. To do this will require the abandonment of its sense of uniqueness. It will also require greater efforts to help the less developed countries, a bolder stance on world peace, and sacrifices of some economic advantages to create a more smoothly operating international economic system. But these are relatively small changes compared with the ones Japan made to achieve earlier goals. There is no reason to believe that a country that has been so successful in attaining its main objectives in the past cannot do so again.

A second reason for optimism is the fact that most Japanese are intellectually aware of the need to be more international, even though they may not be emotionally prepared for it. A host of small moves are being made toward the internationalization of Japan. There is inevitably a degree of self-congratulatory pride and arrogance toward other countries because of Japan's extraordinary economic success, but there are no movements leading toward the strengthening of Japanese separateness from the rest of the world. Such attempts would obviously be suicidal, and even the most flagrantly self-confident Japanese realize that increased international cooperation is the only hope for Japan's future success. It is also quite clear to everyone that a prosperous Japan can

Japanese tourists lining up for their beloved *kinen shashin* ("memento picture"), with London's Houses of Parliament in the background. (*Leonard Freed / Magnum Photos*)

exist only in a prosperous world. There are many current efforts at internationalizing education in Japan, making Japanese more internationally minded, and getting the people out of their familiar national cocoon. These efforts are all admittedly small and feeble when compared to the needs, but all the motion is in the right direction. World conditions also draw the Japanese inevitably outward.

The chief factor, however, that makes one believe that Japan will become more international, and at an increasingly rapid rate, is the shift in generations. Most great changes in the world are basically generational. What older people who knew the old conditions accept reluctantly if at all, new generations, which did not personally experience the past, take up quite unconsciously and often with enthusiasm. Today there are vast psychological differences between the prewar generation and the several successive postwar generations. The younger generations are decidedly more internationally minded than their elders. They eagerly roam the world. They feel themselves part of worldwide youth movements. They accept the differences of the outside world with ease. In fact, they feel bottled up in Japan until they have had a chance to see and participate in what lies outside. They look on their own cities not as different from the rest of the world but as centers of world culture. Just as an American looks on New York and a Frenchman on Paris, they see Tokyo as an international city. The very thought that they feel themselves to be different from others is distasteful or even laughable.

Barring the occurrence of a worldwide catastrophe, it is certain that the Japanese will continue to be a major and increasingly unselfconscious part of the world. The contradictory pulls between uniqueness and internationalism that so grip the Japanese today will be resolved in favor of internationalism. And with the economic power and technical skills of the Japanese clearly lending themselves to that trend, Japan and the rest of the world will come appreciably closer to a viable world order.

40   *Japan Today*

Marius B. Jansen

Recent years have brought enormous changes to Japan and its environment. The pages that follow describe these developments in the context of the traditions, attitudes, and institutions described in this book a generation ago.

Japan reentered international society as a political and economic ward of the United States, at the time when the Korean War was establishing the contours of international politics. Those contours held true until 1993, but they are now beginning to change. The environment within which Japan maintained political stability and regained economic health was dominated by decisions reached in connection with the San Francisco Peace Conference in 1951. Under the terms of the United States-Japan Security Treaty, American troops remained in Japan—they are there still—and American planes provided the nuclear umbrella that shielded Japan from outside harm.

Although the Sino-Soviet alliance and North Korean successes early in the war were threatening to many Japanese at that time, as the years passed they became less so. The end of armed conflict in Korea left the North Korean army in being, but it was badly mauled; the presence of United States and Republic of Korea forces south of the border made further danger from that quarter unlikely. Before long the Sino-Soviet friendship was replaced by bitter confrontation and even border violence; a single, formidable enemy was replaced by two quarreling neighbors. The presence of the Seventh Fleet in the Taiwan Straits and the growing military capability of nationalist forces on Taiwan reduced the likelihood of warfare there. Japan seemed surrounded by powers that had recently defeated it and that had no further claims against it. Japanese sensed little danger and kept military spending to the minimum necessary to satisfy American requests for more. In any case, although

Americans frequently grumbled about Japan's "free ride" in defense, Washington was certainly not eager to see Japan remilitarize, partly from a lingering distrust and partly from fear of endangering Japan's new democracy. The United States was also aware that Asian countries that had known the lash of Japanese aggression so recently felt even more strongly about a new Japanese military. The Security Treaty reassured the rest of Asia as much as it did Japan.

Both parties to the United States-Japan Security Treaty agreed that Japan's economic recovery was the first order of business. The Korean War, with its opportunities for providing services for the United Nations armies, probably marked the beginning of that recovery, but the decisive turn came in the 1960s, during the premiership of Ikeda Hayato, years when Edwin Reischauer was United States Ambassador in Tokyo. Ikeda's "income doubling" plan more than fulfilled its objectives, and as Japan became a world leader in shipping, consumer electronics, automobiles, and hi-tech products the lives of its people were transformed. Urbanization, education, and affluence brought changes that were mirrored in the goals of consumers during successive decades: electric rice cookers, then television, washing machines, and refrigerators, and next air conditioners, color television, and automobiles. Massive population movements brought Japanese from agricultural villages to the cities. Mass transport brought commuters from new housing developments that were ever farther from the workplace. And these changes were not restricted to the great metropolitan centers; better highways, bridges, trains, municipal buildings, schools, and factories opened up what had once been remote and backward sectors of Japan.

Inadequate housing, long commutes, and government policies that favored producers over consumers through forced savings for investment kept most Japanese from full enjoyment of the products of their work, but conditions were so much better than they had been during the decades of war and postwar hardship that people were more conscious of improvements than they were of deficiencies in the quality of life.

In time Japanese prosperity worked to stabilize and energize maritime East Asia. Japan became something of a locomotive of growth among its neighbors or, as some had it, the lead bird in a wedge of geese that pointed the path to a consumer society. The Republic of Korea, Taiwan, Hong Kong, and Singapore soon experienced rapid economic growth that transformed those societies as it had Japan's. Their governments were far more authoritarian than Japan's, but in each a state-led capitalism followed industrial policies that allocated capital, encouraged savings over consumption, and exercised administrative guidance that included protection for nascent industries.

The success of these policies was enormously important to the United States. Not only did the outcome provide object lessons of the advantages of capitalist over socialist development, but it ended the need for formal American assistance. America's informal assistance, by opening the world's largest market to the import of consumer goods, was probably even more important.

The arrangement worked out even better for Japan. By the 1970s the trickle of Japanese imports into the United States had become a torrent that produced a consistent trade imbalance that grew year by year. To some it began to seem that Japan, although a principal beneficiary of the world-wide system of free trade championed by the United States, was nevertheless protecting its own industries until their dominance at home and strength abroad made them invulnerable to foreign challenge. Some Americans began to suspect that, as the memoirs of one Japanese leader put it, Japanese, having failed to achieve economic domination in uniform, were succeeding in business suits. Issues of trade reciprocity that began with textiles and moved on to automobiles and computer chips played an ever more important part in Japanese-American relations. Japan was obliged to accept a series of "voluntary" export restrictions, but the world's fixation with the problems of the Cold War competition meant that nothing was allowed to imperil the Japanese-American security relationship.

Within Japan, the dominance of the Liberal Democratic Party (LDP), a coalition of two conservative parties formed in 1955 to counter the union of the Socialist parties, extended through the thirty-eight years in which those security considerations were paramount. The party operated somewhat like a political *keiretsu*, with factional components arranged to permit limited choice within a monopsonist cartel. It also lived on, and redistributed, lavish favors from supporters and interest groups. During war and occupation periods a web of administrative controls that bound bureaucracy, business, and party had been formed. Inevitably this produced political scandals that surfaced repeatedly before, during, and after the war. But although revelations of improper relations between business and politics shook the government periodically, they never endangered it.

In any case Japanese voters had few acceptable alternatives to the LDP.

It developed skill and flexibility in satisfying special constituencies in agriculture, small business, and distribution that balanced its concern for major industries. The Socialist opposition, denied a seat at decision tables, could not claim credit for the practical adjustments that government bureaucrats made to speed and assist Japan's economic growth. In foreign policy, Socialists clung rigidly to positions calling for a neutral and disarmed Japan, and so guaranteed American support for the LDP. Because there was no real opposition party at hand, the United States with its formidable influence emerged as a major player in Japanese politics. It nudged LDP leaders to liberalize market access and lessen bureaucratic control. Success always fell short of what was desired, but in fact the Japan trade assumed impressive dimensions as Japan began to open its markets. By the 1990s Japan was importing more American products than Britain and Germany combined. Japanese imports of manufactured goods rose by 88 percent between 1986 and 1991, and Japan's per capita imports from the United States (about $400) were slightly higher than America's imports ($370) from Japan. United States influence was so ubiquitous that it functioned almost like an opposition party. Politicians and bureaucrats utilized American pressure to strengthen their own positions in internal disputes, and decisions that were unpalatable to particular constituencies could be explained as having been necessary to placate the United States. In this sense elements of irresponsibility were built into the system that was nurtured by the Cold War.

Still, it would be wrong to overlook the fact that Japan was also well served by its bureaucrats and leaders. The Japanese society that developed under these conditions understandably attracted the admiration and respect of observers around the world. Japanese society "worked." In public transportation, public education, quality of workmanship, and quiet, unpretentious efficiency and cooperation it set standards that few countries could match. Even in public works, where political corruption sometimes exacted its price, money, not quality, was sacrificed. Profits from industrial success went overwhelmingly to investment to increase capacity rather than to improve the quality of life or in dividends to investors, but pride in work and a reasonably equitable standard of living served to still most doubts and diminish protest.

The contours of this landscape changed radically in the early 1990s. In 1989 the death of Hirohito, who was to be posthumously known as Emperor Showa, removed the symbol of Japan's war, defeat, and reconstruction. The Soviet empire disintegrated into its constituent parts. Germany was reunited. In China the communist government suppressed popular calls for political democracy but set sweeping economic reforms in motion. The ideological and military confrontation of the Cold War continued only on the Korean peninsula, where North Korea increased its military capability and gave signs of working toward a nuclear capability. But even there tentative moves toward dialogue between north and south began, and the impending exit of the aging Kim Il-Sung (who died in 1994) held out hope for change.

The Cold War's military confrontations in Korea, Vietnam, and Cambodia seemed at an end. Diplomatic ties were established between Russia and the Republic of Korea, and between China and the Republic of Korea; China entered into diplomatic relations with Indonesia, Singapore, and Vietnam. Taiwanese capital flowed into China and was responsible for 10 percent and more of new enterprises in coastal provinces there. Civil war came to an end in Cambodia. Akihito, the new Japanese emperor, visited Southeast Asia and China. A new economic council, Asia-Pacific Economic Cooperation Council (APEC), formed in Australia in 1989, grew to include China, Hong Kong, and Taiwan. Japan became China's largest trading partner, and China was Japan's second largest. From 1981 to 1991 total world trade increased in real terms by 48 percent; for Japan, and for the rest of East Asia, it doubled. In other words, Japan's world had changed powerfully and permanently.

With the military competition behind them, United States policymakers now placed first emphasis on economic relations and tried to staunch two deficits: a budget deficit that had gone out of control during the 1980s, and a resulting trade deficit of more than a hundred billion dollars a year, more than half of it with Japan. Efforts to deal with the latter in terms of conventional economic theory began with the adjustment of exchange rates in the 1970s to make Japanese exports more expensive and American manufactures more competitive. These steps were sharpened by an agreement (the Plaza Accord) in 1985 that resulted in an upward spiral for the yen that raised its value to around 100 to $1 in 1993. These moves brought some results, but did so slowly and imperfectly. Americans bought less, but the greater cost of what they bought left the totals badly skewed. There was a burst of Japanese investment in American treasury notes; indeed, for some years it almost seemed that Japanese were making possible the ambitious military spending program of the Reagan administration. And Japanese manufacturers invested in offshore production in the United States to guard against protectionist legislation.

More visible were Japanese purchases of American real estate and equities. Although within a few years many of the more spectacular acquisitions by Japanese turned out to have been expensive and unwise, they provoked confusion and uneasiness among many Americans and created the image of wealthy, rapacious Japanese—not unlike earlier Japanese views of Americans. The two countries seemed to have changed roles. Japan had become the world's, probably history's, largest creditor nation, and the United States the world's largest debtor nation.

Japan's economic boom proved of short duration. During the years 1988–1990 a speculative fever swept Japan. In what became known as the "bubble economy" after its collapse, unsound investments based for the most part on wildly exaggerated valuation of land led to competition between banks and lending agencies to lend money. When the bubble burst retrenchment slowed and then stopped economic growth.

As was to be expected, this speculative euphoria was accompanied by political corruption, and on a scale unprecedented in postwar Japan. In 1993 this brought to an end the thirty-eight-year rule of the Liberal Democratic Party and made possible the first steps toward a reorientation of Japanese politics. Political change was in the air everywhere in East Asia; in the Republic of Korea the military government had given way to an elective ("Democratic Liberal") regime headed by an ex-general, who in turn was succeeded by Kim Young Sam, a Democratic politician elected in December 1992. In Taiwan the grip of mainland-born Kuomintang leaders was the focus of popular demonstrations that led to election victories for Taiwan-born leaders, and on the mainland of China a short-lived democracy movement, crushed by tanks in 1989, showed signs of flickering back to life a few years later. On every side, in other words, the generation of war and postwar figures was being replaced by men and women for whom the verities of the Cold War era were no longer set in stone. Japan was no exception.

Japan's Reaction to World Changes

In the 1990s Japan gradually began to take a more active role in world affairs. A number of psychological and symbolic impediments to such participation were removed. More important was the fact that in the post–Cold War world it was becoming difficult for Japan to stand aside from international needs and crises. Japan was now an economic superpower, and its economic clout throughout the world raised expectations in the United States and other industrial democracies that it should participate actively in world affairs. At the same time, however, its feeling that it was being coopted rather than consulted made that participation reluctant and hesitant.

One symbolic impediment to such participation passed with the death on January 7, 1989, of the sovereign in whose name Japanese armies had stormed through Asia. Emperor Showa (Hirohito) had visited Europe and the United States, but he had never travelled in Asia. Although he had visited all other prefectures in Japan, he had never visited Okinawa. Plans for a trip there were taking shape at the time of his death. When Akihito, the new emperor, was enthroned in November 1990, it was easier for him to speak of his "deepest regret" for the course of Korean-Japanese relations, and to interact with East Asian leaders. The fact that seven hundred foreign dignitaries, including President George Bush, gathered at the emperor's interment in February, however, illustrated the degree to which Japan had regained its standing in the world community since 1945.

When Prime Minister Hosokawa took office in 1993 he too was prompted to express his belief that the Pacific War had been one of aggression, a sentiment in considerable contrast to the more equivocal comments of his predecessors, who were afraid that such a judgment might be read as disrespectful of Japan's war dead. Japanese diplomats also assumed a more prominent position in cooperation with their neighbors in Asia. Japan took a conspicuous role in discussions of APEC, the new Pacific economic council. Its relations with the Peoples Republic of China improved. Trade with China and other Asian countries grew, while trade with the United States began to decline. By 1994, although the amount involved was still one-fifth of that with the United States, Japan became China's largest trading partner, and China was Japan's largest after the United States. Security talks with China were also held.

When it came to affairs farther from home and direct national interest, however, Japan's participation continued to be reactive and reluctant. Relations with Russia provided one such example. The Soviet Union had boycotted the San Francisco Peace Treaty Conference. In 1956 the Hatoyama cabinet had negotiated a peace declaration with the Soviet Union, but a formal peace treaty finalizing boundaries eluded negotiators. The stumbling block to further progress was Soviet retention of four northern islands that had been seized in the closing days of World War II and were now administered as part of the Russian Republic. The Soviets had offered to return Shikotan and the Habomai islets in 1956, but with the merger of the Democratic and Liberal parties in that year Japanese negotiators had hardened their position to include demands for Kunashiri and Etorofu as well. The Russians argued that those islands were part of the Kuriles, whose "return" had been agreed to at Yalta. At that time an ailing President Roosevelt, who had not been fully briefed, had dismissed the problem as Russia's natural desire for the return of what had been taken away from it. Japan, however, had not acquired Shikotan, Habomai, Kunashiri, and Etorofu as a result of the Russo-Japanese war, but had held them from the mid-nineteenth century on. Its maximum claim was for the entire Kuril chain, which had been conceded by Russia in 1875 in return for Japanese claims to Sakhalin.

With the relaxation of Cold War tensions it seemed possible that some agreement might be worked out, but this proved illusory. On the eve of Mikhail Gorbachev's visit to Japan in April 1991, Japanese optimism ran high; many anticipated Soviet concessions in return for Japanese economic aid. By the time of Gorbachev's arrival his position was already weakening, however, and a prior visit to the disputed islands by Boris Yeltsin acquainted him with the fears of Russian inhabitants who had moved there. Consequently it seemed clear that Gorbachev could not, and Yeltsin would not, give way on Kunashiri and Etorofu, the two islands that were most in question. Both governments remained locked in position. The return of the northern territories had long been a chief talking point for Japan's bitterly anti-Russian and anticommunist right wing, and no Japanese government could renounce them. On the Russian side, Boris Yeltsin, who became president of the Russian Republic in 1991, faced strong nationalist pressures to retain former Soviet territory, and the surprising strength shown by ultranationalist candidates in the Russian elections of 1993 ensured that there would be further delays in any transfer of the islands to Japan. As was to be expected, Japan was also a cautious contributor in discussions of economic aid to Russia in its transition to a market economy. A visit by President Yeltsin to Tokyo in October 1993 made little substantive difference in that posture, and shortly thereafter Yeltsin's political difficulties at home made his government seem an unlikely recipient of political and economic aid.

In other international concerns Japan's response and participation have also been slow and politically difficult. This was particularly conspicuous in the Gulf War against Iraq in 1990. In October 1990 the Kaifu cabinet announced plans to commit one thousand members of the Self Defense Force as noncombatants, but protests forced it to cancel that arrangement. Plans were then set in motion for the establishment of a special Peace Keeping Organization (PKO) of up to two thousand men. The lower house of the Diet approved, but the upper house, where the Socialist presence had been bolstered by the election that followed the fall of the Takeshita cabinet, blocked the measure. In June of 1992, after the

Kuwait emergency had passed, Kaifu's successor, Miyazawa Kiichi, finally managed to secure approval of the measure. By the time the PKO was created, however, its role was limited by numerous restrictions to guarantee that forces sent would be kept out of harm's way (and from inflicting harm), and the world community was more bemused than impressed. Japan's financial contribution to the United Nations Gulf War was nonetheless impressive. At $13 billion, and financed by an additional tax, it was the largest of any country besides Saudi Arabia.

Despite this impressive sum, Japan's handling of the matter was seen from abroad as hesitant and piecemeal, and it contributed poorly to its position as a major power. It must be added, however, that many Japanese felt that their participation had been taken for granted and that their enormous contribution had brought them little recognition. Even so, the affair ended with a symbolic event of possible future significance. When Japanese minesweepers were sent to help clean the Gulf they took a leisurely route, with a stop in Singapore, that marked the first time the Japanese flag had been seen in those waters since World War II.

One of Japan's long-deferred goals was a permanent position on the United Nations Security Council. Japan had by this time become a key member of the United Nations; in financial contributions it was second only to the United States, and the same was true of its program of overseas aid. The UN Charter, however, a product of the closing days of World War II, makes specific mention of Japan and Germany as "enemy states," and its revision is likely to open the door to requests from other candidates for membership. Japan's position has the formal backing of the United States, and Japan has also solicited the support of Russia and other members. No plan has yet been put forward. It seems logical that permanent members should participate fully in UN peace keeping activities (although the Secretary General, during a visit to Japan, explicitly denied that this should be the case), and in that connection Japan's constitutional limitations would certainly be raised. The larger problem was that much of the world continued to see Japanese contributions to world order as too little and too late. No one was more critical of this than Japanese themselves. Ozawa Ichirō, a principal political strategist for Prime Minister Hosokawa, called for changes to make Japan a "normal country" prepared to participate fully in world affairs, and the influential Kōsaka Masataka wrote in 1993 that "Japan has been lying to the world. We have promised to help prop up the world order by means of economic measures, but we have delivered next to nothing."

In one major settlement in Southeast Asia, however, Japan gave a hint of what might be expected of it in the future. Shortly after its establishment, the Peace Keeping Organization was assigned a role in restoring peace to Cambodia. The UN Transitional Authority was headed by a high UN official, Akashi Yasushi, and the UN High Commissioner for Refugees, Ogata Sadako, was a distinguished academic and former Japanese representative to the United Nations Educational, Scientific, and Cultural Organization (UNESCO). The successful resettlement of Cambodian refugees from Thailand and the monitoring and brokering of elections for the new government in Cambodia marked a conspicuous success for the world organization and indicated ways in which Japan and Japanese could be expected to make a highly constructive contribution without displaying military muscle.

A major development in Japan in the 1990s was an increased Asia consciousness, so strong that some spoke of the "Asianization" of Japan. In part this was a logical result of economic trends. In 1985 Japan traded a third more with the United States than it did with Asia, but by 1993 the reverse was true and Japan's trade with Asia was a third larger than that with the United States. The appreciation of the yen brought a surge of Japanese investment in Asia as well as in the United States, as more and more Japanese industrial production moved offshore. Japan's total direct foreign investment overseas was $4.7 billion in 1980, but surged to $12.2 in 1985 and a high of $67 billion in 1989. Even after the "bubble" burst it registered $34 billion in 1992. With investment of this order Japan was contributing to Asian integration, a trend already in progress through ASEAN (Association of Southeast Asian Nations) and APEC. Japanese intellectuals and readers saw the flood of materials discussing the country's new consciousness of Asia as an important change from the late-nineteenth-century "turn from Asia" to the West. Some saw in this a possible harbinger of a new role for Japan, as bridge between the industrialized, democratic West and a developing and industrializing Asia, though there was little prospect that Japan would want to, or could, give up its place at the councils of developed and modernized states.

The Reform of Politics and the Politics of Reform

The breakup of the pattern of structured confrontation that characterized the Cold War was followed by the breakup of the Liberal Democratic Party. The Socialist opposition had bent, but never broken, its announced preference for a strict interpretation of Article 9 of the Constitution and neutrality in foreign affairs, and, since that position seemed unrealistic and unacceptable to the electorate, the LDP had been the beneficiary. The collapse of socialism around the world, however, meant the collapse of that ideological confrontation, and it opened the way to a new political configuration.

During the four decades in which Japanese politics was dominated by the LDP, matters moved in deeply furrowed channels. For the first half of that period the personal influence and legacy of Prime Minister Yoshida prevailed. The "Yoshida doctrine," as it has been called, stipulated that Japan abstain as much as possible from participation in international affairs, leaving such matters (and its defense) to the United States, and concentrate on economic recovery and growth. By 1972, the end of the premiership of Satō Eisaku, the last member of the "Yoshida academy," as journalists dubbed his disciples, those policies had been brilliantly successful. By then the LDP had also developed a pattern of factions (described in Chapter 24) that permitted and in fact encouraged experimentation and specialization.

Faction leaders helped finance their followers and competed for opportunities for cabinet positions and party presidency; success depended on seniority and size of faction. In the 1970s dissatisfaction with the unyielding nature of seniority resulted in several efforts to democratize this system and open it up to younger politicians through primary elections, but none proved lasting or successful. Each prime minister had to balance faction members in the selection of his cabinet; he seldom served longer than two two-year terms, after which he was succeeded by another faction head. Good relations with Washington constituted the best evidence of competence. They were also central to the concerns of the business community, which provided election campaign war chests. The Japan Federation of Economic Organizations did this systematically by having each enterprise association assign amounts to member firms according to market share. The American market and American approval were of critical importance. The largely successful five-year premiership of Nakasone Yasuhiro (1982–1987), for instance, owed a great deal to his smooth relations with Ronald Reagan, with whom he was on a first-name basis. Japanese pundits wrote of the "Ron-Yasu" connection and often argued that Nakasone's tenure would have been far shorter without it.

Nakasone was also intelligent and articulate; he set as goals a revival of Japanese confidence and pride to permit greater participation in world affairs. Thanks to his good relations with President Reagan he was able to move to the center of pictures of world statesmen at G-7 conferences. He spoke of Japan's international responsibilities instead of stressing its constitutional inhibitions as his predecessors had done, and he called for reforms in the education system to free the curriculum from the tyranny of entrance examinations, make it more creative, and have it conform with his own agenda for a stronger moral and national consciousness. But because his factional backing was weak, he was dependent on the support of the retainers of Tanaka Kakuei; and because his ties within the bureaucracy were inadequately developed, his period in office brought few institutional changes. Nakasone was succeeded by Takeshita Noboru, whose fall in 1989 was triggered by the first of a series of scandals that played a major role in bringing to an end the long dominance of the Liberal Democratic Party.

Although instances of extraordinary individual venality have come to light at times, the problem of corruption in Japanese politics has been largely structural. As in the United States, it centers on the high cost of election. Election laws are strict and limit the length of periods of active campaigning, thus putting a premium on the candidate's ability to establish favorable name familiarity in the shortest possible time. Positive memories associated with a forebear can be extremely helpful; the lower house of the Diet has come to show 40 percent and more second-generation representatives who more or less inherited their seats. Failing that, only expensive vote canvassing can do the job.

Furthermore, most representatives have had to stand for election from multimember districts that elect three to five representatives. The majority LDP has normally had many members competing against each other. As Socialist strength waned, the opposition (who have renamed themselves Social Democrats in English, though not in Japanese) placed only one or two candidates in many districts, indicating their acceptance of a minority role in the Diet. In such cases Socialist candidates have usually been able to rely on the assistance of the party office in their districts. Not so the LDP candidates, as the party office had to maintain neutrality between candidates. Individual support organizations, the *koenkai,* have been established to make up the difference. That nurture, however, requires congratulatory messages for weddings and store openings, consolation gifts for funerals, and a host of additional proofs that the representative "cares." Some of these practices are forbidden by law, but since that law makes no provision for enforcement it is virtually irrelevant. In a society in which gift-giving frequently accompanies requests and expressions of thanks, the possibilities for ambiguity are particularly numerous.

Election to office begins, and does not end, the need for money. The representative now needs money for secretaries to staff offices in Tokyo and in the home district. The national government provides funds for two such employees, but the norm for LDP politicians is closer to fourteen or fifteen employees in four or five separate offices. This is in marked contrast to provisions for legal aides and administrative staff in the United States, where the average congressman maintains seventeen, and the average senator forty-one, staff members at public expense.

To meet these yearly expenses—which run, according to figures released in 1987 by ten newly elected members who were calling for reform, about Y120 million, against an official allowance of less than Y20 million—the Diet representative usually cobbles together a package of party and factional support, political contributions, and "sales" of tickets to special events and testimonial dinners staged for his or her benefit. Japan's economy, like its transportation network, is highly centralized. Business people and entrepreneurs, no less than foreign traders, have to work their way through a maze of administrative regulations. Requests and thanks are frequently accompanied by tangible expressions of gratitude and respect, and the high cost of politics means that money plays an important role in achieving and retaining public office.

The web of influence is further strengthened by ties between the worlds of politics, bureaucracy, and business. Members of the bureaucracy normally retire in their late fifties or early sixties and move on to secondary careers in business, where their knowledge of the administrative process and contacts in government make them invaluable. This process is popularly termed *amakudari* (descent from heaven), perhaps in reference to the Sun Goddess's charge to her grandson to rule over Japan. Able bureaucrats also "descend" to the world of politics, and of course the world of politics deals directly with the world of business. The LDP has developed a series of *zoku*, or "tribes," of Diet members who become known as specialists in a particular area or concern. Reasonably secure in their seats (a larger than usual proportion are second-generation representatives), they acquire enough practical experience and knowledge about a particular area of policy along with seniority in the party to become full participants in the development of ministry policies and budget priorities. It is natural and desirable to have this happen, of course, and the United States Congress is the stronger for many members who develop a comparable expertise. In the setting of Japan's centralization, however, ministries responsible for administrative regulations in areas such as construction, agriculture, and commerce have become particularly important in the political economy of influence and power.

It is therefore not surprising that during the long tenure in office of the LDP there were periodic charges of corruption. Ordinary Japanese went about their business, which prospered, and accepted occasional connivance to defray the costs of office as a fact of life. Most prime ministers announced their intentions to work toward reform without being able to do very much about it. It was assumed that such reform would require two approaches, one to arrange for more small, single-member districts in which campaigning costs might be less, and another to curb political contributions and make them more visible. In 1989, however, a new series of charges and revelations of corruption seemed to go beyond the bounds of voter (and particularly press) tolerance, producing powerful calls for change. Suspicions led to new watchfulness as a series of scandals also surfaced in the worlds of banking and securities. In 1991 these misgivings combined with the bursting of the economic "bubble" and a growing uneasiness about the economy.

The initial stages of the affair centered around allegations about an employment service and recruiting company called Recruit. It published a recruitment bulletin that found a useful niche because Ministry of Labor services covered only about one-fifth of the nation's hiring. Japanese firms interview, examine, and hire workers at the end of the school year. For upper-scale firms, which compete for outstanding students entering the labor force, the decisions made represent a life-long commitment. And since, for demographic reasons, the supply of such entrants has been shrinking, the recruitment process is central to the life of the firm. It is even more important for the individual high school and college graduates entering the labor force, as it represents a single opportunity; henceforth their salaries will for the most part match the salaries of those with whom they enter the firm.

As Recruit's fortunes grew so too did the ambitions of its executives for entry into the business and political elite. They had close access to the "tribe" of Ministry of Labor specialists in the National Diet, paying them annual retainers. Next they came up with large-scale insider trading in new stock issues for the benefit of a wide range of major politicians and their probable successors in several political parties. Individuals important to the company were offered blocks of three, five, and ten thousand shares, many as ceremonial gifts to facilitate the advancement of the company president in the political world. Recruit was also lavish with its purchase of tickets to testimonial dinners for members of the labor "tribe" in the Diet. What was unusual about this was the scale and drive of the campaign, and not the practice. When the details became public a number of leading figures resigned their cabinet posts, and ultimately Takeshita himself stepped down in 1989.

Shortly thereafter, new revelations of corruption surfaced with evidence of a round of gifts and payments by the executives of a rapid express company called Sagawa. Once again the LDP, as the party in power, had been the party most worth soliciting. Meanwhile a number of irregularities in deals by banks and brokerage firms came to light. As revelations continued, it became clear that prominent figures in organized crime (the *yakuza*) had been involved in "sweetheart deals" with brokerage houses that made it impossible for them to lose money. Additional charges of influence peddling and political blackmail by underworld leaders pointed to the very pinnacle of political succession in the LDP establishment.

LDP leaders stumbled badly in responding to these charges. Factions and interest groups seemed to be deeply entrenched and immobile. At first they hoped that an interim caretaker prime minister would divert attention until normal politics could be resumed. An initial experimental foray, with a relatively unknown backbencher as prime minister, foundered almost immediately on charges of character. The leadership then turned to an attractive and able younger figure, Kaifu Toshiki, a former Minister of Education. When it came to matters of importance, however, his hands were tied by the party bosses, and his unsuccessful attempts to institute the Peace Keeping Force and carry out political reform cost him his post in 1991. His successor, the veteran Miyazawa Kiichi, was also blocked in carrying out his promises of political reform. In 1993 he was turned out of office in an unprecedented no-confidence vote in the Diet.

In the meantime new scandals emerged. These centered around the LDP senior statesman Kanemaru Shin, who was long recognized as head of the construction *zoku*. Revelations of bribery payoffs of some $4 million produced an initial court judgment against him of only $1,700. The outrage that resulted led to new searches and the discovery of staggering sums totalling more than $50 million in cash, bonds, and gold bars in apartments he maintained. Kanemaru's political henchmen fell away from him. Spurred by the new evidence they had at hand, prosecutors next raided the offices of major construction companies and seized some 4,600 cases of documents. These documents led to suspicion, and then proof, of bribery that implicated almost every major general contracting firm and led to the indictment of a number of highly visible public officials.

By this time calls for reform were strong. Many of them came from former members of the LDP. One of the first to announce the formation of a "New Party" *(Shintō)* was Hosokawa Morihiro, a former governor of Kumamoto Prefecture and scion of one of the most distinguished aristocratic warrior families of early modern Japan. His ancestors had been feudal lords of Kumamoto, and his maternal grandfather was Prince Konoe Fumimaro, prime minister in the late 1930s. As governor, Hosokawa had taken a strong line in environmental protection with regard to the chemical plant whose pollution caused mercury poisoning (the Minamata case). He had also become convinced that Japan was over centralized and over regulated; one instance he cited was the necessity to refer the change of location for a bus stop in Kumamoto all the way to Tokyo.

Now that the work of reconstruction and recovery had been completed, he argued, Japan needed to reform its politics to place greater responsibility in the hands of legislators instead of bureaucrats, increase choice, enhance local autonomy, and promote greater understanding of diverse cultures in order to be able to undertake initiatives for world peace. At fifty-six, Hosokawa was an appealing and able figure. Despite a dearth of suitable candidates, his New Party did well in local elections and then placed thirty-five candidates in the national elections of 1993. This success led to a series of defections of ambitious parliamentarians from the LDP. At the end of 1992 a group of forty-four Diet members led by Ozawa Ichirō, a former Kanemaru aide, and Hata Tsutomu seceded. Soon Hosokawa's New Party was only one of three new groups, all of which were predominantly composed of former LDP members. When the Miyazawa cabinet proved unable to carry through on its promises for reform and lost a confidence vote, Miyazawa called elections for July 1933 in which the LDP lost its majority. Before long a coalition government was put together under Hosokawa, ending the period of unbroken LDP rule. Voters greeted the new cabinet with enthusiasm. Approval ratings for the LDP rule had fallen drastically, but the new government began with unprecedented favorable ratings of 75 percent.

The new cabinet represented a coalition of eight groups including the Socialists, who agreed to support continuity in the diplomacy and defense measures they had always opposed. The cabinet's center lay with the Ozawa-Hata group that had left the LDP. It was united chiefly in its

Prime Minister Hosokawa Mirihiro.
(Courtesy Japan Information Center)

determination to end the LDP ascendancy and bring about political reform, but it seemed certain that disagreement over economic policies
would guarantee early differences. Events soon showed that its unity did
not even extend to the details of electoral reform, the issue the prime
minister had vowed to settle before the close of the Diet session at year's
end. When the cabinet's legislation for electoral changes was defeated by
Socialist defections in the upper house, Hosokawa had to turn to dissi-

dent factions within the LDP for assistance; he managed to secure Diet approval for a package on the last day of the extended session in January 1994.

Japan's new electoral system calls for 300 single-member districts, instead of the 274 proposed in the original government bill, with the remaining 200 seats to be chosen by proportional representation. For that purpose the country is to be divided into 11 regional blocs. Additional compromises came on the issue of campaign finances. The Socialists had been adamant in ruling out any support for individual candidates from business firms, but under the final terms lawmakers can set up one fund-raising body to accept up to $4,580 a year from each company for a transitional period of 5 years. Public funds are to be provided as subsidies to political parties to make up for the tighter restrictions on corporate contributions.

No one can be confident of the impact of these changes. To some observers the single-member districts seemed likely to favor LDP candidates with substantial funding. Most agreed that women, already a small minority in the national legislature, would find it more difficult to secure enough votes in single-member districts. Others argued that in the future successful candidates would be less obligated to special constituencies such as farmers and small shopkeepers, groups that have resisted liberalization for further market opening. Both sectors have been disproportionately represented under present arrangements, and both are relatively inefficient, of declining economic importance, and made up of senior citizens. Proponents of the changes thus argued that they would lead to a legislature more concerned with urban consumers and more likely to respond to issues rather than special interest considerations.

The events of 1993 seemed nevertheless likely to mark the early stages of important changes in Japanese democracy. It was clear that they were early steps. All the leaders of the new government came to prominence under the old system, having been part of what they now denounced. Furthermore, the prime minister's power remains limited. Liberal Democratic Party prime ministers have served, as an earlier chapter put it, more like chairmen of the board than chief executive officers.

As the leader of a rather shaky coalition, Prime Minister Hosokawa was faced with poor prospects. He was unable to maintain discipline in his coalition, and when the LDP opposition got wind of loans he had contracted with the head of the Sagawa enterprise it deadlocked the Diet with demands for more details. Hosokawa resigned his post after holding it for eight months. The coalition he had formed held together long enough to select the foreign minister, Hata Tsutomu, as his successor, but collapsed almost immediately when the Socialists, charging that they were being marginalized by Ozawa and Hata, withdrew. The maneuvers that followed showed how completely the ideological confrontations of the Cold War had given way; LDP and Socialist leaders joined forces to drop Hata for Murayama Tomiichi, Socialist Party chairman. LDP figures in the cabinet (thirteen) held the posts of Foreign Affairs and International Trade and Industry; eight members of the former coalition were represented, all but one of them Socialist.

Curiously, the LDP-Socialist tie-up proved to have more stability than the two previous coalition cabinets. Steps toward budget formation, defense expenditures, and implementation of the changes in election procedures proceeded relatively smoothly. It seemed that once issues related to the Cold War were resolved, right-wing LDP and left-wing Socialists had a good deal in common. They were eager to protect their base among small producers and farmers, inclined toward protectionism, and they shared doubts about the security tie with the United States.

This did not, however, portend a return to old-style LDP rule. Rather, it suggested that it would take some time before the LDP system that has lasted for thirty-eight years would be replaced by something stable. Work was going forward on the redistricting necessary for an election according to the new system adopted under Hosokawa. The new parties and factions that had formed in the waning days of LDP power were unlikely to survive in their present form, but their appearance provided new opportunities for recruitment and promotion of leaders outside the old seniority system. The LDP seemed likely to continue its disintegration; major figures such as former Prime Ministers Nakasone and Kaifu were openly indignant at the cynical maneuvering taking place, and younger members were no less critical. It could not be said that the Japanese electorate had shown a clear desire for structural "change," but it was significant that all aspirants to leadership vowed to continue the steps toward deregulation, decentralization, and internationalization signaled by Hosokawa. Socialist strength seemed certain to continue its decline.

Japan was likely to develop a more plural system in which single-member electoral district voting would place greater importance on parties and issues. Increasingly, political figures were trying to stake out positions by publishing books indicating their vision for a new Japan. The Hosokawa government, in other words, had signaled a period of ferment and debate about the path Japan should take. Executive influence, however, in the absence of a popular and persuasive figure, would probably be limited, and this promised difficulty for elected politicians in achieving ascendancy over Japan's talented and powerful central bureaucracy.

The Economy: Recession and Surplus

In the early 1990s Japan, after decades of almost uninterrupted economic growth, entered its first serious postwar recession.

Domestic sales were flat, and rapid appreciation of the yen cut into exports, particularly of automobiles, which were already leveling off because of economic turn-downs in other industrialized countries. Japan's trade surpluses remained high, and, as Japanese imports of manufactured goods declined, irritation abroad, especially in the United States, grew. During the years of the Cold War, security considerations had blunted public criticism of Japan in Washington, but the new Clinton administration, which included no experienced Japan watchers in prominent positions, seemed prepared to risk confrontation. Japan's postwar system was entering its first severe test.

On both sides of the Pacific the new administrations tried to proceed in an orderly sequence, but neither government was allowed the luxury of choosing its priorities. Prime Minister Hosokawa, like President Clinton, was clearly intent on domestic changes, but each of them complicated the other's timetable. Hosokawa's talk of deregulation ran into American demands for government assurances of progress in reducing the trade surplus with the United States, and President Clinton's talk of competitiveness and job growth led his advisers to focus on America's trade deficit with new vigor.

Japan's recession was part of a world-wide economic slowdown, but it had a number of distinguishing features that related to developments of the 1980s. Japanese and American efforts to address the trade surplus through correction of exchange rates culminated in the Plaza Accord of 1985. Economic theory held that a higher yen which made Japanese products more expensive abroad would lessen the trade imbalance. The same changes, however, reduced Japanese energy costs, which were denominated in dollars, improving Japan's ability to compete in world markets, and produced more dollars for fewer exports.

The higher yen also contributed to a surge of Japanese investment abroad that had become possible after deregulation measures taken in 1980. Suddenly assets such as hotels, real estate, and even classic works of art were within reach for Japanese investors. Japanese investment in the United States remained behind that of Europe, but the sudden and spectacular nature of the change caught the American public by surprise, and the negative reaction it stirred startled Japanese. Sometimes efforts at damage control became counterproductive; all too often efforts by Japan to cultivate goodwill and encourage understanding of Japan by grants to institutions of learning and museums were condemned as efforts to buy influence. A number of vigorous critics warned readers and listeners that Japanese capitalism, with its ties between state and business, was fundamentally different from American capitalism, and that assumptions of ultimate convergence between the two systems had been badly off the mark. These views found a wide hearing and entered into governmental and press discussions of Japanese-American trade problems.

The problems of the Japanese economy in the early 1990s went far beyond those of trade. The 1980s were years of bonanza growth with particularly startling rises in the valuation of land. As a result, home mortgage companies near the great cities developed multigeneration mortgages, and companies with access to land used it as collateral for loans that pyramided to ever higher levels. Along with this came striking rises in the valuation of securities; major firms invested in each other's stocks with profit. At times deregulation resulted in laxity, as with the savings bank scandals in the United States. Japanese banks grew in size and numbered among the world's largest; they competed to make loans that sometimes received remarkably little scrutiny (the Ministry of Finance, as a matter of policy, did not allow banks to fail), and secondary financial institutions like loan companies were able to secure funding for even more marginal loans at higher interest rates. The relatively equitable distribution of income on which postwar Japan had prided itself also began to disappear, and it seemed as though an era of speculative robber barons had launched Japan into new and untried waters.

In the early 1990s this "bubble" economy burst. Japan's rate of growth plummeted. In 1993, when adjusted for inflation, it was one-tenth of a percent, the lowest since the oil crisis year of 1974. The Tokyo Stock Exchange, which had climbed to dizzying heights, lost well over half its value. Banks, forced to meet new Ministry of Finance requirements for reserve funds just as they struggled with loans that had turned bad, were unable to rescue customers who needed money to stay afloat, and the count of bankruptcies rose steadily. It proved that many of the overseas investments, particularly in prestigious real estate, had cost too much, and in the depressed real estate market of the United States they were not salable.

As purchasing power declined and consumption remained stagnant major firms, especially automobile manufacturers, found themselves saddled with excess capacity. In the United States manufacturers faced with similar problems brought in new executives who cut the work force and closed down excess capacity. In Japan, however, postwar labor peace had been built upon expectations of permanent employment for major sections of the work force, and manufacturers were reluctant to sacrifice trained workers in a diminishing supply of labor. United States firms could be ruthless in streamlining support structures of office staff, but Japanese offices, far less productive and efficient, were more difficult to restructure.

The postwar system began to change. Workers were encouraged, and sometimes shamed, into taking early retirement. Long-treasured institutions of Japanese capitalism—permanent employment and seniority pay—proved inflexible. Many companies moved production to offshore locations, where labor was cheaper. Six percent of Japanese industrial production was produced offshore in 1990, and some predicted that this would rise fivefold by the end of the century. Cohorts of new workers entering the labor force were smaller than they had been, and graduates, particularly women, found it much more difficult to find employment. Japan's new economic institutions were experiencing their first serious strain.

The Tokyo government needed to stimulate its economy for domestic and foreign policy reasons. It was important to restore prosperity, not least because imports, the measure of American expectations, were drying up and worsening the trade imbalance. And so it experimented with several packages of economic stimulus, most involving greater public sector spending, to try to "jump start" the economy, but each package proved insufficient to do the job. The Ministry of Finance was afraid that increased public spending and lower taxes would cause a new round of inflation, and it wanted a raise in the consumption tax (an unpopular measure that had been instituted under Takeshita) to keep things on even keel. Expansionary fiscal policies produced a 13.3 percent growth in public fixed asset formation in 1992 and 17.1 percent in 1993, but even the last figure was only 1 percent of Japan's giant GNP.

Things were made more difficult for Prime Minister Hosokawa by United States warnings that Japan was not doing enough to get the economy moving. Few governments can make decisions without considering foreign reaction, but in the postwar world none have been as conscious of the watchful eyes of Americans as Japan. The reasons for this lie partly, though in decreasing measure, to the half century of American presence and leadership in Japan, and more particularly to the aggrieved posture Americans had by now adopted toward the Japanese trade surplus. During the hectic negotiation that marked the closing days of Diet deliberation of the political reform bills in Tokyo, Prime Minister Hosokawa had to take time off to receive disapproving comments from visiting U.S. Secretary of the Treasury Lloyd Bentsen, and the ink was scarcely dry on the government's announcement of a one-year, 20 percent reduction in income taxes when the measure was dismissed in Washington as unsatisfactory because it was temporary.

The trade problems are real enough. Economists see them as a natural outgrowth of the U.S. deficit and rate of savings, but as they are associated in the public mind with "lost jobs" they are unsustainable politically. Japan's pattern of reluctant concession in the face of American pressure has also done little to help. Beginning in the early 1980s the United States changed rapidly from a creditor to the world's largest debtor nation. Its trade imbalance with Japan, the largest and most conspicuous part of the American trade deficit, grew until it averaged $50 to $60 million yearly. A series of U.S. administrations had struggled to lessen this imbalance by pressuring Japan for greater market opening and liberalization, and these efforts achieved significant results before Japan's recession brought them to a halt. Between 1986 and 1991 the volume of Japanese imports overall rose by 50 percent; Japan was importing more American goods and products than the United Kingdom and Germany combined, and Japan's per capita imports from the United States neared $400 and were slightly higher than U.S. per capita imports from Japan. Yet it remained true that foreign manufactures had to run a gauntlet of administrative regulations and that the Japanese distribution system, cumbersome and highly structured, added disproportionately to the cost of foreign products. There were, for instance, regulations about the mix of products that ordinary retailers could offer, and the Large Stores Law set barriers of neighboring shop owner approval in the way of large-scale retailing.

Under President Bush, Japan and America mounted a series of discussions labelled the Structural Impediments Initiative to consider these difficulties. American negotiators pointed to bureaucratic regulations, the distribution system, and the nature of industrial alignments in Japan as barriers to greater trade, whereas the Japanese stressed the importance of the American budget deficit, inadequacies in American public education, and insufficient efforts to penetrate the Japanese markets. These were long-term problems, however, and they did not provide answers to the conviction of most Americans that the Japanese market was not truly open.

Japan's long-standing refusal to permit the importation of foreign rice was another stumbling block, both to American negotiators and to successful completion of the "Uruguay round" of international agreements. In 1993, nature, in the form of an unsuccessful rice harvest in Japan, gave the Hosokawa government the excuse it needed to ignore farmer complaints and permit the importation of rice. The details of this concession, however, illustrate the difficulties facing Japanese consumers. Japan is to import 400,000 tons of foreign rice the first year, and 800,000 tons by the end of a six-year period before ordinary import tariffs are to be negotiated. The Food Agency of the Ministry of Agriculture, Forestry, and Fisheries will continue to control rice prices, and domestic and foreign rice will cost the same, although growing rice in Japan costs ten times as much as in the United States and thirty-four times as much as in Thailand. Furthermore, instead of deciding just which rice they would like, consumers have a choice between native rice (which, in short supply, disappeared as long lines formed to buy it in March 1994) and a "blend" that is 50 percent Japanese and 50 percent divided between rice from China, Thailand, and the United States. Clearly profits accrue to the Food Agency, and not to anyone else.

A new stage in trade disputes began in 1993 with Prime Minister Hosokawa's first meeting with President Clinton. The new American administration stressed the necessity for "objective indicators" of gains in specific markets. The two met again six months later, in February 1994, to define and announce their agreement. In the interim, however, negotiations had come to a deadlock. The Japanese resisted identification of "objective indicators," considering them the equivalent of "targets" that had been interpreted as "guarantees" for the Americans in earlier negotiations, and they wanted no part of having to nudge buyers to meet deadlines. Japanese negotiators were thus taking the high ground and arguing from sound economic theory that such matters had to be left to market forces, while Americans retorted that administrative arrangements kept market forces from working.

The Hosokawa-Clinton meeting in February broke the pattern of earlier meetings. Instead of the bland agreements that had come out of such discussions in earlier years, the two leaders now expressed their regret that none had been forthcoming. American negotiators, who were accustomed to having the Japanese concede as little as possible as late as possible in order to save agreements, discovered that Japan, in the words of a controversial book that had attracted much attention earlier, could now steel itself to say "no." Japanese negotiators in turn sensed the new mood that accompanied the end of the Cold War, and they returned to Tokyo aware that they would have to proceed with additional steps for deregulation and facilitation of market access. However courteous the parting of the prime minister and the president, it was clear that a divide had been crossed in the postwar relationship between the United States and Japan. The Japanese-American relationship was now one of full equality, and the age of condescension on the one hand, and of deference on the other, had come to an end.

Japanese at Home and Abroad

Patterns of society change more slowly than patterns in politics and economics, but the last half decade has been remarkable for accelerated change in several areas in Japan. As noted earlier in this book, Japanese have been compulsively concerned with the way they are perceived in other parts of the world. With the maturation of Japan's economy and society "internationalization" became an obsession with many. In English the word is an improbable adjective-become-noun, but it is not uncommon in Japan, where it has meant many things to different groups.

To liberals it meant liberating Japanese from parochialism. To conservatives and those in power it meant making Japanese aware of, and preparing them to participate in, world trends now that they had time to look up from the treadmill of economic effort. Departments of international affairs sprouted up on campuses across the land. Publishers vied with each other in the production of books about Japan's place in world history and society. The term could also contain nationalistic overtones. It was just as important for the outside world to understand Japan as it was for Japan to know that world. Such communication was, in fact, part of "internationalizing" Japan. Politicians and educational bureaucrats also wanted young Japanese to regain the pride in self and country they felt postwar education had taken away from them, so that they could be prepared for the world they were to enter. Textbook publishers, with Ministry of Education approval, found more in the old Japan to praise and also softened their criticism of the 1930s. Publishers produced an endless series of books about being Japanese, a category known as *Nihonjinron*. In most ways there was a greater awareness of the outside world, though there was also astonishment that that outside world should interest itself in the content of Japanese schoolbooks. Japanese leaders found it necessary to make apologetic explanations for what they had thought were family matters carried out within the confidentiality of the nation-household.

The burgeoning tide of Japanese investment abroad greatly increased the number of Japanese who had to manage offshore factories or real estate ventures. Management requires a quite different set of skills and much deeper knowledge of the other than ordinary trade and commerce do, and as a result there began to emerge a large number of Japanese who were widely experienced in other cultures. Unfortunately the reverse was true of United States investment in Japan; the higher yen, added to higher profits elsewhere in Asia, resulted in net American disinvestment in Japan and, in consequence, a smaller group and weaker voice to influence government policy.

The same yen appreciation increased Japanese travel. Millions more Japanese were going abroad; by 1992, the number of trips—not people, to be sure—outside Japan was nearing 10,000,000. In 1992 Japanese (at 3,643,000) were the most numerous international visitors to the United States, with almost 1,000,000 more persons coming than from the United Kingdom, which was second. Although most of these trips were undertaken for business or within the security of the tour group, there was also striking growth in the numbers of young Japanese studying abroad, with close to 40,000 in the United States alone. Those young people, like their counterparts in other countries, seemed to have relatively little consciousness of national borders, taking a world of airports and jets for granted. So did many of their elders. At holiday time in 1993, in fact, there were press reports of groups of Japanese who came on almost turnaround pilgrimages to take advantage of shopping bargains available in major American malls.

Children of Japanese assigned abroad often found reentry into Japanese society a bruising experience. In foreign-language classes some might even be marked down for pronouncing foreign words correctly; often their teachers, lacking the students' advantages, transmitted English sounds as they had learned them, through Japanese syllabaries—which constitute an almost insuperable bar to foreign language pronunciation. Having lost one or more years of systematic vocabulary building in written Japanese, the students risked being hazed or derided by their peers as stupid and incompetent. A number of special high schools were established in an effort to ease such students' reentry. Some Japanese educational institutions established high schools in the United States so that managers sent overseas could take their families with them without risking their childrens' chances for the all-important admission to schools that would qualify them for the ladder of success in Japan. As the gauntlet of entrance examinations neared, however, Japanese fathers more often than not left their children at home with their wives to prepare full time for the examinations. Japan remained a tight little island, and it was understandable that many young people sometimes lost enthusiasm for breaching its walls after having experienced the freedom of discussion and participation in overseas, particularly American, schools.

Foreign immigration into Japan is little noted. Very little of it is formal, for Japan, with its assumptions of homogeneity, remains more inhospitable to immigration than almost any other country. But the rising income, educational status, and expectations of Japanese have created a need for blue-collar labor that has been partly met by workers from other lands. Those who come with Japanese blood receive the best treatment. In 1990 the Immigration Control Law was changed to give permanent resident status—which carries with it the right to work—to first-, second-, and third-generation Japanese from South America, where their forebears immigrated after the United States closed its doors in the twentieth century. In 1992 there were some 145,000 such persons in Japan. There are probably as many or more illegally present from other Asian countries, particularly Bangladesh and the Philippines.

In recent years the inability of farmers in northern Japan to find wives willing to share their hardships has also led to efforts, often village-wide in scope, to recruit spouses from the Philippines, Thailand, Korea, and as far away as Sri Lanka. Although modest in scale, this partial "internationalization" of rural villages, which represented the "real Japan" for nationalist theory, is not without its interest. Absent Japanese blood, however, immigrants and even those born in Japan of Korean or Taiwanese parents continue to battle for full civil rights. Japan-born Koreans, some the children of immigrants who came as laborers after the annexation of Korea in 1910, and more who were impressed as labor during the Pacific War, have only now gained rights of permanent residency and freedom from the humiliation of the identification card with fingerprint. The recession of the early 1990s, with its diminished opportunities for employment, made legal status more difficult to attain for all non-Japanese.

Nowhere are changes greater than at the two extremes of the generational chart. Japan's population is aging more rapidly than that of any other country. The proportion of those aged 65 and over will reach 16.6 percent of the total population in the year 2000, 20.3 percent in 2010, and 24.5 percent in 2020, making Japan the "greyest" of the advanced economies. By comparison, those 65 and over numbered only 12 percent in 1990. The reasons are many; families have fewer children because they are no longer needed in agriculture as before, and because other forms of social security exist. Japanese now have the longest life span in the world. All this has important consequences for social and taxation policy, and it may affect future election strategy if politicians court the "grey" vote. It also guarantees that foreign workers will continue to be needed and that more production will be shifted to other countries.

At the other extreme of the generational divide, children who grow up with fewer siblings in households where the father is seldom in evidence because of his long commute and evening hours are often coddled, coached, and spoiled by mothers who probably exhaust themselves psychologically more on one son than their grandmothers did on several. The Japanese language grows constantly with loan words that are no longer recognizable to those who "lent" them, and *mazakon*, or "mother complex," is now a common term. In mature years a man pampered in this way may find it easier to pour out his troubles to a motherly barmaid than to get home to help with the dishes.

On the maternal side of the coin the present system makes it easier for the woman to return to work once the children are out of the house, so that an "M" curve finds the years of motherhood the valley between two periods of employment. For most women friendships are likely to be with other "single" women, as the husband is away long hours; social life is seldom for couples. The corporate breadwinner is rarely home, and the thought of having him return on a full-time basis sometimes prompts a divorce at the time of his retirement. It is clear from the endless surveys and questionnaires that Japanese compile that women are more independent than they ever were, that their lives are much more their own than they were, and that a fair number decide to avoid marriage and motherhood altogether.

Yet for most women options remain limited. In 1990 the largest percentage of the 15.5 million women who worked held clerical positions, with crafts and production process jobs next common. That same year the average age of working women was 46 years, up 10 years from the figure for 1960. In 1986 the Equal Employment Opportunity Law that was supposed to even out employment opportunities and assignments went into effect. Because it had no enforcement arrangements, however, it brought few changes. Pay for women has remained well below that for men, and as Japan entered recession in the 1990s women, the last to be hired, were also the first to be let go. Admission applications to private women's colleges declined sharply, and women college graduates had particular difficulty in finding employment. Despite this, the appearance of an occasional woman prepared to take her employers to court to gain fairer treatment indicates that the struggle is far from over. In politics Doi Takako, the former leader of the Socialist Party and subsequently Speaker of the House of Representatives, provides one example.

What of the young? Japanese, like other people, profess great difficulty in understanding the values and attitudes of their juniors. There is now a generation of young people that seems to its elders unappreciative of the enormous effort that has gone into making Japan what it is, that takes material things for granted, that wants vacation and relaxation time as much as it does work, and that wants that work to be interesting as well as properly compensated. If the Japanese economy recovers in the early future, and if wages, bonuses, and profits regain an even keel, one can probably expect this pattern of self-indulgence (as the elders see it) to continue. Sustained economic difficulties, however, may find management having an easier time imprinting Japan's corporate culture on those fortunate enough to find good jobs. The young radicals who stormed through the streets to denounce the Security Treaty in 1960 often ended up as pillars of the establishment, particularly in construction trades, which require leadership and strength on the job. It is quite possible that a generation later something similar lies ahead, and that a stronger sense of nation and of past can develop because of, and not despite, Japan's greater consciousness of the outside world. The nature of that world, and the way Japan relates to it, are still very much in question.

Throughout several decades of negotiations with the United States, Japanese have urged Americans to be patient; time, they argued, was on the side of the changes that the United States was pushing for. They were probably right, though it is also clear that American insistence helped speed things up. Nevertheless, by 1994 it was clear that some irreversible changes were under way in Japan.

One was demographic and relates to the aging of Japanese society that has been described. Japan, even more than other industrial countries, will have to make allowance for this by extending the retirement age, increasing contributions and expenses, and developing an infrastructure of residence for aging Japanese who can no longer expect to have their children around them. Subsidies of many kinds for farmers and small shopkeepers have been an important part of the political and economic policies that have kept Japanese society reasonably harmonious during decades of cataclysmic change, but support and necessity for this will diminish as the new electoral changes take effect. Fifty-one percent of the farming population is over sixty years of age, and the desperate efforts of farm villages to maintain themselves illustrate the problem. It has been possible to regard the protection of this sector of society as a form of social security; and certainly those policies have helped to cushion the social dislocation that might otherwise have followed the massive shift to the cities. Now that that shift has been completed, increased emphasis on the needs and interests of urban consumers can probably be expected. The new electoral system will carry that further.

Cautious deregulation of elements of the distribution system is also producing new large-scale and discount shopping facilities in many areas. Clearly the economies and convenience associated with deregulation and imports will have increasing support, unless they are seen as imposed by overbearing outside negotiators.

Deregulation is also in the interest of the Japanese business community, which is tired of administrative controls and the financial contributions expected in some fields like construction. Business opportunity to influence politics by funding the LDP will decline with the LDP; the Japan Federation of Economic Organizations *(Keidanren)* has announced that it will stop coordinating political contributions from 1994. Business, too, wants a more transparent system than the one Japan has had. Thirty years ago the desire of business for political stability was a major ingredient in creating and sustaining the power of the government party, but in recent years big business's doubts about LDP and bureaucratic intransigence helped provide the context in which LDP rule came to an end.

The bureaucratic presence in Japan is far more pervasive than it is in the United States, though not greatly more so than in most European countries; in this respect it is the United States that is unique. Bureaucratic power grew during the command economy of the war years, and Occupation reforms were strained through the bureaucracy. Japan was well served by its bureaucrats during the emergencies of postwar reconstruction.

Japan's bureaucracy is by no means monolithic, however, and there are signs of bureaucratic initiatives that can promote internationalization and liberalization. In 1993 leaders in the Ministry of International Trade and Industry authorized plans for a dozen "foreign access zones" as part of a plan to decentralize industry and energize the economy. These widely scattered enclaves might, if they are set up, operate in somewhat the way the nineteenth-century "treaty ports" did to provide direct access to foreign goods without having them go through the pipelines of the existing distribution centers. In the 1860s the government of the shogun tried to counter this by ordering that everything be channeled through the authorized guilds of its major metropolis, and in so doing helped to fuel the indignation that led to the Meiji state. This time one senses a more modest bureaucratic attempt to short-circuit the controls of rival agencies. The parallel may be extreme, but in the context of calls from many Japanese for a "third opening," to complete the work of Perry and of postwar reform, it provides one more way of looking at contemporary Japan.

It will require some time for the political setting to stabilize once more, and in the interim the bureaucracy will be slow to lose influence and power. But the long-range trends are in the direction of a Japan more open, more responsive, more consumer-oriented, and even more interesting.

Suggested Reading

STEVEN ERICSON

There are many excellent books for those who would like to do more detailed reading on some of the aspects of Japan treated in this book. For an overall view of modern Japan, Frank Gibney's *Japan: The Fragile Superpower*, rev. ed. (New York: New American Library/Meridian, 1985) makes good and reliable reading, and Zbigniew Brzezinski's *Fragile Blossom: Crisis and Change in Japan* (New York: Harper and Row, 1972), Masataka Kosaka's *100 Million Japanese: The Postwar Experience* (Tokyo: Kodansha, 1972), and Roger Buckley's *Japan Today* (Cambridge: Cambridge University Press, 1985) can all be recommended.

Many books deal with Japan's relations with the outside world and particularly with the United States. Among the better ones are Stephen D. Cohen, *Uneasy Partnership: Competition and Conflict in U.S.-Japan Trade Relations* (Cambridge, Mass.: Ballinger, 1985); John K. Emmerson, *Arms, Yen, and Power* (New York: Dunellen, 1971); Harrison M. Holland, *Managing Diplomacy: The United States and Japan* (Stanford: The Hoover Institution, 1985); James W. Morley, ed., *Forecast for Japan: Security in the 1970s* (Princeton: Princeton University Press, 1972); Lawrence Olson, *Japan in Postwar Asia* (New York: Praeger, 1970); Robert S. Ozaki and Walter Arnold, eds., *Japan's Foreign Relations: A Global Search for Economic Security* (Boulder, Colo.: Westview, 1984); Robert A. Scalapino, ed., *The Foreign Policy of Modern Japan* (Berkeley: University of California Press, 1977); Ezra F. Vogel, *Japan As Number One: Lessons for America* (Cambridge, Mass.: Harvard University Press, 1979); and Martin E. Weinstein, *Japan's Postwar Defense Policy, 1947–1968* (New York: Columbia University Press, 1971).

There are a number of books describing Japanese government and politics; among the more recent ones are Bradley M. Richardson and Scott C. Flanagan, *Politics in Japan* (Boston: Little, Brown, 1984), and J. A. A. Stockwin, *Japan: Divided Politics in a Growth Economy* (New York: Norton, 1975). In addition, there are some excellent studies on specific aspects of the Japanese political scene. Especially notable are Gerald Curtis, *Election Campaigning Japanese*

Style (New York: Columbia University Press, 1971); Haruhiro Fukui, *Party in Power: The Japanese Liberal-Democrats and Policy Making* (Berkeley: University of California Press, 1970); Ronald J. Hrebenar, *The Japanese Party System: From One-Party Rule to Coalition Government* (Boulder, Colo.: Westview, 1986); Margaret A. McKean, *Environmental Protest and Citizen Politics in Japan* (Berkeley: University of California Press, 1981); Steven Reed, *Japanese Prefectures and Policymaking* (Pittsburgh: University of Pittsburgh Press, 1986); Kurt Steiner, Ellis S. Krauss, and Scott C. Flanagan, eds., *Political Opposition and Local Politics in Japan* (Princeton: Princeton University Press, 1980); and Nathaniel B. Thayer, *How the Conservatives Rule Japan* (Princeton: Princeton University Press, 1971).

In connection with Japanese society, note should be taken of Tadashi Fukutake, *Japanese Society Today,* 2nd ed. (Tokyo: University of Tokyo Press, 1982) and *The Japanese Social Structure: Its Evolution in the Modern Century* (Tokyo: University of Tokyo Press, 1982); Takeo Doi, *The Anatomy of Dependence* (Tokyo: Kodansha, 1971); Chie Nakane, *Japanese Society* (Berkeley: University of California Press, 1970); R. P. Dore, *City Life in Japan: A Study of a Tokyo Ward* (Berkeley: University of California Press, 1958) and *Shinohata: A Portrait of a Japanese Village* (New York: Pantheon, 1978); Ezra F. Vogel, *Japan's New Middle Class: The Salary Man and His Family in a Tokyo Suburb* (Berkeley: University of California Press, 1971); and Gail L. Bernstein, *Haruko's World: A Japanese Farm Woman and Her Community* (Stanford: Stanford University Press, 1983). The best studies on Japanese education are Herbert Passin, *Society and Education in Japan* (New York: Columbia University Press, 1965); Thomas P. Rohlen, *Japan's High Schools* (Berkeley: University of California Press, 1983); and Merry White, *The Japanese Educational Challenge: A Commitment to Children* (New York: The Free Press, 1987).

On Japanese economics and business there is a wealth of fine books. Among the better introductory works are Kunio Yoshihara, *Japanese Economic Development: A Short Introduction* (Oxford: Oxford University Press, 1979), and G. C. Allen, *The Japanese Economy* (New York: St. Martin's, 1982). A masterful study emphasizing the role of government planning is *MITI and the Japanese Miracle: The Growth of Industrial Policy, 1925–1975* (Stanford: Stanford University Press, 1982), by political scientist Chalmers Johnson, while the prodigious *Asia's New Giant: How the Japanese Economy Works* (Washington, D.C.: The Brookings Institution, 1976), edited by economists Hugh Patrick and Henry Rosovsky, tends to stress market forces. Recent works with an international focus include Thomas Pepper and Merit E. Janow, *The Competition: Dealing with Japan* (New York: Praeger, 1985); Thomas K. McCraw, ed., *America versus Japan: A Comparative Study* (Cambridge, Mass.: Harvard Business School Press, 1986); Daniel I. Okimoto, ed., *Japan's Economy: Coping with Change in the International Environment* (Boulder, Colo.: Westview, 1982); Kunio Yoshihara, *Sogo Shosha: The Vanguard of the Japanese Economy*

(Oxford: Oxford University Press, 1982); and M. Y. Yoshino, *Japan's Multi-national Enterprises* (Cambridge, Mass.: Harvard University Press, 1976). Among the several outstanding books on Japanese management and labor are Rodney C. Clark, *The Japanese Company* (New Haven: Yale University Press, 1979); Michael A. Cusumano, *The Japanese Automobile Industry: Technology and Management at Nissan and Toyota* (Cambridge, Mass.: Council on East Asian Studies, Harvard University, 1985); W. Mark Fruin, *Kikkoman: Company, Clan, and Community* (Cambridge, Mass.: Harvard University Press, 1983); R. P. Dore, *British Factory, Japanese Factory: The Origins of National Diversity in Industrial Relations* (Berkeley: University of California Press, 1973); Andrew Gordon, *The Evolution of Labor Relations in Japan: Heavy Industry, 1853–1955* (Cambridge, Mass.: Council on East Asian Studies, Harvard University, 1985); and Taishiro Shirai, ed., *Contemporary Industrial Relations in Japan* (Madison: University of Wisconsin Press, 1983).

For the historical background, the revised edition of *Japan: The Story of a Nation* (New York: Knopf, 1981) by Edwin O. Reischauer gives fuller coverage than do earlier editions of this book, and a still more detailed treatment is to be found in John K. Fairbank, Edwin O. Reischauer, and Albert M. Craig, *East Asia: Tradition and Transformation* (Boston: Houghton Mifflin, 1978). Basically the same text also appears in Reischauer and Craig, *Japan: Tradition and Transformation* (Boston: Houghton Mifflin, 1978). In addition, there is John Whitney Hall's *Japan: From Prehistory to Modern Times* (New York: Delacorte, 1970). On premodern Japanese history there are George Sansom's classic work, *Japan: A Short Cultural History*, rev. ed. (Stanford: Stanford University Press, 1952), and his massive three-volume *History of Japan* (Stanford: Stanford University Press, 1958, 1961, and 1963); Conrad Totman's *Japan before Perry: A Short History* (Berkeley: University of California Press, 1981); and Bradley Smith's gorgeous *Japan: A History in Art* (New York: Simon and Schuster, 1964). On modern history there are many good works, including W. G. Beasley, *The Modern History of Japan*, 3rd ed. (New York: St. Martin's, 1981); Peter Duus, *The Rise of Modern Japan* (Boston: Houghton Mifflin, 1976); and Harry Wray and Hilary Conroy, eds., *Japan Examined: Perspectives on Modern Japanese History* (Honolulu: University of Hawaii Press, 1983). In *Samurai and Silk: A Japanese and American Heritage* (Cambridge, Mass.: The Belknap Press of Harvard University Press, 1986), Haru Matsukata Reischauer offers a unique view of Japan's modern development through biographies of her grandfathers. Charles E. Neu's *The Troubled Encounter: The United States and Japan* (New York: Wiley, 1975) and William L. Neumann's *America Encounters Japan: From Perry to MacArthur* (Baltimore: Johns Hopkins University Press, 1963) are two broad accounts of the history of Japanese-American relations, and general studies of the American occupation of Japan are to be found in Kazuo Kawai, *Japan's American Interlude* (Chicago: University of Chicago Press, 1960); John C. Perry, *Beneath the Eagle's Wings: Americans in Occupied Japan*

(New York: Dodd, Mead, 1980); and Edwin O. Reischauer, *The United States and Japan*, rev. ed. (Cambridge, Mass.: Harvard University Press, 1965). The story of the political convulsions that swept Japan in 1960 is well told in George R. Packard, *Protest in Tokyo: The Security Treaty Crisis of 1960* (Princeton: Princeton University Press, 1966).

A number of excellent conference volumes dealing with various aspects of modern Japan have also appeared in recent years. Among the best are Albert M. Craig, ed., *Japan: A Comparative View* (Princeton: Princeton University Press, 1978); Ellis S. Krauss, Thomas P. Rohlen, and Patricia G. Steinhoff, eds., *Conflict in Japan* (Honolulu: University of Hawaii Press, 1984); and Ezra F. Vogel, ed., *Modern Japanese Organization and Decision Making* (Berkeley: University of California Press, 1975). The most useful reference and bibliographic works on Japan include Janet E. Hunter, *Concise Dictionary of Modern Japanese History* (Berkeley: University of California Press, 1984); *Kodansha Encyclopedia of Japan*, 9 vols. (Tokyo: Kodansha, 1983); John W. Dower, *Japanese History from Earliest Times to 1952: A Bibliographical Guide* (New York: Markus Wiener, 1986); Association for Asian Studies, *Cumulative Bibliography of Asian Studies, 1941–1965*, 8 vols., and *1966–1970*, 6 vols. (Boston: G. K. Hall, 1969–70, 1972–73); and the annual *Bibliography of Asian Studies* (Ann Arbor: Association for Asian Studies).

The list above offers only a small sampling of the more general books on Japan. More detailed and narrowly focused works exist in profusion, as do beautiful books on Japanese art and fine translations of Japanese literature.

New Books

The volume of publication and debate about Japan reflects the growing recognition of the intellectual and political challenge that Japan presents for Americans. The appearance of Chalmers Johnson's *MITI and the Japanese Miracle* in 1982 stimulated an important debate about the role of government in Japanese economic growth. Recent contributions to that discussion include Kent Calder, *Crisis and Compensation: Public Policy and Political Stability in Japan, 1949–1986*, and *Strategic Capitalism: Private Business and Public Purpose in Japanese Industrial Finance* (Princeton: Princeton University Press, 1988 and 1993). An interesting discussion by two seasoned participants is that of Paul Volcker and Toyoo Gyohten, *Changing Fortunes: The World's Money and the Threat to American Leadership* (New York: Random House, 1992).

The most thoughtful and thought-provoking discussion of the way postwar Japanese policies evolved is the admirable book by Kenneth B. Pyle, *The Japanese Question: Power and Purpose in a New Era* (Washington, D.C.: American Enterprise Institute, 1992). One example of Japan's response to world changes is the subject of Gilbert Rozman's *Japan's Response to the Gorbachev Era, 1985–1991: A Rising Superpower Views a Declining One* (Princeton: Princeton

University Press, 1992). Andrew Gordon has edited sixteen essays that cover all aspects of contemporary Japan in *Postwar Japan as History* (Berkeley: University of California Press, 1993). Among fine new books on Japanese society is Sumiko Iwao, *The Japanese Woman: Traditional Image and Changing Reality* (Cambridge, Mass.: Harvard University Press, 1994). Reference works also continue to proliferate and improve. The nine-volume *Kodansha Encyclopedia of Japan* now has a two-volume version (*Japan: An Illustrated Encyclopedia*) that appeared in 1993, and there is also a fine one-volume alternative in Richard Bowring and Peter Kornicki, eds., *Cambridge Encyclopedia of Japan* (Cambridge, England: Cambridge University Press, 1993). Also of note is the handsomely illustrated *Cultural Atlas of Japan* (New York: Facts on File, 1988), by Martin Collcutt, Marius Jansen, and Isao Kumakura.

Index